Earthly Bodies, Magical Selves

Earthly Bodies, Magical Selves

*Contemporary Pagans
and the Search for Community*

Sarah M. Pike

UNIVERSITY OF CALIFORNIA PRESS
Berkeley · Los Angeles · London

University of California Press
Berkeley and Los Angeles, California

University of California Press, Ltd.
London, England

© 2001 by
The Regents of the University of California

Library of Congress Cataloging-in-Publication Data

Pike, Sarah M., 1959–
  Earthly bodies, magical selves : contemporary
pagans and the search for community / Sarah M. Pike.
        p.   cm.
  Includes bibliographical references and index.
  ISBN 0-520-22030-7 (cloth : alk. paper)—
ISBN 0-520-22086-2 (pbk. : alk paper)
    1. Neopaganism—United States.
2. Neopaganism—Rituals. 3. Festivals—United
States. 4. United States—Religion—1945–
I. Title.
BL2525 .P55 2000
299—dc21   00-042616

Chapter 6 appeared in an earlier version as a chapter in James R. Lewis, ed., *Magical Religion and
Modern Witchcraft,* State University of New York
Press, 1996. Reprinted by permission. All rights
reserved.

Manufactured in the United States of America

09 08 07 06 05 04 03 02 01

10 9 8 7 6 5 4 3 2 1

To my parents,
Lucy Grey Pike and Thomas Howell Pike III,
and to the memory of Ricky Lee Schill

Contents

List of Figures   ix

Preface   xi

Acknowledgments   xxv

Introduction: We Cast Our Circles Where the
    Earth Mother Meets the Sky Father   1

1. Driving into Fairie: Place Myths and Neopagan Festivals   11

2. Shrines of Flame and Silence: Mapping the Festival Site   41

3. The Great Evil That Is in Your Backyard:
    Festival Neighbors and Satanism Rumors   87

4. Blood That Matters: Neopagan Borrowing   123

5. Children of the Devil or Gifted in Magic?
    The Work of Memory in Neopagan Narrative   155

6. Serious Playing with the Self:
    Gender and Eroticism at the Festival Fire   182

Conclusion: The Circle Is Open but Never Broken   219

Notes   227

Bibliography   259

Index   273

Figures

1. Community webweaving at the 1999 Pagan Spirit Gathering   8
2. A festival goer wearing a cow-pelvis mask   26
3. Neopagans circling the Sacred Fire at the opening ritual of the 1995 Pagan Spirit Gathering   30
4. Elf Lore Family elder Peh   34
5. Wiccan handfasting (wedding)   36
6. Maps of Lothlorien nature sanctuary in Indiana   46
7. Altar for a Neopagan's dog   61
8. Goddess altar   68
9. Goddess altar   71
10. Buddha altar   72
11. Don Waterhawk with his handmade ritual knives and rattles   76
12. Shopper on Starwood's Merchant's Row   77
13. Neopagan symbols on the Elvis altar   79
14. Clay images fashioned at a Sacred Art workshop   124
15. Louis Martinie of the New Orleans Voodoo Spiritual Temple and friend   129
16. Participant in "Flags of the Loa" ritual at Starwood   143
17. Priestess Miriam of the New Orleans Voodoo Spiritual Temple   152
18. "Tripsy" the fairy   164
19. Candle Labyrinth   184
20. Elf Lore Family masking workshop   199
21. Masked ritual participants   200
22. Starwood's ritual fire circle   208

Preface

This is a study of a new religious movement defining and creating itself
in the second half of the twentieth century. It is about the festivals that
Neopagans hold to celebrate their communities and to experiment with
personal religious identities.[1] I wanted to learn the ways that Neopagans
make sacred spaces, create rituals, tell stories about themselves, and act
out their religion through music and dance at festival sites removed from
their daily lives. In this work I explore the ways in which festival space
both expresses and shapes the religious yearnings of participants who
are searching for spiritual intensity and utopian community. This is also
a study of the way Neopagans make meaning out of their lives at festival sites by working on a series of boundaries. It is on the boundaries
between festival communities and their neighbors, between Neopaganism and Christianity, between sacred and profane spaces, and between
self and other that Neopagans create new religious identities through
conflict and improvisation.[2]

Neopagans occasionally appear in the news, and it is not unusual for
their image to be distorted by ill-informed reporting or in reference to
struggles over religious-freedom issues. Terry and Amanda Riley, members of the Southern Delta Church of Wicca, owned an occult bookstore
in Jonesboro, Arkansas, which, like many such bookstores, was stocked
with "books, incense, candles, amulets, talismans, herbs, wands, caul-
drons."[3] *The Commercial Appeal* (Memphis, Tenn.) reported, "It all
began on June 23, 1993, the day Riley's landlord came into his occult

supply store with two Church of the Nazarene ministers and told him he had two weeks to get out." The ministers appeared on television and claimed that Riley was "infringing upon the religious freedom of the landowner." They then announced to viewers, "We the evangelical churches of Jonesboro want it known far and wide that Jonesboro, Arkansas, is basically Christian and will stand together against any teachings that pollute or distort the Christian belief. . . . We want our city and especially our children protected."[4] Many Neopagans voiced support for the Rileys, who had trouble finding a new location for their store—most townspeople refused to rent to them—and traveled to Jonesboro to participate in a march protesting religious persecution. Between demonization and trivialization this thriving religious movement is working to counter negative representations with their own media campaigns. This study also looks at the conflicted space between self-representation and cultural representation of less commonly known religions. This is another boundary site at which meaningful selves and communities are made.

I entered the world of Neopagan festivals in the summer of 1992, when I attended three festivals that season in southern Indiana, central Wisconsin, and western New York. In the eight years since then, I have attended at least one festival a year in the United States: ELFest, Wild Magick Gathering, Sun Fest, Summerhawk, Chants to Dance, Circle Harvest Fest, Pagan Spirit Gathering, Starwood, Rites of Spring, Winterstar, Pantheacon, and Ancient Ways.[5] Neopagan festivals are celebrations and community gatherings of the Neopagan movement that emerged in the 1960s in North America and Great Britain. Most Neopagan communities experienced growth during the seven years I worked on this project (estimates of the number of Neopagans in the United States range between 150,000 and 200,000), and festivals have grown so steadily that some of them began limiting attendance and requiring preregistration.[6] The most significant numbers of Neopagans live in the United States, Canada, Great Britain, western Europe, Australia, and New Zealand. Neopagans from Iceland, South and Central America, South Africa, and former Soviet bloc nations have also participated in Neopagan Internet discussions and festivals. Groups and individuals calling themselves "Pagans" or "Neopagans" began organizing the first festivals and defining themselves as a large movement in the 1970s. Most Neopagans consider themselves part of a movement to revive and recreate what they understand to be pre-Christian, nature religions. They also draw from the religious practices of American Indians and non-Western religions such as African-based Santeria and Tibetan Buddhism. Neopaganism is extremely eclectic, and includes both those who interact with a pantheon of Greek deities and others who favor one great goddess; members may be separatist lesbian-feminist Witches or heterosexual and inclusive; and still others represent science fiction fandom and former followers of the Grateful Dead. According to a 1991 survey taken at Pagan Spirit Gathering in Wisconsin, festival participants identified themselves with thirty-two religious and cultural traditions as diverse as Witchcraft, Egyptian, Mayan, Greco-Roman, New Age, Native American, and Yoruba. They had turned to these other religious idioms because they had found traditionally existing religions no longer tenable. By borrowing from other cultures, Neopagans create identities that are personalized and current, but also rooted in ancient traditions.

Because Neopagans read themselves out of family groupings and the religious faiths of their parents, they generally choose new definitions of kinship, family, and religion. Festivals make available the materials for creating these new identities. At festivals, self-creation takes place within and alongside group activities: workshops on astrology, tarot cards, mythology, magic, witchcraft, Native American medicine, African drumming, large rituals, and late-night bonfires. Most of the workshops and rituals focus on healing and self-improvement "techniques" as well as the myths and beliefs of diverse world cultures.

The vast majority of Neopagans are late twentieth-century Americans trying to make sense of their lives with beliefs and practices that differ from the Judaic and the Protestant and Catholic forms of Christianity that most of them knew growing up. Why they have left more widely accepted religious cultures for those perceived to be exotic and threatening, or that are simply dismissed as superstitious, is one of the questions this study will address. Some Neopagans would say that spiritual power and commitment to community are absent from most Protestant and Catholic churches. These members believe that institutionalized, European-based religions, especially Christianity, depict the body and sexuality as sinful, perpetuate homophobia and misogyny, and cause ecological damage because of their emphasis on the afterlife and spirit rather than body and natural world. Neopagans are committed to pursuing religious options that they think will bring about harmony between humans and nature, sacralize the body and sexuality, heal wounds caused by intolerance, and create healthy and peaceful communities.

The origins of Neopaganism are complex and to a large extent still debated in books and articles by Neopagans, at festival workshops and in Internet forums, as well as in historical studies by scholars. I have concluded from my research that there are four main sources in the West that have contributed to the Neopagan movement as it manifests at festivals:

1.   Pre-Christian and other European "folk" traditions, including fertility and seasonal rites and herbal knowledge. The European witch craze, the rise of medicine, and the spread of scientific knowledge resulted in many of these practices going underground or being lost. Many were reinvented by anthropologist Margaret Murray in her book *The Witch-Cult in Western Europe* (1921) and British civil servant Gerald Gardner in *Witchcraft Today* (1954), who also incorporated "elite" sources in his writings on witchcraft.[7]

2.   European "elite" or ceremonial "magic" can be traced through Renaissance alchemy and the works of Renaissance writer Marsilio Ficino and included the reading of Greek, Roman, and Jewish texts. These earlier occult traditions were sources for the creation of the Golden Dawn, a ritual magic group that also borrowed material from Egyptian and Asian religious traditions. The Golden Dawn included for a time William Butler Yeats, the Irish poet, and Aleister Crowley, an occultist whose writings have influenced many festival rituals.[8]

Old World magic, astrology, and occult practices arrived in America with early colonists, as documented by historians David Hall and Jon Butler.[9] Many of these practices faded during the eighteenth century as increasing emphasis on science and rationality displaced them, but interests in magic and occult practices revived again in different but related forms during the nineteenth century—in spiritualism and Theosophy, for example.[10]

3.   The third source for American Neopaganism is what historian Catherine L. Albanese has called "nature religion": a wide range of ideas and practices, including American Indian traditions and New England transcendentalism (practiced by Ralph Waldo Emerson), that make nature their "symbolic center."[11]

4. The fourth source for contemporary Neopagan festivals is what might be loosely called the 1960s "counterculture": cultural and religious expressions that emerged in the 1960s as protests against dominant American social institutions. Aspects of the "counterculture" that contributed to American Neopaganism include: experimentation with psychedelic drugs, the feminist movement, growing ecological awareness, science fiction and fantasy novels, and fascination with Asian religions, including Zen and Tibetan Buddhism and various forms of Hinduism.[12]

Most Neopagan festivals are outdoor camping affairs that are held at private campgrounds or state parks and involve anywhere from fifty to a thousand people. In the 1990s approximately sixty festivals took place annually across the United States between May and September. Some festival participants attend only one or two festivals each year; others, mostly artisans or ritual specialists, visit several different festivals each month. Neopagans come from a broad range of backgrounds. Some festival goers live on nature sanctuaries like Lothlorien in southern Indiana, but many more live in New York City, Pittsburgh, San Francisco, Boston, and Chicago. Some are nomads living out of vans and renovated school buses, roaming the country, and others are artists, massage therapists, Reiki practitioners, and college students. And there are also computer programmers employed by large corporations, city council members, architects, nurses, teachers, an engineer for a major American car manufacturer, enlisted men, and college professors. Some of the men and women who attend festivals accompany friends or family members and do not identify themselves with the larger Neopagan movement, although they may share in its ecological or religious freedom concerns. But most festival goers attend festivals to experience living for a brief time in a wholly Neopagan community.

I base my understanding of Neopagan festivals on four kinds of primary sources. The first is participant observation at the festivals themselves. When I went to a festival for the first time, I either wrote to the festival organizers explaining my project and giving them the opportunity to ask about my approach and discuss issues of confidentiality, or I alerted them to my presence when I arrived at the festival. As I met other festival goers, I explained that I was at the festival for my research project. I found that most people soon forgot that I was researching their community and began to treat me as a friend and fellow Neopagan. Because festivals are typically open to anyone who is willing to pay the fees and follow their rules, I was not the only curious outsider in attendance. My role as participant-observer, then, was problematized by my invisibility. Festival goers knew that I was a participant, but they were not always aware that I was observing them for this project. Like many, though by no means all, Neopagans, I am white, middle class, and well educated and therefore did not stand out from them in any significant way. I entered their world as a curious outsider, but as I talked to Neopagans about their ritual experiences, childhood memories, and concerns for their children and the future, I found the boundary between insider and outsider slipping away, even while in my mind I tried to shore it up.

I found myself privy to gossip and the intimate details of people's lives: their marriages, sexual orientation, and conflicts with their parents. In my capacity as participant-observer, I entered their lives in ways I had not anticipated and, I believe, came to understand their concerns on a much more profound level because of this. When Neopagans forgot I was an academic and revealed themselves to me, I believe that I gained insights that would not have been possible if the attendees were constantly reminding themselves that I was there to study them. This slippage of identities was more a problem for me than for the Neopagans I came to know, as one of my informants reminded me after reading my comments here.

When this book was almost finished, I attended a Neopagan conference in San Francisco, where I was asked to clarify my commitments: "Are you one of us?" and "Do you call yourself a Pagan?" were what they wanted to know. Academic audiences, on the other hand, usually asked me, "What did you wear?" or "Did you take your clothes off?" These two sets of questions represent the concerns of the two worlds I moved in and out of while researching this book. This is also a study about the research process itself, and I have turned the analytic lens on my own experience of festivals at those points where I learned something important about Neopaganism. These moments of insight often came about during or shortly after I forgot my outsiderness and became a full participant. I do not claim to be a Neopagan or to represent this religion as an insider might, but I have been transformed by my experiences in Neopagan communities, and this transformation is surely reflected in the way I tell their stories.

I found that writing field notes was a difficult process because it interrupted my participation in the flow of festival events. I developed the habit of leaving the main festival area for an hour or two in the middle of the day to walk alone in the woods until I found a place to sit down and write notes. I outlined rituals and jotted down short quotations and anecdotes, which I filled in on my return home from a festival and in later conversations with other festival goers. During my first year of festival going, I carried along a tape recorder with which I recorded festival workshops and formal interviews with festival participants. After the first two festivals, I decided that because of the short duration of the gatherings and the densely packed schedule of workshops and rituals, the hours I was spending interviewing and setting up interviews were preventing me from participating fully in festival life. From that point on I conducted interviews with festival organizers and other festival participants outside of the festivals.

I gathered ethnographic information in several other ways. I met Neo-pagans in coffee shops and in their homes for both taped interviews and untaped conversations. I also had ongoing discussions with two festival organizers who were particularly helpful. Peh, an Elf Lore Family (ELF) elder, met me in a coffee shop in Bloomington, Indiana, about once a month during 1993–94 to discuss various issues involved with putting on ELF festivals. From May to November 1992, Kenn Deigh, editor of the Neopagan journal *Mezlim,* communicated by letter and telephone with me about his efforts to organize a new festival, Lumensgate. I also attended the "Sunday night ritual group" at Peh's home every week for two years (1994–95). At the end of each ritual I took copious notes on preritual planning, the rituals themselves, and postritual discussions over meals. These experiences deepened my understanding of the other kinds of rituals that Neopagans are involved in beyond the time and place of festivals.

I supplemented these two primary ethnographic activities with data gathered from six electronic forums: listserves femrel-l ("open discussion of women, religion, and feminist theology"), Arcana ("discussion and study of the occult"), natrel-l (Nature Religions E-mail List), Pagan-Digest, and newsgroups alt-magick and alt-pagan.[13] I subscribed to Pagan-Digest, Arcana, and femrel-l. In all three cases I posted introductory notes describing my research interests. I occasionally participated in discussions that took place on the lists, but I mostly "lurked"— Internet lingo for silently listening to conversations but not joining in. When topics relating to my research interests appeared, stories of religious persecution, for example, I saved them or downloaded them for later use. Messages from the subscription-only listserves are quoted with permission, unless I was unable to track down the message writer because he or she was no longer at the same e-mail address. In most cases, listserve data can be retrieved by searching the list archives. I also sent out two e-mail questionnaires about childhood experiences (in 1994) and body art (in 1996).[14]

Some of the advance planning and networking for festivals as well as postfestival discussions take place on the Internet, where contact information, festival journals, and photographs are shared. An extended festival narrative of words and pictures exists through links from website to website, allowing festival participants to keep their community alive across the country. The World Wide Web, notes Janet Murray in her study *Hamlet on the Holodeck: The Future of Narrative in Cyberspace,* "is becoming a global autobiography project. . . . pushing digital narrative closer to the mainstream."[15] Neopagan festivals are only one of many real world events that are extending their life through the Internet and creating new forums for narrative.

Neopagan publications were my fourth primary source: *Green Egg* (published by the Church of All Worlds in Ukiah, California), *Circle Network News* (published by Circle Sanctuary in Mt. Horeb, Wisconsin), *Mezlim* (published by N'Chi in Cincinnati, Ohio), *Fireheart* (published by the EarthSpirit Community in Massachusetts), *Enchanté* (published by John Yohalem in New York City), and the *Elven Chronicle* (published by the Elf Lore Family in Bloomington, Indiana). Disputes that I observed at festivals involving cultural borrowing, persecution by Christians, and festival rules surfaced in these publications and were debated on their pages, airing criticisms in a broad public setting (*Green Egg,* for instance, ". . . is now read by 30,000 people worldwide," states a 1997 issue).

The sun had finally come out in the Berkshires where I was attending Rites of Spring, and I took advantage of the nice weather to photograph merchants' displays. The owner of one of the booths, a woman named Cerridwen, sat for me with her parrot on her shoulder in front of a display of tie-dye clothes. She suggested that I speak to Jeff Koslow, the staff photographer for Rites. "Just look for the old hippie carrying a camera on his hip and wearing a staff badge." Later in the afternoon I spotted Jeff standing by the festival operations building. I introduced myself and as we walked together through the festival site, I described my research project to him as a study of the ways individuals and communities create new identities, the sources and other cultures upon which they draw, and the conflicts that emerge in the process of identity construction.

Jeff asked if my emphasis on practice and conflict might be called "architecture of belief." He suggested we try an experiment. He placed his mug of coffee at one end of a short fence that ran along the lakeside and my cup at the other end of the fence. He asked me to walk along one side of the fence while he walked along the other side, and we continued our conversation. Now we were talking at a greater distance from each other with a visible boundary between us. Jeff suggested that our relationship changed as we moved into a different physical relationship with each other. Festival space structures and shapes how Neopagans relate to each other and interact with the spirits and deities that are important to them.

This study looks at the way "the architecture of belief," as Jeff called it, is constructed in space and how beliefs are lived and practiced at festivals. It is not so much about belief itself, as it is about religious experience, because it is in techniques of the body—such as trance states and fire dancing—and ritual action that Neopagans most clearly diverge from other religious communities in North America. My study is about relationships among humans and between humans and their deities. It explores how people build up, tear down, and live in the architecture of belief. As Jeff and I walked along in conversation, our thoughts evolved with the movement of walking. Or, as he observed after his experiment, before we were separated by the fence we were gently bumping into each other as we made our way along the rocky path, moving close to and then away from each other, holding a conversation with our bodies as much as with our words. This experiment revealed the difference between the participant's bodily contact with the subjects of her study and the observer's position on the other side of the fence.

Everything changed about my understanding of Neopaganism after I began attending festivals. I was no longer looking at Neopagans from "across the fence," but sitting in circles and chanting with them, talking over meals, looking into their faces when we danced across from each other, and hearing about the losses in their lives. As I talked with Neopagans in their homes and over coffee, planned rituals with them, listened to their stories, and kept company with them at festivals, several issues emerged that shaped the direction of my research as it progressed over these five years. I came to see that *conflicts* within the Neopagan movement and within local Neopagan communities I worked with often pointed to the most profound and deeply felt desires of the men and women in these communities. Quiet confrontations and heated battles came about as Neopagans tried to make sense of their experiences, as they put the structures of their beliefs in place. I discovered that conflicts usually addressed the meaning of Neopagan identity—both personal and collective.

Some of the deepest conflicts had to do with representation, how Neopagans appear to and are understood by the general public, neighbors, other cultures and religions, and each other. At the heart of the project of reclaiming ancient traditions is the problem of representation. It is empowering to reclaim images of the witch or druid that have accumulated centuries of fear and associations with evil and perversity, but because these are powerful images they are powerfully contested. I discovered that the problem of representation was most clearly defined in practice—through the body and in building sacred places.

This study, then, is practice centered. As Neopagans attempt to practice their feminist, tolerant, inclusive, and ecological ideals at festivals,

they believe they are creating themselves anew. But their newly invented
self and community identities do not always match the ideals with which
they describe themselves in books and other publications. What I have
learned about Neopaganism has been a result of bringing together what
Neopagans say about themselves with how they act. It is in the process
of trying to put their ideals to work in real life, building communities in
which they can support each other in times of persecution, celebrate
births and marriages, and mourn the dead, that Neopagans are at their
most creative. In these practices they most clearly reveal what it means
to be a religious person searching for community in the late twentieth
century.

Neopagan self-creation at festivals bears directly on contemporary debates about the meaning of subjectivity and the self in the late twentieth
century as well as the tension between individual expression and the
needs of community. Neopagan assumptions about the self emerge from
shifts in American religiosity that took place during the 1960s. Neopagan
festival communities like Starwood and important Neopagan organizations like the Church of All Worlds have their recent origins in the 1960s
counterculture and exemplify changes in the relationship between religion and self-identity that took place during that decade. Many scholars persuasively argue that the 1960s were marked by a shift to more
personalized religious commitments, in which moral and religious authority increasingly became located in the self rather than in external
sources. Robert Ellwood observes that beginning in the sixties, "External religious authority is widely rejected in favor of one's right to find a
religion that meets one's own perceived needs."[16] As they create the self
anew, Neopagans play out in the 1990s the "progressive democratization of personhood" and a search for personalized religion, which cultural historian Peter Clecak argues were particularly central to the sixties counterculture.[17] Clecak characterizes religious seeking in the 1960s
as "the quest for personal fulfillment. . . . Everyone had to compose his
or her own story; autobiography threatened to displace history as a dominant way of making sense of things." This emphasis on the authority of
the self replaces the importance of a community of others and institutional authorities, according to Clecak and Ellwood. Like other observers
of the 1960s, sociologist Phillip E. Hammond contends that involvement
in church life was normative until "the social revolution of the 1960s
and 1970s" greatly increased "a phenomenon we will call 'personal autonomy,'" which Hammond claims resulted in the "third disestablishment" of institutional religion. By this he means that religion in late

twentieth-century America "is more likely to be *individually* important and less likely to be *collectively* important."[18] As conscious supporters of this disestablishment, Neopagans aggressively resist centralization and turn to the authority of their personal experience. Festivals are religious spaces that offer participants the opportunity to explore aspects of the self that cannot be experienced in ordinary life. Dimensions of self that are otherwise intolerable, inaccessible, or disallowed are encouraged at Neopagan celebrations.

Festival goers compose their own stories through costume, body art, masking, altar building, and ritual dance. They share with each other autobiographical accounts of childhood experiences and past traumas. Narratives of childhood are much more predominant in Neopagan communities than historical accounts, and the historical accuracy of personal stories is rarely questioned. Festival workshops are set up to nurture the "real self," and rituals are organized around the pursuit of self-knowledge. When they travel to festivals, Neopagans say they are making "a pilgrimage to self." This festival self is shaped by childhood stories, Neopagan interpretations of pre-Christian European religions, and the incorporation of religious idioms from Native American and African American cultures. The authenticity and appropriateness of these sources are debated, but many Neopagans claim that their usefulness is judged by the needs of the self—"what works," to use their words. Neopagans turn to the self as a measure for moral certitude in response to ethical disputes about borrowing and the attacks of some Native American critics.[19] What is "good" or "bad" is measured by effects on the self, rather than against any absolute standards of judgment.

For Neopagans, personal experience is not something that can be disconnected from the community or actual site within which experience takes place. Neopagans say that religious belief and practice in the late twentieth century must focus on healing ourselves, our communities, and the planet. And this healing, they believe, must take place through relationships—with deities, the land, and each other. What "relationship" means in this case is not simply a conversation between self and other, but an intimate connection with the natural world, with a goddess or god, and with one's community. Neopagans embody their gods and goddesses in ritual, rather than only addressing them. And if the deity represents a force of nature or the earth itself, Neopagans believe that they are becoming one with the world. They go about this process of healing in festival workshops and rituals, which, for instance, "send energy" to Gaia, the earth as goddess. And the healing power that they conjure up is more powerful because of its collective amplification than if they were working individually, which is one of the reasons festivals are very important. Self-expression and self-transformation accomplished within the framework of a religious community more effectively heal or change the world as we know it, as well as transform the self.

My analysis of Neopagan self-construction is based on an understanding of the self as multifaceted and context specific.[20] Neopagans see some aspects of self to be universal—the astrological self, for example, which is destined from birth to have certain characteristics—while others are culturally constructed and thus more malleable to human will. Neopagan views of the self are diverse but usually assume that:

1. The self includes a conscious performance of who one is and wants to be; it is the self that emerges in interaction.

2. It has a personality that is both given at birth—Neopagans usually turn to astrology to identify these characteristics—and is shaped through interactions with important others.

3. It has an "astral" self that can be accessed through particular techniques such as guided meditation. This self has no boundaries and is engaged in the search for oneness with universe or deity.[21] This is the part of the self that moves through spirit worlds and interacts with deities and spirits with life-changing results. This view of the self draws from Jung's psychology of archetypes.

4. The self also includes the soul or part of the self that has continued through many past lives. Here Neopagan beliefs link to Hindu and Buddhist understandings of reincarnation and karma. Not all Neopagans would agree on these four facets of the self, but festival workshops and rituals proceed as if these were shared assumptions.

In its festival form, Neopaganism furthers our understanding of what the turn toward a self-centered religion means three decades after the sixties. If Neopaganism is in some ways a characteristically post-1960s religion, it also requires a rethinking of what kinds of self styled religiosity emerged during and after the 1960s. I suggest that what emerged was a utopian desire for self-realization and personal forms of spirituality within a meaningful community. Festivals provide a locus where cultural problems, and especially problems of ultimate meaning, are expressed, analyzed, and played with. Observers of the contemporary American religious landscape argue that secularization and disestablishment of religious institutions characterize the current state of North American religion. Scholars of American religion have judged the decline in church attendance to signal a disestablishment, or the increasing personalization of religion,[22] while others have noted the shift from mainline churches to conservative, experiential forms of Protestantism such as Pentecostalism and independent evangelical churches.[23] What is often seen as the triumph of secularization is in fact a displacement of the sacred onto spaces that once were not thought of as "religious," such as Neopagan festivals. The festival is an important cultural and religious site that exemplifies the migration of religious meaning-making activities out of American temples and churches into other spaces. Large-scale cultural and religious events like Neopagan festivals, raves, women's music festivals such as Lilith Fair, the Burning Man festival in Reno, Nevada, and Rainbow Family gatherings offer alternatives or place themselves in critical opposition to ordinary life.[24] These religious options offer an experiential intensity that participants find lacking in other religious institutions. I suggest that attention to these religious sites is essential to an understanding of contemporary issues and future trends in American cultural and religious life.

These collective events are approached by many participants as opportunities to feel a sense of belonging to a community, to have ecstatic and powerful experiences that cannot be had elsewhere, experiences that are possible only in large groups of people with a shared vision. Neopagans see gatherings as opportunities to let their "real selves" come out in places far removed from everyday life. This study suggests some ways in which these collective events are being shaped by desires not met in other religious communities, as well as what they express about contemporary American spirituality in the late twentieth and early twenty-first centuries. I make some tentative observations about what Neopaganism can tell us about the "third disestablishment" of American religion "on the ground"—in the lives of Neopagan festival participants. In so doing, I offer a complex and ambiguous view of religious self and community in post-1960s American culture.

Acknowledgments

Without the help of many people and institutions, more than I can possibly thank here, this project would not have been pleasurable, or even possible.

California State University, Chico, awarded me a research grant that provided me with the luxury of a semester's release from teaching that allowed me to finish this manuscript, as well as providing me with faculty development grants that amounted to three course releases. The American Academy of Religion also supported my work with an individual research grant. Indiana University provided me with two grants that supported the first period of research during the summer of 1992 and spring of 1993.

Many faculty colleagues around the country have been unfailing in their support and generous with their friendship. I have benefited from my conversations with them and want to particularly thank Micki Lennon, Jason Beduhn, and Liz Faier for our graduate-school days. Sabina Magliocco and Adrian Ivakhiv have been conversation partners from our first encounter as fellow interlopers in the Neopagan world. Calvin Roetzel at Macalester College and Joel Zimbelman at California State University, Chico, cheered me on and found ways to lighten my teaching load so that I could finish this book. My colleagues at Chico State, especially Kate McCarthy, Bruce Grelle, and Sarah Caldwell, have been supportive through the later stages of the project, and their pointed questions have sharpened my thinking.

I want to thank Douglas Abrams Arava for his early faith that this book should be published and Reed Malcolm at the University of California Press for his ongoing help and ready support. Thanks also to Jean McAneny and Ellen G. Browning for their careful editing and probing questions. Bron Raymond Taylor, Michael York, and Tanya Luhrman contributed importantly to the book with their helpful suggestions on the entire manuscript.

I am grateful to many teachers for their inspiration and encouragement through my years as a student, especially to Michael Jackson and Mary Jo Weaver at Indiana, to William Poteat and David Stark, who, during my years at Duke, set me on this path, and to my dissertation committee: Stephen Stein, David Haberman, and Beverly Stoeltje. Special thanks go to my dissertation advisor, Bob Orsi, for his unwavering support and friendship throughout all phases of my work and for reading and asking provocative questions about many versions of this material.

My deep gratitude goes out to friends and family who nurtured and believed in me as I was working on this study; without them it would have been a lonely task. I have sought always to follow in the footsteps of the women in my family who pursued their intellectual interests: my mother, Lucy Pike, my aunt, Sally Thomason, and my grandmother, Marion Griswold Grey. I am also grateful to Ursina Hastings-Heinz, Jan Tarlin, Christy Cousineau, Francine Lorimer, Ransom Haile, John McCall, and Robin Murphy, for their faith in me and for their care. My parents, Tom Pike and Lucy Pike, have always made me feel that learning and teaching are important, and for this I will never be able to thank them enough. This work is dedicated to them, with all my thanks for their love.

Work always went home with me, and for their graceful tolerance, I thank my children. Dasa accompanied me through this project from beginning to end and Jonah and Clara came on board in the later stages, but all of them made the work more pleasant when they sat in my lap as I typed or insisted that I take a break to play. My greatest debt and most profound thanks are to them.

Neopagans around the country welcomed me into their homes, kept me company at festivals, and told me their stories. To all of them I owe a special debt, and for sharing with me more than words can possibly convey, I am particularly grateful to Laughing Starheart, Clare McCall, Louis Martinie, Mishlen Linden, Marty Laubach, Gwendolyne Wyldeheart, and Kenn Deigh. Without their willingness to talk to me and graciously include me in their rituals, this project would not have come into being.

We Cast Our Circles
Where the Earth Mother
Meets the Sky Father

The carved sign on the driveway reads "Lothlorien." This nature sanctuary amid the wooded hills and valleys of southern Indiana, a site for many Neopagan festivals, takes its name from J.R.R. Tolkien's *Lord of the Rings,* a popular book among Neopagans.[1] In his fantasy masterpiece, Tolkien named the enchanted land of the wise and ancient elves Lothlorien. On first encountering a Lothlorien festival in full swing, it seemed that Neopagan festivals were a feast for the senses.

My first foray into the world of festivals was in May 1991, when I attended ELFest, an annual spring festival sponsored by the Elf Lore Family (ELF) at Lothlorien. The site was a convenient forty-five minute drive from Bloomington, Indiana, where I was a graduate student at the time. Soft drum beats and notes from a flute mingled discordantly with the sounds of "flying saucer rock" as I walked through "Avalon," the main festival field. Clusters of colorful tents were set up under the canopy of trees. Small campers and vans lined the circular gravel driveway. Festival goers were roaming informally around campsites, gathering at tables covered with books on witchcraft and long, hooded robes for sale or talking with and greeting friends. A woman who smelled of incense and roses and whose naked body was more than half covered with tattoos of flowers and dragons, smiled broadly at me. Two men wearing black leather boots and dark cloaks walked by, deep in conversation. Farther along the road, a young man with bronzed skin juggled balls as he talked to another man wrapped at the waist in a tie-dye cloth and carrying a rainbow-colored parasol. The festival field was alive with music, quiet conversation, naked skin, and bodies adorned with costumes and elaborate jewelry. I passed an aura reader and merchants selling jewelry and crystals as I followed signs to Thunder Shrine, the dome-covered ritual circle where a group of drummers had gathered and a woman dressed in chain mail was dancing around the fire to an African beat. How does a place like this come to be, I wondered, and that is what I began asking my new festival acquaintances.

Of the festival sponsors that I am familiar with, ELF is typical in that it centers around two or three experienced spiritual leaders and relies on a core group of people to organize festivals and coordinate festival volunteers. These men and women are the ones who put in the long hours necessary to bring the festival into being, and in doing so are centrally important in creating the mood of a festival.[2] The Elf Lore Family, which organizes ELFest and Wild Magick, has fluctuated in structure over the years that I have been acquainted with it (1991–96) but has generally functioned as a volunteer organization directed by a group of elders. ELF was founded by Terry Whitefeather and a small group of friends, who organized their first small festivals at state parks in southern Indiana. Because of ELF's growth and the difficulties involved with using state-owned public lands, Terry and his friends began looking for wooded land to purchase and in 1987 bought the land that would be named Lothlorien. During the years I attended ELF festivals, ELF was organized in hierarchical levels. The "elders" were the most powerful decision makers and generally had been active in the community for the longest time. They oversaw land use, festival planning, publicity, registration, publication of rules and guidelines, and festival security. They also dealt with conflicts that arose during festivals, such as a charge of sexual harassment that I will discuss later. ELF "clan" worked as "apprentices" to elders and helped with the various kinds of work necessary to run the festival, such as clean-up and security. Elders, clan, and other volunteers planned the festival program in advance by corresponding with men and women who wanted to conduct workshops and rituals. They also organized work crews that prepared the festival site in the weeks preceding festivals. During festivals, "Parking Trolls" directed off-loading and parking while other ELF clan members organized volunteers and registered incoming festival goers.

Festival planning begins months in advance when announcements are sent out and posted on Neopagan organizations' websites, then circulated via e-mail by members of listserves and newsgroups. Calls are sent out seeking workshop presenters to submit their proposals; well-known Neopagans are invited to be guests and sometimes offered a small stipend for their participation (most workshop presenters are not paid, although they receive free or discounted admission). Most festivals require that all participants contribute to the community in some way, from presenting workshops to emptying recycling containers. These jobs typically include registration, kitchen staff (when there is a kitchen), fire building, recycling crew, and first-aid assistance. Festival goers may barter longer work shifts in exchange for free admittance or discounted festival fees. Volunteer work crews clear and mark trails through the woods, set up recycling containers and toilets, rope off and mark ritual and workshop space, and collect firewood.

There is no Neopagan governing body or central organization to set festival guidelines, and the variations between festival locations, workshop topics, and religious commitment can be striking. Nevertheless, most festivals follow an ordered pattern of activities, which include the following: opening ceremony; workshops scheduled in the mornings and afternoons; evening rituals and performances; late-night drumming and dancing, fire circles and coffeehouses; a community feast; and a closing ritual.

Festival goers often travel long distances, usually by car in order to carry camping supplies and costumes. Welcome centers and gateways are set up near festival entrances. On arrival, all participants go through a formal check-in procedure during which they pay festival fees, sign up for work shifts (four hours of "work sharing" at Pagan Spirit Gathering [PSG] is typical), pick up festival programs, and receive some kind of identification. At PSG 1994, all participants were given a "spirit bag," a necklace composed of a piece of yarn tied around a tiny cloth bag that held herbs, a stone, and a tiny crystal. The festival guide explained that "this special amulet is a symbol of the PSG community spirit. . . . It was assembled and blessed at the Earth Keeper's gathering held at Circle Sanctuary just prior to this year's PSG." These necklaces were to be worn at all times to identify festival goers and prevent outsiders from sneaking in, but they also served as a symbol of the festival that participants could take home with them. After checking in at the festival entrance, participants were directed to find a campsite. Campsites are occasionally set aside for groups of people with common interests or concerns, such as "family camping" or "12-step support camp," but usually festival goers camp with friends. Some people prefer to camp on the outskirts of the festival community, while others choose to pitch their tents near the late-night fire circle, where they can be sure to hear drumming all night long. Soon after arrival, festival goers change into their festival clothes and their Neopagan jewelry or remove their clothes, and walk through the festival grounds looking for old friends.

Almost all Neopagan festivals include an opening ceremony during which spirits and deities are called and requested to be present at the festival and to protect the festival space. The language of "community" is also invoked to remind festival participants that they are part of "the web of life," to borrow a metaphor from Rites of Spring 1997, where a web was woven by festival participants in the central festival field. Pantheacon 1997 started off with an opening ritual to "call in blessings upon this gathering of the tribes," according to the Pantheacon program.

Rituals of many kinds are included in a festival, ranging from small private ceremonies at campsites to large public rituals.[3] Rituals also take place within the festival workshops that are scheduled throughout the days of a festival. The Women's Healing Circle and the Grief Ritual were two of the workshop rituals at Rites of Spring 1997. Night is reserved for concerts, performances, dances, and large rituals. Although contests are rarely part of Neopagan festivals, perhaps because they conflict with the egalitarian focus of festivals, festivals usually include a variety of performances that are planned in advance.

Festival participants spend their days attending workshops, talking to friends, receiving massage therapy, getting their bodies painted, shopping for new ritual wear, and browsing through the merchants' area. At large festivals, several workshops run simultaneously throughout the mornings and afternoons. Anyone with a certain amount of experience in the community and a good idea for a discussion topic or skill to share with a group can run a workshop. The Starwood 1998 program listed seventy-eight presenters and two hundred workshops, performances, and rituals scheduled over five and a half days. Workshop topics included healing ("The Healing Drum for Everyone" and "Alchemical Healing"), ritual skills ("Sacred Theatre" and "Abortion Ritual Design"), education about Neopagan and other cultural traditions ("Druidry Ancient and Modern," "Goddess of Hebrews, Goddess of Jews," and "Buddhist Mandalas and the Cosmic Symbolism of the Tibetan Stupa"), crafts or tool making ("Amulet-Making Workshop" and "Batik Prayer Flags and Banners"), and alternative lifestyles ("A Bouquet of Lovers: Open Relationships in a Pagan Tribal Context" and "Living in Community as an Act of Revolution").

Meal arrangements at festivals range from food grilled over individual campfires to a YMCA summer camp dining hall filled with hundreds of Neopagans. Festivals generally require participants to take their own food and cook at their campsites. At the large festivals like Starwood and ELFest, free food or food vending was available, and Rites of Spring offered cafeteria-style dining. Most festivals also include a communal feast of some kind. ELFest 1992 featured a community potluck and Pagan Spirit Gathering 1992 included an astrological feast/potluck. Rites of Spring organizers invited all festival goers to their Medieval feast, which was cooked in the camp kitchen and served as a sit-down meal with multiple courses. Neopagan meals tend to include more vegetarian options than other American collective events, but the feasts I attended were diverse, offering hamburgers, gourmet vegetarian dishes, and ethnic food—Middle Eastern falafel or Indian curries. Unlike festivals that celebrate regional or ethnic identity, there is no pattern to the foods or any attempt to make them symbolic of group identity.

Neopagan identity is primarily expressed at festivals through music and dance. Drums and percussion instruments are common at many workshops and chanting often occurs at the beginning and end of workshop sessions. There are hundreds of Neopagan chants, some newly invented and others makeovers of older songs. Chants originate with one community then spread throughout the North American Neopagan community to the extent that often no one knows who started the chant in the first place. For example, I had heard "Air I Am, Fire I Am, Water, Earth and Spirit I Am" at several Midwestern festivals before hearing it at Rites of Spring in Massachusetts and learning that it is attributed to Rites of Spring organizer Andras Corban Arthen. Formal concerts and informal drumming sessions take place at most of the larger festivals. Starwood featured Jeff "Magnus" McBride's magic show before the procession and lighting of the Saturday night bonfire. (McBride, who was named Hollywood's Magic Castle Magician of the Year and NBC's World's Greatest Magician, according to the Starwood program, has appeared at several Neopagan festivals.) Pagan Spirit Gathering 1993 featured a talent show, and Rites of Spring 1997 included a Neopagan soap opera called "All My Avatars" and an indoor concert by percussionists Circle, Skin, and Bone. Starwood XV presented seven musical acts, ranging from Behavior, a "free-form Rock instrumental combo," to Djoliba, featuring "Lansana Kouyate from Guinea, West Africa, where his family have carried on the tradition of their Malinke tribe through music as Griots: sacred storytellers."[4] Dances can be planned, as was the Guiser's Ball, a costumed dance at Rites of Spring 1997, or they can be impromptu.

Major festival rituals usually take place on Friday and Saturday nights and are open to all festival goers. These rituals involve much planning because they include hundreds of people from a wide range of Neopagan traditions and ritual experiences—complete beginners who have never before participated in a ritual and seasoned ritual leaders. Major rituals may be planned by a small group usually led by someone who is well known among the local or national Neopagan community as an effective ritual facilitator. Ritual planners often ask for volunteers and plan the ritual through workshops or meetings with volunteers before the ritual takes place, though the main theme is established in advance. Preparations include writing scripts for invocations of deities and spirits into the ritual circle and making costumes and masks. Ritual organizers must balance the importance of participation—everyone wants to experience the ritual, not simply watch—with a carefully structured ritual that powerfully affects all participants, is beautiful to witness, and communicates something meaningful. These formal rituals can be complex, theatrical performances with a stated focus or theme like "The Descent of Persephone" at ELFest 1991 or "Remembering Salem" at Pagan Spirit Gathering 1992. These rituals are more like performances or ritual theater conducted by a coven—Children of the Laughing Greenwood coven organized the Remembering Salem ritual at Pagan Spirit Gathering in 1992—or a small ritual group that is accustomed to working together and spends a considerable amount of time planning and preparing in advance of the festival. Many main rituals include two phases: a carefully planned performance by a small group of ritualists and a participatory activity that involves everyone.

The Web Ritual at Rites of Spring 1997 was a successful example of this kind of ritual. It began with a performance during which various powers were called into the ritual circle by core members of the EarthSpirit Community. During the second part of the ritual, everyone present contributed in some way to the "web of community." In preparation for the participants' contributions, festival programs were sent out with maps to festival goers after they preregistered (most, though not all of, the larger festivals require preregistration). "The Official Program Oracle of Rites of Spring XIX" described the ritual as follows: "Our web takes root this year as Pagan land-based communities manifest around the country and we bring our spirituality concretely into our everyday lives. We will listen to the rhythm of the earth and affirm these changes and the awareness that they bring of our deep connection to the land. We will fill the web with our passion to nourish and sustain these bonds. Come with your own strands of yarn to weave into the web and with any objects you have brought to add to it." As with most Neopagan rituals, participants in the web ritual entered ritual space through a marked entrance—in this case a wooden bridge with branches arched over it. Often participants are smudged with sage or sprinkled with water as they enter—a form of purification and a signal to them that they have entered ritual space. Drumming and other kinds of percussion usually take place as participants gather at a ritual site. When several hundred people had formed into a circle around the Rites of Spring ritual field and were chanting softly to the drumming, Andras Arthen, EarthSpirit's founder, strode into our circle carrying a long, carved staff with a deer's skull on the top. His body was draped with animal skins, his face was painted, and he wore a long, flowing skirt and leather boots. Andras silently "cast" a circle, marking the ritual space by walking around the assembled circle of people and raising his staff to the four directions.

Casting a circle is the standard opening for most rituals and is performed in many ways, depending on the preferences of the ritual's organizers. The circle bounds ritual space to create a safe and sacred area in which participants can focus on the ritual performance and their own experience of the ritual. After the circle has been cast, deities and elements of earth, air, water, fire, and spirit are usually called into the circle to lend their powers to the ritual. In the web ritual this was done by performers who were dressed as particular elements. Andras's wife, Deirdre Arthen, next entered the circle and walked around it a few times passing in front of the participants, singing as she went. She had covered herself with earthly things: bark, moss, and leaves. Representatives of elemental spirits soon followed her dressed in black leotards and wearing large masks that symbolized the four elements. The first wore a tree mask made from large pieces of bark; a fire mask followed, then a water mask with blue and green streamers; finally a participant wearing a white air mask danced into the circle. Each elemental spirit moved around the circle several times, performing its own unique steps and gestures, followed by percussionists playing different beats. Deirdre, the priestess, then initiated the weaving. People from the circle began to move forward to pick up the ropes that extended from the maypole to stakes in the ground. They stood holding the stakes as other participants wove yarn and string in and out of the ropes. The drumming continued throughout this process while everyone repeated a weaving chant: "Weavers,

Figure 1.   Community webweaving was a part of the blessing of the sacred
mound created at 1999 Pagan Spirit Gathering. Courtesy Circle Sanctuary
archives. Photo by Selena Fox.

weavers, we are weaving the web of life." Some people danced as they
wove and tied small feathers, beads, and other decorative objects to the
string. Others traded yarn and twine with each other or threw them up
over the ends of the ropes near the top of the maypole, catching them on
the other side of the rope. This process continued until everyone's twine
and yarn were woven and a colorful web had been created (see fig. 1).

   All ritual events are optional and some festival goers prefer to sit
around their small campfires visiting with friends and discussing magical techniques for hours. Festival evenings may be simply social or may
combine serious and focused ritual work. At night the campground resembles a medieval village with candles and fires burning, populated by
men and women in long, hooded cloaks. Some festival goers gather late
at night in coffeehouses for storytelling and socializing, while others
join the drumming around the festival fire. Late-night festival fires usually occur after formal rituals and sometimes extend through the night.
They tend to be loosely organized, without a stated goal. Rites of
Spring's fire, however, is more tightly organized; it is billed in the festival program as "the place to go for impromptu tribal drumming and
dancing especially between dawn and dusk. . . . Please don't use this fire
for casual socializing." As the drumming gathers momentum and
dancers bare their skin at late-night fires, a circle of festival goers gathers
around the fire to watch, and, if they feel so moved, to join the circle of
drummers and dancers.

Most festivals include a closing event of some sort. At Rites of Spring's closing ritual, everyone formed a large circle around the maypole, where the community web was still suspended over the field. We collapsed the web by pulling up the stakes that held the string and yarn. Participants were told that after the ritual they could cut off pieces of the collapsed web to take home with them. The festival organizers called some of the people who had made significant contributions to the festival community to the center of the circle, where they were thanked: the drummers, the "next generation," and the staff. Then everyone participated in a Spiral Dance that wound around the field while chanting "Carry it on to the children, carry it out on the street, carry it to the ones you know and to the ones you meet. Carry it light on your shoulders, carry it deep in your soul, for we have been blessed with magic, and the magic will make us whole." This closing chant was an attempt to bridge festival events with the outside world. As the spiral of festival goers holding hands wound its way to the edge of the field and it was time to depart from the ritual grounds, each person stopped by the pile of dirt that was formed during the opening ritual by the handfuls of dirt that each festival participant was asked to bring from home. A hollow had been dug in the mound and within it were colorful stones for each person to carry home with them. After participants picked up their stones, they walked to the top of the hill and passed through the same gateway where they had been greeted when they first arrived.

CHAPTER ONE

Driving into Faerie

Place Myths and Neopagan Festivals

During several years attending festivals, I found that Neopagans everywhere describe their festival experiences in much the same way. Each festival has unique features, but Neopagans approach all festivals as opportunities to participate in a community of others who share some of their religious beliefs and practices. In later chapters I discuss in detail distinct characteristics of particular festivals. Here, however, I explore similar ways in which the festivals—Starwood, ELFest, Wild Magick Gathering, Summerhawk, Rites of Spring, Spiral, Lumensgate, and Pagan Spirit Gathering—are imagined as places of contrast with the rest of the world.

During ELFest 1991, I met Kenneth Deigh, a man who plays many roles in the national Neopagan community. Kenn has been attending festivals in the United States for more than ten years, organizing and directing large group rituals and presenting workshops on various aspects of ritual work: Magical Mudras, a workshop on physical postures and gestures, and Invokation and Evokation, techniques of spirit possession, are two workshops Kenn offered at Starwood, a large festival that takes place at Brushwood sanctuary in southwestern New York. He also edits and publishes *Mezlim,* a Neopagan magazine. Kenn and a few friends organized their first Lumensgate festival in 1992, which was held on the summer solstice (June 21) at Brushwood. "Lumensgate," Kenn wrote me, "means 'gateway to light,' gateway to a place where we can transform, a place where possibilities are open to us." As a festival organizer Kenn is particularly conscious of what makes festivals different from the everyday world.

> There is something magickal about simply *going* to a Festival. Especially if the journey is a long and rigorous one, to some "uncharted shore." I remember my first trip to Spiral. . . . After an all day trip through the beautiful scenery of the Kentucky and Tennessee mountains, we spent a couple hours finding our way past Atlanta and down a long, straight road as the sun began to set behind us and we struggled to stay awake and alert. A final turn off took us onto a winding, wooded track that brought us into an increasingly surreal tangle of pines, shadows and red clay illuminated by our headlights. I began to sense a change in the feel of the landscape, as if we were driving into Faerie, with the trees closing behind us.

Like many other festivals, Spiral takes place on a wooded site far from the lights and sounds of the cities from where most festival participants come. Kenn goes on to describe his arrival: "Finally we reached the campground and the welcoming yellow lights of the dining hall and registration table. I parked the car between tall pines and stepped out onto the blanket of fallen needles, feeling completely awake, alert and filled with joy." Festivals are uncharted shores emotionally as well as physically; Kenn remembers,

> I could feel myself opening to the experience that lay before me, and I knew that it would be a Magickal one. Anything that happened there could not help but transform me. That was the first time I remember being so consciously aware of the transition to "festival space," but I don't think I've ever attended a gathering—before or after that first Spiral—where something similar didn't occur. Now I'm simply more aware of the process, and help it along at times by visualizing/sensing/feeling veils hanging in the air, which we pass through on our way into the site.[1]

The veils that Kenn imagines moving through mark the boundary between the everyday world and the "Magickal one" of the festival. Festival goers anticipate that festival space will be transformational because it is different from their workplaces and homes. Kenn's vision of trees closing behind him separates Spiral from the quotidian world and marks his departure from daily routines.

The process of being transported to a different reality and changing states of consciousness is made possible by magic, an important factor of self-transformation at festivals. The notion of magic is central to Neopagan belief and practice. Whether they believe that magic is something that happens psychologically or in the physical universe, the explanations that Neopagans give for the concept of magic almost always include "change" and "transformation."[2] One of the most famous definitions is occultist Aleister Crowley's (1875–1947): "The Science and Art of causing change to occur in conformity with Will."[3] Florence Farr (1860–1917), one of the members of the Golden Dawn, a Victorian occult group that Crowley also belonged to and whose rituals have been important for many Neopagans, describes magic as "unlimiting experience," by which she means, "Magic consists of removing the limitations from what we *think* are the earthly and spiritual laws that bind or compel us. We can be anything because we are All."[4] In its various meanings, magic is essentially a method of consciously separating oneself from the world of the everyday and moving into a realm where possibilities are open for physical or psychological transformation, which is what festival goers experience when they attend festivals.

Some outsiders and first-time festival goers—"festival virgins"—find Neopagan festivals strange and disorienting, while others feel immediately at home. Participants describe festivals as "magical" and "surreal" places for drumming all night, dancing naked around fires, going into trances, and traveling out of their bodies. They report intense emotional and physical experiences and say that they return home somehow transformed—their bodies marked with new tattoos, their minds with new ideas and memories. Neopagan stories and descriptions of festivals are shaped by the fantastic expectations people bring to them, especially the belief that festivals are "rehearsals for a hoped-for real future."[5] How do Neopagan festivals come to be imagined and experienced as such different places from the world outside them? What must Neopagans do to change wooded farmland or campgrounds into "fairyland" and how do they make such a place feel like home? Or, in the words of geographer Yi-Fu Tuan, how does a space that is "open and undefined" become a "secure and familiar . . . place" for festival goers?[6]

As Neopagans work to make festivals transformative places, they confront two potential contradictions. Neopagans escape their homes and familial responsibilities when they journey to the festival "forest far, far away," and at the same time they expect festivals to be the location of "home" and "family." They also look forward to the festival as an opportunity for self-expression as well as an experience of community. It is in the process of drawing boundaries between the festival world and "mundania," a term Neopagans use to refer to the world outside, that these contradictions most clearly emerge and are addressed. And it is through this work, in response to these dilemmas, that festivals are turned into special places, where, as Kenn puts it, "Anything that happened there could not help but transform" participants.

FESTIVAL ANTECEDENTS
IN THE NINETEENTH CENTURY

Neopagan festivals generally strike outsiders as a radical new phenomenon in American culture. Some say the occasions represent frightening, even demonic trends in American religious expression. But in a number of ways—in their relationship to nature, spiritual eclecticism, nonconformity—in both form and religious content, pagan festivals are not that unusual in American religious history. Neopagan festivals belong to a tradition of collective events that first flourished in the "spiritual hothouse," to borrow historian Jon Butler's phrase, of the nineteenth century. Chautauqua Institutes (nineteenth-century Protestant conferences that blended religion and leisure), outdoor revivals, camp meetings, lyceum programs, and Spiritualist conventions were all intended to transform the mind and spirit.[7] Like contemporary Neopagan festivals, these events of earlier eras were consciously experienced apart from the rhythms of daily life and drew boundaries between the participants' gatherings and the rest of society. Such gatherings were also places or events at which a multitude of meanings and desires converged; they served as vacation retreats, as opportunities for conversion experiences, and as avenues to new and radical ideas. Three North American religious and cultural trends from the nineteenth century best demonstrate the importance of the contrast between the ordinary world and the "place apart": Spiritualist conventions, evangelical camp meetings, and tourist attractions.

Neopagan festivals not only share several features with nineteenth-century Spiritualist gatherings, but Neopagans also count Spiritualists among their many ancestors. An anonymous participant in Arcana observes that "the best 19th-century social equivalent of the modern Wiccan/Neopagan groups is the Spiritualist movement," because, like contemporary Neopagans, Spiritualists "were largely a loose network of small, self-organizing circles without a central hierarchy." And for this reason, he says, both were "incapable of forming a widely-agreed upon theology or ritual."[8] Neopagan festivals are akin to the gatherings of nineteenth-century Spiritualists in their eclecticism and the challenge they represent to more orthodox and established religious practices.[9] Loosely defined organizational structures resisted institutionalization and allowed both groups to accommodate participants from a wide variety of faiths at their gatherings.[10]

Some Neopagans also claim Spiritualism as part of their ritual lineage to legitimate their own medium-like practices. Sandy, a "third-generation Spiritualist" I met at Pagan Spirit Gathering, is married to a medium.[11] Rhianna, a participant on the electronic forum Pagan Digest, recalls that her grandmother, a spiritualist medium, held seances in her living room.[12] At their gatherings, Neopagans also engage in mediumistic rituals during which they commune with spirits. During large rituals, ancient deities, tree spirits, angels, and the dead are invited to guide and help humans in their spiritual endeavors as well as their more worldly pursuits, such as, for example, reclaiming a stolen car. Spiritualists and Neopagans position themselves in imaginative ways in relation to invisible beings whose existence others fear and deny. Both movements might be characterized by hunger for more direct interaction with an invisible world of spirits and deities, also populated with loved ones who have passed away.[13] In both cases ritual practices and assumptions that the spirit world was easily accessible diverged from more widely accepted religious behavior.

Like Spiritualists, many Neopagans have multiple religious commitments, interact with invisible realms of experience and personality, and encourage female leadership and social activism.[14] In their attempts to be inclusive, Neopagan gatherings have attracted many people not as interested in contacting the world of spirits as they are in gaining support for alternative therapies like biofeedback or unconventional relationships such as polyamory. Historian Ann Braude propounds in her study of Spiritualism and women's rights that this was also the case for Spiritualist newsletters, lectures, conventions, and camp meetings that brought together "large audiences for promoters of radical causes" like women's rights, abolition, and free love.[15] Abolitionists, women's rights activists, and other types of social reformers advanced their causes in conversation with each other, just as today Witches, Druids, Taoists, Zen Buddhists, and practitioners of religions from all over the world attend Neopagan festivals. Gatherings like these have become zones of cross-fertilization and hybridization where individuals with varied interests and backgrounds meet and interact, and share information about rituals, myths, and deities, bringing forth new religious forms.

Emergent religions whose practitioners worship at "alternative altars," in Robert Ellwood's phrase, define themselves in contrast to established religions like the larger Protestant Christian denominations. Neopagan festivals also contest accepted cultural norms by openly supporting gay rights and sexual freedom, female leadership, and nudity. Both men and women may wear black hooded cloaks or leather bondage gear and explore unusual practices such as out-of-body travel and psychic healing. Particularly important to both Neopagan festivals and nineteenth-century Spiritualist gatherings have been women's rights issues. Historian Ann Braude argues that Spiritualist gatherings exposed their female participants to new possibilities for women's social roles and that suffragism and Spiritualist activities were closely related. Neopagans are likewise concerned with equality for women, and women are prominent heads of Neopagan organizations (Selena Fox of Circle Sanctuary), editors of important Neopagan publications (Diane Darling of *Green Egg*), priestesses and authors (Starhawk) and festival organizers (Ceil, of Wyrd Sisters, who produces Spiral Gathering).

Because of their support for radical social causes and their resistance to institutionalization, both Neopagan and nineteenth-century Spiritualist gatherings have been looked on with suspicion by outsiders who assumed the participants were either organizing subversive activities or indulging in "perversions" such as "free love."[16] The many Christians who participated in Spiritualist conventions may not have rejected their Christian backgrounds to the extent that Neopagans do theirs, but they were still suspected of being "fundamentally opposed to a Christian worldview."[17] In this way, Neopagans and Spiritualists are located by themselves and others on the margins of American religious culture, and indeed, define themselves in rejection of it.[18] Some Americans, including the nearby neighboring conservative Christian congregations, imagine Neopagans to be satanic child abusers. Ironically, the evangelical forebears of Neopagans' Christian critics engaged in religious activities themselves that were viewed suspiciously by *their* neighbors and that also seemed to anticipate Neopagan festivals on the American religious landscape. Nineteenth-century evangelical camp meetings and revivals were "theatrical" and "carnivalesque," to the dismay of their critics but to the delight of participants. "Critics complained . . . but the setting of the revival, for the space of the few hours or days, often protected practices that were elsewhere forbidden," such as women preaching.[19] Nineteenth-century men and women attended camp meetings for varied and often contradictory reasons, often as much to indulge the senses as seek conversion. Neopagans attend festivals for similarly diverse purposes. Merchants attend to sell their wares, spiritual seekers hope for intense experiences, and other Neopagans look forward to socializing with old friends. "I used to come to festivals to learn about ritual magic; now I come to hang out with friends," said Howie (as he was driving me home from ELFest in 1992), who has been attending the annual ELFest for many years.

Evangelical camp meetings and Neopagan festival sites, particularly ones in out-of-the-way places, draw together the contradictory values of camp-meeting followers and festival goers and allow them to coexist temporarily, if uneasily.[20] As sites of religious work and pleasure, these gatherings are given the task of coordinating the multiple interests and expectations of those who attend them. It is the very diversity of participants' backgrounds and interests that made nineteenth-century camp meetings—and today Neopagan festivals—suspicious to outsiders but attractive to participants. Critics of camp meetings "perceived a manifest subversiveness in the form and structure of the camp meeting itself, which openly defied ecclesiastical standards of time, space, authority and liturgical form." These outsiders felt threatened by "the intense enthusiasm of congregated masses, the unbridled communal force and overwhelming power that swept over these occasions," but were ineffective in preventing camp meetings from taking place because the meetings were so successful.[21] Critics and supporters of camp meetings alike agreed that these were powerful experiences of "unbridled forces," and had very little in common in form and appearance with religious gatherings in mainline Protestant or Catholic churches.

Camp meetings took place in nature, distinguishing them from gatherings in urban lecture halls. Because their wild surroundings heightened the contrast to everyday life, controversial behavior like ecstatic dancing and swooning was exaggerated in these settings. Neopagan woodland gatherings and camp meetings in the hills of Kentucky seem strange and wild to city dwellers because they provide a sensual and aesthetic contrast to the everyday world—"be prepared for a crash course in Mother Nature" reads one Neopagan festival announcement.[22] The establishment of national parks like Yosemite and Yellowstone in the 1870s and 1880s made possible a new kind of relationship to the natural world. These parks became destinations for pilgrims "with the leisure to 'rough it' for pleasure."[23] As sites where city dwellers could more directly encounter the natural world than at their homes, these nineteenth-century attractions also anticipated Neopagan celebrations. Natural sites like Niagara Falls became attractive locations for tourists and pilgrims because they addressed a range of needs, functioning as pilgrimage sites, family vacation spots, and honeymoon destinations. Neopagans also take advantage of leisure and vacation time to get sunburned and mosquito bitten at primitive festival sites. Camp meeting grounds, state and federal park land, and Neopagan festival areas, are all sites that belong to a different reality than city dwellers are accustomed to; "roughing it" helps create the contrast that makes these places compelling.

Neopagans' view of festivals as spiritual frontiers in the wild is drawn on a thematic that powerfully characterizes American attitudes toward this land.[24] Neopagans tap into the frontier myth that is at the heart of American religious diversity because it held the promise of endless imaginative space within which to create a new religious life and community. The wilderness is one of the most powerful symbols of the American frontier, although it has figured ambivalently in the American religious imagination as a place of danger as well as spiritual promise. The Puritans thought it was in the wilderness that they could carve out God's kingdom, a "city set upon a hill," to quote the Massachusetts Bay Colony's first governor, John Winthrop (1588–1649).[25] Europeans like Alexis de Tocqueville, who visited America in the 1830s, were fascinated by the wilderness as a place of contrast to European civilization and urban life.[26] The American Romantics Thoreau and Emerson believed that "Wilderness symbolized the unexplored qualities and untapped capacities of every individual."[27] Neopagans approach their festival retreats in the woods as places of personal testing and spiritual renewal.

These comparisons with earlier American idioms raise interesting questions about the future of Neopaganism. Camp meetings and Spiritualist conventions seem to have been antinomian stages in emergent religious movements that later became more rigidly structured and institutionalized. If religious Americans assume they have inexhaustible religious options—an open spiritual frontier—then where will Neopagans go next, and what other religious movements will emerge from Neopaganism? Will Neopagan festivals lose their subversive exuberance? The answer depends, in part, on how successfully they shore up the boundary between festival world and mundania. It is by establishing their identity in contrast to the outside that festivals become powerful places of meaning making. Neopagans thus follow a familiar American path of constructing spiritual space by rejecting the meanings and rituals proposed by culturally dominant Christian churches. Christianity becomes essential as that which is rejected—and which rejects—to establish Neopagans' own identity.

When Neopaganism is brought into the current American religious scene, several features of these other religious idioms come into sharper focus. The wilderness where gatherings took place and the woods where today's Neopagan festivals occur establish a sensual contrast to churches filled with orderly pews. The woods function as a sacred locale where men and women take their hearts and bodies to be made anew in what they see as an uncivilized and virgin wilderness. Certainly, successful revivals were held in ordinary buildings as well, but by setting the camp meeting next to Neopagan festivals, the religious importance and creative power of wilderness sites emerges more clearly in itself, as does the process by which the wilderness experience is made different from other domains of life.

Contemporary scholarship leaves unexamined key phenomenological issues about nineteenth-century religiosity; for example, how did certain spaces become sacred? And what does it mean to various participants to say that a space is sacred? These comparisons across the centuries suggest that the process of boundary making between festivals and the outside world is as important as what goes on within. These boundaries are not created by emerging religions alone; they are mutually constituted by the community within and that without. What forces and desires on both inside and out create the space of experience as special and different? Comparisons of nineteenth-century camp meetings, Spiritualist conventions, and tourist sites with Neopaganism help establish a kind of geographical genealogy for nineteenth-century sacred space. I turn now to examine more closely the specific ways in which Neopagan festivals are set apart from the rest of society, engaging these questions of comparison in a way that will contribute to the study of nineteenth-century religions and more generally of American religious culture.

THE FESTIVAL AS A PLACE APART

Festivals become places separated from the everyday world not only because of their physical settings, but primarily because of the ways in which festival goers perceive them.[28] Throughout festivals, participants work to make an experience set apart from their lives "back home." They create place myths: composites of rumors, images, and experiences that make particular places fascinating. These myths may extol a place's vices as well as its virtues.[29] Neopagans tell stories designed to locate the festival in "an imaginary geography vis-a-vis the place-myths of other towns and regions which form the contrast which established its reputation as a liminal destination."[30] But how do festivals take on these connotations of magical otherworlds and what makes them "liminal destinations"?

When they separate festival from mundania, Neopagans follow a pattern they share with other ritualists and festival participants around the world. The festival is what ritual theorists, beginning with Arnold van Gennep's work in 1909, have labeled "liminal": a "transitional" or "threshold" experience. Van Gennep discusses the order of rites "within ceremonial wholes" like festivals, which he breaks down into three phases: rites of separation from a previous world, or "preliminal"; rites of a transitional stage (threshold or "liminal" rites); and ceremonies of incorporation into a new world, or "postliminal" rites.[31] The structure of Neopagan festivals includes these three phases, the first of which I discuss in this chapter, along with some consideration of the final phase of reincorporation. According to van Gennep, the transitional or liminal period is characterized by "a suspension of the usual rules of living," which may include "excesses" and sexual license.[32]

With their opposition of festival to mundania, it would seem that Neopagans expect this kind of liminality to characterize the festival experience. They also expect to experience a sense of oneness with other festival goers and the feeling of belonging to a tribe or an extended family: "a state of oneness and total unity . . . the very opposite of social structure with its emphasis on differentiation, hierarchy, and separation." In the liminal stage of rites of passage, "Moral choice, creativity, and innovation are possibilities that emerge from the agony of isolation and the joy of communitas."[33] Certainly these are conditions that Neopagan festivals try to produce. According to festival belief, when participants return home, they are no longer the same people who walked through the gates several days before. Neopagans present a dualistic model of ritual and festival as liminal, antistructural spaces opposed to mundania—highly structured everyday society.[34] Because of this set-apart quality, many festival goers approach festivals with an "anything goes" attitude, imagining them to be an occasion for dressing and behaving in ways that are unacceptable in the world outside festival grounds. Folklorist Beverly Stoeltje explains that "in the festival environment, principles of reversal, repetition, juxtaposition, condensation, and excess flourish, leading to communication and behavior that contrast with everyday life."[35]

Festival worlds are fantastic and enchanting, say Neopagans, because they offer everything that mundania denies. After having observed the development and growth of Neopagan festivals, Margot Adler added a section on festivals titled "Pagan Festivals: The Search for a Culture or a Tribe" to the 1986 edition of *Drawing Down the Moon,* her classic study of Neopaganism. In it she gives a brief account of the history of Pagan festivals and responds to the question "Why did festivals catch on?": "Probably most critical was the fact that outdoor festivals established a sacred time and space—a place apart from the mundane world, where pagans could be themselves and meet other people who, although from a variety of traditions, shared many of the same values." Neopagan festivals offer a shared reality different from what Neopagans experience in mundania. Adler reports that one festival organizer described the difference this way: "It's a trip to the land of faery, where for a couple of days you can exist without worrying about the 'real' world."[36] Salome, a college senior who has been involved with Neopaganism since she was a teenager, told me, "Everything seemed so vivid there. It was like a psychedelic experience. When we came back it was like back in the real world."[37] Here "real" takes on the more common usage of "get real" and "real job"—in other words, being a responsible adult, or in this case, fulfilling the responsibilities of a college student. But Neopagans think festivals are *more* "real" because they embody an ideal reality, an intensity of experience unconstrained by practical considerations such as making a living or finishing one's college degree.

Mundania is cast as the antithesis to festival, as a world in which Neopagan values are rarely expressed and Neopagans must hide their identities. The contrast aimed for is moral and ontological, but this opposition between sacred and profane, carnival and work, festival and mundania is as much the production of a different reality as it is the negation of the everyday. Neopagans establish—through narrative, ritual, and fantasy—a contrast between the festival world and everyday society, in which the former takes on a heightened reality and represents for participants a world made over by Neopagan views of gender, ecology, and the nature of the divine. In this sense, festivals "operate not merely as models of and for society that somehow stand timelessly alongside 'real' life. Rather they construct what reality is and how it is experienced and understood."[38] Jeff Rosenbaum, one of the principal organizers of the successful Starwood and Winter Star gatherings, believes that festivals are opportunities "for people to have sort of 'space stations' or safe places where they can go to learn and to become illuminated, to recapture that sense of being in reality rather than being asleep and dreaming in this world of illusion."[39] For Rosenbaum, festivals offer a "reality" that is unattainable in the outside world. Australian Neopagan Vyvien shares with readers of *Green Egg,* published by the Church of All Worlds and one of the oldest Neopagan magazines in the United States, an impression from her first festival: "Everything I did was as the first time and therefore seemed clearer, more focused, more real."[40] For Neopagans like Rosenbaum and Vyvien, festivals are different from ordinary life because they are "more real," allowing for a more direct experience of "reality" and sharpening the senses in ways that are not possible in everyday life. Neopagans say that going to a festival is like traveling to a more real world of heightened experience and perception. "People feel starved for something real in their lives," I overheard in a conversation at Wild Magick 1992 about why Neopagan festivals are growing in number. Peh, an ELF elder who dresses in black clothes and long robes at festivals, expressed relief at leaving his work clothes behind. In contrast, when I met him in mundania during his lunch hour he was dressed in a business-like trench coat over khakis and a polo shirt, his silver pentacle necklace hidden beneath his clothes or left at home.

So what is more *real?* Neopagans' expectations that festivals will be especially "real" point to their intense dissatisfaction with the everyday world and the depth of their desire for something more. The power of festival space is in the possibility for natural and supernatural experiences otherwise unavailable. The stronger their rejection of mundania, the more vivid the festival world becomes for them. They highlight at festivals what is lacking for them in mundania—religious tolerance, for instance—in order to focus their desires and energies on making the festival special. In order to create a "super-real" festival world, Neopagans imbue the festival space with meanings absent from the workplace and urban landscape. They set aside spaces for "healing" and "trance-work." These spaces, often unavailable in the outside world, make possible "real" healing, healing that is spiritual as well as physical and that is helped along by friendly spirits. Massage tables are set out in the middle of wooded campsites and marked with signs offering massages for low cost or barter or for free. Pagan Spirit Gathering includes the "Centering Dome" for people who need emotional support or a quiet place to sit and relax. The free community kitchen is another festival feature that is part of an attempt to gain a fresh perception of community by offering an alternative to the outside world's consumerism. A group of volunteers at ELFest 1992 set up a community kitchen that offered free food and coffee to all festival participants. Another way in which the festival holds out an ideal, "more real" existence is by drawing festival participants into an awareness and appreciation of their connectedness to the natural world. A popular festival chant attests to the important relationship between human and nature: "Earth my body, water my blood, air my breath, and fire my spirit."[41] Neopagans make an effort to create, for a week, reality as they think it should be, a world that heals body and soul and encourages interaction with nature.

By emphasizing the sacredness of the natural world and the boundaries of ritual and festival space, Neopagans make material the belief that the divine is "immanent," meaning that the gods and goddesses live in the earth and trees and are more accessible in forests and farmlands removed from the distractions of urban life. Some Neopagans use the term "nature religions" or "earth religions" in order to be most inclusive and to emphasize the more socially acceptable elements of magical groups, that is, their nature-centered identities, rather then spell making and magical work.[42] Ritual leaders draw on the belief that spirits surround them. At Ancient Ways 1997, the "Hermes and Hecate" ritual included a call "to the spirits of the land" to join the ritual. At the end of the ritual, everyone was asked to breath out "ahhh," in order to "send off all our energy to the spirits of the land." At ELFest 1991, participants in the "Descent of Persephone," a ritual based on the Greek myth of Demeter and Persephone, had to make their way blindfolded through dark woods where they encountered a Persephone figure—a priestess dressed in a Greek-style gown. Festivals are disorienting because they are very different from the spaces most festival goers frequent. Even more disorienting is the dark; no streetlights illuminate the paths, and a step away from campfires and candles is the dark of the woods which some might feel threatens them as much as it promises transformation.

Like many other religious people, Neopagans emphasize the importance of "sacred space" for effective and powerful rituals. Festival sites are "sacred" because they are "dedicated to or set apart for" specific practices.[43] In an introduction to "Reader's Forum" in *Circle Network News* (a quarterly newsletter published by a Neopagan church) on "Sacred Space," Moonstar writes, "Sacred space provides the setting and contributes to enhancing the mental set necessary for connection with the deeper spiritual aspects of the human psyche. By deepening these connections, we become able to channel the Spiritual Energy of the Inner Self for healing ourselves, for healing others, and for healing the planet."[44] Sacred space is what links the individual to realities outside the self and makes enduring changes in self and world, according to Moonstar. In the same issue of *Circle Network News,* Caitlin observes that "a special place for Magickal workings becomes the ground, becomes the World, where we can focus and intensify our power, where we can affect reality, where we can experience the ecstasy of oneness with the Divine."[45] Festival participants expect that sacred space will make it possible for them to both go deeper into the self and to act more powerfully on the surrounding world. In this way sacred space is a method of manifesting "interconnectedness," the belief among Neopagans that the layers of the self, including past lives, are vitally connected to the rest of the planet and its inhabitants.[46] Sacred space is meant to be active. It acts on ritual participants and shapes their experience at the same time that they act on it, inscribing space with meaning.

Establishing festival sites as special and powerful places begins in promotional material. A flyer for Spiral 1994, a gathering held near Atlanta, Georgia, tempts potential festival participants with a description of "two hundred acres of enchanted woodlands with a 275 acre lake" and "a private road with locked gates." Inside a mailing about Lothlorien events, I also received a brief description of the site itself: "Lothlorien—a vortex of life tucked away amongst the forested hills, fertile valleys and limestone quarries of South Central Indiana. . . . Lothlorien is a 'stargate between worlds', a mythic memory being recalled, a haven for Flora and Fauna, a spiritual gathering point." In ELF's "Wild Magick 1993 Bulletin," Lothlorien is described as "a Rainbow Bridge, an interface . . . a magickal nature sanctuary" that "fills a gap between the tame and the wild." Festival sites also may be seen as special and unique because of physical or geological features. Circle Sanctuary, where Circle's smaller festivals and workshops are held, is "located in southwestern Wisconsin in the Driftless area, which often is called 'enchanted' because it was the only place in North America to be totally surrounded by glaciers and never touched by them." Because Neopagans are practitioners of what they describe as earth religions, these aspects of a land's history invest the festival site with special meanings that shape religious beliefs and practices.

The isolation and hiddenness of most festivals also facilitates their separation from mundania, further enhancing their sacredness. Festivals differ significantly from the cities and suburbs festival goers come from because they take place in isolated wooded sites like Brushwood in New York, or on nature sanctuaries like Lothlorien in southern Indiana, or Wotanwald ("Odin's Forest") in northern California.[47] Each of the three festival sites I visited during my first year of research was reached by traveling off main thoroughfares and through forests or down quiet country roads. Going to the woods to establish a relationship to the land itself is an important part of the festival experience for Neopagans. Hidden deep in woods far away from home, festivals allow Neopagans to forget the rigors of the workplace and families that are antagonistic to their chosen religious identity. In his interpretation of Brazilian *Carnaval,* anthropologist Roberto DaMatta writes: "What explains the style of Brazilian *Carnaval* is the necessity of inventing a celebration where things that must be forgotten can be forgotten if the celebration is to be experienced as a social utopia. Just as the dream makes reality even more vehement, *Carnaval* can only be understood when we discover what it must hide in order to be a celebration of pleasure, sexuality, and laughter."[48] Festivals create a sanctuary in which festival goers can escape the discrimination and harassment they face outside, just as in the outside world they repress desires and hide the identities that they explore and release at festivals. Their view of festivals as intensely real and special events makes easier the task of forgetting the persecution and suspicion of conservative Christians or dismissal by an American public that associates "witches" with *The Wizard of Oz* and "magic" with David Copperfield's elaborate stage performances.

At festivals, Neopagans also try to escape mundania's attitudes toward nature, spirituality, sexuality, and the body. Body and movement, as well as forest settings, facilitate the shift from mundania to the festival community. Festivals promote sensual enjoyment and self-expression, and in so doing they enable participants to go beyond their usual ways of carrying themselves and acting toward others. Changes in bodily actions such as moving more slowly help festival goers forget "what needs to be forgotten," such as the fast pace of their everyday lives. Festival guides and programs encourage people to treat the festival as a place of play and relaxation, in one example revealing in public what is usually hidden—lingerie: "After the Opening Ritual we will gather in the Dining Hall for Ragnar's Pub, a wild and wonderful party that allows us to get down and loosen up, to let everything out and leave the mundane world behind. Bring your favorite dance music, get all decked out in your most outrageous lingerie (men and women) and be prepared to dance like a fool to shake off the outside world."[49] For festival goers, "dancing like a fool" is not something that is possible in the mundane world, but it is perfectly appropriate in the festival setting. Festivals are "more real" because at them Neopagans feel safe to express themselves in dress and behavior that would be considered excessive or bizarre elsewhere (see fig. 2). Anthropologist Loretta Orion explains it this way: "Neopagan

Figure 2.   A festival goer wears a cow-pelvis mask in preparation for activities at Starwood. Photo by Ransom Haile.

gatherings, like other pilgrimages, are retreats from the constraints of quotidian existence. In sacred space it is safe to shed clothing and other conventions linked with the secular world, as it is safe and efficacious to assume a different appearance by wearing masks or costumes."[50]

Festival goers describe the festival as a place of enhanced sensory perceptions or altered awareness. They also say their experience of time changes. Michael, an architect from the East Coast puts it this way: "Starwood is long enough so that you live there. Your time frame just shifts down and becomes more attuned to the day. You walk slower, act slower. . . . There's a sense of just being outside of time. . . . You forget that there's an outside world."[51] "Pagan Standard Time" takes over at festivals, indicating that events will take place eventually, but often not at the hour when they are scheduled. Nude and costumed, dancing and chanting, festival participants express a reality that sharply contrasts to their mundane lives. Festival participants shake off assumptions about time and the body, about proper behavior and social roles. But the party is not simply a celebration; it also functions as a rite of passage from one kind of world to another.

PILGRIMAGE THROUGH SPACE TO SELF

The separation of festival world from mundania is also accomplished by making festival attendance a pilgrimage. Neopagans often journey to far-away places when they go to festivals, and they see this journey as a pilgrimage or a rite of passage that will transform them. Neopagans' accounts of their trips to festivals are similar to the stories of other religious people described in studies of pilgrimage.[52] Neopagans envision the festival as a pilgrimage destination, and they approach the festival site as a place of miraculous experiences. When they attend festivals, Neopagan pilgrims set out on "sacred journeys" toward ideal communities and ideal selves.[53] Festivals promise a world made over by Neopagan values because they involve "pilgrimages to nature," sacred to "nature-worshipping pantheists," as Neopagan psychologist Dennis Carpenter calls Neopagans.[54] Loretta Orion explains that festival goers travel "to Earth—the goddess who is everywhere, everything. . . . Nature is not the setting for the pilgrimage but the destination and object of the pilgrim's quest."[55] In contrast to pilgrimages to saints' shrines or deities' temples, Neopagan pilgrimages are not to places connected by myths to the life of a saint or deity (although Neopagans do make pilgrimages to ancient sites like Stonehenge). Rather, at festival sites like Lothlorien, the land itself, the trees, and the earth are invested with the desires and dreams of festival goers and become "sacred" destinations for festival participants.

Neopagans are also pilgrims through "landscapes of the self." Neopagans say they constitute "new selves" on the trip between festival and mundane worlds. Neopagans see festivals as both passageways and destinations. Kenn Deigh describes Lumensgate, the festival he runs, as the way to a place apart as well as that place itself. In this view, personal changes and spiritual experiences take place during the festival, but are ongoing. For instance, when I asked Leaf, a member of ELF, about her experiences at Lumensgate, she told me that she was still experiencing profound changes brought about by a Lumensgate ritual two years earlier. For her, the Lumensgate ritual and the changes it instigated were all part of an ongoing journey of self-exploration. Festival goers speak of going to a festival as a journey to what festival "pilgrim" John Threlfall calls "spiritual homeland." In "Pagan Gatherings—Discovering Spiritual Homeland," which appeared in *Circle Network News*, Threlfall discusses his first trip to Pagan Spirit Gathering as a pilgrimage across the country: "I have come to see my journey across

America that summer of 1989 as my own Hajj . . . I was drawn forth on a pilgrimage of my own making, seeking a holy land that, ultimately, I could find only in myself."[56] For Neopagans, festivals make possible a journey to a "true" self, which is a territory to explore. As one festival organizer puts it, these gatherings are "a wondrous revival of the old regional fair except that this region is one of the mind."[57] Metaphors that integrate place and self commonly appear in Neopagans' descriptions of self-discovery at festivals, a topographical sense of subjectivity that echoes the psychoanalytic theories of Sigmund Freud and Carl Jung. Freud in particular saw himself as the "emotional excavator" of his patients, and in a similar fashion Neopagans excavate themselves at festivals. Neopagans draw on a common set of modern metaphors to craft an account of their multileveled journeys to pilgrimage sites.

This is not to say that Neopagans are Freudians. They are more likely to participate in group therapy than psychoanalysis. But like Freud, they make use of spatial analogies when they work on the self in workshops and rituals or when they describe traveling to festivals as "a pilgrimage to and through self." They sift through their personal histories and past lives for information about themselves, and they organize rituals intended to heal broken selves and to bring about changes in behavior. At ELFest 1991 Kenn Deigh's ritual of self-transformation required participants to take a token to represent some part of the self that they wanted to cast out of their lives. During the physical and emotional journey of this ritual, participants were given seeds symbolizing those aspects of the self they wanted to nurture. Because ELF literature pictures the festival site populated by the spirits of trees and plants, the land itself was imagined to aid participants who followed Kenn's directions to "journey to the self's underworld"—in actuality to be led blindfolded through the dark woods. As they stumbled along the path and were guided by ritual helpers, participants felt disoriented in time and space, but they leaned on the arms of their guides and focused inward on the changes the ritual had set in motion.

Festival sites are imagined in such a way as to facilitate this self-excavation or "topoanalysis": "the exploration of self-identity through place." Festival spaces specifically set aside for healing and for contemplation of death, for example, present these aspects of human experience to festival goers in concrete visual forms.[58] Dimensions of self and space are interconnected for Neopagans; boundaries are fluid between self and other, imagination and reality, and human and nature. Festival space dissolves these boundaries by telling participants through their senses that the space belongs to them and is different from the other spaces they live in. The very appearance of festivals—handpainted signs welcoming them to Lothlorien, a colorful banner with ribbons flying in the breeze, and the sound of drums or flutes—signals this difference.

FESTIVALS AS HOME, TRIBE, AND FAMILY

Neopagans engage in self-exploration and commune with nature at festivals, but they also establish important friendships and intimate relationships with other festival goers. If they want to be archaeologists of the self, then they want to do so in the company of others and under the auspices of a Neopagan community. Observers of the relationship between self and community in the contemporary United States have argued that Americans tend to emphasize the needs of the self over those of the community. Robert Bellah and his colleagues point out in *Habits of the Heart* that when Americans describe their spirituality they talk most about personal empowerment and self-expression rather than the requirements of community.[59] In contrast, Neopagan festivals emphasize both self-transformation and the creation of community. Festivals provide a unique opportunity to observe the ways in which these apparently conflicting projects are carried out.

A flyer advertising a festival in Georgia illustrates the explicit strategies incorporated into festivals to create communities that can coexist with and enable self-transformation.

> The Opening Ritual on Thursday evening will be a time to create a magickal place of safety and protection. To build a sacred fire in the center of our universe. . . . We ask that once you arrive that you acknowledge and affirm your place within this Magickal Circle, thus beginning your participation in the active current. Realize that you are within a Circle surrounded by the SPIRAL Family. . . . The Opening Ritual will bring us together once again under the Full Moon in September. We will create a safe and free space to work our Magick. A place where you can be free to explore the magickal self that lives within.[60]

Circles are central to Neopagan beliefs and rituals and are particularly important in defining sacred space (see fig. 3). Circular spaces are in keeping with Neopagan emphasis on cycles of the moon, seasonal festivals, and reincarnation. Their attention to circles may also explain in part how Neopagans see the relationship between self and community. In this relationship, the circle of community is what makes possible work on the self. An announcement for Pagan Spirit Gathering describes one model for this relationship:

Figure 3.   Neopagans circle the Sacred Fire at the opening ritual of 1995
Pagan Spirit Gathering sponsored by Circle Sanctuary in Wisconsin.
Courtesy of the Circle Sanctuary archives. Photo by Robert.

> This Gathering is about experiencing Community—creating a Pagan Tribal
> Village together at this special place—sharing songs, meditations, rituals,
> dreams, food, ideas, fun, magic—sharing work as well as celebration—teaching
> and learning from each other—sharing our visions of the past, present, and
> future—examining ourselves collectively and individually as part of the
> Pagan/Nature Spirituality movement manifesting on Planet Earth. It is about
> living fully as our magical Pagan selves in this spiritual place for a week. . . .
> This year's Gathering focuses on Sacred Circles—with special emphasis on
> honoring circles as symbols of sacred time and sacred space, wholeness and
> balance, Nature's rhythms and life cycles, community, and the interconnect-
> edness of all life.[61]

At Pagan Spirit Gathering, circles are collective forms that encourage
individualistic Neopagans to collaborate on a common project. Circles
of this sort are most successfully created at festivals— "this special
place"—that are explicitly separated from and opposed to ordinary life.
After the Rites of Spring 1998 web ritual, Andras Arthen spoke about
the importance and meaning of community embodied by the ritual circle.
He asked participants to touch the ground, to note where it was hard or
soft, wet or dry— "like life." He reminded us that we are dependent on
community and responsible for maintaining and caring for our communities. He suggested that over the weekend everyone come to the web,
which was left in place until the festival's closing ritual, to "take some
power" and "give some," or walk into the intricately woven web. But

he cautioned as well: "Be careful how you tread the web, because that is how you tread in community."

Neopagans attend festivals to experience a sense of belonging to a community, but it is in part their experience of marginality that unifies them. Festivals become meaningful places as extensions of participants' own feelings of marginality. Many Neopagans see themselves as social outcasts and their Neopagan lifestyle as a rebellion against mainstream society. The separateness of festivals allows for a community-wide recognition and a communal self-affirmation of Neopagan marginality and its historical roots. Often, events are commemorated at festivals that identify the Neopagan community with other ostracized and persecuted groups. One of the main rituals at Pagan Spirit Gathering 1992 was a memorial for people executed as witches in seventeenth-century Salem, Massachusetts. As I discuss in chapter 5, many Neopagans recall being ostracized by their peers during adolescence because they dressed strangely or spent too much time reading books, but in adulthood they find a place of belonging and a sense of community in the Neopagan movement and at Neopagan festivals. At festivals Neopagans who have felt ostracized celebrate their outcast status and make it into a defining identity in a space constituted as powerful because it is outside the ordinary, as they are.[62]

The relationship between Neopaganism and mundania, like the relationship between New Religious Movements (NRMs) and more established religions, is not simply one of binary opposites. Rather, it is a far more complex and dynamic relationship. Festivals are both distant from and closely connected to the world against which they constitute themselves, and the boundary between festival and mundane worlds is more fluid than is generally admitted by festival goers. Kenn observes that festivals provide

> an opportunity to step out of our usual model of social interaction. Some of the same things applied, but when you got out there they made it clear that as long as you didn't hurt yourself or anybody else, basically whatever you wanted went. Now, when it comes down to it, that's not true. There were certain things that still held, but it was a lot more open, a lot more free. And even though it wasn't focused, it was providing an atmosphere, a place, a social mechanism by which people could express more of themselves and discover and explore more than they could back home and in their usual motif.[63]

Here Kenn affirms the contrast between "back home" and the festival. But he problematizes the notion of the festival as an ideal place. Festival goers do not simply leave their old habits at home, he warns. They arrive at festivals with wildly conflicting ideals and expectations about what a festival home and family should be like. When I asked Peh to describe the meaning of "community" at Neopagan festivals, he explained to me that festivals are places where the community a person brings with them—by which he meant their social status, relationships in the mundane world, career, and upbringing—encounters the festival community.[64]

Festivals are not only strange places apart from everyday life, but also Neopagans' home and family. Annual journeys to festivals are simultaneously adventures to exotic "uncharted shores" and to familiar, home-like, memory-laden places. The world Neopagans represent as the fringes of mainstream culture becomes the center of their most meaningful activities. Self-described festival pilgrim John Threlfall puts it this way: "There is a family out there, ready to embrace me whenever I feel lonely or out of touch. All I need is to find a Pagan gathering and I'll be home."[65] "Welcome home" reads the sign on the registration booth for Wild Magick 1992. Festival goers set out from their mundane homes and often journey long distances in order to reach their festival home. At festivals, Neopagans make marginality more real than the real world that excludes them and travel to festival sites in order to be home. They excavate themselves precisely amid such ambivalence and contradiction.

For many participants, festivals are an ideal way of being with others, and for this reason the participants relate more intimately to each other at festivals than in other social environments. Festival goers expect festival communities to be egalitarian, tolerant, nurturing, creative, and supportive of personal expression. At festivals they find sympathetic friends who listen to stories of their personal lives and give them advice for dealing with family members who do not understand their religious beliefs. One participant in Pagan Spirit Gathering 1994 particularly appreciated "living in our family/tribal community, in perfect love and perfect trust, without fear of ridicule or reprisal."[66] The intensity of festivals also encourages greater and more immediate intimacy. At Wild Magick 1992, ELF's fall festival, tattoo artist Laughing Starheart camped next to three women from Pennsylvania and Cherokee tribe member Don Waterhawk, an artisan and prominent workshop leader at many of the festivals I attended. As the festival progressed these neighbors began to spend time together talking about their lives, sharing food, and doing small and intimate rituals—a pipe-smoking ceremony and a gift ritual. During the summer festival season the following year they continued to meet and camp together at several festivals; they spent holidays at each other's homes, and they helped each other through crises—a skiing accident and a divorce. In the year following Wild Magick 1992, I met Laughing Starheart at another ELF festival. His tent was decorated with a colorful batik banner that read "Ohana." When I asked him what the banner meant, he explained that it was "the name for 'home' in Cherokee" and referred to his festival family: the three women, Don, and several other close friends who had become "like family" at festivals.

I have repeatedly watched festival "families" develop in this way. Festival goers who were strangers at the beginning of a festival, by the end have become like family members who visit each other at their mundane homes, who phone, write letters, e-mail each other regularly, help each other through difficult times, and celebrate important rites of passage. Certainly not all festival goers become members of small families. Some prefer to camp alone, while others attend festivals with covens or ritual groups from their home towns, and some Neopagans refer to the entire festival community as their family or home.

Orion relates a powerful story about the importance of the festival family to Neopagans who feel they do not fit in the broader society. She witnessed a handfasting (Neopagan marriage ceremony) between two gay men: "Although they had been sharing their lives for several years, Nat and Garland decided to ask the 'Spiral family' to acknowledge their union after it became clear that Nat would die of AIDS within a few years. The community was empowered to create the union . . . that mainstream society would not acknowledge." She reports that two years after the handfasting and a month before Nat's death, the couple returned to Spiral so that Nat could "say good-bye to his 'Spiral family.'" These rites of passage demonstrate that Neopagans have developed their own kinship systems: "To some Neopagans these bonds are peripheral, to others they constitute the most significant of their social relationships, surpassing and substituting even those based on kinship by blood (consanguinity)."[67] A flyer for Lumensgate festival reads: "The overall focus of Lumensgate is creating and working with Magickal Community—our Chosen Family!"[68]

Festivals become home-like places where participants can be the kind of children they want to be, can share intimate secrets and play in the ways schools, parents, and religions in the outside world deny them. The festival is constituted by desire for a family to accept them as witches and magicians, a family who will appreciate their arcane knowledge and admire their tattoos and jewelry. In *Drawing Down the Moon*, Margot Adler identifies the central role of Neopagan festivals in Neopagans'

Figure 4.   Elf Lore Family elder Peh speaks at ELFest council meeting at
Lothlorien in Indiana. Courtesy Marty Laubach. Photo by Bethany Curtiss.

search for a home in the world: "Many festival organizers have told me
that the most frequent feedback they receive is the comment 'I never
knew there were other people who believe what I believe, let alone several hundred at one place. I never knew that I could come totally out of
the closet and be what I am openly.' The feeling of being at home among
one's true family for the first time is the fundamental reason that festivals have spread throughout the country."[69] At festivals, Neopagans discover and create families that nurture new identities and allow them to
reveal parts of themselves that they usually hide: "I come here to see family," asserted one woman at an ELF council meeting at ELFest 1992
where the purpose of the festival was being debated. ELF elders like Peh
facilitate these meetings, solicit comments, criticism, praise, and stories
from festival participants in order to make them feel that they have a
stake in their festival family and a voice in the creation of the festival as
a home-like place (see fig. 4). Festival organizers actively promote these
images of the festival as family. Fliers and pamphlets for Starwood, Wild
Magick, and Pagan Spirit Gathering advertise "a global tribal village,"
"spiritual community," "family," and "home." Announcements of festivals try hard to be inclusive. For example, a flyer for a pagan retreat
called Harvest of Light in Missouri welcomes "all races, traditions, alternative family structures, and sexual orientations."[70]

Participants feel that they can be their "real selves" in the festival families they have chosen. They can dress as they please, worship foreign

goddesses and gods, explore their sexuality, and express their sexual orientation as they are unable to do in their given families. Festivals also make possible a community space where political organization around issues of religious and sexual freedom or "alternative" families can take place.[71] Starwood XIV (1994) offered workshops on "The Path of Polyamoury" and "Dysfunctional Families and Group Energies: The Gaia Conspiracy," and Pagan Spirit Gathering 1992 held workshops on "Bisexual Spirit— Bisexual Pride" and "Out of the Broom Closet: An Open Discussion of Craft Homosexuality." At festivals I witnessed gay as well as straight handfastings, and a handfasting between two men and a woman. In the festival setting, invented families are a haven from the struggles of daily life, and they call into question accepted norms such as heterosexuality and monogamy. Handfastings are typically defined as commitments for "a year and a day," but they are also legally recognized marriages when performed by Neopagan clergy like Selena Fox (see fig. 5).

Festival organizers promote this sense of festival as family or tribe in their literature: "Coming from a variety of spiritual orientations and ethnic heritages, participants cooperate to create a global tribal village in which they live, work, play, and do ritual together for the week of the Gathering. This special Gathering is the Pagan Spirit Gathering (PSG). . . . PSG focuses on developing the sense of spiritual community and global tribal culture. PSG is a chance to live a holistic Pagan lifestyle on a totally Pagan space. PSG is an opportunity to attune deeply to one's own Inner Self in a natural, magical environment." Pagan Spirit Gathering's organizers identify the double nature that is central to Neopagan festivals: PSG is a place for self-expression, but it also offers an experience of community and a sense of belonging to a common "tribe." The notion of a "global tribal culture" clearly expresses Neopagans' desire to include diverse individuals and cultures in one community. Festivals are imagined by their organizers and participants as opportunites to develop multicultural and tolerant families and provide accepting and supportive environments in which everyone can attune to their "Inner Self."

Festival gatherings may be the only communities where Neopagans feel fully themselves, and for this reason, ironically, festival communities are necessary for the individualism that Neopagans value. "These festivals restore my faith in humanity," I overheard one Starwood 1992 participant say. Rose explained to me that being at gatherings allows people to feel support and to recognize others who share their own values and experiences. At these events, she said, "My higher self can connect directly with other higher selves without going through a lot of preliminaries."[72] For

Figure 5.   A Wiccan handfasting (wedding) takes place at 1997 Pagan Spirit Gathering in Ohio. Kyra and Cygnus are wed in a rite by Selena Fox and Dennis Carpenter of Circle Sanctuary. Courtesy Circle Sanctuary archives. Photo by Jeff Koslow.

Rose the "higher self" is a side of her personality unconstrained by every-day roles, a self that emerges most easily in an accepting and supportive group context. A festival goer at Summerhawk festival in New York con-curs; what he likes most about festivals is "leaving the masks behind." Peh is an ELF elder, cofacilitator of the Bloomington, Indiana, Covenant of

Unitarian Universalist Pagans chapter, and a magician who has organized
and participated in countless festivals. He describes a similar sense of being
free of constraining roles during festivals. As Peh was driving me to
Summerhawk, he discussed his relief to be far away from the strains of his
marriage and the stress of his job at a university computing center. Peh
looked on the festival as an opportunity to escape from his daily familial
and work responsibilities as well as to connect with old friends and to gain
a fresh perspective on his life. "I wear many hats," he explained to me,
"and lately they have become reified." He expected the festival could
change all that, but only because he defined it in contrast to the things in
his life that needed to be fixed. By going to Summerhawk, he felt he would
be able to enjoy a more fluid identity unconstrained by role expectations.
He believed the festival would enable him to explore those parts of the self
that were obscured by marital and vocational concerns. The relationships
among "higher selves" create community for Peh and others. But such a
community is possible only in a place where the usual "masks" and "hats"
are unnecessary, but at which new masks and robes can be tried on.

AT THE BOUNDARIES

Neopagans say that self and community are more fully realized in a place
safely bounded and metaphysically removed from the everyday world.
Emphasis on boundaries between inside and outside is a constant theme
at Neopagan festivals and essential to understanding how festival goers
experience community belonging and personal freedom. At boundaries,
definitions are made, and the elements that constitute self, community,
and family are identified. Home and festival as well as specific places
within the festival, such as ritual circles and healing shrines, are defined
against each other as their boundaries are negotiated by festival participants. Neopagan boundary work follows a pattern described in an extensive literature by folklorists and anthropologists on festivals as places
where conflicts develop and are resolved.[73]

An uneasy dynamic that develops at festivals reveals the tensions between individual and community that festivals are intended to harmo-
nize. Neopagans gather to share a common experience, but in so doing
they may discover the many differences that separate them. By emphasizing first their separation from the outside world and, second, their
unity as tribe and family, Neopagan festival communities try to downplay inner differences and contradictions. They cling to the symbolic
identification of the festival community with the circle and assert their

unity in the face of inner dissent. But a festival goer may find that he or she is as different from others in the festival community as from the outside culture. For instance, some participants are more willing to be rebellious than others. Most Neopagans are to some extent countercultural simply by their presence in this marginal festival space, and most of them identify to some extent with a common inheritance of persecution and otherness. On the other hand some festival goers live in ways that compromise with the expectations of mundania, while others live further outside mundania. Some Neopagans are completely "in the broom closet" about their practices, but others display pentacles around their necks and let their coworkers know that they are Neopagans ("born-again Pagans," in the words of one popular button). Another tension emerges between those who are looking for a "wildly imaginative party" and others who want to work hard to change and heal society. Orion suggests that on occasion, festivals perpetuate the social problems they want most to change, such as rigid and hierarchical structures.[74] Participants expect festivals to embody their ideals, but festival communities do not always live up to such expectations.

The festival bounded in time and space, then, becomes a place in which all sorts of imagined festivals intersect and conflict with each other. Thus the opposition between festival and mundane worlds is often complicated by the many differences among festival goers. I return to these internal tensions in later chapters, as I continue to problematize the distinct boundary Neopagans attempt to draw between festivals and mundania. Whether festival virgins or veterans, festival goers arrive at a festival site with a range of desires and expectations. Memories of past festivals on the same site and of festivals at other locations, as well as festival stories told by friends or appearing in Neopagan publications, all contribute to a festival's history. The Neopagan festival as a place takes shape in the encounter between representations of festivals and people's actual festival experiences.

If there are many differences within festivals, there are also points of connection between festivals and the outside world. Participants from different geographical areas take with them pieces of their local communities, covens, or other magical groups. They also take home their festival experiences, rather than leaving behind their "new" selves and communities. The Pagan Spirit Gathering Village Guide suggests that festival goers take home ashes from the ritual fire after the closing rites. People also leave the festival with new books, clothing, or jewelry bought from merchants, made in workshops, or given to them by other members of the festival community. In her account of "Womon-gathering," a women-only festival in southern Pennsylvania, Watersnake describes feeling sad as she prepared to return home, but reassures herself that the festival experience will remain with her: "I knew I would be taking home with me many experiences to share with others, and a new sense of self that will be with me for the rest of my days." After the closing ritual, all the women say their good-byes and pick up "small stones from the sacred circle to take back with us to our homes . . . keeping the energies created that weekend alive in the rocks in our hands . . . and in our hearts."[75] These souvenirs provide material links between the disparate worlds of festival and everyday life. At a workshop on the Santeria *orisha* (elemental powers personified as spirits; in Vodou they are called *Pwa*) at Starwood 1992, the workshop facilitator suggested that the *orisha* Oshun was directing the "bridge-working that's being done at Starwood," helping festival goers carry "feeling" back to cities where no one is making sacrifices to connect themselves to the spirits.

In some sense, then, Neopagans meet new deities at festivals. These may be deifications of parts of self or spirit presences believed to inhabit the land or those invited into ritual space. While closing rituals are intended to say "thanks and farewell" to guardian and other spirits, festival goers often feel that they take something residual with them from the encounter. In some sense, these spirits go home with participants just as the feeling of community stays with them when they leave. Neopagans also take home the changes they go through during a festival. As Watersnake describes it, she returns to mundania with "a new sense of self," perhaps less tangible than "small stones from the sacred circle," but nonetheless real. Neopagan festival goers say that emotional and spiritual changes stay with them after they leave a festival site. Vyvien puts it this way: "For a few weeks afterwards I felt that same summer sky spaciousness inside my head, and I trust that some corners of it still sing in me somewhere."[76] At the end of her first gathering, Orion reflected on what festival goers take home with them and what they leave behind: "These pilgrims returned home from a pilgrimage site that existed only in their memories, leaving their seeds to sprout in the deserted straw field."[77]

Home and festival exist in a dynamic relationship, never truly separated. Festivals provide a space to work out problems of home, and home is where the effects of festival experiences will continue to be felt and reincorporated into life there.[78] Using words and images, Neopagans build up boundaries between festivals and mundania at the same time that in practice they break them down. They leave "their seeds" in offerings to shrines at festival sites, and they take home tokens of the festival community—ashes from the fire—along with memories of their festival selves and newly acquired spirit helpers.

Festivals are full of tensions and contradictions. They are set apart from mundania for self-realization and for intimate encounters with others; they are intended for communion with nature as well as for envisioning an alternative society; and they are safer than the hostile outside world. However, the woods and fields of festival sites are populated by mysterious and unknown spirits. Neopagans summon supernatural beings in rituals back at their home temples, but at festivals they may not feel familiar with spirits of the land or with the deities invoked by other festival goers during rituals. Gardnerian witches whose rituals involve a goddess and god, may not be comfortable with the spirits invoked by Vodou practitioners camped next to them. Festival goers may also be uncomfortable with the fact that there is no established tradition to define the relationship between the festival community and spirits whom they believe to populate the woods and hills where festivals take place. Neopagans must not only deal with the complex relationships and power struggles that exist in all human communities, but they must also confront the mysterious relationships between themselves and the supernatural beings whom they call upon for protection and self-transformation.

Festival spaces are powerful in part because they are in the process of becoming; they are being defined at the same time that they are experienced. Order is brought to bear on the unpredictable nature of festival experience by bounding and defining smaller spaces within the festival site. The dynamic aspect of festivals is particularly clear in the processes by which Neopagans map festival space as they set aside certain areas for healing, camping, workshops, and ritual dancing. I turn next to look more closely at the ways in which Neopagans express their identification with other religious idioms in the spaces within festivals and, in so doing, work out relationships with the spirit world.

CHAPTER TWO

Shrines of Flame and Silence

Mapping the Festival Site

A group of mourning festival goers moves in a procession away from the festival field and descends a steep hill into the woods named "Faerie" on the map of Lothlorien. They follow a winding path past tiny shrines of crystals and roughly carved god and goddess figurines nestled in the roots of trees and enter Faerie through an arch of bound tree branches. They gather in a grove of maple trees, some of which have been recently felled. One of the group paints tar on a tree where a large branch has been cut off. Some of them place crystals and other offerings in the tree's "wound." The mood of the group is somber and angry, and a few people are weeping. They have come here to offer reparation to a tree in their sacred woods that an erring community member has injured. They gather in this grove to mourn the loss of the fallen trees and to heal the injured one.

Johnny, a longtime festival goer, related this story to me when I mentioned to him that I wanted to learn about the processes by which spaces within festivals are created.[1] It all began when Andrew, an ELF member who was doing some jobs on the festival site, volunteered to put together a crew to build a small wooden structure that would function as a community kitchen at festivals. Without telling any of the elders what they were going to do, Andrew and his work crew went into Faerie, the section of woods on Lothlorien considered to be a sacred nature sanctuary, and cut down some maple trees. They neglected to go through formal decision-making procedures, such as asking one of ELF's elders which trees could be cut down. A festival was going on at the time and many festival participants were outraged when they heard about the tree cutting. Johnny described people sobbing and becoming "hysterical." Andrew was then "tried" for breaking ELF's long-standing rule that trees on Lothlorien cannot be cut down without permission. His punishment was to plant trees on the festival site and to participate in a healing ceremony to atone for the trees he had cut. In this way, the ritual affirmed ELF's communal integrity and secured Faerie's special place on the festival map.

At festivals, spatial boundaries such as the fence between a festival site and neighboring property, and the boundaries between Neopagan culture and mundania are where Neopagans express and define self and community. But conflicts and tensions *within* the festival community are also revealed when participants negotiate the boundaries of smaller spaces in festival sites. In this way the inner locus of definitional work at festival altars and shrines parallels the processes of self-constitution at the outer edges. Conflicts over place meanings within festival sites reveal some of the ways in which festival communities struggle to define themselves and the issues that are at stake in these struggles.

In the case of Andrew's tree cutting, festival participants came together over an incident of boundary transgression to make clear the meaning of Faerie and of their festival community. The incident identified important values of the community, especially respect for nonhuman life. In their responses to Andrew's actions, the festival goers claimed for themselves the role of Lothlorien caretakers. They also affirmed the existence of life in the land and the reality of the tree spirits that ELF promotional literature often mentions: "The Green Man is alive and dancing through the forest," reads ELF's "Wild Magick Guidebook," for instance. From its inception, Lothlorien has been intended as a sanctuary to protect "the Green Man" and other spirits of the forest. The disciplinary action against Andrew further demonstrated distinctly Neopagan values; his judges gave him community-centered tasks, thus incorporating him back into the community. The breach in community ethics gave ELF members a chance to clarify their ethics to everyone at the festival, just as in public struggles with neighbors or debates about cultural borrowing, Neopagans define themselves and clarify the meanings of their religious practices.

As places within festival sites are invested with meaning, issues of authority emerge that reveal the dynamics of a festival community's power relations.[2] The tree cutters overstepped the boundaries of authority as well as the boundaries of a sacred woods. While Andrew's offense was the destruction of and damage to these special trees, also at issue, according to several festival goers I spoke with about this incident, was Andrew's neglect to consult community elders before proceeding. The elders were the ones who made such decisions and took it upon themselves to mete out punishment. Andrew took the elders' decision-making authority into his own hands and in so doing challenged ELF's egalitarian rhetoric. ELF has constantly promoted the theme at festivals that "Everyone is a star": "There ain't no 'secret chiefs' in Lothlorien, no one but individuals, friends in the circle . . . in the circle we are equal," reads a flyer for ELFest 1991. But Andrew's experience suggests that there are in fact "secret chiefs" who make important decisions and act on behalf of the entire community. The ideal festival community as it appears in festival goers' expectations and in festival literature is not always experienced as such. This discrepancy between the real and the ideal is inscribed in the spaces of a festival and can best be studied through a close analysis of the ways in which sacred and not-so-sacred spaces are created. I lift out these issues of conflict from Neopagan festivals in order to look carefully at eruptions of hidden power relations, such as those exemplified by the tree-cutting incident at Lothlorien.

Spatial relations themselves express, enact, and are shaped by contests over power or the fact that the spaces within festivals can be as different from each other as the festival itself is from the everyday world. It is when Neopagans work to differentiate festival spaces that they expose hidden forms of authority and contests over power within the festival community. I follow philosopher Michel Foucault's focus on the relationship between power and space in *Discipline and Punish* and other works for my definition of "power."[3] Here power is constitutive of the social world—it is that that establishes both meanings and the possibility of their subversion. For Foucault, power moves fluidly through social relations, but also becomes sedimented in spatial arrangements and pressed into the bodies of ritual participants. Neopagan power relations are embedded in festival spaces and in festival goers. Neopagans say that they reject forms of "power over" to use Witch and political activist Starhawk's term.[4] But in their attempts to practice alternative power relations within their communities, they often simply hide old forms of power under new guises and generate new forms of authority. By exploring how space is defined and experienced at festivals, I have uncovered the meanings of these hidden forms of power.[5]

WHAT NEOPAGANS MEAN BY "SACRED SPACE"

When the ELF community purchased Lothlorien, its first action was to give places on the land specific identities and designated purposes that expressed the community's values and interests. Faerie Woods was one of the first sites to be mapped, and over time many other spaces were similarly bounded and given meaning. On a map of the site that accompanied festival promotional material, the following areas within Lothlorien were labeled: Silence Shrine, Lightning Shrine, Steam Shrine, Mud Shrine, Song Shrine, Radiance Shrine, Mist Shrine, Crystal Shrine, Flame Shrine, Rain Shrine, Dust Shrine, Ancestors' Shrine, Heart Tree Circle, Robins Wood Circle, Eco-Science Circle, Shaman Circle, Holistic Healer Circle, Psychic Circle, Music/Theater Circle, Children's Circle, Warrior Circle, Sacred Rhythm, Troll Circle, and Faerie. How did these spaces within the festival site acquire such specific identities and what do their identities tell us about Neopaganism?

Most areas on the site take on associations and stories that continue to shape and reshape their meaning as annual festivals come and go. Festival goers inscribe the festival site with references to myth, fantasy, and the other cultures they have adopted as their own. Every year or two, new additions appear on the Lothlorien map and are marked on the site itself by hand-carved signs, usually because members decide that they need a place that expresses their emergent perspectives and activities (see fig. 6). Specific areas are also defined by the experiences that people have in them. On one of my first trips to Lothlorien, several ELF members told me they became disoriented and then both physically and mentally lost when they ventured off the path through Faerie. Jeffrey remembered what happened when he strayed away from the path: it began to rain and he lost his sense of time, he then found himself uncharacteristically dancing and singing in the rain.[6] According to Jeffrey and other ELF members, Faerie is a particularly effective place for personal communion with "the spirits of the land." One ELF member had what she called an "out-of-body experience" in Faerie and another heard voices. Salome told me that during ELFest she found herself in Faerie "with two people, one who did not exist and had on this rainbow mask. We looked up and saw UFOs. I completely forgot where I was."[7]

The first time I walked through Faerie I could not help but remember these stories. I noticed a shift in the sound and feel of the woods when I stepped through the entrance gate. Because of the lay of the land, I could only hear distant and muffled sounds from the festival field and camping areas, even though they were quite nearby. Faerie seemed completely set apart from the rest of the festival site and the lively festival community just on the other side of the hill. It seemed as though I had walked through a gateway into another world, green and quiet. Surely the festival goers who reacted so angrily to the tree cutting had felt something similar about this place. For visitors to Lothlorien, Faerie is an enchanted site within an enchanted land, and for this reason, festival goers' ideals are particularly focused there.

While spaces marked off within festival sites may separate festival goers from each other, they also connect them to the earth and especially to the flora and fauna of the festival site. Intense emotional reactions to the tree cutting attest to the importance in this community of maintaining what festival goers imagine to be a harmonious relationship between humans and nature. Neopagans also try to draw closer in this way to their adopted cultures, which they say have more intimate relationships to the earth. Most of the shrines are identified with natural elements and forces—rain, thunder, etc. Neopagans who frequent Lothlorien make altars in the woods out of crystals and found objects like birds' skeletons, label areas with decorative signs, plant flowers and herbs, and clear brush and make paths through the woods to express their commitment to the land. In similar ways, Circle Sanctuary encourages visitors to interact with the site's natural characteristics. The sanctuary site is mapped out in a *Circle Network News* special issue on "sacred sites" and includes descriptions of the following designated areas and their purposes: "Ritual Mound and Stone Circle . . . a gateway to the Otherworld and a place of healing"; "Ritual Ridge and Temple of the Earth Mother . . . a wonderful place to commune with Gaia"; "Mugwort Circle" and "Troll Hole, . . . named for the nature spirit in Scandinavian mythology"; and "Spirit Rock," used for "meditation and vision quests." Circle's owners view Neopagans' relationship to natural places as dynamic and interactive. Instead of forcing their own place meanings onto the land, Circle advises visitors to let the land "speak" to them.

Neopagans demonstrate a wide range of attitudes toward ecological and environmental issues, resulting in confusion and disagreement, as in the tree-cutting incident at Lothlorien. In a discussion on "Nature Religion: A Scholar's Network," listmembers disagreed about Neopagans' environmental commitments. Neopagans' belief that nature is sacred seems conducive to a sense of stewardship toward land and animals. Nicole argued that theory—nature as sacred—and practice must be consistent, which for her meant that "the sacred connection which I feel with

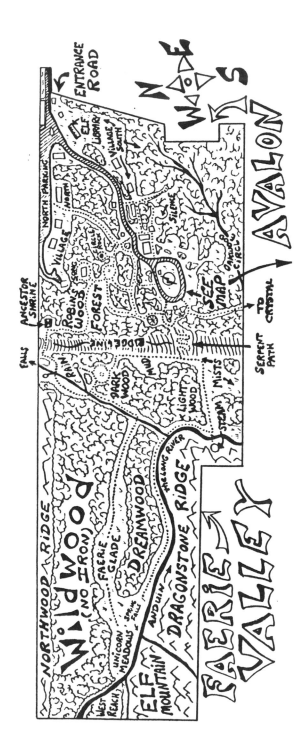

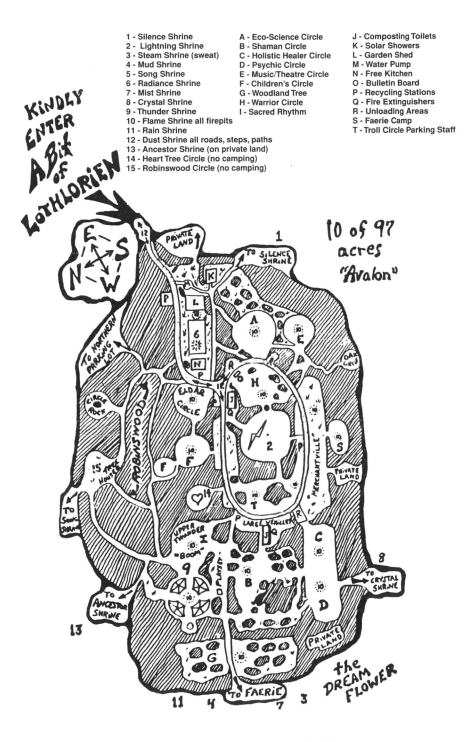

1 - Silence Shrine
2 - Lightning Shrine
3 - Steam Shrine (sweat)
4 - Mud Shrine
5 - Song Shrine
6 - Radiance Shrine
7 - Mist Shrine
8 - Crystal Shrine
9 - Thunder Shrine
10 - Flame Shrine all firepits
11 - Rain Shrine
12 - Dust Shrine all roads, steps, paths
13 - Ancestor Shrine (on private land)
14 - Heart Tree Circle (no camping)
15 - Robinswood Circle (no camping)

A - Eco-Science Circle
B - Shaman Circle
C - Holistic Healer Circle
D - Psychic Circle
E - Music/Theatre Circle
F - Children's Circle
G - Woodland Tree
H - Warrior Circle
I - Sacred Rhythm

J - Composting Toilets
K - Solar Showers
L - Garden Shed
M - Water Pump
N - Free Kitchen
O - Bulletin Board
P - Recycling Stations
Q - Fire Extinguishers
R - Unloading Areas
S - Faerie Camp
T - Troll Circle Parking Staff

Figure 6. These maps are examples of those provided by Elf Lore Family for festival attendees of Lothlorien nature sanctuary in Indiana.

the earth is manifest in organic/biodynamic gardening, support for alternative technologies, solar passive housing, etc. These lifestyle choices also have a natural political implication, somewhat idealistic no doubt, but something to strive towards."[8] Anna agreed that in her community (in the San Francisco Bay Area), "Most people walk their talk about transportation, recycling, use of old-growth wood, and so on."[9] Another participant in the discussion countered that "Neopagans pretty well reflect their larger societies, and most people do not sit down and think about the ecological/political consequences of buying a product made in this country versus that country."[10] Neopagans I have visited and talked to seem to be more environmentally conscious than the general population, but not many of them are environmental activists, preferring to make changes in their individual and community lives such as building a solar house or composting toilets on a festival site, rather than becoming involved with political action.

However, there are exceptions to this tendency to withdraw from politics, and a certain amount of overlap exists between Neopaganism and radical environmental organizations like Earth First! For example, a subscriber to the "natrel" e-mail list forwarded a call to action to the list recipients, urging Neopagans and other interested people to join an action to stop the logging of old-growth redwood. On 30 November 1999, a Witch from the San Francisco Bay area sent out an announcement on the Internet about sixty Witches from the Starhawk's Reclaiming Coven who were participating in the World Trade Organization protests in Seattle, Washington. A week later Starhawk circulated her account of the protests and arrests, and the rituals she and other Witches participated in while they were in jail.[11] Perhaps their lack of political involvement with ecological issues contributes to Neopagans' sense of responsibility for the places where they hold rituals and festivals. Interactions with spirits of the land in ritual space or at shrines allows the many urban residents who travel to festivals to feel that they are living out their commitment to respect nature.

At festivals Neopagans also have an opportunity to situate themselves in relation to cultures that they believe are more ecologically sensitive. Festival sites are attractive and meaningful to the festival community as a whole because of the part they play in recreating ancient pre-Christian practices, when, Neopagans believe, humans honored the changing seasons and lived more harmoniously with their surroundings. For the people who work ritual in them, festival spaces represent an imagined historical connection with ancient earth religions. In their study of Neopagans' sacred spaces, Don Campanelli and Pauline Campanelli put it this way: "As the ancient Britons did on the Salisbury Plain, we cast our circles where the Earth Mother interfaces with the Sky Father. We salute the four directions which symbolize the four elements and at the circle's center, where all things meet their opposites, we place our altar. Beneath a canopy of stars, bathed in palest moonlight, we dance the sacred round dance, our bare feet read joyfully upon the Earth while our spirits soar."[12] Ancestors' Shrine at Lothlorien holds, among other things, an image of a Viking ship and goddess figurines; the Druid "nemeton" (a ritual mound) at Brushwood is designed from reconstructions of ancient Druidic practices. To further their claims on pre-Christian and non-Western cultures, Neopagans mark symbols of their chosen identities on festival spaces.

Neopagans say that because they want to identify with Native Americans or ancient Druids, rather than following the religions of their parents, outdoor ritual spaces are more appropriate to their religious practices than built environments like houses and churches. Making shrines in the woods and participating in rituals outside contrast with the practices of the religions they grew up in: "As the sacred nights of the sabbat approach, we are drawn to do our rituals out of doors, whenever possible, just so that we can be affected by the elements. . . . While others bow and kneel in temples and cathedrals, insulated from the elements, we who follow the Old Ways choose to worship in green forests or at the ocean's edge. While others are uplifted by the voices of a choir or sermons preached from a pulpit, we on the hidden path hear voices in the wind, in forest, field, or city park."[13] Although Neopagans imagine ritual spaces bounded by stones or trees to be the opposite from the churches of their youth, both kinds of spaces bring humans together with their deities.

Designated sacred places like Faerie become sites of conflict because they are where human and divine meet. It is at these sites that Neopagans want to feel and express an ideal relationship with their deities. At these sites, festival goers must encounter and revise their understandings of the meanings of festival, deity, and nature. If a goddess is to be honored by not allowing tree cutting in her woods, then it is the goddess herself and not just the community who is violated when the rules are broken. "The Lady of the Lake calls from Avalon. She calls her children home. Merlin awakens" and "The spirits of ancient Druids inhabit this circle" reads the introduction to Lothlorien in "Wild Magick Guidebook." For Neopagans, it is in the presence of these mythological figures and "the faeries

and elves" that acts of violation must be judged and specifically Neopagan ethics affirmed.

Because Lothlorien and other sanctuaries are inhabited by Neopagans'
gods and goddesses, the structures of these sites embody Neopagans' most
important values, especially the identification of earth as a goddess. De-
Anna Alba explains this relationship in an article about Gaia that appeared in *Circle Network News:* "This planet, the body of the Mother,
is sacred space and should be treated as such at all times." Because the
world around us is divine, writes Alba, "the only real difference between
the sacred space of the Earth Mother and the Universe and the sacred
space we mark out by inscribing a Magick Circle on the ground is that
we use our Magick Circle as a container and focalizer of the power we
raise before we release it to do its work."[14] In this way, shrines, ritual
circles, and special places like Faerie become "containers" and "focaliz-
ers" to use Alba's words, of the divine "energy" that Neopagans believe
is all around us.

The creation of specific spaces within festival sites is also affected by
whether festivals are located on public or private land. Private or Pagan-
owned sites that host festivals are *physically* marked with community
identities and traces of previous festivals. Festivals at temporary public
sites such as state parks or campgrounds, on the other hand, express histories and identities that tend to be located in memory instead of at the
festival sites themselves. Permanent shrines and circles for festival rituals, for instance, can be cleared only from the woods or constructed on
privately owned land. At Lothlorien and Brushwood, both sites that are
privately owned and host a variety of Neopagan gatherings, creating and
maintaining permanent shrines are important festival activities. Neopagans who regularly attend festivals at these sites generally expect to
participate in ongoing relationships with the land: planting and caring
for herbal and flower beds, trimming weeds and thorns along woodland
paths, building boundaries around shrines, and arranging altars.
Michael, an architect from the east coast, found this aspect of his first
ELF festival to be particularly appealing.

> One of the things that made Elf Fest special and was different than any fes-
> tival that I'd been to before was that it was their land. And when I arrived
> the first afternoon I felt that. People asked if they could help. People acted
> like this was an ongoing community that they were part of. This is a place
> that has energy being put into it and it's becoming part of a life . . . And the
> little shrines that are out in the woods . . . are a simple childlike expression
> of their connection with the land. To leave a piece of you or a small statue or

some beads to say this I did to this place and to those who come after me, is very different than a festival that is on a rented piece of land. Elf Fest felt like someone's home.[15]

The ongoing process of caring for and adding to these shrines is one of the reasons permanent sites have more of a sense of history and continuity than festivals held at public campgrounds and state parks. Relationships that are inscribed on the land help create a sense of belonging and being at home among festival participants.

Festivals held at public campgrounds have no visual record of festival histories like the shrines at Brushwood and Lothlorien and must use different methods to demarcate ritual and shrine spaces. They depend on participants' memories of past festivals and their skill at creating the atmosphere that makes festivals seem special. Space is sacralized either with concrete elements, like the ashes that are saved from one festival to the next, or with other mnemonic devices such as storytelling. When I attended Pagan Spirit Gathering in 1992 and 1994, a fire was lit in the same location, and the ashes of the previous year's fire were spread beneath the kindling and logs. Important areas are also located by maps and labeled with signs and ropes. Attending festivals at temporary sites is not as Michael puts it, like going to "someone's home," but means that festival goers have to take more responsibility for making the site feel like home. The PSG 1993 Village Guide describes the festival community's responsibility for their "Ritual Circle, Sacred Fire, and Community Altar":

> The Ritual Circle is the main ritual site and Community sharing area of the Village. . . . In the center of the Ritual Circle is the Village's Sacred Fire. It represents the Spirit of the PSG Community and should be treated with respect. We hope to keep it burning continuously throughout the Gathering. It will be lit as part of the Opening Ritual on Monday night and extinguished on Sunday as part of the Farewell Ritual. Feel free to feed the Sacred Fire with wood provided for it and with dried herbs, paper talismans and other sacred offerings. Do not burn trash in the Sacred Fire . . . The Community Altar is a meditation place at the Ritual Circle. Personal items can be placed on the altar to be energized during rituals.[16]

PSG's organizers invite festival goers to participate in creating special spaces within the festival site. Herbs and other offerings brought from home as well as the attitudes of festival goers in caring for the site transform the campground into Neopagan space.[17]

Stories of remarkable events, for instance the tornado that swerved around Pagan Spirit Gathering in 1992, situate the current gathering within a history of previous gatherings at the same site. The 1993 issue of *Circle Network News* that advertised the upcoming PSG included stories and poems about the previous year's festival, several of which mentioned the tornado: "There were many circles formed at this Gathering. Within our Sacred Circle we shared our energies, ideas, love, and yes, sometimes our tears. . . . We circled the camp in our processions, we circled each other with our arms. We held hands in circles as we faced Nature's furious spiral, the tornado; our reminder of Her power."[18] At this gathering Neopagans used the circle, a familiar tool for creating sacred space—and narrative practices centered on the circle—to understand and explain their experience with the tornado. The circle protected them and reflected their sense of success in coming together as a community to deal with an emergency situation.

Stories and powerful images of this sort aid in the process of making a public or non-Pagan–owned land into a meaningful space. Visualization is a key ingredient in many Neopagan rituals and one of the skills that most festival participants can be expected to bring with them. A pamphlet for Spiral, a Neopagan gathering held at a campground in northern Georgia, instructs participants on what to do upon arriving at the site:

> After you have arrived and unpacked, please go to the Ritual Area and begin placing your Magickal energy within the Ceremonial Circle. The Circle will be bordered with four banners representing the four directions within Nature. . . . At SPIRAL the portal into the Circle is entered in the South, through the Red Banners. . . . Take a moment at the gateway to balance and ground yourself and then enter this sacred space with reverence and call upon your Gods and Goddesses, your Higher Self, to come and be with you and everyone attending SPIRAL; ask that they surround this site with a beautiful blue crystal bubble of light that will protect everything and everyone within.

The boundaries and shapes of ritual spaces at temporary sites are more likely to be made in relationship to the four directions and to the world of spirits and deities, than in regard to physical aspects of the land. Participants are asked to "call upon *your* Gods and Goddesses, *your* higher self." In this way, Neopagans work together as a community to personalize the site, to transform a public campground into a sacred and protective place. As they put into practice their theology of immanence— the view that "spirit and transformative power [are] embodied in the natural world"—participants reinforce a collective Neopagan identity.[19] Neopagans' definition of "sacred space" then, is a site that offers intimate contact with nature and is believed to have active powers—as the home of fairies, gods, tree spirits, and ancestors. It also creates connections with what Neopagans see as an ideal past when humans lived in harmony with nature and were aware of an enchanted world around them. It is a site that must, in as many ways as possible, announce its departure from mundania's religious structures and sacred spaces.

PLACES OF CONFLICT

"I didn't come out to the woods to listen to Jimi Hendrix. I mean, I like Hendrix, but not here," complained Laughing Starheart during one ELF festival. Amplified music in Lightning Shrine—the center of the festival site where community meetings, performances, and some rituals are held—could easily be heard from Starheart's tent along the main drive. Starheart had brought several marble stones to the festival to donate to a new sweat/purification shrine, but at that moment the stones were sitting in Lightning Shrine. Starheart and his friends decided that the stones should be moved because the "party" and "electronic energy" were not appropriate for stones intended for a space of purification. I helped them carry the heavy stones into Heart Tree Circle—a peaceful space in the middle of the woods—where we placed them at the four directions. Starheart and his friends felt that this was a satisfactory place for the stones to wait until ELF decided on a new sweat site.

Neopagans have high expectations that spaces they create within festival sites will be powerful. But not all ritual spaces are created equal and some become more "sacred" than others. The Faerie woods of Lothlorien are one example, as are the spaces used for community rituals at large festivals. Most festivals have one or two areas, such as the Ceremonial Circle at Spiral Gathering and Thunder Dome at Lothlorien, that are set aside for the festival fire and major festival rituals. Ritual spaces also function as the festival in miniature. The struggles over meaning that are found there represent larger festival struggles. It is at these ritual circles that the entire festival community comes together to define itself and to experience its unity. Inevitably, these are also the spaces where differences between participants are brought to light. Community disputes about particular festival practices usually center on ritual spaces that are multipurpose and serve the largest numbers of people. Festival conflicts about purity and the proper use of a space are more likely to be about the main ritual area than anywhere else, and they illustrate Neopagans' desire to identify and exclude the impure as part of the process of self-definition.

Peh provided me with several examples of how tensions over the purity of ritual space come about. He explained that some festival participants expect they will be able to use festival space in the same way they would at home in their own temple or ritual area; this is simply impossible at large festivals. At Starwood a few years back, he remembered, a group of ELF members went together to drum near the front of the festival field every night. When Peh and his friends were preparing for the main bonfire, another group of festival goers came and "cleansed" the space. Peh was "deeply offended" when they cleansed the space before beginning their ritual, because this act introduced a negative and mean-spirited atmosphere into the festival. The cleansing ritual involved such actions as burning incense and performing incantations to drive away what the group thought were destructive spirits. Peh believed that the festival should be an eclectic space in which participants must tolerate each others' differences. The cleansing signified disapproval and intolerance, according to Peh. "How can people attend a big eclectic gathering like Starwood and expect they will be provided with a quiet meditative space?" he asked.[20]

Similar disputes arose at Pagan Spirit Gathering's Eagle Cave site. At this temporary site, a large community altar was adjacent to the main ritual space, and a fire in the center was kept burning throughout the festival (and even covered with large plastic tarpaulins during rainstorms). Festival organizers and some festival goers assumed that everyone at the festival was concerned about keeping the space pure. But judging from complaints about "trashing" the festival fire, this was not always the case. At Pagan Spirit Gathering 1993, several of the daily village meetings included warnings about improper uses of the fire, particularly treating it as a party space—leaving beer cans and other trash around it. Ron, who had attended several previous PSGs, addressed this problem at the meeting: "I'm a Druid and I like partying," he confessed. But he reminded other festival goers that there are many campsites where drinking is acceptable, if not encouraged: "Just don't sit around the ritual fire drinking beer—go elsewhere." Another community member spoke up to remind festival goers that the fire is for drumming, dancing, trance work, and meditation, and that they should not leave their cigarette butts lying around it. One article in an ELF newsletter complains about people roasting hot dogs over the sacred fire pit, but I have heard other festival participants describe the cooking and sharing of meals, even over the festival fire, as a "sacred" act.

In order to encourage festival goers to act appropriately (however this is defined), festival organizers must think up ways to alert festival goers that they are entering ritual space. Gateways set major ritual spaces apart from the rest of the festival, marking the entry to a world of self-transformation

and at the same time channeling and drawing attention to community concerns. At Rites of Spring XIX, a wooden bridge and gateway of gnarled tree
branches marked the entrance to the ritual field. Ritual spaces focus and intensify a sense of separation from the outside as well as from quotidian activities like eating and sleeping, which also take place on festival sites. They
are spaces set aside within the festival for specific rituals of celebration, such
as the Greenheart Revel at Lothlorien to honor spirits of the land or rituals of self-transformation, such as the enactment of Persephone's descent
into and release from the underworld that took place at ELFest 1991. Many
large group rituals use gatekeepers and gateways to mark and guard entrances to ritual space. Often at the beginning of a ritual, gatekeepers pu-
rify each person who enters the ritual space by smudging them with the
smoke of burning sweetgrass or sage, a ritual practice Neopagans borrowed
from American Indians.[21] This is usually done by lighting a braided or
tightly bound clump of the herb, blowing it out, and then fanning the smoke
over the bodies of participants as they come into ritual space.

Gatekeepers keep disruptive people out, prepare or mark those who
enter, direct latecomers to their places, or tell them they cannot enter at all
because the ritual is already underway. They provide the boundary control that is necessary to make a ritual space safe and secure. The gateway
to the Rites of Spring XIX fire circle was watched over by a gatekeeper
who smudged each drummer or dancer before they entered the fire circle.
Gateways of this sort serve to sharpen the intentions of those who pass
through them. They provoke the immediate awareness of passing from
one kind of space into another. When I walked along the winding path at
midnight to find the Rites of Spring fire circle, I felt safe and alone in the
dark woods, free to talk to anyone who came along the path or to keep
my thoughts to myself. I noticed the shadows in moonlight and heard the
noises of chipmunks in the woods. When I finally arrived in the clearing
where the fire circle was set up, the gate keeper fanned sage smoke up and
down the front and back of my body. I smelled the sage and its heavy
sweetness as it filled my lungs. Then I stepped through the gate and my attention was immediately focused on the fire and the group of people gathered around it—nothing else seemed important.

PLACES OF ACCUMULATION: SHRINES AND ALTARS

Neopagans are a contentious group of individualists who argue about every
aspect of festival experience. But not all festival spaces are characterized by
conflict. When they are not disagreeing about how to proceed, festival goers

work together to create beautiful places on festival sites. Shrines are among festival communities' most successful collective productions. Shrines within a festival site usually accumulate meaning piece by piece instead of by a single, deliberate act of planning. These shrines and altars are what I call "places of accumulation," and do not seem to attract the same kinds of tension and conflict as festival ritual circles. Like Lothlorien's Thunder Dome and Pagan Spirit Gathering's Ritual Circle, they embody a collective identity, but they allow more space for individual expression without discord.

A shrine is a sanctuary, a sacred space marked off from other festival activities and set apart for ritual or meditation. Shrines are larger and often less clearly demarcated than altars, although altars are often placed within them. They are found at the interface between the realms of human and nature, while the places inside human domains—homes and other buildings—that are marked off for ritual are usually called temples. Both shrines and temples are places established to facilitate communication between humans and other worlds as well as experimentation with different forms of consciousness, such as trance or meditation. Caitlin Johnson argues in *Circle Network News* that a shrine is "a special place for Magickal workings [that] becomes the ground, becomes the World, where we can focus and intensify our power, where we can affect reality, where we can experience the ecstasy of oneness with the Divine."[22] Shrines bring together in space and time festival goers and their important others: the broader Neopagan movement, deities, fellow festival participants, and ancestors.

Neopagans witness and participate in life passages at shrines: newborn-naming ceremonies, handfastings (Neopagan commitment ceremonies or marriages), and commemorative rites for the dead. Memorial rites for dead relatives and friends and interactions with ancestors take place at Lothlorien in Ancestors' Shrine or at Heart Tree Circle; rites of passage such as handfastings and child blessings are also celebrated at Heart Tree Circle. Heart Tree is located just off the main drive around Lothlorien's festival field, near the center of festival life and is "the spiritual core of Lothlorien" according to ELF's Wild Magick Guidebook. During Wild Magick 1993 I attended a "fairy blessing" for a newborn baby girl at Heart Tree. The ritual was open to anyone who wanted to participate. It was attended by about forty people, some of whom were close friends of the baby's parents. Laughing Starheart, the ritual facilitator, paraded around the festival site "heralding" the event. He gathered people in a procession that wound through the festival and under a bough-covered tunnel that led to a circular area cleared in the woods in the center of which stood the Heart Tree. Everyone slowly walked into the shrine and formed a circle around the mother, Talian, and her baby daughter, Marion. In the center of the circle of trees, the baby was sitting in her mother's lap next to a mound of earth built up at the base of a heart-shaped tree trunk, an earthen altar covered with the remains of previous ritual offerings. Starheart explained how the ritual would proceed and asked for volunteers to summon the spirits of the elements earth, air, fire, and water and to act as "guardians of the circle." The circle was "cast" after each volunteer said a few words about the characteristics associated with their element. Starheart then asked all the participants to quietly call on their own "conception of deity."

While the formulation "their own conception" seems to further the impression that Neopagans are highly individualistic, in most festival rituals calling on one's own god or goddess takes place as part of an explicitly collective enterprise. Neopagans consistently put their individualism in relation to community at festivals. At a ritual like this they enter a clearly marked ritual circle for a common purpose: to simultaneously bless the baby *and* their broader festival community. Neopagans feel comfortable including each other's deities in rituals; they believe that the gods and goddesses of the religious cultures they have adopted "know how to get along together." Commenting on his experiences in witchcraft and Santeria rituals, Gardnerian elder Gary, whom I met when he presented a workshop on "Nature Religion and the Modern World" at Pantheacon 1997, suggests that "the Goddess is on good terms with Yoruban deities."[23]

Most Neopagans are polytheists, and as Margot Adler puts it, "Polytheism is grounded in the view that reality (divine or otherwise) is multiple and diverse. And if one is a pantheist-polytheist, as are many Neopagans, one might say that all nature is divinity and manifests itself in myriad forms."[24] The assumption that deities are different faces of similar realities or forces in the world undergirds justifications for cultural borrowing and assures Druids, Witches, Shamans, and Norse Pagans that their deities too are included in festival rituals.[25] Because they are eclectic by necessity, festival rituals are flexible in content. The quarters are called, which involves turning to the four directions and their corresponding elements (these correspondences can vary from group to group, but common sets are: east/air, south/fire, west/water, north/earth), and a deity is invoked. The names by which elements and gods and goddesses are called also varies tremendously. As with many Neopagan practices, there is not a "right" way to call the quarters; this is left to individual preference or specific Neopagan traditions.

At the baby blessing, the circle was marked in just this way, with a different participant inviting the spirits of each direction to attend the ritual. Starheart explained to the crowd that had entered Heart Tree Shrine that the baby blessing was to benefit all children present at the festival, as well as "the child within" each adult participant. He requested that everyone give a specific gift as a blessing for the baby. These gifts, he added, could be aspects of themselves that they had in abundance, such as an inner strength or a special talent they wanted to share. Moving clockwise around the circle, each person said their blessing out loud. Many participants offered "the gift of love," other gifts included forgiveness, passion, creativity, wishes for "the many friends a little Leo needs" and wishes that Marion would "embody the goddess, the divine feminine." Finally the last person in the circle blessed the baby with "the gift of mirrors to see the strengths in herself and to see both sides of any issue." Starheart then asked children participating in the ritual to come into the center around the "fairy princess" and give her a blessing. Most of them were too shy to speak but one of them sang the theme song from "Barney," a children's television show about a purple dinosaur. The blessings were distributed by "blowing them" out to the children, across the circle and onto the baby. After the circle dispersed a few people gave little gifts to the baby: a wand made of lavender flowers, a colorful necklace decorated with mirrors and beads, a poem, a ceramic sculpture of an angel, and a tiny flower crown made of dried flowers and ribbons with a tiny pentacle tied on it. Like many festival rituals, the effects of this one were not confined to the space of Heart Tree. At the next large festival following the "fairy blessing," I heard two festival goers reminiscing that this rite of passage was one of the most "beautiful" rituals they had attended and that they still could "feel its effects."

The places within festival sites help create a sense of family by serving as the loci for crucial life events of the sort otherwise conducted in government offices and churches.[26] Neopagans demonstrate an alternative view of civic culture as tied to nature and practiced by small communities or "tribes." On 30 June 1991, a memorial service was held in Heart Tree Circle for Rinsa, an ELF elder, reported *The Elven Chronicle:* "The service was held in council form with the passing of the 'Talking Rattle' to allow each in attendance to express special feelings about Rinsa. . . . Following this gathering there was a procession to Thunder where an altar of offerings was burned. The ashes were later collected as part of an ongoing Shaman's Guild tradition of collecting ashes from sacred fires at gatherings."[27] Baby blessings, handfastings, and memo-

rial services at festivals become part of festival history that are reported
and talked about at festivals for years afterward.

Through an accumulated history of ritual memories and objects left
at its altar, Heart Tree and other festival shrines acquire a collectively
constituted identity. As in the case of Heart Tree Shrine, the Druid nemeton at Brushwood and the Ancestors' Shrine at Lothlorien were set up
to invite visitors to leave behind offerings to ancestors or deities.
Through the efforts of entire festival communities, shrines take on shape
and definition over time. Lothlorien's Ancestors' Shrine, a disintegrat-
ing log cabin covered with moss and located along a trail in the woods,
lies far away from the center of festival activities. Visitors allow the
forces of growth and decay to eat away at trinkets and other human-
made objects left there. The winding path to Ancestors' can be made
nearly impassable in summer by poison ivy, yellow jackets, spider webs,
and blackberry brambles. Its doorway and three of the walls are rotten
but still standing. A roof of corrugated metal covers most of the shrine's
interior. On a weather-worn altar in the middle of the structure are a
variety of offerings: sculptures of goddesses, a brass chalice, seashells,
crystals, candles, feathers, metal jewelry, a turtle's shell, animal bones,
dried flowers, fruits, and herbs. Tokens to honor ancestors are placed
on the altar, tied to the walls of the shrine, or hung from its decayed
ceiling. Full beer bottles confirm that festival goers come to the shrine
to offer libations of beer and other spirits to their ancestors. A couple
of carved staffs lean against the far corner; handmade masks and a plastic bag full of herbs hang on one wall; and a plaster circle affixed to the
wall is painted with "You and I are earth." Ancestors' bears the traces
of many visitors as it accumulates their mementos and shelters their private rituals.

As they create shrines that both accumulate and express meaning,
Neopagans interact with what anthropologist James Fernandez calls
"architectonic" spaces: active meeting places of human and divine
worlds. For a sacred space to be an architectonic, "It must contain both
an extension of personal body images and an intension of mythical and
cosmic images."[28] Shrines and altars are more than just places where
people leave personal mementos and offerings; they are alive with interactions between Neopagans and their ancestors or the spirits of the land.
Neopagans take objects into their shrines to honor and attract ancestors.
These objects often have personal significance—a deceased parent's pos-
sessions—or are symbolic to the Neopagan community as a whole—
small stones from Stonehenge, for example.

Ancestors' Shrine is a place where deceased community members, friends, and relatives are mourned and honored. Neopagans also connect the families they were born into with their created festival families at Ancestors' Shrine by remembering dead parents and grandparents who might not approve of their Neopagan identities. At the end of Wild Magick Gathering 1992 after most of the festival participants had left, Laughing Starheart and I walked out to Ancestors' with some gifts. Starheart then meditated in front of Ancestors' central altar and spoke silently to his father and grandmother. He looked to see what had happened to his grandmother's college pins that he had left at the shrine during a festival the previous spring. He found one of the pins and after looking at it, put it back on the altar. Starheart then spread the rose petals he had brought around the inside of the shrine as he bid good-bye to his departed relatives, promising to visit the shrine again at the next festival. While we were walking back to the festival field he told me he wants to have his own ashes scattered at Ancestors'. Over the many years he had attended festivals at Lothlorien, the shrine had become for him a place for contemplating death and for examining his own life in connection with his dead relations. Ancestors' Shrine seemed to Starheart the most appropriate place for his friends to remember him someday.

Some elements of the altar are connected to specific individuals—a dead parent's identification card and a mother's sorority pin. Other objects such as animal skulls and dried flowers allude more abstractly to the dead. A pipe and tobacco in a pouch hang on a rotting log with a plastic-covered letter that invites all who enter the shrine to make use of the pipe. The author of this page-long letter explains that the pipe should be smoked to share in and celebrate the peace she finally made with her dead grandfather, the original owner of the pipe. During ELFest 1994, festival goers held a memorial service in Ancestors' for "Owl Woman," who sold stones and crystals at festivals and was killed in an accident while traveling in Jamaica. Her friends conducted a small, private ceremony for her during a festival and left crystals, stones, a doll, and other tokens at the shrine in her honor. When I returned to Ancestors' in 1999, I found the original shrine completely collapsed, the many objects in it buried deeply in the mud. The shrine area had been expanded to include a recently built dog altar. Visitors had already begun to add objects to the dog altar next to the old altar site, and no attempts had been made to repair the shack that originally had marked Ancestors' Shrine (see fig. 7).

Neopagans see death as part of "the wheel of life." From a Neopagan perspective, human life cycles correspond to seasonal changes. For most

Figure 7.   An altar for a Neopagan's dog stands next to Ancestors' Shrine at
Lothlorien Nature Sanctuary in Indiana. Photo by Ransom Haile.

Neopagans, death is not the end of life but the beginning of another life
in the cycle of reincarnation. "Pagans generally follow the cycle of the
year," explains an informative Neopagan website.

> The turning pattern of the seasons is seen as a wheel. Each aspect of seasonal
> change is understood as a mystery of the Divine. As the wheel turns, so Na-
> ture reveals the many faces of the Gods. Pagans shape rituals to express what
> they see and feel in Nature. In doing so, they share in the mystery of the turn-
> ing cycle and join more closely with the vision of their Gods. In their seasonal
> rites, Pagans pass on a deep vision of human life as part of the natural cycle.
> Pagans take delight in their vision and reach out to embrace ever more deeply
> that whole of which they are a part. Just as Nature is both male and female,
> so the seasonal celebrations describe the dance between Goddess and God
> throughout the Wheel of the Year.[29]

The Pagan wheel of the year begins at Samhain (what most Americans
call Halloween) when, according to Neopagan belief, the boundaries between the world of the living and the world of the dead are thinnest. For
Neopagans and Witches who worship the goddess in what they call her
"triple aspect," the third stage of life—the crone—corresponds to the
end of the year after which the wheel begins anew with the maiden goddess. The late autumn harvest marked by Samhain also contains the
promise of new crops for the next year. By celebrating the turning of the
wheel, Neopagans situate themselves in what they understand to be a
long tradition of pre-Christian seasonal events.

Festivals are designed to connect festival goers to the pre-Christian cultures they seek to emulate as well as to personal pasts. These connections
are particularly evident at shrines that express a collective desire for historical roots, as well as offer a space for personal experiences like Starheart's. On my first trip to Starwood, I attended the long-anticipated public opening of the Druid nemeton, a sacred circle with a central altar
mound enclosed by mountain laurel.[30] The June-July 1992 issue of *News
from the Mother Grove,* 4, no. 6, a publication of Ar nDraiocht Fein, "A
Druid Fellowship," reported on the private, Druid-only consecration of
the nemeton at a Druid gathering held at Brushwood earlier that year at
which I was not present.[31] This report brings together many of the themes
in shrine making that I have been discussing:

> After the workshop on Sacred Enclosures, a group of us trooped to the site
> to begin work. The site was dedicated to sacred service, and offerings were
> made to the land, the plants and trees, the animals, and the spirits of nature.
> A bush forming a living arch directly east was determined to be the entrance
> to the site and it was noted which trees were due north, south, east, and west.

Almost all the trees on the site were left standing. Moss was collected to be placed on the central mound as the land was leveled. Other Druids collected stones and rocks for the central mound and made a ring of brush around the site. The mound took shape around a central fire pit, which will surround a central pole, or Bile. . . . The next day holes were dug around the central mound for altars to the Land, Sea, Sky, Nature Spirits, Ancestors, and the Gods. Brush was worked over the altars, and dirt and moss placed above them and around them. The nemeton took shape with amazing speed, and it was clearly evident that the land was working with us. . . . The site was consecrated in a full ADF liturgy under the aforementioned full moon. . . . At the climax of the three-hour ritual Isaac planted a shard from Stonehenge in the central mound.

Like many other shrines and ritual spaces, the nemeton was oriented in relation to the four directions; it incorporated natural elements found at the festival site as well as objects brought by its creators. Like ELF's Ancestors' Shrine, the Druid nemeton embodies personal and community stories as well as a historical past, in this case an imagined Celtic Druid past. A piece of Stonehenge that represents stories about and evidence for British Druid rituals is connected at the nemeton with contemporary improvisations that blend what little is known of the Druids from archaeological records with imaginative reconstructions.[32]

In the same issue of *News from the Mother Grove,* "Chief Artificer" Bryan Perrin, the artist responsible for designing the nemeton, talks about his vision for it, emphasizing the experimental and accumulative nature of the project: "We're trying to do something of a re-creation based on archaeological information, but also combine it with our modern vision in ADF, of how we believe Celtic cosmology works." The nemeton embodies Neopaganism's ritual and theological eclecticism by combining myth, history, the visions of Ar nDraiocht Fein members, and the individual traditions of all who visit and contribute to the shrine, returning from festival to festival or year to year to see how their offerings have become integrated into the larger shrine project.

We can open ourselves up to new types of devotional practices. I'm trying to encourage people to do simple votive offerings, whether you just carve on a little piece of wood, like a lot of people already have, or paint on stones. . . . And it will all be organically growing and flowing and changing with us . . . when you do an idol or something like that, when it goes totally organic and you start getting a kind of chia pet effect. What's it mean when mushrooms start popping out of the mouth of the green man you carved a few years ago? Hopefully the thing will become a fascinating garden full of all these different people's energies.[33]

The nemeton is a collective creation that brings together festival goers with mushrooms and moss, reminding them of the fluid boundaries between human and nature. At the same time, it serves as a visual reminder of the ancient past and peoples they have claimed as their own.

Through magical practice, Neopagans interact with specific places to produce specific effects. In an article in EarthSpirit Community's journal *Fireheart,* Scott Pollack discusses "building for an earth-oriented spirituality": "Magic is fundamentally neutral. It is the intentions and results that determine what its flavor is. It is, therefore, important to understand that when we build, we willfully change the landscape, and that we must accept and control those changes. When we put a building in a place, we forever change the understanding of that place."[34] Woodland shrines are incorporated into festival culture and thus stand out from their wild surroundings, even as they are exposed to rain and wind, insects, and other creatures. At shrines like Ancestors' and the nemeton, visitors interact with each other's offerings, individuals with their pasts, and humans with nature: "When you do a large nemeton, or sacred enclosure earthworks like this, it turns into a dialog with the Earth Mother. . . . A geomancy is a magical working, and we might find out that when we set up our directional fires that the spirits of the land there cause things to happen in those different directions, and we might start getting different associations because of that. It can become a teacher to us."[35] At Ancestors' Shrine and the nemeton, people add their own objects to existing pieces, thus allowing the conversations among human participants and between humans and nature to take on meaning over time.

Like Ancestors' Shrine and the Druids' nemeton, collective altars that appear at festivals serve diverse purposes and accumulate meanings over a short period of time by providing points of focus in the midst of the visual complexity of festivals. The Pagan Spirit Gathering community altar brought together pieces of individual identities in a community setting. The altar was created on a picnic table covered with purple cloth and placed near the main ritual area. Festival participants were told at the opening ritual to place anything on the altar that they wanted to "charge with energy." In this way the "energy" that accumulated at the altar was a collective project that produced a unique result at every festival. The altar was located in a public area so that festival participants could enjoy looking at it as well as "charging" their "ritual tools." When I visited it on the fourth day of the festival, it was almost completely covered. On the seat of the picnic table were two large metal swords carved with designs. In the center of the table was a cloth ball made to look like the earth, and next to it a sculpture in the style of the Egyptian cat goddess, Bastet. Several staffs leaned across the back of the table and, like many things pagan, were personalized—decorated with beads, feathers, and personal tokens. On the top of one staff a fox's tail was attached, on another a goat's skull. On the table itself, apparently mundane things lay next to more elegant and valuable sculptures or crystals. A Hershey bar signified the cult of chocolate (a humorous parody of ritual groups to which an entire workshop was devoted at PSG). A Barbie doll seemed somewhat incongruous, but less so because she was garbed according to the Neopagan aesthetic in a maroon cloak and gown and a crown; she was standing at an altar of proportionate size and holding a plastic sword. Next to Barbie and her altar lay candles in candleholders, a crystal scepter, a bunch of dried carnations, crystals of all shapes and sizes, other kinds of rocks, necklaces, chalices, stone and metal goddess figurines, a wreath of vines, a statue of Pan playing pipes, and a cloth doll wearing a pink dress with triangles on it (signifying gay and lesbian identity). Also displayed were a replica of the Statue of Liberty, large seashells, a mask made almost entirely of feathers, a brass statuette of a woman holding a crescent moon over her head and with snakes coming out of her feet, and dried ears of Indian corn. These objects and the interests they express might not work together harmoniously in a ritual, but here they seemed to get along fine. Altars, then, provide a nonconfrontational means of expressing unique individual identities within a community space.[36]

Altars are also set up for specific rituals or specific deities and provide a resting place for items to be used by ritual participants such as chalices, candles, incense, images of goddesses, ritual scripts, athames (ritual daggers), swords, and wands. Raymond Buckland, a priest of Saxon Witchcraft, explains that personalized tools are important because they are "extensions of the operator. . . . The real magic comes not from the tool but from within the magician."[37] Any place can be designated a shrine: a grove of trees, a dilapidated shed, a walled circle, a basement room, or a tent. Altars, on the other hand, usually are constructed on a horizontal surface, most often a table, a tree stump, or a bedroom dresser. Altars themselves are ritual tools—easily created, moved around, prepared for different purposes, or destroyed by their users. Neopagans construct altars in their homes, dormitory rooms, cars, or temples as places to draw their attention to their relationship with particular deities and to invite their ancestors to join them. "Altar-building is a form of talk," claims one altar builder.[38] Like praying and chanting, altar making is a way of conversing with spirits, deities, parts of the self, and ancestors.

Altars are the smallest and most personal festival places, but they are also important to Neopagans' lives outside the festival. They serve as semipermanent structures in a person's home that maintain consistent form, although they may change in small ways from year to year. Cheri, a frequent participant at ELF festivals and a graduate student studying English literature, has kept an altar on her dresser since becoming a Neopagan four years before I met her. She shows me objects from her past: a photograph of her grandmother and tiny wooden animals that she inherited when her grandfather died. Personal altars like Cheri's are similar to home altars in other cultural and religious communities in that they locate the individual in a network of kinship relations. In "Conjuring the Holy: Mexican Domestic Altars," Ramon A. Gutierrez observes that unlike the objects on church altars that "tie one to the communion of saints, to the angels and apostles in heaven, and to the history of the church triumphant, on home altars the photographs, trinkets, and mementos construct family histories that visually record one's relations to a lineage and clan."[39] Altars are a site of connection between the living and the dead as well as between human and deity, but home altars also situate the individual in particular kinship arrangements among the living.[40] Neopagans place objects on their altars that express kinship relations within the Neopagan community as well as in their birth families. Alongside the things from Cheri's family are candles, incense, crystals, and stones given to her by men and women who became her friends at festivals. Altars like this are condensed stories that are told only when the altar maker is asked about them. They are decorated with figures of deities and mnemonic aids that recall people and events that have been important in the altar maker's life. In this way, altars can become histories of the self. Cynthia Eller describes the altars that Witches and the other "spiritual feminists" she studied make in their homes: "The altar is the self, symbolized and idealized, and set in right relationship to the world."[41] Altars externalize and reveal their makers' inner lives and when displayed at festivals allow festival goers to share hidden parts of the self with a community. Shrines, altars, and ritual areas are aesthetically compelling, often beautiful in design and presentation. Both the visual effect of the finished product and the creative process of making altars and shrines contribute to the quality of the festival experience.[42]

Neopagans often take objects from home altars and temples to festivals as a way of connecting the festival world to their lives outside festival. I turn now briefly to Neopagan shrines and altars outside of festivals in order to highlight some qualities of Neopagan sacred space in general. Neopagan home temples are like festival shrines and circles in that they often have altars set at the four directions, but they are stamped with the identities of the individuals who created them, even in those cases where an entire ritual group used the temple. I have visited temples that were bedrooms, corners of rooms, or a floor in any room cleared of furniture and marked as ritual space with a circle or altars. The most elaborate temples I have seen are those belonging to teachers or priests who frequently host ritual groups. Peh's large basement temple housed altars for each direction, and its carpeted floor was marked with tape that traced out the lines of the kabbalistic tree of life. A good-sized closet opened onto the room and was used exclusively for storing ritual aids such as herbs, candles, incense, and cloth. Temples are often set up for specific ritual occasions or regular coven meetings. At first I thought that their power was temporary, that the existence of the temple as a place where spirits came and went was bounded by the beginning and ending of the ritual. But I came to see that this was not always the case (see fig. 8).

The magical workings of a temple, its role as a space in which change happens, in which energy is exchanged, may continue even when no one is actually in the temple. For instance, I noticed that friends would leave ritual items, particularly new ones they had recently purchased, such as a new athame or staff, to charge on the altars in Peh's temple. This seemed to mean that the item would take on the energy of the temple and of the many ritual workings that had taken place within it. I came to wonder whether the spirits themselves could be said to exist in the temple apart from the rituals we conducted, because this then would account for the charging. Were the entities responsible for charging tools left on the altars, or was the charging accomplished from a vague energy left over from ritual work?

Another festival goer shared with me a story about his temple that shed some light on this issue. He accused a woman in the local community of astrally projecting to his temple and psychically attacking him. It seems that a temple, like an altar, can function as an extension of the self, a place where human meets spirit. Kevin, a longtime festival goer and Neopagan priest, described the problems he was having in his life—depression and emotional pain—as a consequence of his work with the

Figure 8.   This altar is an example of those found in Peh's home temple. The face on the goddess statue is covered by a black cloth to allow practitioners to project their own images. Photo by Ransom Haile.

goddess Anath (ancient Canaanite war goddess): "Perhaps it has something to do with the work I've been doing with the goddess Anath. She shows up in my Temple on a regular basis; visits for a moment and then leaves."[43] Here, it seems that Anath is a part of the self not under conscious control, a view that fits into Kevin's view of the deities: "Unlike most self-proclaimed Pagans, I do not consider myself or what I do to be of a religious nature. At least not in the sense of worshipping a specific external deity. I am more interested in the authentic depths of the human experience, as delved by Magick, Jung, shamanism, and anything else that works."[44] Kevin's self-explorations usually take place inside his temple, but they have ramifications in his everyday life, as he suggests here. Festival goers take with them to festivals ritual tools and experiences from their home temples.

Another space outside of festivals that expresses aspects of the self that might otherwise be hidden is a Neopagan's car. Neopagans' cars carry their identities from home through public space and also onto the festival site. At Rites of Spring 1997, I noticed many cars, in appearance like other Americans' cars, but covered with bumper stickers that expressed religious and political positions if not outright Neopagan identities: "The Goddess is Alive and Magic if Afoot," "Good Planets are Hard to Find," "War is Costly, Peace is Priceless," and "I Support the Women's Movement." In a discussion on Pagan-Digest, some participants described their cars as a combination of altar and billboard, a place of sanctuary, and an outward reflection of self for the world to see. "What do you have in your car to tell the rest of the world that you are pagan" asks Lunae Mica Alicia. Syrylyn responds, "I have a Rowan twig Dream catcher on my rear view mirror, a little Crystal garden on the ledge of my speedometer, bumper stickers 'Magic Happens,' 'We're Everywhere' and 'Love Your Mother.' "[45] Cars can embody an entire history of their owner's Neopagan identity. Shadowfox's car reads "Something Wiccan This Way Comes" on the bumper and the Wiccan Rede ("Do as thou will as long as thou harm none") on the dash board. . . . "This is the way I let my passengers know and anyone behind me . . . know that I am proud to be a pagan." Shadowfox also put a fox tail on the rearview mirror, "given to me when I first entered the craft, and the first 2 flight feathers of a sick crow that I could not save."[46]

Surprisingly, the car that publicly expresses their Neopagan identity in an antagonistic world can also be a safe and secure place: "My car is a full out pagan-mobile. I drive a little station wagon with a woven pentacle I made and put in the rearview. I have four stickers in the window on the hatchback that say 'Keep your rosaries out of my ovaries,' 'My goddess gave birth to your god,' 'Eve was framed,' and 'Freedom of religion means any religion.' I love my car. It's my magickal hiding place, I always get in it and drive when life becomes a bit too hectic."[47] The contrast between altars hidden in temples and cars broadcasting Neopagan slogans reveals Neopagans' ambivalence about their identity within the broader culture.

Like cars, altars function as an extension of personal identity for their creators. They are public expressions of self within the festival community if not for a broader audience. An altar in front of a campsite is presented as a work of art as well as an externalization of its maker's identity expressed in symbols for the community to see. Pieces on the altar may be made by hand, bought, or found; they may be tokens from a ritual or gifts from a spiritual teacher. Private altars at campsites are intended to be admired, but not touched without permission. J. Perry Damarru warns first-time festival goers in his "Gathering Primer": "There may be a number of altars set up around the gathering site. These altars are sacred to the people who put them in place. Honor their space. Don't touch anything on the altars without their express invitation."[48] Some festival goers set up altars in their tents where they can be seen only by friends who are invited in, rather than by anyone passing by. At Pagan Spirit Gathering, Laughing Starheart invited me into his tent where he was putting on colorful silk scarves for an evening of dancing around the fire. He was kneeling in front of his "angel altar," which contained many different small angels, incense, herbs, and candles. Objects like the angels on Starheart's altar are never arbitrarily put there; they are always invested with meaning by the altar's creator. Starheart explained to me that angels link his Christian background to his current fascination with mythological figures from Greek, Egyptian, and other non-Christian cultures. Private altars are put together within or next to tents or campsites and limited in use to the friends of the altar builders, whereas public altars may be displayed in merchants' booths or ritual spaces and be accessible to passersby to leave offerings or take blessings. Personal altars create a clearly bounded place for self-expression within the larger festival community (see figs. 9 and 10).

IMPROMPTU PLACES

Religious meaning is not always found at the most beautiful festival sites or at those specifically set aside for ritual activity. Festival communities tend to be spontaneous and improvisational, and they make

Figure 9. A goddess altar in front of a merchant's tent at Starwood festival offers fruit to the goddess. Photo by Ransom Haile.

special the most unexpected places. Even places designated for other than ritual purposes, such as eating areas and toilets, become potential sites for community-building efforts. Ironically the most private of built places—the restrooms, portable latrines, and composting toilets—are especially important for socializing and expressing both collective and personal identities. These are the places where the boundary between self and world is most exposed, at the orifices where humans are most vulnerable. These places break down the boundary between private— only inside one's tent at festivals—and public spaces where one meets and interacts with others.

Toilets are dealt with differently at private sites like Brushwood and Lothlorien and public ones where portable latrines are brought in for the duration of the festival, such as the campground where Pagan Spirit Gathering is held. But on both public and private sites, these places designated for the most basic of bodily functions can express specifically Neopagan characteristics, such as their collective commitment to a more ecologically conscious lifestyle. Ecological concerns impelled the Elf Lore Family to build two sets of composting toilets at Lothlorien. While the

Figure 10.   This Buddha was set up in the Roundhouse nightly drumming
circle at Starwood festival. Photo by Ransom Haile.

portable latrines at Pagan Spirit Gathering differ visually from Lothlorien's handmade composters and Brushwood's weathered wood outhouses
decorated with cut-out moons and stars, even these ugly public conven-
iences can be personalized. Both of the years I attended PSG, the twenty
portable latrines that lined the driveway to the festival field were each
hand-labeled with paper signs reading: "Philosophers and Metaphysicians
Only (be prepared to wait)," "Five Items or Less," "ABDs: we know who
and what we are," "Discordians" (written upside down), "Moon Lodge,"
"Tull Fans," "Solitaries," "Couples Only," "People Who Love Zola,"
"Sex Goddesses," "Druids," and "Witches." In this way, the smallest,
most ordinary spaces express Neopagan identities. The self-referential labels are posted for the amusement of the festival community and convey
a sense of Neopagans' playfulness in creating identities.

Meals, another physical necessity, can also express a distinctively Neopagan identity and offer an informal site for socializing. Pagan Spirit
Gathering includes an astrological feast at the main ritual circle, where
wooden signs are marked with the different astrological signs and par-

ticipants are asked to sit with other festival goers who share their sign rather than with friends and family. These small groups of strangers asked each other about their hometowns and their jobs, but they also discussed their charts and astrological traits, and their experiences getting along with others born under different signs. Like conversations in the waiting line for toilets, these get-togethers are characterized by what I call the intimacy of strangers. The festival ethos encourages quick intimacy because festivals are clearly constrained by limitations of time and space. At ELFest 1992 I was eating lunch at Phil's Grill (located in the heart of the festival) with Crystal and Jade, two women I had recently met. As we finished eating, they began talking about methods of healing from sexual abuse and rape. Crystal demonstrated to Jade a technique for shielding herself from abuse, a kind of psychic self-protection. No one seemed to find it awkward to discuss such a private topic in a public setting—a table at Phil's Grill—in front of me—a stranger. I often encountered this intimacy of strangers, which is a characteristic of festivals in general, at the most unexpected places where I would have expected privacy to prevail. In mundania's restrooms and restaurants, people generally avoid eye contact and conversation with strangers or watch them surreptitiously. But at festivals, strangers look each other in the eye and speak to each other out of an understanding that as Neopagans they venerate the body and its functions as sacred and divine.

Several kinds of public eating areas exist on the main festival field where food can be purchased. A late-night cafe (one table with a prep area) at Starwood served coffee and pastries to dancers and drummers taking a break from the late night fire. One year at ELFest, the Java Cafe marked off a space in the woods where hot and hungry festival goers could escape the sun and feast on tabouli salad and several other vegetarian offerings.[49] Other Lothlorien festivals have featured Phil's Grill, with choices for both vegetarians and meat eaters. But at ELFest 1992 the free ELF kitchen took away some of Phil's business, and I did not see him at Lothlorien again. The ELF kitchen intentionally set itself apart from the commercial nature of the outside world by serving free meals. And it was not situated near the edge of the festival, but rather in a three-sided shack near the center of the festival field. The kitchen made coffee in the morning, cooked up big stews in the afternoon, and provided a strategic social site at the fork in the festival field road where almost all festival goers were likely to pass by on the way to the solar shower and pump for water.

Another important space that focuses on the personal needs of each festival goer, but in a public area that is available to the entire community, is the healing tent. In places like ELF's Healer's Circle and PSG's Centering Dome individual needs are once again met in a specifically Neopagan context. Skilled healers care for the physical and emotional welfare of festival goers at Healer's Circle. Regular medical first-aid is available for wounds and minor physical ailments, but what makes Neopagan festivals' offerings unique is their incorporation of healing alternatives to orthodox medicine such as herbal remedies, homeopathic medicines, Reiki practitioners, and herbalists. Festivals address sickness and pain on many different levels and in many places: in main rituals on healing the rifts between men and women, in workshops on healing past lives, in discussions of alcoholism and sexual abuse, and in conversations about damaged relationships. The discourse of healing is a central aspect of festivals and comes into sharper focus at these small spaces where people seek help for a variety of ailments. The entire festival is designated as a special place for healing by many festival goers, but healing is focused and intensified at these smaller sites.

Pagan Spirit Gathering set up two separate healing tents in 1992 and 1993. The first-aid tent was available for physical medical emergencies such as sunburn, heat exhaustion, or allergy problems. The nearby Centering Dome, run by a professional psychologist and her staff of volunteers, dealt with "festival burnout," depression, relationship problems and breakups, and other psychological troubles brought on by the sometimes intense atmosphere of festivals. When I worked a volunteer shift at the dome, people came in for all of these reasons, or they simply wanted to talk to someone who was available specifically to listen to them. At Centering Dome, festival goers could choose between a picnic table outside at which they could sit and talk to the dome's volunteer staffers or the dome-shaped tent into which they could retreat to spend some time alone or to talk more privately with a trained counselor. Cynthia Eller describes a similar kind of place at a "spiritual feminist gathering": "The womb room," she writes, offered a " 'peaceful, sacred space' where participants can spend time alone or with volunteers who are 'caring listeners.' "[50] If festivals as a whole are intended to heal and transform person and community, then Centering Dome is one place where these festival concerns are clearly practiced.

Merchants' Row also provides services—massage and aura healing are two examples—that promote healing. But the vendors' or merchants' spaces are approached more ambivalently by festival goers. Even though many Neopagans say that festival space contrasts to mundania's consumer mentality, and they occasionally promote bartering as an alternative, these are commercial spaces often with high-priced goods that beckon festival participants who want to dress more elegantly or possess fancier ritual tools than their neighbors. Occasionally festival goers and organizers debate the presence of merchants and try to restrict vendoring, but these spaces continue to fulfill a variety of functions within the festival community. Especially at large festivals, merchants play an important part by being available to newcomers and making them feel part of the community as well as providing them with educational materials and ritual tools. Vendors' ambivalent position in the community is also caused by their range of participation. Some are recognized as full participants in the festival and their goods and skills often supplement workshops that they offer, while others do not offer workshops and may not even be Neopagans.

Although some merchants probably take advantage of an opportunity to make money, others are trying to support a Neopagan lifestyle. Laughing Starheart, for example, told me that he had quit his job as a window dresser at a Detroit department store to try to make a living selling his T-shirts and applying tattoos at Neopagan festivals across the country. Merchant's Row at festivals makes it possible for some participants to offset festival expenses by selling or bartering their skills and merchandise. It is also a place to find objects for altars and ritual work, tools for festival goers to care for and enhance their bodies, and information about Neopagan beliefs and practices different from one's own. Much of the healing, networking, socializing, and educational interaction that takes place formally at workshops and during rituals also occurs more informally on Merchants' Row. Merchants' Row is the Neopagan marketplace, usually located in the most central and accessible area of the festival site, where festival goers can purchase ritual tools, clothing, books, jewelry, and other products (see fig. 11). Some of the merchants who take wares to sell and barter are professional artisans who work at their craft full time, others make only a few pieces of clothing or ceramics they can sell to defray festival expenses. Professional jewelry and ritual tool makers may leave a festival with money in their pockets, but many merchants do not attend festivals to make a huge profit, preferring to barter their wares for any number of goods and services.

Merchants' Row is a place where the boundary between mundane and festival worlds is flexible, and the overlap between Neopagan and other subcultures, such as the Society for Creative Anachronism (a medieval reenactment society), is clearly expressed. At Pagan Spirit Gathering 1993, the following items were available for purchase on

Figure 11.   Don Waterhawk arranges his handmade ritual knives and rattles in his temporary shop on Starwood's Merchants' Row. Photo by Ransom Haile.

Merchant's Row: books on tarot (with tarot cards), magic, mythology, world religions, and fantasy or science fiction; instruments such as drums, pipes, bells, flutes, and rattles (see fig. 12), many of them handmade; paintings and sculptures of deities including Hindu and Egyptian gods and goddesses; tie-dye clothing; handmade cloaks and long, flowing gowns; chain mail; crystals, stones, and beads; goddess jewelry, pentacles, and Celtic style (knotted) brooches; ritual tools such as candle holders, athames, and wands (these tools are often made from animal parts, even road kill at one merchant's booth, or from materials like bone, feathers, horn, semiprecious stones, crystals, brass, and copper); "Light Force" spirulina (a health supplement); herbs for medicinal, culinary, ritual, and cosmetic use; cassette tapes of Celtic music and Native American, African, and Neopagan chants and drumming; tattoo magazines; lesbian erotica; jewelry for body piercings; stained glass; herbal massage oils; homemade soap and incense. Not all the things for sale are specifically magical or occult—herbal cosmetics and clothing, which can be used for ritual, can also be worn by non-Neopagans. Merchants' Row is one of the few sites within the festival where such varied interests

Figure 12.   Shopper on Starwood's Merchants' Row tries out some of the drums for sale. Photo by Ransom Haile.

coexist without conflict. In this way it encapsulates the utopian vision of eclectic Neopagan festivals by "building tribal community and culture across a diversity of traditions and paths," as Circle Sanctuary describes one of its goals for Pagan Spirit Gathering.[51]

Merchants also provide much free information on a wide range of topics. The slow and relaxed pace of festivals usually means that merchants are available to chat more leisurely than they would be able to at their stores or workplaces. They exchange knowledge and skills as well as goods with their customers. In an hour's stroll down PSG's Merchants' Row, I learned about a new method of natural birth control and the best type of incense to use for ritually cleansing a new house. At Starwood 1992 I sat down at a display of perfume oils and the merchant, Silver Moon, spent ten minutes explaining to me the process by which she produces her custom blends to suit the needs of each individual's personality and astrological chart. Merchants are usually happy to recommend tarot decks and books or to discuss custom work for specific ritual purposes, such as rings for a handfasting or the appropriate tattoo for a specific initiation. Festival merchants also sell how-to books that facilitate education and ritual work as well as products like spirulina and herbal remedies that they claim will rejuvenate and heal the body.

Merchants who depend on selling their wares for their livelihood try to appeal to the diverse interests of their clientele, which extend well beyond the Neopagan movement. Some of them attend arts and crafts fairs, gay and lesbian events, science fiction conventions, tattoo and body piercing conventions, biker gatherings, and Society for Creative Anachronism events. In this way, they serve as networkers between Neopagan festivals and closely related or overlapping communities. Larry, for example, who also travels to science fiction conventions, sells costumes, dark robes, beads, rings, and necklaces with fairies on them, soft-sculpture dragons, small fur purses, Dungeons and Dragons magazines, and science fiction and fantasy books. Beth, a ceramicist, sells her sculptures of angels and goddess figures at women's music festivals as well as at Neopagan events. Laughing Starheart tattoos, offers the T-shirts he designs, gives tarot readings, and presents song and chant workshops at male-only Radical Faerie gatherings.[52] Neopagans locate themselves in relation to these other subcultures as they pick and choose T-shirts silk-screened with pink triangles, books by Robert Heinlein, Celtic cloaks, or chain mail from merchants' tables. An Elvis altar at Starwood is one example of how American popular culture coexists with reconstructions of ancient religions at festivals (see fig. 13).

Figure 13. North American pop culture combines with Neopagan symbols at the Elvis altar (with chia Elvis centerpiece) on Starwood's Merchants' Row. Photo by Ransom Haile.

The informal sociality of Merchants' Row is in part due to the fact
that merchants' shops are usually their festival homes as well. At Wild
Magick 1992, Laughing Starheart had a large two-room tent with a bedroom in back and a tattoo parlor in the front room and wares under a
canopy in the front with a rainbow-colored sign reading "Laughing Starheart's Traveling Three-Ring Gypsy Tattoo Parlor." The front section is
his work space, the back his "temple," decorated with colorful cloth
hangings, table, altar, and inflated mattress bed. A longtime festival goer
who spends most of the year attending festivals all over the eastern half
of the United States, Starheart's merchanting site combines a private
home/temple sanctuary with a public area for economic transactions.
Like many of the other merchant spaces on Merchant's Row, Starheart's
is a social hub.

During two hours at Starheart's tent/temple at ELFest 1994, I observed a constant stream of visitors and clients stopping by, only occasionally to buy something. Ely stopped by to show Starheart how the
recent pentacle tattoos on the soles of his feet had faded and to make
an appointment to have them touched up during the festival. Like other
festival goers who run into each other in front of merchants' tables, Ely
and I had met at another festival and took this opportunity to renew
our acquaintance. When I first met Ely at ELFest 1992, he was a car
salesman, but at this ELFest two years later, I found out that he had left
the used-car business and was majoring in religious studies and psychology at a Midwestern university. While Ely was describing to me his
recent coursework, a man I had never met burst into the "tattoo parlor" to tell Starheart that he had found his "lost ring." Ely and Starheart consulted about the tattoo, as this man whose name I never
learned told me about the hopes and devastations of his tragic love life.
The ring, a valuable gold band engraved with runes of some sort, was
one of a pair—his ex-lover still wore the other one around her neck.
They had broken up just a couple of months before but he assured me
that he was still hoping to get back together and "have five children"
with her. The "casual" conversation that takes place along Merchants'
Row and throughout any festival tends to focus on the most personal
aspects of life, particularly relationships and health problems. Merchants are in a position to befriend anyone who walks by, whether they
want to or not, and because of this, they play an essential role in creating community at festivals. As a festival newcomer during my first
summer of research, I had no "family." When veteran festival goers

gathered at their friends' campsites, I sought out the ever-available merchants for company and conversation. In this way, like many other newcomers, I was gradually brought into the festival community by merchants introducing me to their friends and customers.

HOMES AWAY FROM HOME

Private campsites, like shrines and altars, also serve to situate individual identities within the broader context of the entire festival "village" or "tribe." They are more separated and distinctly bounded than impromptu gathering places like Merchants' Row and festival toilets. They also tend to be highly personalized. Festival participants might arrive in slick new cars and vans or in made-over school buses, painted campers, and dilapidated cars covered with bumper stickers. Vehicles parked along Merchants' Row at ELFest 1993 were typical of this diversity: a new van, a pre-1970 VW bus hung with Egyptian-style paintings displaying slickly produced Pagan magazines and jewelry, and a small hand-painted purple camper with black trees stenciled on it. At most festivals, participants set up and decorate their own personal camping spaces in tents, vans, teepees, and pavilions. Some campsites appear quite ordinary and could be seen at any public campground. Dwellings range from nylon tents bought at discount and sporting good stores to canvas teepees and handmade medieval-style pavilions. Individuality is encouraged at these festival homes: "To help locate each other's camps more readily and to add to the Village's tribal atmosphere, participants are encouraged to wear ritual garb and decorate their camp areas with banners, altars, symbols, ribbons, and other art," advises a brochure for Pagan Spirit Gathering. Some campers make their festival homes in particular trees or around rock formations, while others create their own distinctive temporary homes out of fairly ordinary sites.

When I first arrived at Starwood 1992, I walked down a wooded dirt lane adjacent to the large and open festival field. A Volkswagen camper van was parked behind some comfortable-looking chairs grouped around a fire pit. Facing outward toward passersby and in front of the campfire was a bull altar decorated with a variety of bull figurines and freshly cut gladiolas. I was told this was an altar for the Cult of the Bull. A few campsites beyond the bull altar, I came upon a woman setting up her tent under the thick overhanging branches of an apple tree. Of all the campsites at Starwood that year, hers was the most like a sanctuary. Her tent was completely hidden beneath the leafy tree and could be reached only by crawling through a tunnel of branches. On one side of my campsite at Pagan Spirit Gathering 1993 was a neon-blue nylon tent and a kitchen area covered in nylon mesh and furnished with new plastic and aluminum camping gear; no feature distinguished it from countless similar campsites on campgrounds all over America. I helped my neighbors on the other side set up an elaborate cream and white canvas pavilion, with thick wool rugs and a full-sized futon inside. Candles in wrought iron candle holders hung on tree branches outside. For most festival goers, the whole process of setting up and personalizing campsites is an important expression of their festival identity and how they want to present themselves to the broader community. Campsites and the personal altars displayed at campsites develop out of personal aesthetics as well as community expectations.

Campsites are where festival history is made, new "families" form, and old friends share plans and memories around their camp fires. As I sat down with Amelia and Willow at their campsite, they began catching up on the events of each other's lives since the last festival. They talked about their relationships with men and about their jobs, and they talked about changes that had been wrought in their lives by the previous festival. Even temporary campsites like Amelia's become important gathering sites within the brief duration of one festival. Campsite intimacy is facilitated by the separation of campsites from more formal festival activities, in the same way that the entire festival is seen as a sanctuary from the outside world. At times, festival goers need to retreat from the intensity and social demands of festival activities just as they need to escape from mundania. While I attended festivals, my tent was a space that helped me temporarily separate myself from the festival to write field notes and process the day's events.

As personalized spaces, campsites serve as homes away from home and as escapes from festival overload. They offer home-like sanctuaries in a strange and, for newcomers, often disorienting environment. Campsites even receive special designations on festival maps: "quiet zones" or "family camping" are two common ones. Starwood's quiet zone is far removed from the festival field, as are the fairy woods and the chemical-free camping area. By marginalizing these areas, festivals signify that there will be late-night drumming and loud boisterous parties that might not be to the liking of all participants. Lothlorien also features campsites for different interest groups: elders, children, healers, shamans, scientists, and in the center of the festival field, Troll Camp. In the years I attended ELF festivals, the camp established by parking Trolls, whom Johnny called the ELF's "proletariat," was a "party zone" complete with bar and bar stools. Lothlorien festivals have included "Cincinnati" and "Detroit" camps for groups of friends attending from these urban areas. Other camps are organized as "festival families"—groups of friends who see each other only at festivals. Festival families often gather around campfires in the middle of a group of tents, creating small personal spaces where they invite friends and neighbors for shared meals or music. Small communities are especially important at large festivals like Starwood, where it is easy to feel lost among the thousand or more participants.

I spent an evening during ELFest 1994 around the Ohana campfire, somewhat hidden in the woods behind Starheart's large tent. As they waited for Starheart to appear and lead the chants, the informal circle of festival goers got acquainted. First they talked about their occupations: Amelia teaches music; Terese works for a defense corporation; Cally for a temporary employment agency; one of the women had been a teacher, but told us that she could not keep her job once she "came out of the closet" as a Neopagan. On common ground now, other people around the fire discussed their own experiences of being "in" or "out of the closet" with their families. Several came from conservative Christian families who still had no idea that they were Neopagans. Sitting around this campfire were men and women who had been raised as atheists, Unitarians, Catholics, Presbyterians, and Pentecostals. Cally who came from a Pentecostal family told the others that there was "no way" she would say anything about Neopaganism to her family: "They would have me kidnapped and brainwashed." Terese talked about secrecy on the job and described her surprise at meeting another Witch at the large corporation where she works. "We are everywhere," several people agreed. Tammy said "This is much more of a family than my other family." Around the campfire others agreed that their festival friends are more of a family than the blood relatives with whom they cannot share their Neopagan identities.

My second night at Starwood, I ventured out beyond the central merchant and camping area to find a friend I had come to know on the Internet but had never met in person. She had been attending Starwood for several years in order to camp with a small group of friends from all over the country, and they had claimed a private wooded area well away from the center of the festival. Before I reached my friend's camp, I passed by the edge of the forest where campers had strung colored Christmas lights through the tree branches. After I joined my friends at their campsite, I discovered that this was the "fairy woods," claimed by gay men, lesbians, and their friends.[53] Neopagan festivals are one of the few public contexts where gay and lesbian relationships are affirmed and celebrated. Gay, lesbian, and bisexual (and a few transgendered) people made up a sizable and visible minority at every festival I attended. Pagan Spirit Gathering's "1992 Tribal Survey" reported the following statistics on sexual orientation: out of 354 responses 71.8 percent marked heterosexual, 14.1 percent bisexual, 5.4 percent gay male, 2.5 percent lesbian, 2.2 percent celibate, and 4.0 percent "other."[54] While heterosexuals make up the majority of festival goers, heterosexuality is less emphasized as the norm in the Neopagan community as it is by most Americans. Gays and lesbians say they feel safer at Pagan gatherings than in the outside world, but still not as safe as at gatherings where they are the majority, such as the Michigan Women's Music Festival (not a Neopagan event, yet attended by many women who identify themselves as witches or goddess worshippers) and Radical Faerie gatherings. To enter the "fairy woods," it was necessary to leave the festival field behind and pass under the colorful lights into a dense growth of trees and brush where tents bearing banners of pink triangles were nestled.

It would seem that the private spaces within festivals would be the least contested and most devoid of the tensions that erupt in large ritual areas like Thunder Dome or Lothlorien's enchanted Faerie woods. When they are not located deep in the woods or otherwise secluded locations, they often seem to welcome visitors, but this is not always the case. Festival etiquette for community ritual areas can also be applied to campsites and small gatherings around campfires. J. Perry Damarru makes this point clear in his advice to first-time festival goers: "As you roam around the gathering site, you may come across a small group of people forming a circle. They may or may not be performing a healing. They may or may not want to maintain a measure of privacy. Be sensitive. Don't enter or break an existing circle."[55] Boundaries between spaces within the festival are as crucial to festival goers' security and enjoyment as those between the festival and mundania.

At Wild Magick 1993, Starheart, David, Willow, and several other friends gathered together for a pipe ceremony led by David, which was modeled on American Indian pipe ceremonies. They sat in a circle on woven rugs spread between their campsites which happened to be on the edge of Merchants' Row, an area that was only semiprivate because of the many people passing by. Once the ritual had begun, tensions arose when someone who was only a vague acquaintance wandered by and asked to be included. He was told that the ceremony was already under way, and he walked off with a scowl. But several minutes later a close friend of David's arrived, and she was invited to join the group, even though the ritual was even further along. In this case, the boundary between the public merchants' area/festival field and the private campsite was not clearly marked. The boundaries between sites may become clear only when they are transgressed, as in the tree-cutting incident in Faerie woods. As these incidents suggest, festivals often appear to be more open and free form than they actually are. Festival goers establish boundaries within the festival itself that function to distinguish themselves from other festival participants and enable them to feel secure, to define their own ritual groups and circles of friends, and to mark off their private territories.

There is almost no place on festival sites that has not been subjected to arguments over its meaning. In fact, it would seem that the "place-myths," to borrow Rob Shields's term, within festivals are constantly undergoing a process of negotiation. A sense of community builds up in spaces as a result of the kind of interactions I have described, but it also breaks down at their boundaries. Even merchants' displays are treated with conflicting attitudes. Most festival goers enjoy looking at merchants' goods, if not buying items for the main ritual or perhaps gifts to take home to friends, but other Neopagans are unhappy with what they see as the commercialization of festivals. At the ELFest 1991 Grand Council, Diana voiced her disapproval for the increasing size of the merchants' area at ELFest. "The festivals are starting to feel like malls," she complained, and the community should remember, she advised, that these "are festivals, not 'shows.' "[56] Neopagans invest festival places with their ideals, and because of this they often come into conflict over the meanings of these places.

In the American religious imagination, Neopagan festivals serve as the locus of conflicted images and expectations. Religious communities that Neopagans have rejected in order to join their festival families, and particularly those communities that see Neopaganism as a form of devil worship, make shaping and defining festival space even more urgent. Because they feel embattled from without, festival goers are more likely to insist on controlling the festival from within. Festival goers believe they have little control over outsiders' perceptions of their religion, and thus, defining the spaces within festivals allows them to feel they have some control over the meanings that are being made out of their religious lives. Festivals are exotic spaces hidden in the woods and explicitly opposed to ordinary life, so festival neighbors are concerned about what takes place at festivals. I turn now to look at this larger struggle over meaning and suggest some of the ways in which broader American religious and cultural struggles impinge on festival experience, again crossing the boundaries that Neopagans work so hard to maintain.

CHAPTER THREE

The Great Evil
That Is in Your Backyard

Festival Neighbors and Satanism Rumors

"Satanic Rites Held at Yellowwood Forest" reads the headline news story about a Neopagan festival in southern Indiana. "Festival neighbors and local churches fear that festival bonfires and drumming are signs of satanic sacrifice."[1] Neighbors with "overactive imaginations" (as Neopagans put it) spread rumors of festival goers who engage in "blood letting and other acts of horror."[2] For conservative Christians who fear festivals in their midst, Neopaganism is a close-to-home example of Satan's resistance to the armies of God. But Neopagans see themselves as a misunderstood religious minority, with a "history of suppression and abuse" by "hysterical fundies" and law enforcement agencies.[3] "Biblical bigots," Neopagans complain, express pervasive cultural ignorance and prejudice about witchcraft and engage in widespread persecution of non-Christian religions.[4] As a result of unfounded rumors that they are carrying out satanic rituals, festival goers are harassed by neighbors and members of local churches; festival sites are vandalized by teenagers and searched late at night by local police. In response, festival organizers invite neighbors to tour festival sites and explain to reporters that they are folklorists and ecologists not child abusers.[5]

Important issues of Neopagan self-definition are raised at the geographical and cultural boundaries between festivals and their neighbors. The festival community's identity, founded in the contrast with mundania already, is further shaped by Neopagans' responses to rumors that they are "devil-worshipping slimeballs who commit atrocities in the name of Evil," as Neopagan Llyselya put it in a letter to *Green Egg*'s Forum.[6] Festival policies about dress, behavior, and noise that cause conflict within festivals often originate in efforts to deal with complaints of neighbors outside the festival boundaries. Neopagans adopt a number of different strategies to secure and define festival boundaries against outside attacks: they police themselves more carefully; they exclude avowed Satanists; they contrast their religious tolerance to neighbors' intolerance; they complain about and criticize local communities, while they also find common ground on which their neighbors can understand them.[7] But all of these impinge on the meanings and experience of festivals. Festival goers must at the same time identify who they are in the festival community—Wiccan, magician, Druid, shaman, etc.—and who they are in relation to outside perceptions. Neopagans reveal important concerns about their religious lives when they respond to conflicts with neighbors, and it is in part through their responses to persecution that Neopagans carve out a place for themselves on the North American religious landscape. These conflicts reveal how Neopagans imagine their place in the larger world of American religions, and how other religions respond to their presence there.

A FESTIVAL AND ITS NEIGHBORS

In 1985, the *Brown County Democrat* ran a story based on interviews with two police officers who had been sent to investigate alleged "devil worshippers" at Yellowwood State Forest in southern Indiana. These "satanists" were in fact Neopagans who had gathered for a weekend of workshops and rituals organized by the Elf Lore Family. Undercover police officers roamed through the forest keeping an eye on the festival goers throughout the weekend. The policemen told the *Democrat's* reporter that they saw "emblems that have been connected with devil worship" and ceremonies that "resembled satanic rites." The story went on to describe the officers' reports of ritual participants dressed in "devil-like costumes" who were "drinking what appeared to be blood Saturday morning and eating raw flesh." Police "heard the group planned to sacrifice a goat," although such a sacrifice never took place, and officers found no reason to arrest anyone at the gathering.[8] The Sunday edition of the Bloomington, Indiana, *Herald Telephone* carried a follow-up story on the Yellowwood incident in which a pastor from nearby Bean Blossom Baptist Church described his congregation's response to the alleged satanic gathering: "Members . . . deposited anti-satan literature at the Yellowwood gathering after his wife received a call that satanic rituals were occurring there."[9]

In the days following these initial stories, the *Herald Telephone* carried responses from ELF members outraged by the article in the *Brown County Democrat* and demanding a retraction. ELF also issued a press release presenting its side of the story. Festival organizers treated police officers in a polite and friendly manner, according to the press release, because they were confident that they were not breaking any laws. ELF invited officers to tour the campsite, confident that "everything was in order." In contrast to their own cooperative attitudes, festival goers complained of constant surveillance and disruption of their rituals by police: "Throughout the gathering, various Sheriff's and Conservancy vehicles repeatedly cruised the site, up and down the road, prowling through the parking lot, occasionally shining headlights onto the assembled tents and campers. One car parked silently in a hidden drive adjacent to the site. Police dogs were in evidence and, at one time, two officers, at midnight Saturday evening, entered the gathering with their animal. Most folks, including the children, were asleep at the time. . . . Various ELF members were repeatedly questioned as to whether a goat was to be sacrificed. None was in attendance." ELF's press release also pointed out that the only destructive act committed at Yellowwood that weekend was by their harassers: "The Bean Blossom Baptist Church did send members by the gathering to deliver Bible tracts. These were thrown out of a window, scattered upon the earth, and generally wasted upon the ELFs who picked up the litter."

RUMORS OF SATANISM

"We are not evil. We do not worship the Devil. We don't harm or seduce people. We are not dangerous. We are ordinary people like you. . . . We are not what you think we are from looking at T.V.," responded Margot Adler's informants when asked what they most wanted to tell the public about Neopaganism.[10] When Neopagans explain their religion to outsiders, the first thing they tell them is "We aren't Satanists." They know that neighbors' perceptions of Neopaganism are constructed from negative media images of contemporary Pagans as devil worshippers and child abusers. There are three primary ways in which Neopagans are cast as evil others by their Christian neighbors, and more generally by conservative Christians in the broader culture: scapegoating, by which

Neopagans are to blame for a host of social problems such as teen violence; fear of captivity, which suggests Neopagans are to be feared because they will catch you or your children; and apocalypticism, which results in the belief that Neopagans both signify and will cause the coming apocalypse described in the Book of Revelation.

The demonization of Neopagans has taken place in part because of a campaign against what some conservative Christians, law enforcement agencies, and social workers have labeled "satanic ritual abuse." Satanic ritual abuse was a topic of discussion at the 1991 American Psychological Association's annual meeting in Los Angeles: "The APA conference focused on this issue and decided that the entire 'ritual abuse' scare was started by a few therapists. . . . They indicated that genuine cases of 'ritual abuse' are extremely rare, and are as likely to be inflicted by Christians as by anyone else."[11] But the findings of professional organizations seem to have little effect on popular perceptions of ritual abuse. Scholars of religion also challenge misconceptions about satanism. They make a distinction between the two most significant divisions of satanism: 1) the psychologically disturbed or criminally minded; and 2) serious Satanists such as members of Anton LaVey's Church of Satan, who have more developed theological systems and disavow any criminal wrongdoing.[12] Scholars who distinguish between Satanism as a religion and the appropriation of satanic symbols by criminals are also ignored.

Neopagans and religious satanists are victims of "the satanic panic," as sociologist Jeffrey Victor calls widespread fears about satanic ritual abuse.[13] Victor argues that rumors of satanism are spread by social workers and police detectives as well as conservative Christians. These Americans identify everything from the role-playing game "Dungeons and Dragons" (a topic covered by law-enforcement seminars on ritualistic crime), to the rituals of contemporary witches as evidence of a demonic conspiracy.[14] Victor notes that recent conspiracy theories about an organized underground network of satanists explicitly recall anticommunist hysteria in America during the 1950s. Bennett Braun, who treats "purported Satanic-abuse victims" at a Chicago clinic, claimed in a 1988 speech that "we are working with a national-international type organization that's got a structure somewhere similar to the communist cell structure."[15] Victor contends that paranoia about Satanic forces at work in American society is given credence by psychologists, social workers, and police officers trained in workshops led by Christian fundamentalists. " 'Devil worshippers' have been socially constructed as scapegoat deviants to blame for the social turmoil and moral crisis in American society. The possible existence of earthly agents of Satan is entirely consistent with the ideological fears of religious traditionalists. It does not require a great leap of faith for many of them to believe that devil-worshipping agents of Satan are at work behind much of the immorality and perversion in American society." But "satanic panic" has spread beyond the confines of Christian churches: "What is more curious is that many people who do not hold a traditionalist religious ideology are also swept up in the Satanic cult scare. The explanation may be that the Satanic demonology remains a powerful metaphor for the workings of evil even for some professionals, who are, after all, socialized in American culture." Rumors of satanism are so widespread that they do not simply affect Neopagans' freedom to hold their rituals at state parks or other public places. The explanatory power of satanic conspiracy theories threatens Neopagans' lives on many fronts and impacts child-custody cases, employment, and educational experience.[16]

Neopagans charge that among those people who have been "swept up" in this "scare" are social workers and the courts who take their children away in custody battles.[17] Rachel, one of the first Neopagans I met and interviewed in 1989, told me that she often called herself a "psychic" instead of a "witch" because she was afraid of losing her son. In each issue of *Circle Network News*, the "Lady Liberty League" column typically lists several cases in which religious issues affected custody disputes. In the summer of 1995, three separate items involving custody battles appeared in this one-page column: "Within four days of coming out to the local newspaper as the high priestess of a Wiccan coven, Jessica Spurr's three foster children were abruptly removed from her home. . . . A case worker made an unannounced visit to her home and asked Jessica why she had not told anyone . . . that she was a witch."[18] Social workers and other state-appointed guardians of children's welfare who do not jump to the conclusion that Neopagans are devil worshippers, nonetheless often see them as unfit parents.

"Hysteria mongering" by Neopagans' neighbors is a result of fears about satanists in their own backyards. As Chris, writing to Arcana, sees it, "Neighbors have been known to harass folks for such tiny causes as 'dressing funny,' wearing 'peculiar jewelry,' having too many books (occult or otherwise), etc. Rituals held by Neopagans in their backyards or living rooms can also serve as provocation. Neighbors have trespassed on occultists, stolen and vandalized their property, threatened to have their children taken away by social services, and even shot at them."[19] Films and T.V. shows which portray Neopagans, especially Witches, as satanic, encourage fear of difference. After the Lifetime cable network ran an antiwitchcraft movie called "To Save a Child," Jehovah's Witnesses stopped by one Neopagan's house to look around and later "grabbed neighbors to tell them that Pagans lived in this house."[20] The case of Iron Oak Coven in Palm Bay, Florida, widely publicized on Neopagan electronic forums, is an excellent example of the trouble Neopagans' neighbors occasionally cause. High Priestess Jacque Omi Zaleski tells it like this: "Early in 1994, a distant neighbor drove by our acre homesite and saw us in our yard celebrating Imbolc with some friends. Probably remembering all the Saturday night horror shows she had ever seen, she complained to the City. The police knew there was nothing wrong here and took no action. Rebuffed by the police, she contacted Planning and Zoning officials who were willing to go further with the complaint. Two city officials threatened us with fines and arrest if we had more than five people on our property for worship or prayer, even 'over a birthday cake.'" The neighbor had complained to the city that Jacque and her husband were holding events at their house in violation of city zoning laws that prohibited "churches" in residential areas, so the city sued. This woman was apparently far more concerned about the suspicious gatherings in her neighbors' back yard than in the offending cars of their coven mates, which the Zaleskis claimed were not parked anywhere near her house nor blocking the road in any way.

The city spent $60,000 to prosecute Iron Oak, and the Zaleskis spent $22,000 of their own money for their defense. After three days of hearings, the Code Enforcement board voted unanimously in favor of Iron Oak. But the Zaleskis were infuriated by this violation of their religious freedom. Because they had publicized the case in newspapers and over the Internet, Neopagans nationwide as well as other religious organizations concerned about freedom to worship, came to their support. They decided to take the City of Palm Bay to federal court under the Religious Freedom Restoration Act (RFRA). In 1996 they engaged in aggressive fundraising over the Internet and held a festival in Florida; Jacque Zaleski traveled to Pagan Spirit Gathering for further support from other Neopagans.[21]

Neopagans complain that Christian neighbors are always vigilant, always on the lookout for local satanists. Peh showed me a news story in *The Martinsville Reporter* in Martinsville, Indiana, that included excerpts from an interview with Larry Reck, a professor at Indiana State University who was scheduled to speak at the Martinsville (Indiana) High School (about fifteen miles from Yellowwood forest) on the topic of "satanism." Reck, for example, provokes fears of captivity when he reports, "In 1982, I wrote about the possibility of satan worship in Morgan County. At that time, I had several reports of area residents seeing dark-robed, torch-carrying groups in and around Morgan-Monroe Forest. I also had some reports of animal sacrifices in the same area. . . . Our own plant superintendent, Rick Morrison, told me that he had gone to fish in Cherry Lake one night with a friend. They heard voices and saw people carrying torches. They didn't wait to see if they were satan worshippers. They got the devil out of there."[22] "That was us!" Peh announced, laughing, when he showed me this news clipping. Surface similarities between Neopagans dressed in ritual garb and satanic worshippers in popular films like *Rosemary's Baby* (1968) and *The Omen* (1976), who also wear dark robes and carry torches, are sufficient to arouse fear. Reck conveys to a large public audience what he sees as a serious warning about the dangers of local "satanists": "Watch out, there really are robed devil-worshippers waiting for you in the woods at night." But Neopagans protest that while they may wear dark hooded robes and perform their rituals deep in the woods, they have little in common with the satanically possessed murderers of popular horror movies. Neopagans respond to satanic rumors by saying that they are members of real communities, neighbors and fellow employees, not fictional characters designed by Hollywood.

Ignorance and fear of the unknown other cause some contemporary Americans to identify Neopagans as enemies of society who are responsible for a set of social problems. Scholars of new religions are quick to point out that this kind of scapegoating has been a constant theme in American religious history. "Paranoid perceptions of 'the enemy' have led to irrational accusations concerning beliefs, obscenities, profanities, rituals and behavior patterns" since the colonial period, according to J. Gordon Melton, editor of *The Encyclopedia of American Religions*.[23] From the earliest European presence in North America, fear of difference has been an important characteristic of American society.[24] As relatively recent arrivals with tenuous ties to this land, European-Americans have had a strong need to situate themselves as important shapers of American religious culture. New religions and recent immigrants alike are perceived as threats to Christian cultural and religious dominance. This was the case in relations with cultures indigenous to the Americas as well as with Asian religions that first arrived on American shores in significant numbers between 1840 and 1924, according to historians Thomas A. Tweed and Stephen Prothero.[25] While many Americans assume that late twentieth-century American society is tolerant of difference, the experiences of Neopagans and members of other new (or new to North America) religions suggest otherwise.[26]

The persecution of religions perceived to be strange or dangerous displaces blame and points to important cultural issues or fears in the persecuters. Rumors of satanic conspiracy offer "bible-believing" Christians, to borrow sociologist Nancy Ammerman's term, and other concerned adults an explanation for their children's inclination "towards violent and anti-social behavior." Wiccan priest and elder Don Frew, who has been a police consultant on occult crime, argues that, "Once an individual has 'snapped' and committed a crime, parents and others are much more willing to look for the cause and affix blame on an evil enemy at the edge of society than they are to look inside the home. Related to this, it's a lot easier to accept that your child was molested by a Satanic cult than to think it might have been Uncle Frank."[27] Following this line of reasoning, Neopagans believe that they are being blamed for social problems that have nothing to do with them. They believe that the real problems contemporary American families face, such as poverty and divorce, teenage pregnancy and drug abuse, are blamed on local and visible targets like Neopagan neighbors. Widespread hysteria about satanism, which led to the harassment of ELF members at Yellowwood, is also supported by sensationalistic stories on television. In October of 1988, for instance, Geraldo Rivera devoted a program to "Devil Worship: Exposing Satan's Secret Underground," and "Americans in 19.8 million homes tuned in." How has satanism, and anything that hints of satanism, such as dressing in black and dancing around bonfires at night, become the evil other for so many Americans?

Social, economic, demographic, and religious changes in post–World War II America have raised new questions and problems for conservative Protestants and Catholics. These changes include the following: the lack of any central religious authority; an influx of immigrants; an increasingly corporatized world; transformations in social and personal life, such as the high rate of divorce; and rapid technological change—the computer revolution. What sociologist Robert Wuthnow terms the "restructuring" of American religion has resulted in uncertainty about the moral status of America—especially a fear of sexual license, alternative family structures, and changing gender roles—among conservative Protestants and Catholics, as well as the tendency to construct evil others who threaten America's future. Symbolic boundaries have shifted the public dimensions of religious culture, so that discussion of moral issues such as gay rights and abortion has become polarized in new ways.[28] In these boundary shifts, Neopagans are aligned with the forces of liberalism and pluralism that conservative Protestants and Catholics fear will continue to bring about moral and spiritual decay.[29]

Neopagans have become one of several focal points (abortion is another one) for conservative Christian critiques of contemporary American life and morality. Critics of Neopaganism range from Pentecostal ministers and conservative Protestant political lobbyists to Catholic priests and followers of Marian visions. They include southern Baptists who attacked an Arkansas occult bookstore, Pentecostal church members in southern Indiana who showered Bible tracts on ELF members worshipping in Yellowwood forest, and conservative Catholic writers who instruct their readers to avoid the danger of satanism in its New Age and Neopagan guises. They have little in common doctrinally or in the area of ritual practice, but they can agree on one thing: Neopaganism and new religions like the New Age movement are evil threats to the moral and religious character of American life.[30] Coming together against a non-Christian foe allows these fractured Christian communities to experience coherence and a sense of cultural authority they do not possess apart from this necessary other.

The eclecticism and cultural borrowing that attract many participants to both New Age and Neopagan movements are symptoms of Satan's plan to take over the world, according to some Christians. For the purposes of their attackers, the Neopagan and New Age movements are interchangeable. The New Age Movement is even more difficult than Neopaganism to define and identify. It has roots in the "positive thinking" approach of Norman Vincent Peale and others, includes the holistic health movement, and draws heavily on Asian philosophies and practices, although it also includes many Christians. *Natural Health* (formerly *East-West Journal*) and *New Age* magazines reflect some of the concerns of this movement. Although Neopagans borrow from some of the same sources, they root themselves in pre-Christian nature religions, early 1900s ceremonial magic in Great Britain, and post-1940s British witchcraft, none of which is important to New Agers. Neopagans have much in common with New Agers' interests in alternative healing practices, astrology, and personal transformation, but the two movements have distinct emphases and practices. Neopagan ritual practices—"calling the quarters"—and the centrality of nature and seasonal cycles in their rituals is not shared by many New Agers, who are more likely to be drawn to books about angels or channeling. Although these movements diverge on many points, they share beliefs and practices that many conservative Christians find dangerous: visualization, sacralization of nature, "occult" techniques such as divination and astrology, and interest in American Indian and other non-European religions.[31]

Conservative Christians who oppose what they see as satanic influences on American religious and cultural life, strengthen their own position by exaggerating the evils of the other side, in this case represented by their Neopagan neighbors. They believe that Neopagans have satanic potential because they belong to a different moral universe and are aiding the forces of Satan, even if they are not actually sacrificing babies and drinking blood. Descriptions of festivals by fearful neighbors are replete with images of deviant practices—flesh eating, drug abuse, group orgies, child sacrifice, and other similar activities. One of the battles to be fought, argues Jay Rogers, a member of the Christian Coalition, is against contemporary Pagans who provide "the spiritual force behind the politics of abortion."[32] Rogers admits that when he investigated his Wiccan neighbors' rituals, he was "not able to ascertain whether or not Witches use the blood of aborted children in their sacrifices." But he suspected that "since the child is not considered human according to our liberal abortion laws, it stands to reason that such a sacrifice, protected by law, could be used by witches." Rogers claims that, like the "ancient Israelites . . . 20th century Americans were first enticed by the sexual revolution of the 1960s." Soon thereafter, he reminds his readers, abortion became a "fundamental right." Rogers concludes that revivals of paganism are dangerous precisely because he identifies witchcraft with killing children: "Whenever pagan sexual immorality is accepted, abortion and child sacrifice becomes a necessity in covering up the fruit of sin." As this argument goes, sexual permissiveness identified with Neopaganism by necessity leads to child sacrifice. "Satan has you all by your genitals," Christian Gladiator Ministries' Eric Pryor warns *Green Egg* readers.[33] The connection between witchcraft and abortion is another symptom of America's declining morality and widespread sexual debauchery.

Stories about satanic possession put the blame for America's social and moral decay on those religions that are taking shape outside a biblical framework. Conservative Christians face off against Neopagans, New Agers, and other non-Christians in a battle for religious control of America's moral universe. Protestants may still feel challenged by Catholics and even by other Protestants, but antagonism toward Neopagans results from the fear that Americans will continue to seek meaning outside of biblical religion entirely. Judging from conservative Christian polemics against "witches" and "satanists," Neopagans are more demonic and constitute an even greater threat to young Americans than secularism. There is a sense in which Neopagans really are "satanic" from the perspectives of their conservative Christian neighbors. On one Big Ten campus, the Campus Crusade for Christ called Neopagans "wolves in sheep's clothing," and refused to work with them on ecumenical issues because "Satan might be working through them."[34] Neopagans generally do not believe in and worship the Christian God, which from some Christian perspectives locates them with Satan's minions: "Witchcraft falls into Satanic worship because it does not acknowledge the existence of God," argued one minister.[35] The owners of Brushwood shared with me their favorite comment by a hostile Christian neighbor: "The nudity doesn't bother us; what we care about is how people think."

Neopagans are not "born-again" through Christ, and they are often polytheists. The Neopagan world is inclusive of many spirits, ancestors, and gods and goddesses who live side by side. In Neopagan belief, humans are responsible for their own lives, although they may call on spirits, ancestors, and deities for guidance. Neopagans engage in transactions with spirits and deities, using ritual offerings to garner help and support. A contributor to Pagan Digest describes the Christian view of her deities this way: "The problem exists because Christians believe in good and evil beings. A Christian who contacts/is contacted by a spirit or god has to go through an IFF (Identification Friend or Foe) procedure, and their only frame of reference is God and Satan. That priest or preacher has no handle on where to put Apollo, so he falls back on the old 'Satan can disguise himself as an angel of light' routine and rejects what you say. Of course, most pagans don't believe in the 'good god, evil devil' setup, so they find it harder to understand the Christian's actions."[36] Rumors of satanism thus emerge from the context of belief in an ongoing struggle between good and evil in which Neopagans and their deities are delegated to the forces of darkness.

For many Christians, the spirits of the land and ancient deities that Neopagans call upon are demonic, and they are doing Satan's bidding, not God's. Conservative Christians charge that New Age spirituality and Neopaganism substitute many gods for the "one, true God" and attempt to make the human, material world as sacred as the divine world. Practices such as tarot reading and meditation, which seem to draw on sources of power other than God, are also seen as satanic. For conservative evangelical Protestants, Neopagans are the unsaved whom they must either convert or protect themselves against. In so doing, these

Christians "stand verbally on God's side in the battle against an evil world."[37] This war is in part a struggle between conservative Christians and what they see as competing *religious* beliefs about the nature of ultimate reality, the relationship between human and divine powers, and the unfolding of history.[38]

Festivals embody an alternative vision of society, and it is not a vision most conservative Christians feel comfortable with. Neopagan moral stances and religious beliefs are troubling enough to conservative Christians, but it is specifically sexual morality and the sacralization of sexuality that make Neopaganism most objectionable to these Christians. Even if their stories of evil orgies are sensationalistic and inaccurate, Christian critics correctly perceive that Neopagans mix sex and religion, and it is this mix that troubles them, that they find most threatening to their attempts to raise children in a safe and Christian world. Most Neopagan festivals welcome gay marriages and offer workshops on safe sex, open marriage, bisexuality, "sacred prostitution" (the idea that women or men may engage in sex as part of a commitment to a god or goddess), and many other topics that explore various forms of sexuality and the relationship between sexuality and spirituality.

Neopagans have been created in the image of the evil other, and their festivals have been demonized, in order to give a face to the causal factors behind frightening social and moral conditions—especially those pertaining to sexuality—in late twentieth-century America. Stories like *Michelle Remembers* about satanic rituals pit the victim/survivor against an evil religious other—in this case, a satanic cult. While each claims that the other is a powerful force threatening their lives, both conservative Christians and Neopagans see themselves as marginal cultures struggling for religious identity and control over their children in an increasingly secular and rational America.[39]

FESTIVAL AS SPECTACLE

Late twentieth-century American parents are clearly worried about their children, and for good reason. Teenage pregnancy and teen alcohol and drug abuse are serious social problems, and they are high on the list of cultural dangers that Christian critics associate with Neopagans.[40] They are also problems that teens keep hidden from their parents. Neopaganism, parents are warned, may be a part of their children's secret life that parents have no access to, and it may also explain children's furtiveness and their strange hairstyles and clothing. Distorted stories

spread by fearful neighbors provide lurid details of the dangers at Neopagan festivals that may tempt their teenage children. Fred, Brushwood's
owner, related a recent incident in which his own son and the son of a
professor at the local community college were accused of being involved
in satanism because of their "weird hairstyles." Fred also shared with
me a letter sent "To The People of Sherman [New York—the closest town
to Brushwood] Or Who[m] It May Concern." In it, the author, who signs
himself "A Friend in God," warns Brushwood's neighbors to "protect
your children from the great evil that is in your back yard . . . a strange
pagan gathering." He explains that earlier in his life he found himself
"before the Altar of satanism." He confesses that at that time he "took
part in rituals covered in blood, I drank blood sometimes mixed with
wine, and did drugs. . . . As a result of what I did in this cult I am condemned to die from sicknesses which I acquired from this life style." The
author takes a voluptuous delight in recounting his former "wickedness."
By describing his actions with horror-movie imagery, he hopes to gain
support for his fight against "the pagans."[41] This "friend in God" tells
of visiting one of the festivals at Brushwood. He says he saw there some
people from his days "in the Ohio coven," but he describes no specific
practices that he witnessed at the festival: "We did not stay very long,
but long enough to see my worst thoughts about this situation. . . . These
people are some of the worst active satanists in the country today. . . .
All I can say to the people of Sherman is 'do not let your children get involved with these people. They will brain wash them, turn them into
drug addicts, show them all the immoral and deviant things you can
dream of. . . . bet you will not get in during their darkest rituals, but your
children might."[42] The author warns parents who live in the area surrounding Brushwood that their teenage children are most at risk, thus
playing on popular images of satanic ritual abuse from films like *Rosemary's Baby*. Parents' fears for their children's safety are easily manipu-
lated as a powerful strategy against Neopagans.

When Neopagans are demonized by Christians who are genuinely
afraid for their children, their festivals become sites of engagement where
Christian forces test Satan's strength. Festival neighbors may suspect that
Neopagans are looking for vulnerable young people to hold psychically
captive or are perhaps laying the groundwork for Satan's next battle with
God. Circle Sanctuary in southwestern Wisconsin near the town of
Mt. Horeb, which sponsors a variety of festivals year-round, got a re-
straining order against a "fundamentalist Christian televangelist" in
order to protect their Samhain festival (held annually on October 31)

from harassment. The Reverend Jeff Fenholt campaigned against festivals held at Circle as part of "nationwide ministry against Witchcraft." During a rally of fundamentalist Christians the day before Halloween, Fenholt "proclaimed that Mt. Horeb was under attack and spoke of his intent to return to this area as well as to go to other sites around the United States he also has targeted as part of his ongoing campaign against Witches and the Wiccan religion." Fenholt's attack on Circle was supported by fellow televangelist Pat Robertson. On his *700 Club* television show, Pentecostal preacher "Robertson denounced the one mile 'no witnessing' zone around the Sanctuary" that a court had granted Circle.[43] Curiosity and fear aroused by negative media images of Neopaganism and witchcraft turn festival sites into places of hidden and mysterious activity.

When Neopagans travel to festivals they expect to leave behind the suspicions that surround their religion in neighborhoods and workplaces. They forget that festivals do not really take place in an enchanted fairyland separate from surrounding communities and nearby churches. Indeed, festivals often take place in rural areas where people are less accustomed to the extreme religious and cultural diversity of the large urban areas where many festival goers live. Starfeild, who had recently moved to the North Carolina mountains, writes, "I have moved to the Dark Ages. . . . The Wiccans rallied in Asheville. The Baptists called them Satanic!"[44] Festival neighbors suspect their home territory is being invaded by evil outsiders with perverse ritual practices and strange beliefs. Judging by letters to local newspapers and their requests for police protection, Neopagan festival neighbors who consider themselves "respectable Christians" look warily on the festive atmosphere of Neopagan gatherings and think the noise they hear is evidence that their worst fears have been realized. Neighbors intrude on festivals because they feel threatened by what they cannot see, but also to find out if their wildest imaginings are true.[45]

By keeping their religious identities to themselves and holding their festivals at isolated sites, Neopagans make their religious practices even more fascinating to outsiders. By the very act of hiding what they are doing, they draw attention to themselves. The "hiddenness" of many new religions accounts in part for the negative ways in which they are viewed. Sectarian and communitarian movements that withdraw from society, such as the International Society for Krishna Consciousness (New Vrindaban, West Virginia), the Church Universal and Triumphant (Corwin Springs, Montana), the Branch Davidians (Waco, Texas), and Neopagans who retreat to summer gatherings in the woods, seek "to reduce tension with the wider society," according to sociologist Bryan Wilson. And yet "near neighbors inevitably become aware of them. . . . The very fact of withdrawal into a sequestered enclave arouses suspicions of sinister purposes."[46] The combination of hiddenness and carnivalesque display is what makes festivals something to wonder about and to see. If festivals are a space of imaginative possibility for festival goers, where different ways of being in the world can be experimented with, it is hardly surprising that they are also an opportunity for other Americans to let their imaginations run free.

Rumors of satanic sacrifice have no basis in fact, in my judgment and experience. I never witnessed any physical abuse of humans or animals by Neopagans. I never saw Santerian or Vodou animal sacrifices at any festivals (though a few Neopagans participate in these practices elsewhere). Sexual promiscuity and drug use were subdued at some festivals and at others no more excessive than at a rock concert. Festivals are celebrations, and their raucousness is as much due to dancing and drumming as to mind-altering substances. Participants make a lot of noise and act in ways they probably would not in another environment. The atmosphere of some festivals encourages excessive behavior, but others are more sedate and family oriented. Although the factual content of neighborly fears is thus open to question, rumors are key to the dynamic by which festival communities and neighbors play off each other's fears in the processes of self-definition in electronic and print media.

The press release ELF issued in response to the allegations in the *Brown County Democrat* states humorously: "It seems that the officers allowed too many horror movies, cheap novels, and 'fire and brimstone sermons' to color their perceptions. They saw no 'three young women' who 'danced naked around the fire.' It sounds like a case of wishful thinking."[47] Fascinated neighbors capture on film or describe in writing the things they are most afraid of finding at festivals: "satanists" drinking blood, abusing children, and engaging in orgiastic frenzy. When I was at Brushwood for Starwood 1992, a member of the festival security force told me that several years ago a fundamentalist group had infiltrated another Brushwood festival and with a video camera filmed a ritual of what they thought were people drinking blood (actually wine). The trespassers were caught as they tried to leave the festival site, and the film was confiscated and destroyed. Another frequent visitor to Brushwood told me of a recent incident in which some local fundamentalists wearing combat fatigues managed to sneak into Summerhawk festival and steal the festival program. From an outsider's view Summer-hawk is probably the most "satanic" of festivals because it includes an inverted Christian mass, the "Gnostic Mass," and is based on rituals designed by Aleister Crowley.[48] The ritual centers around a priest and priestess (sitting naked on the altar) and includes prayers to Egyptian deities as well as Christian language, such as bread and wine as sacrament.[49] The Gnostic Mass and other rituals, which seem sure to provoke the fears of local Christians, have taken place at festival sites like Brush-wood and Lothlorien.[50]

Rumors about satanic activities and nude orgies at Neopagan gatherings attract the attention of local teenagers (some of whom find themselves accused of being "satanists") as well as reporters, curious vacationers, and conservative Christian ministers. Fred told me of the time he caught several local teenagers trying to sneak into a festival in the middle of the night. He showed them around the festival grounds and took them to a ritual fire so that they could see there was no sacrifice or group orgy taking place. The Association for Magical and Earth Religions put together an information pamphlet for teenagers involved in the occult and their parents that "details stereotypes and genuine hazards of the occult." In their more realistic evaluation of what teenagers would find in Neopagan organizations and witchcraft covens, the pamphlet writers explained that "a teenager seeking sex, drugs and rock and roll in an occult group is much more likely to find hugs, home cooking and new age music."[51] Festival organizers imply that more often than not teenagers' fascination with Neopagan neighbors is motivated by curiosity about the exotic strangers in their neighborhood rather than malicious intent.

But in another incident some adolescent curiosity became an opportunity for vandalism. A Neopagan community in Georgia sent out an article to Neopagan organizations describing their experience of becoming a spectacle.[52] They had set up a ritual site on a friend's land—"a rural spot outside Atlanta" and spent many hours clearing the site, building a stone altar, ringing the circle with stones, erecting cornerstones, planting herbs, etc." A few months later they discovered that vandals had destroyed much of their work and had stolen a few ritual tools. They shared with their readers what they had learned from the incident: "Don't leave removable items unattended . . . especially in a place that is infested with red-neck teenagers!" Weeks later this site was vandalized again: "Two of our members went out to the site to do a bit of 'housekeeping.' To their horror they found that someone else had been there and much damage had been done to the circle, a cross had been erected in the center of the fire pit, the place was in shambles, and the words 'Jesus Saves' and 'In God We Trust' were scratched into the Earth in front of the Altar." When they called police to report the vandalism, they were told that "neighbors at the site had formed a coalition 'to stop the Witches' and had called a press conference that evening to complain about the Witches." The private ritual site had been transformed from an attraction for teenage vandals into an evil threat to "citizens" whose protests against "the witches" were given legitimacy by Atlanta television stations.

The following evening a group of community members watched local television coverage of the protests about their ritual site: "On one station we were treated to full views of the site with police, reporters and 'curious spectators' (as quoted by the media) crawling all over the circle. . . . Then we turned to another station and were even more shocked—they showed basically the same scenes, but with shots of people desecrating the circle site!" In what was a nightmare for this Neopagan community, television viewers as well as the actual intruders gazed at the "exotic" site and investigated its alleged secrets. They simultaneously sated their curiosity and destroyed the site's dangers by taking it over: "One man was shown in the act of dismantling the Altar, stone by stone, 'to find out what is in there' . . . while everyone stood by, watching, and allowed him to do so! Another was shown picking up stones from the circle ring 'as a keepsake.' We were outraged not only by the actions of these people, but by the fact that others stood by and watched as they desecrated our place of worship." A place of intimate and sacred rites was exposed on television in images with many possible meanings, most of them shaped by public fears and suspicions about "satanism." The altar was imagined as a place of bloody sacrifice rather than nonviolent religious worship. The stones placed carefully to mark off a sacred circle were lifted to see if the remains of sacrificial victims were buried underneath.

Exposing what is concealed at festival sites stimulates viewers' media-saturated imagination and stirs their appetite for forbidden thrills. Festivals have the draw of sideshow attractions and traveling exhibits to curious neighbors, since they embody the strange and mysterious realm of "the occult." Onlookers watched from the safe distance television provided as others pried out the sacrificial site's evil secrets. But the Neopagans watching their ritual site eroticized and then destroyed on the evening news were horrified by the parallel with Stephen King movies and popular television series like *The X-Files* (in which a pair of FBI agents tries to discover the secret forces behind grotesque murders and suspicious rituals). These Neopagans had created a sacred circle in which they could interact with the forces of nature and participate in communal rites. This sacred and special place was destroyed by neighbors who suspected that the Neopagans, not themselves, were the evil defilers.

It seems likely that titillating stories will continue; "black magic" and "satanism" attract more of an audience than accounts of "good witches." Neopagan festivals are serious religious occasions for some of their participants and for others a good time to party with like-minded friends. But as long as they are clearly such places apart from the ordinary world, they will continue to make fascinating and frightening viewing from outside.

"PLEASE DON'T FEED THE LOCALS": RESPONSES TO PERSECUTION

Neopagans respond to harassment by tightening the boundaries of their communities through increased security measures at festival sites and sharper self-definition. In so doing, they distance themselves from their persecutors by disparaging Christians. Their own misunderstandings of Christian worldviews and their failure to distinguish between different brands of conservative Christians—they are all cast under the rubric "fundies"—seems strikingly parallel to the ways in which conservative Christians treat *them*. In anger, Neopagans express their own resentment of "red-necks" whom they assume to be uneducated. For all their supposed tolerance, some Neopagan organizations treat their less well-read neighbors with antipathy and condescension. Their persecutors are an enemy to identify themselves against and to challenge in the public arena with press releases explaining that Neopagans are not devil worshippers, but victims of undeserved slander. Charges that Neopaganism is a satanic conspiracy have also resulted in the need for this decentralized movement to organize and protect itself against threats to its religious freedom. Neopagans often find themselves drawing together and putting aside their differences in order to fight a common enemy. They work hard to reverse negative news stories and educate neighbors. Festivals provide an opportunity to share strategies and relate stories of persecution to a sympathetic audience. All of these activities help create a sense of shared experience and a common Neopagan culture.

To spread information about religious discrimination, Neopagans turn to any form of communication that reaches large numbers of people; festivals and Internet listserves work well for this purpose. In the spring of

1993, I read on both Arcana and Pagan Digest the story of the Rileys in Arkansas, who were forced by a coalition of citizens organized by local ministers to close their occult bookstore. The Rileys sought financial and political support via e-mail. They spread the word that they were looking for sympathetic lawyers to sue for religious discrimination, and they requested donations to aid their legal battle. Neopagans on the Internet responded to the story with outrage and anger. They kept track of the Rileys' struggle, continued to discuss it, and forwarded news of the case to other Neopagans. Some Neopagan supporters even attended a rally in Arkansas. They marched up the town's main street to the courthouse where they heard speakers present sympathetic descriptions of Neopaganism. At Pagan Spirit Gathering 1993, festival participants gathered for the village meeting and listened to priestess Selena Fox describe the Rileys' predicament. When she came to the end of the story, Fox asked everyone to send their blessings to Arkansas. In this way, festival participants joined in a common cause, fighting a common foe.

Neopagan responses to persecution both create solidarity and set off conflict within their own communities. They come together to strategize and to offer each other support in the face of persecution. In the very process of deciding how to present themselves to the public and respond to accusations of satanism, their own differences emerge. Brushwood's owner responded to intrusions at festivals by hiring his own security force. At Starwood 1992, I talked with the head of security at Brushwood, an ex-police officer, who assured me that his responsibility was not the inner peace of the festival community, but protection of the boundaries against intruders. Nevertheless, many festival participants were offended by security requirements and saw Brushwood's rules as evidence of authoritarianism. Starwood organizers responded to the problem of intruders by requiring everyone to wear special festival tags on their bodies in full view, in order to identify them as festival goers. One Starwood festival goer complained in *Green Egg*'s Forum: "During my first evening at the festival I was stopped on two occasions by security staff who demanded that I display my plastic tag to show that I had paid to be there. I was informed that such tight security was necessary to ensure that outsiders did not gain entry."[53] "It doesn't go with my look," grumbled another festival goer, who was wearing a costume elaborately decorated with sequins and glass beads. The celebration of difference and desire for freedom from restrictions conflict with the need to protect festival boundaries from unwelcome intruders. A folklorist I met there told me that she heard several complaints about the festival's security force who were running the camp " 'like the Gestapo. . . . They felt it set a very bad precedent to let a single group of individuals have this much power over the course of several festivals."[54] In a festival setting that is supposed to be egalitarian, Neopagans resent any show of power or force, even if it is for their own protection. Dress codes and other curbs on festival behavior and personal expression are also received with hostility. Many people attend festivals to escape an oppressive outside world, and particularly cherished is the opportunity that festivals provide to walk around naked, bare-breasted, or costumed, without attracting unwelcome attention.

Since their harassment at the hands of Christian neighbors and local police in Yellowwood Forest, ELF has experienced similar internal conflicts over how best to secure boundaries and get along with neighbors. Following the local paper's accusations that they were satanists sacrificing animals in Yellowwood Forest, ELF acquired its own land (what is now Lothlorien Nature Sanctuary) and began holding festivals there. But rumors persisted and neighbors accused participants in Lothlorien festivals of performing satanic rituals.[55] They also continued to complain about the noise made by festival drumming. After several unexpected intrusions by police, some of ELF's members decided that they should take the initiative for a change and invited the local sheriff to tour Lothlorien. They explained the tenets of Neopaganism to him and the kinds of activities, such as drumming and dancing, that take place at festivals. ELF members also talked to reporters from local newspapers who countered neighbors' rumors with more accurate stories of festival events. ELF's tactics had mixed results. The sheriff seemed more tolerant, but tensions remained: neighbors still complained about the drumming, and local police once again arrived unannounced at a festival and drove around shining their lights "in people's faces."[56]

Other strategies have emerged from ongoing tensions between ELF and its neighbors. In 1991 an ELF "warrior's guild" was formed in response to visits by police investigating noise complaints. In *The Elven Chronicle*, Larry, a regular festival goer, described his reasons for forming the warrior's guild: "I was leaving late Saturday night. Just as I pulled up to the gate three squad cars pulled in. . . . They had come to investigate a noise complaint (yes, the drumming). This brings us to the last festival. This time the police opened the gate, didn't check with anyone, and drove three squad cars through the festival grounds (this occurred between 3:00 and 4:00 a.m.). I, for one, am outraged by this blatant disrespect by the police of private property and constitutional rights."[57]

Citing his experience working security at an annual convention of eight thousand to ten thousand motorcyclists held in a nearby county, Larry proposed a guild, resembling Brushwood's security force, that would not police the festival community, but would secure festival site boundaries. At the festivals I attended, several ELF members could be seen walking around with walkie-talkies all night long—one of them stationed at the gate house near the entrance to the festival site, and others patrolling the main festival field. The security patrol at Lothlorien remained low key, but it called into question the presentation of festivals as worry-free vacations from the outside world.

All the festival sites I have visited take precautions to keep appearances at their boundaries as "normal" as possible in order to allay neighbors' suspicions. At Lothlorien, nudity is only allowed in the woods away from the public road, and an adjustable sign is posted that reads "no skyclad allowed" or "skyclad allowed." At one festival in a public park, participants were told to obey park rules, which meant, among other things, keeping their clothes on. Of course while this allowed men to take off their shirts, women were prevented from doing so. A group of male festival goers decided to protest this "sexist" rule by parading around the festival site wearing bras.[58] At Pagan Spirit Gathering's Eagle Cave site, no nudity was permitted in the public area of the campground near the bathroom and dining house or at the campground's lake. Brushwood has similar restrictions: no nudity is allowed at the top of the hill near the dining hall and the county road. "Wear clothing when going to the ice coolers, cook house, and/or parking area . . . . Tone down in town. If you go into town keep your Starwood gear, clothing and image at Starwood. Please do not feed or tease the locals," requested the Starwood 1995 program. Warnings of this kind would not be necessary if festival goers had not previously flaunted their festival gear in the rural New York town where they stopped for gas and supplies. Some festival goers surely go into towns dressed in such a way as to affirm neighbors' prejudices: long, black robes with hoods, black leather, tattoos, and pentacles are all popular festival wear.

"CHRISTIAN-BASHING"

Casting themselves as the persecuted victims of ignorant and zealous Christians, Neopagans identify themselves with history's marginal and oppressed populations. In this way they establish a tradition and history for their religion that make sense of their own experiences of persecution

and legitimates their opposition to conservative Christians. Personal experiences of persecution and identification with others who have been
victims of persecution are important aspects of Neopagan self-definition
and are discussed at festivals.[59] When they describe their experiences as
a religious minority, Neopagans distance themselves from Christianity
in a variety of ways that disparage Christians. They say Christian history is characterized by "the degradation of women and nature" and the
persecution of other religions: "they really screwed us over in the past,"
writes Noadia in *Green Egg.*[60] ELF's press release in response to the article on their Yellowwood festival accuses their harassers of "inquisition-
like slander."[61] Similarly, a Neopagan student at Brown University "can't
understand how a religion which is supposed to be about love and respect can condone the senseless murder of worshippers of other beliefs
(as in the Crusades), or the ruthless suppression of Africans, Mexicans,
South Americans, and other 'heathens' who needed to be saved by Christianity and have their land and riches taken away."[62]

Victims of religious persecution often respond by fitting their enemies into the stories they tell about themselves, and for Neopagans, this
story goes back to the Christianization of Europe and the witch craze
of the sixteenth and seventeenth centuries. Neopagans seek to recover
religious practices that they believe were crushed or irreversibly transformed by Christian missionizing. "The search for such spiritual heritage," Neopagan scholar Dennis Carpenter writes, "is complicated by
the fact that Christian religious and political dominance resulted in the
destruction of much of the pre-Christian Pagan heritage."[63] Margot
Adler writes that "the myth of Wicca" teaches that "churches were built
on the sacred sites of the Old Religion. The names of the festivals were
changed but the dates were kept. The old rites continued in folk festivals, and for many centuries Christian policy was one of slow co-
optation."[64] Neopagans like to point out that some practices associated
with both Christian and secular holidays—Easter eggs and Yule logs—
have pagan origins, as do occasions like Halloween (which corresponds
to the Celtic holiday Samhain). Some Neopagans believe they are re-
viving the practices of pre-Christian European cultures, even if their
recreations are more imagined than historically accurate.[65] It is these
ancient cultures, Neopagans charge, that were suppressed by an aggressive Catholic Church and persecuted in early modern Europe by
both Protestants and Catholics. Neopagans argue that their Christian
accusers, like witch hunters of seventeenth-century Europe who wanted

to suppress rebellious women, midwives, and other "threatening people" in the community, have constructed lies about Neopagan rituals to
suit their own agendas.[66]

Angry reactions to harassment and resentment over restrictions imposed
by festival organizers for their protection contribute to what one Neopagan
calls "Christian-bashing." By equating their own persecution by Christians and police with other victims of persecution, Neopagans write themselves into the history of "this long holy war." Neopagans, like conservative Christians, use the language of warfare to talk about their persecutors.
They do this by reversing accusations. In the stories Neopagans tell, it is
Christians who are guilty of "our Pagan Holocaust," suppressing dissent
and killing innocent people.[67] Other Neopagans point out that contemporary Christians are not innocent victims of abuse, but in fact are more
likely than Pagans to be abusers.[68] Chris Carlisle, representative of the Al-
liance for Magical and Earth Religions, told me that her research showed
Christians to be as likely to inflict ritual abuse: "Yes, Christians!! What
would you call a child being beaten while the Bible is read?"[69]

> I have a friend whose father is a baptist preacher, who molested her through
> her entire adolescence. . . . So it kind of seems to me that all of these wild sa-
> tanistic stories are a form of misdirection, and the people we need to be re-
> ally concerned about are the extremist "Christians". . . . There are probably
> a few sickos out there who do ritualistic child abuse, yes, but I think there are
> far more "normal, upright pillars of the community, active in church" types
> abusing their kids than "satanists" . . . and pagans and similar groups do not
> condone child abuse or use it in their rituals. . . . I guess blaming things on
> satanist cults is more interesting than facing the real problems.[70]

Neopagan antipathy toward Christians develops, at least in part, as
a response to being harassed by Christian neighbors. In order to prove
their own innocence, Neopagans make "militaristic fundamentalist
loonies" into villains. To emphasize their tolerance and inclusivity, they
describe Christians as rigid and zealous religious fanatics. Neopagans
also argue that it is Christians, not Pagans and Witches, who are responsible for "the increase in drugs, mass murder, pornography, sexual
license, and everything else that is evil in this country." Witch Leo
Martello believes that Christians blame the occult and witchcraft for social problems in order to evade their own "responsibility for the spiritual sewer that exists today."[71] A major point of contention in Neopagan
discussions of religious discrimination is this tendency to label all Christians as rigid and dogmatic persecutors.[72]

Melissa, an Arcana participant, chides list members for collapsing all types of Christians into a unified group: "You see, I've been following various electronic forums on paganism and the occult for some years now, and I've noticed that, in many cases, the non-Christian participants tend to lump *all* Christians into one group, forgetting that there indeed exist Christians who are practicing mystics and occultists."[73] Melissa is suggesting that Neopagan antagonism toward and generalizations about Christians are very much like Christian attacks on "Satanists" and Neopagans. Neopagans who mock all Christians are just as guilty as the Christians themselves of lumping together distinctly different religious communities, she claims. Neopagans work hard to make the general public and their Christian attackers distinguish Witchcraft and Neopaganism from the Church of Satan, but in their own discussions neglect to separate conspiracy-minded conservative evangelicals from more tolerant Christians.

Neopagans refer to Christian fears of satanism and the rumors their neighbors spread to ridicule Christian "superstitions," in order to highlight the differences between Christians and Pagans. One Arcana member wrote in response to a message detailing the "sinister" aspects of the card game "Magic: the Gathering":

> This is about as funny as the classic Jack T. Chick fundamentalist comic-book tract "Dark Dungeons," which claims that Dungeons & Dragons is a Satanic cult in which you learn REAL spells as you advance levels—one of which is "mind control," to get your parents to buy you more D&D stuff . . . and that Tolkien and C. S. Lewis were "occult" authors who are pals with the Big Red Guy. . . . I wonder what would happen if people took Christianity as literal-mindedly? "You say your parents indoctrinated you into a cult that worships a god who committed incest with his own mother, by eating his flesh and drinking his blood? Someone call County Child Services, quick!"[74]

With humor, Neopagans draw attention to what they think are absurd Christian perspectives on their religion. When they relate to each other Christian misrepresentations of and ignorance about their religious practices, Neopagans affirm their own sense of belonging and their status as insiders who "get the joke." Chris Carlisle suggests that perhaps Christian-bashing is just a kind of Neopagan irreverence for all traditions and individuals who take themselves too seriously and are intolerant of difference. "I recall an earlier thread about prejudices and Christian-bashing. I confess that at our group meetings we sometimes indulge in humorous Christian-bashing, but we also make fun of other Pagans and our own group too."

Not surprisingly, on electronic forums nasty comments about Christians do not go unchallenged by other participants, and Christian-bashing has become a point of contention on Neopagan listserves and newsgroups. In electronically mediated discussions, "Christian-bashers" receive angry messages from other Neopagans as well as from Christian participants. One critic of Christian-bashing notes: "In chatting with 'Neopagans' I've found a wide variety of responses and prejudices. The most common is . . . the anti-Christian feeling which to my mind is as distasteful as any past Christian persecution. About half of those who I've found to have prejudices against Christianity seem to take the stance of any Christian as a personal affront to them." In this way, "Christian-bashing" puts Neopagans on the same level as their persecutors and becomes an obstacle to public outreach. "We are our own worst enemies," writes Pete Pathfinder Davis to *Green Egg*'s Forum: "We need to forego our adrenaline addictions, give up controversy for controversy's sake . . . and stop adding to the mythology of persecution."[75] But it is this mythology that seems to give strength and fire to Neopagans' struggle for broader acceptance of their religion.

When confronted with Christian-bashing, some Neopagans become disillusioned with the entire Neopagan movement, which they expect to live up to the ideals of tolerance by which it measures other religions. Wol, a Pagan Digest subscriber, is disheartened by the large gap between Neopagans ideals and the attitudes of "Christian-bashers":

> I've often been disappointed that the pagan world has not yet, either, been able to rid itself of the religious arrogance inherent particularly in the U.S. and I've wondered whether this isn't a subtle indication of our Puritan heritage, a heritage rife with delusions of the "one way" the "true path" and of a "manifest destiny" in which God has granted us this land as "heaven on Earth" regardless of those who might have dwelt peacefully here before us. That heritage is so deeply ingrained in each and every one of us, it is no surprise than when we adopt another faith or belief system we once again find ourselves claiming to be the "one true" way etc. Pagans might not like to admit it, but I see it clearly, and it might be the first sign that paganism is becoming orthodox in its own way—those who aren't of our belief are viewed with disdain, as ignorant, and moreover, as needing to be "saved." For what it's worth, I would hope that pagans could rise beyond the old paradigm into a new one in which all faiths could be accepted (since ultimately that is what is preached), but such is not an easy path considering the place we live in.[76]

The belief that Neopagans can "make themselves anew" is widespread at festivals and on electronic forums. It follows then, that those who mirror the very crimes with which they charge Christians have failed to transform themselves completely into Neopagans. Instead, they are the Pagans who, acting out of insecurity, distance themselves from their "natal monotheisms" simply to strengthen their own position as outsiders.[77] In so doing, they bring themselves closer to the Christians they criticize. As Wol points out, the "religious arrogance" of Neopagan commentary on Christians is similar to rather than divergent from the American exceptionalism of Puritans and other American Christian cultures.

Occasionally Neopagans who are dismayed by intolerance in their own ranks and attacks on Christians withdraw completely from contact with other Neopagans. Sherry, another critic of "Christian-bashing" writes: "Pagans, ideally, I felt should practice what they preach in tolerance and understanding of humans of all walks of life whether pagan or not. However, I have discovered this isn't always the case and therefore, I've chosen to be solitary until the Goddess guides me to the right 'group' if ever."[78] By choosing to remove herself from the larger Neopagan community, Sherry rejects a Neopagan identity constructed out of opposition to Christianity. Another critic of Christian-bashing reflects on what function it serves the "bashers": "There are also plenty of 'pagans' out there for whom being so is more a political statement than a spiritual one. Vocal for no obvious reason, then upset when people who are Christian tell them to be quiet, or react in a negative way. They are even more surprised when other pagans tell them to be quiet too. I'm not convinced that it upsets them to get a rise out of Christians at all, because it means that they can bitch about how they have been oppressed. 'Oh, me oh my, I have struck out at authority and look what it has done in return!!' "[79] The boundaries between Neopagans and their Christian persecutors are not as clear cut as some Neopagans would like them to be.[80]

Critics of "Christian-bashing" argue that attacks on Christianity result from ambivalence about one's own Christian upbringing, as much as from the realities of persecution. This is Rowan's argument in *Green Egg's* readers' Forum: "Tolerance is a two-way street. You cannot run around whining about how persecuted you are by Christians, condemning them for single-handedly raping the Earth and enslaving women and native peoples . . . then expect them to welcome you into their lives with open arms. . . . Those of us with ex-Christian backgrounds must come to terms with our past."[81] Some Neopagans also discover that attacks by Christians trigger doubts about their own Neopagan identity. Ellenie told Pagan Digest subscribers about a Christian friend who had been helping her with housekeeping and left suddenly one day after finding Ellenie's books on witchcraft lying around her room. Ellenie was particularly upset by the woman's accusations that she was "leading [her] family to Hell." She was so upset in fact that she confessed to Pagan Digest readers, "I was forced to admit to myself that my fearful reaction had to mean that deep down inside, all those Sunday School lessons were still lurking."[82] "Recovering Christians" like Ellenie discover that their newly chosen Neopagan identity is constantly challenged. For this reason they may find it reassuring and reconfirming to focus on differences between Christianity and Neopaganism.

GOOD WITCHES, BAD WITCHES

Neopagans also distance themselves from self-proclaimed Satanic religions, such as LaVey's Church of Satan and the Temple of Set (founded by former Church of Satan member Michael Aquino), and controversial occultists such as Crowley.[83] Mary-Ann, a Pagan Digest contributor, argues that it is safer for Neopagans to separate themselves from any practices that might be construed by outsiders as satanic or abusive, such as animal sacrifice in Santeria and Vodou worship. She remembers one message she came across on the Internet that "seemed to have more to do with individual ambition than with worship or a group connection to nature." Why align themselves with extreme individualism, she asks, when Neopagans want to practice a peaceful nature religion. But Neopagans are ambivalent about the place of extreme individualism in their communities. Just as they are unsure when to curb disruptive behavior or how to define deviance at festivals, so they do not know what to do about Satanists. Neopagans do not all agree on whether they want "self-labeled 'Satanists' included in our number, since we like to be inclusive, but we have enough trouble already with mundanes understanding the word 'witch.' "[84] Neopagans cannot come to a consensus on absolute distinctions between their religion and Satanism. Festival goers—OTO members being the most obvious example—who follow Crowley's "Do What Thou Wilt" ("A divine mandate to discover one's own true will") do not sound much different from participants in LaVey's Church of Satan.[85] If Crowley-style magicians are to be included among their numbers, then why not Satanists?

Mary-Ann highlights two common distinctions Neopagans make between Neopaganism and Satanism. First, Neopagans point out that followers of the Church of Satan emphasize individual will and development of individual powers while Neopagans ideally put more stock in collective efforts. And second, the one characteristic that almost all Neopagans share is the worship of nature, which is not important in the Church of Satan.[86] Neopagans argue that Satanists are "photo-negative Yahwists," who construct rituals and follow beliefs that are the direct inverse of Christian rituals and beliefs. By these accounts Satanists are in fact closer to Christianity than they are to Paganism.[87] Leo Martello, a witch "by heredity" and a longtime Neopagan activist, contends that "every Christian is a potential Satanist. And vice-versa. . . . " Similarly, witch Starr Goode sees Satanism as "a psychotic branch of Christianity."[88] It is only Christians, claims Martello, who believe in the reality of the devil, and he quotes Billy Graham saying "the Devil follows me every day. He tempts me. He is a very real presence to me."[89] Martello explains that witches never worship the devil, and that their horned god was transformed into Satan by Christians: "Witches don't believe in the Devil or Heaven or Hell. The only people who can be true Satanists are Christians. . . . Devil-worshippers are nothing but reverse or perverse Christians."[90] Martello and other Neopagans distinguish their horned male deity from the Christian devil. For them, this horned figure often depicted with a large, erect phallus, represents the Greek god Pan or the Celtic Cernunnos, which Neopagans believe had large popular followings before the deities were transformed into evil figures by Christianity. According to an international Neopagan organization, the Covenant of the Goddess, "The concept of 'the devil' . . . is a creation of Middle Eastern thought which is fundamental to some religions of that region, including Zoroastrianism, Christianity and Islam. Worship of this being as 'Satan' is a practice of profaning Christian symbolism and is thus a Christian heresy rather than a Pagan religion. The gods of Wicca are in no way connected to Satanic practice."[91]

The view that Satan is a Christian invention and a perversion of ancient fertility deities is common among Neopagans. Reporter Helen Knode was told by coven members she interviewed for her *L.A. Weekly* piece "Out of the Broom Closet," that the *Malleus Maleficarum* "gave the devil the physical appearance of Pan and then accused Pagans of worshipping the Christian idea of absolute evil. Which is what Satanists still do today: they invert Christianity's most cherished notions."[92] Satanists may have a valid religion, admits Martello, but he insists that it bears no resemblance to Neopaganism or contemporary witchcraft. Neopagans are generally quick to point out that Satanists make use of a Christian construction—Satan—while they themselves are interested in *pre*-Christian religions. Most Neopagans also reject the inversion of Christian beliefs and rituals that is characteristic of Satanism.[93]

Neopagans draw ever tightening circles of self-identification around themselves, excluding anything "other," as they respond to incidents of persecution and accusations of child abuse. Just who gets excluded though, is a matter of controversy. Neopagans not only separate themselves from the Church of Satan, but also place other Neopagans outside the bounds of their communities. Ironically, the criteria they use to exclude other pagans from their midst are similar to the crimes Christians charge *them* with, such as sexual perversion and child abuse. Leo Martello accuses some Neopagan authors of introductory witchcraft texts of drawing from "their own masturbatory fantasies" in advocating that "an adolescent boy has his penis circumcised by his mother and a girl has her hymen broken by her father using an artificial phallus." These witches, claims Martello, "are nothing more than common criminals" who "sold out for thirty pieces of silver and capitalized on the sex-crazed fantasies of those who have a malicious or repressed reason for wanting to believe the worst about Witches."[94] Martello asserts that, like Satanists, these witches give credence to Christian perceptions that he and other Neopagans are trying to change.

Attempts to draw distinctions between "good" and "bad" witches and between Neopaganism and Satanism often result in "infighting, back stabbing, and 'Witch Wars' " about who should or should not be included in the Neopagan community, and this becomes a source of distress to many Neopagans.[95] As Denise, one correspondent to *Green Egg's* Forum, complains, "Fundamentalists don't care what we call ourselves or who we worship; we all belong to magico-religious systems that they consider evil. Chick Publications has a tract called 'Wicca— Satan's Little White Lie.' Followers of Lyndon LaRouche were seen during the Gulf war with posters that read, 'Burn witches—not flags.' They don't care if we worship nature, the Goddess, Old Horny, or whatever—we are 'other,' and 'different' = 'bad' to them." Wiccans and Neopagans, continues Denise, who censor other witches or members of the Church of Satan, are handing victory to Christians: "I'm sure fundies are delighted to see us fighting amongst ourselves, keeping our attention from what they're doing to outlaw our religions and bring back the burning times."[96] Denise worries that Neopagans, who are the most defensive and most concerned with making exclusive self-definitions in response to criticism from Christians, are the ones who are aiding the "fundamentalist fascists' " campaign to wipe out Neopaganism.[97]

CONFLICT WITHIN FESTIVAL COMMUNITIES

Neopagans' self-definitions are debated in electronic forums and in Neopagan publications, but acted out in person at festivals. Members of a particular festival community rarely agree on how best to deal with antagonistic neighbors or present themselves to the public eye. Their responses to neighbors are not consistent and result in tensions within the festival community as well as between the festival community and outsiders. Disagreements at festival boundaries are like those concerning specific sites within festivals, such as Lothlorien's Thunder Dome and the main ritual space at Pagan Spirit Gathering. They reflect conflicts and tensions over community self-definition. The public appearance of a festival, like the atmosphere of a ritual space, symbolizes a community in its entirety, which is a problem for a new religious movement as diverse and decentralized as Neopaganism.

Festival organizers often respond to neighbors' suspicions by presenting their festivals to the public in ways that downplay their divergence from social norms. In promotional literature and press releases they describe themselves as harmless, religiously tolerant, law abiding, and drug free. In private discussions Neopagans cast aspersions on Christianity and mundania in general, but in their dealings with neighbors they are more likely to focus on points of connection. ELF's press release after the story on Yellowwood was outlined in the *Sunday Herald-Telephone* headline story "Folklore Group Denounces Link to Satanism," in which they highlighted their interest in mythology and cross-cultural studies. In the press release, Terry Whitefeather, one of ELF's founders, explained ELF's goals this way: "Ecology and a healing of the Earth—eradicating pollution, restoring damaged forests, cleaning up toxic waste—is core to what we're about." Throughout the article, ELF's leaders used the term "folklore" to describe ELF's activities: "As the group's name suggests, members are interested in folklore and each specializes in a different aspect. Members address one another by names they have selected from folklore."[98]

Certainly these claims reflect important aspects of many ELF members' identities. But ELF's group of elders has also included individuals who identify themselves as "ceremonial magicians" and "Witches." By describing their community of Neopagans as folklorists, ELF members linked their activities to a more respectable and less culturally charged identity than Witchcraft or Paganism. Terry Whitefeather repeatedly states in festival literature that ELF festivals are open to all faiths, including Christians. He explicitly rejects the label "Pagan": "ELF is not a Pagan organization. . . . ELF members may practice every religion from Agnostic to Zen Buddhist including Christianity," reads one ELF brochure. Another ELF member was quoted in a news story as saying, "We have some Christians and Buddhists, agnostics, Taoists—a little bit of everything. But we're really short on Satanists right now." In this way, Neopagans move to the sidelines of a religious war between Christianity and "satanic" forces, a struggle they want no part of. ELF hoped that by using this strategy, its activities would be less threatening to local Christians and more acceptable to the public.

But many ELF members were exasperated by others' avoidance of the label "Pagan" or "Neopagan." One frequent participant in Lothlorien festivals remarked, "They didn't consider themselves Pagans; they wanted to be 'elves'. . . . It just struck me as being really hokey."[99] Peh told me he was outraged to receive a letter in which another ELF elder, Tindome, who had just returned from Disney World, complained about Lothlorien festivals' "public image." In the letter, Tindome proposed that ELF make Lothlorien events more accessible to the general public. "Tindome wants to transform Lothlorien into a theme park," grumbled Peh.[100] Festival organizers and campground owners are more likely to present themselves as "normal" to outsiders because they want to maintain friendly relationships with surrounding communities. Some participants' concern about presenting a normal and friendly face to festival neighbors are in tension with others' desire to express themselves through costume and behavior at festivals in ways not possible elsewhere.

Two issues of contention that have repeatedly come up in the four years I have been attending festivals at Lothlorien are drumming and drugs. Debates on these topics hinge on tensions between individual and community, festival world and mundania. A promotional flyer for ELF 1995 events reads: "No offense intended if we ask you to observe respect for the surrounding neighborhood by growing quiet after 11 p.m. (and before noon on Sunday) while visiting Lothlorien. It is impossible to please everyone all of the time. No matter what one does someone else will not like it. It is easy to blow strangers off and turn potential friends into enemies by perceiving their way as 'less than your own'. Good old boy hunters and quiet farming neighbors are not bad people." This warning forced festival goers' to face their biases and assumptions about their neighbors. Several competing explanations for the controversy about late-night drumming circulated through the festival community as restrictions became more rigid. ELF members who were concerned with the festival's public face argued that drumming needed to be subdued in order to "be good neighbors" and to put to rest suspicions that some type of satanic orgies were taking place late at night. Others claimed the drumming issue was simply being used by ELF members who themselves do not like the noise and party atmosphere of late-night drumming and dancing.[101] A flyer for "Lothlorien Events 1994" reads: "We've met plenty of people who would like ELF to provide an exclusive Neopagan party zone. Others desire a nudist camp, hippie commune or a 'drum as loud as you want' (and the neighbors be damned) heathen war camp."

In order to solve the noise problem, ELF also made changes that did not entail severe restrictions on late-night drumming. In a *Bedford Times-Mail* article entitled "Elf Lore Family Taking Steps to Be Seen as Good Neighbors," the reporter interviewed members of the local community as well as ELF festival organizers. An ELF member told the reporter that "during our September festival last year one of the people and I got in cars and drove around the roads. At a couple of points more than a mile away, we could hear the drumming as though we were right there."[102] Because of this discovery, ELF decided to construct a dome as a sound barrier over the ritual drumming circle. Design flaws and the unpredictability of volunteer labor resulted in a variety of construction problems; nevertheless, the dome was finally finished in 1994. But by this time regulations on drumming had become too limiting for some festival goers. Several veteran festival drummers started avoiding ELF festivals because they felt that ELF's leaders were becoming too controlling of the festival experience and particularly of the free-form late-night drumming that is a major attraction for many participants.[103] The meaning of the festival and its popular late-night fires was clearly an issue in these conflicts about being "good neighbors."

Like the drumming debate, drug and alcohol use is as much an area of tension within the festival community as between festivals and outsiders. Because there is often no community consensus about these issues (even where festival rules forbid illegal drugs), festival goers can be somewhat paranoid. One evening during Starwood 1995, the sheriff arrived with a "canine unit" near the entrance to the festival site and rumors began circulating that the police planned a drug bust. Although illegal drug use may occur on occasion at festivals, it is not widespread. I was told that some people who heard the rumor actually destroyed drugs in their possession before they discovered that the rumor was false and that police were at the festival site as a safety precaution. They came at Brushwood's owner's invitation and not to search festival goers. Mundanes can easily get the wrong impression, and for this reason some Neopagans are more concerned than others to keep a subdued public image. A letter to the *Green Egg* Forum complains that a non-Pagan friend brought her teenage boys to visit, and when they saw a copy of *Green Egg,* which has run articles on sacred prostitution and the "religious" use of psychedelic drugs, they said to him, "Hey, man, these Pagans are sex fiends and drug addicts!"[104] It is this view of their religion that Neopagans are trying to change.

Neopagans' openness to sexuality and hallucinogenic drugs is not the aspect of their community they want neighbors to notice first. In their written policies, all festivals strictly forbid the use of illegal substances, but in fact do not enforce those policies. The Circle Sanctuary Guide to 1991 Pagan Spirit Gathering listed under "things not to bring": "Illegal drugs, firearms, pets, friends not pre-registered." Even if such warnings have little effect on the use of illegal substances at festivals, at least they display for neighbors festival communities' attempts to these issues. But restrictions can also be perceived as a challenge to the ethic of free expression. During Winterstar 1993, Isaac Bonewits discussed substance abuse in his workshop "Pagan Taboos." Bonewits suggested that because they are such individualists, many Neopagans are afraid to criticize others for alcoholism and drug abuse. As evidence of their attention to these problems, some festivals have set aside areas for "pagans in recovery," and the Starwood 1995 program listed a workshop on "Twelve Step/Sober Support." At ELFest 1992 community council, several ELF elders voiced concern about rumors of drug busts. They claimed that festival attendance was down because some ELF members were circulating rumors that there was to be a drug bust at the festival that year.

In contrast to policing the boundaries of Neopagan identity—"dress down when you go to town"—and securing their festival sites against intruders, festival organizers and other Neopagans also emphasize points of connection with their neighbors to improve community relations. Such strategies suggest a willingness to remain connected to society instead of becoming totally isolated from and antagonistic toward Christians and local communities. These "public relations" Neopagans go beyond correcting misperceptions about their religion and actively work to find common ground for communication with neighbors.

Peh described to me the outreach work he had done with local police. One of the ways he was able to get them to understand what was happening at festivals was to say, "It's like a bunch of old hippies getting together to camp." He identified unknown Neopagan behavior with "hippies," whose unconventional appearance and behavior he hoped would be more familiar to them. Festival neighbors in southern Indiana may not approve of what hippies of the 1960s represent, but they can at least see them as part of a familiar episode in America's cultural history. In this way, some of the mystery and hiddenness of festivals is cleared up, even if neighbors continue to be critical of Neopaganism. Peh went on to explain to me how he dealt with neighbors' discomfort with nudity at ELF's festivals. He approached a common understanding with neighbors on the issue of nudity by asking them if they ever swam naked at the local swimming hole—"What's the difference?" he asked them. Peh related to me a conversation on the topic he had had with Fred, the owner of Brushwood, who explained festival nudity to his neighbors by saying, "Well, you like to sit around your house without any clothes on— it's the same thing." Rather than trying to explain festival activities in the context of Neopaganism, which holds that the body is sacred and celebrates sensuality, they used examples that they hoped suspicious outsiders could identify with. As a public relations strategy, making the strange familiar may help to defuse some of the antagonism between festivals and their neighbors. But in a religious culture where the "strange" is so central to personal and group identity and security, such a strategy entails serious risks.[105]

CONCLUSION

The Yellowwood Forest encounter between the Elf Lore Family and their fearful and suspicious neighbors makes for a good story of rural intolerance. Persecution stories have more entertainment value than accounts of neighbors cooperating, and they sharpen the boundaries of one's own identity in contrast to the "other." But neighbors do not always live up to Neopagans' worst expectations of them. During Summerhawk 1992, I talked with Fred of Brushwood about his relationship with the locals. Fred is on the public school board and active in other areas of his small rural community. He believes that local people's attitudes about events at Brushwood are changing: "They're coming around," he told me. For instance, a neighbor who worked in the kitchen where food is sold during festivals was impressed at "how nice people are here," and she subsequently confronted another neighbor who was talking about the festival in a derogatory manner. Fred told me about another episode where supposedly bigoted neighbors surprised him with their tolerance and acceptance of Neopaganism. The previous year he and his family gathered with a group of friends to attend a lecture on "the occult" at a local Methodist church. They went to the church anticipating that they would need to defend themselves and Brushwood festivals against charges of satanism. They expected to hear the usual stories of child abuse and sacrificial rituals. Fred and his friends made up a group of thirteen and were surprised to find when they arrived that they were not overwhelmingly outnumbered; only fifteen church members attended the lecture. The regular minister introduced a younger minister visiting their congregation from another church, who proceeded to give a presentation that Fred claimed was as positive and informative "as if some Neopagans had hired him themselves." The minister presented clear and accurate definitions of Neopaganism, distinguished it from "satanism" and "satanic cults" and called Neopaganism a "real religion."

The dynamics of power in the politics of persecution are much more complex than they at first appear. Neopagans often find themselves cast in a role prepared for them by conservative Christians in a cosmic drama of the battle between the armies of God and those of Satan. The Christians believe that America's moral world is at stake in this struggle, and particularly the sexual morals of young Americans, who are perpetually threatened by the presence of Neopaganism—a religious choice that embodies contemporary spiritual and moral dangers. Stories of satanic captivity and the abuse of children limit Neopagans' attempts to enjoy freedom from religious persecution. But when Neopagans return Christians' fire by "Christian-bashing" and insist on aligning themselves with other victims of persecution, they perpetuate rather than alleviate their involvement in the spiritual war for America's future. In this way, they participate in the broader social construction of their role as "the other," and in general of the American cultural politics of alterity. But they also adopt the discourse of otherness and persecution as they look toward the future, as they attempt to shape the kind of world they would like to live in. This is a world, they say, that Christians have suppressed and feared because it is a world populated by spirits and strange deities, a world where one god is not the authority, but rather where authority is fluid and dispersed among humans and their supernatural helpers. Neopagans speak out against the persecution and misunderstanding they experience not only to end the persecution, but also because they want to spread knowledge about different moral, sexual, economic, and religious options.

One of the most important strategies by which Neopagans affirm their place in contemporary American religious culture is by identifying with Salem witches, ancient Druids, and marginalized cultures like American Indians. Neopagans carve out a place for themselves on the American religious landscape by creating boundaries to distinguish the festival world from the mundane world and Neopagan communities from their Christian neighbors. At festivals they create a place apart to make anew their identities with the religious idioms of other, non-European cultures. In order to distinguish themselves from their Christian pasts and the mundane religions they grew up with, Neopagans look to pre-Christian and non-European cultures. To sharpen the boundaries between their past and present identities, they cross the boundaries between themselves and racially or historically "other" communities—African-American Vodou and American Indian cultures, for instance. But at the same time, they want to move the margins—spirit possession, divination, and the sacralization of sexuality and pleasure—into the center of American religious life. It is these marginal lifestyle and religious choices, Neopagans argue, and not the ways of conservative Christians, that would create a better and more humane world. I turn next to explore in greater detail the ways in which this identification with marginal others takes place and what it can tell us about Neopaganism. Along the way, I place Neopagan strategies of identification with the "other" into conversation with contemporary debates about identity, cultural purity, and multiculturalism.

CHAPTER FOUR

Blood That Matters

Neopagan Borrowing

At Pagan Spirit Gathering, the priestess asks hundreds of ritual participants to address their "own" deities. "Artemis!" "Kali!" "Ogun!" "Isis!" "Pan!" and "Great Spirit!" are called out from the circle of participants, as they summon their adopted gods and goddesses. At the end of the ritual, figures clothed in deerskin and feathers or masks and capes dance through the firelight and dark shadows of the woods chanting, "We are the old people, we are the new people, we are the same people, stronger than before." At festivals, Neopagans celebrate the identities they have borrowed from ancient or non-Christian religions, such as Santeria. They hold workshops on such topics as "Native American: Spirits of the Land," "Creating Smudge Fans . . . in the Native American Tradition," "Medicine Shields," "Moon Lodge," "Birthing Your Animal," sweat lodges "rooted in Native American Shamanic traditions," "The Way of the *Orisha*," "Yoruba Theology," "Initiations in East African Traditions," "Sufi Dancing," and "Tibetan Time Travel."[1] Participants design and take part in rituals that pay tribute to the religions they have claimed. But the colorful diversity of Neopagan festivals and rituals masks the cultural uniformity of its members. Most Neopagans are middle-class European Americans who are seeking alternatives to the Christianity, Judaism, or atheism of their parents (see fig. 14).

Neopagans' desire to identify with other cultures is the inverse of distancing themselves from mundania and from Christianity. The exotic

Figure 14.   Clay images fashioned at a Sacred Art workshop at 1995 Pagan
Spirit Gathering reflect diversity in personal spiritual expression among
Neopagans. Courtesy Circle archives. Photo by Selena Fox.

"other" becomes as attractive to them as Christianity is undesirable, providing the contrast to everything that they have rejected in their own
pasts and mundane lives. To distance themselves from Christianity, Neopagans appropriate the practices of these others with total, and frequently uncritical, acceptance. They seek to replace the past they have
cast off with ritual objects, clothing, symbols, and ceremonies such as
those of the Tibetan Buddhists or Native Americans. But in the same
ways that Neopagans resist Christian missionizing, others, most often
Native Americans, resist Neopagan attempts to appropriate practices
that the groups feel belong to them.

Just as they disagree about how to defend themselves against intolerant Christian neighbors, Neopagans argue among themselves over the
politics of cultural appropriation. These charged discussions point to the
emotional intensity with which Neopagans make themselves anew. Profound issues of self-identity—kinship, sexuality, and spirituality—are at
stake in conflicts about cultural borrowing. Borrowing from American
Indians and practitioners of Santeria is debated among Neopagans at
festivals, in newsletter articles and Internet conversations about searching for spiritual roots. It is criticized in recent scholarly works such as
The State of Native America and *The Invented Indian* and condemned
by some Native Americans in published statements like "A Declaration
of War against Exploiters of Lakota Spirituality" on the grounds that it
is "cultural genocide."[2] Critics from non-European cultures accuse Neo-

pagans and others of stealing the cultural property of communities who have already been once dispossessed by white Europeans. The critique encompasses not only Neopagans, but also appropriators of American Indian art and jewelry, New Agers, literary imposters, and environmental activists who look to Native cultures to model appropriate relationships with the natural world. Not surprisingly, many American Indian critics are unsympathetic toward middle-class white people starved for cultural authenticity, and hostile when "white-indians" threaten their traditions by cultural absorption, dilution, and misinterpretation.

Despite criticism, cultural appropriation is encouraged by the smorgasbord of workshops at Neopagan festivals. Neopagans continue to incorporate elements from Native American and other non-European cultures into their rituals and religious identities. As one workshop leader, a member of the Cherokee nation suggested, "Should Native American practices be shared, adapted, circulated, and thus kept alive? Must blood determine membership in a particular culture or can cultural identity be decided by other factors, such as extensive knowledge and experience with sweat lodge rituals or drumming techniques?" Neopagans say they are personally empowered by "becoming" members of cultures that are not theirs by birth. By adopting the practices of these cultures, they develop a spirituality that "works" for them as individuals. But the very focus on self-invention is what most offends opponents of cultural borrowing who charge that "whiteshamans," to use anthropologist Wendy Rose's term for white borrowers, threaten Indian survival. Perhaps Neopagans are complicit in the latest episode in the devastation of America's indigenous cultures as the last reflex of European colonialism. Since Neopagans claim to honor and revere these cultures, how do they perceive their own complicity? If Neopagan borrowers are simply the latest North American spiritual con artists, as their critics would have us believe, then what motivates them? What meanings do Neopagans derive from their own borrowing—by their own account?

The debate over cultural appropriation exemplifies contemporary Americans' ambivalence about the meanings of "culture," "authenticity," "self," and "ethnic identity." It also reveals the intensity of Neopagans' desire to construct meaningful identities from a confusing array of possibilities and to have their new identities recognized by other Americans. But they discover that these goals are fraught with difficulties. When Neopagans reject their parents' religions and become "shamans" or "Taoists," in some sense they no longer clearly belong to any particular culture or tradition. They are not "Christians," nor do they completely belong to their adopted religion, whose communities may not accept them. On these contested boundaries between cultures, Neopagans work creatively to make themselves anew. I look now more closely at the ways in which Neopagans shape borrowed practices into meaningful religious identities in the midst of general cultural confusion about who owns the past and to whom religious practices "belong."

RE-MAKING THE SELF
IN THE IMAGE OF AN OTHER

At festivals and in their religious practices at home, Neopagans work to create new self-images that separate them from their neighbors and from their own Christian backgrounds. At festivals, they take particular care to visually identify with ancient or non-European cultures by adorning themselves with hooded cloaks, buckskin skirts, chain mail, and eagle feathers. They devote years to studying their adopted cultures, they tattoo the adopted religion's symbols on their bodies, they place its symbols on their altars, and they turn to its rituals to help them through difficult times. They work hard to create new selves rooted in ancient traditions such as Druidism and religions they see to be closer to nature than Christianity, especially American Indian traditions. Neopagans imagine that these non-European traditions possess the wisdom and knowledge that is absent from their own lives. "In our melting-pot world," Pagan Digest contributor Moongold writes, "we need to search out spiritual truths."[3] Moongold herself searches in Native American culture for knowledge about the earth and spirits of the land that she and other pagans believe European culture has lost. Neopagans remake themselves in the images of other cultures out of a deep frustration with what is lacking in the Christian culture they were raised in. Because they believe that Christianity and many Western modes of thought have destroyed the earth and abused women, they look hopefully to non-Christian cultures to be in harmony with nature and to treat women with respect.

Neopagans seek methods to reinvent themselves wherever they can find them: at festivals, in books, and over e-mail. Neopagans imagine that teachers will give them a measure of authenticity. Teachers are proof of a Neopagan's membership in an oppressed culture—inverting the search for power through identification with the most dominant social group. Sherry, who taught Neopagans how to use the crystals they bought from her at festivals, often referred to her teacher Sun Bear, a medicine man who grew up on a Chippewa reservation. It was Sun Bear, she explained, who helped her connect her interest in stones to Native American healing techniques.[4] One of the first large festivals I attended in 1992 advertised a "traditional" sweat-lodge ritual that was to be facilitated by Roland, a European-American who was traveling the country holding sweat lodges for different communities. I arrived a day early to help other volunteers finish the final preparations for the festival. At the end of the day I spoke with Jerry, one of the workers who was in charge of building the sweat lodge, about his initial meeting with Roland. He was upset because when Roland arrived on the festival grounds he insisted that the existing sweat lodge would not work for his purposes. He wanted the festival community to build a new sweat lodge in the "proper" manner and claimed that *he* had been doing sweat lodges for years and had extensive training in "authentic Native American sweats." Roland's assurance of his own expertise was based on his contact with "real" Indians and years of experience.

Instruction by an "authentic" teacher who inherited her tradition from parents or grandparents, or is unusually knowledgeable or experienced in it, renders Neopagans' chosen religions more authentic. Their constructed identities seem less arbitrary when they are legitimated by a "real" medicine man or Vodou priestess. Louis, whom I first met in the African drumming workshop he presented at Summerhawk festival, related to me his initial difficulty finding a teacher. When he first moved to New Orleans, he remembers visiting an old "Afro" woman: "I went to see her 4 or 5 times and I would just be sitting there for hours and she wouldn't say anything or look at me. After about the fifth time, she said "yep" and she told me all this stuff. . . . And she said, 'sometimes I want to talk and sometimes I don't want to talk and you have been here enough that it's time to talk.' So me being an Anglo didn't have a lot to do with it, I think it was simply that she's not going to talk to just anybody who comes in off the street."[5] Louis's introduction to the New Orleans Vodou community was possible because of his persistence and a teacher's willingness to tell him "stuff," in this case, African-based healing practices. From a Neopagan perspective, Louis's African American teachers in New Orleans or a medicine man living on an American Indian reservation "belong" to their cultures by race and locale. Neopagans seek out these teachers because they see them as racially and religiously authentic guardians of ancient knowledge that European Christians have ignored or suppressed. By studying with "authentic" teachers they become part of an ancient lineage that replaces their Christian cultural heritage. They then use their teacher's authenticity to further their own authority at festivals and within the larger Neopagan movement.

Adopting another culture may seem arbitrary, but Neopagans' narratives make sense of their choices. Neopagan stories address questions of authenticity by explaining why they "belong" to a specific religious tradition and culture, as in Louis's account of how he came to be a Vodou practitioner. He told me that he discovered personal connections with Vodou through his relationship with the spirit Legba.[6]

> Legba . . . would come to me as an older black man who was very kind and there was something about the French in Vodou that attracted me. . . . And I knew that my mother's maiden name was Martinie, then I found out that it was pronounced Martin("yay"), not "martini," then I got a card from these people who want to trace your lineage and they said, "did you know that the first Martinies came from New Orleans in 1848?" So maybe there is some sort of genetic or ancestral connection going on there. I was walking on the same streets that my ancestors walked on. They probably went to Congo Square and walked down Rampart Street.[7]

Here Louis's personal quest returns to matters of "blood." Neopagans pursue those parts of their own heritage that open up into non-Christian cultures they want to emulate. Family ties to other cultures are one justification for borrowing that appears in Neopagan narratives of self-discovery. Louis's attraction to Vodou is the result of a personal search that includes blood connections, African American teachers, and ritual experience, a complex authentication of his spiritual choice.

When Louis relates the story of his involvement with Vodou, he seems to be making it up as he goes, constructing a coherent narrative while he tells his story. Louis's sense of belonging to the New Orleans Vodou community emerges from this story. At the same time his understanding of his heritage is a result of his growing involvement with the New Orleans Vodou community. Louis explained to me the origins of his participation in New Orleans Vodou: "It really started with the drumming. . . . I was looking for some sort of experience that would give me the intensity that I found playing with a secular band, playing gigs in clubs. . . . Then I started making trips down to New Orleans on a fairly frequent basis to seek out the Vodou current. . . . I just kept on going down and talking to people. . . . and decided why don't I look for a job here."[8] Like the spiritual autobiographies of other Neopagans, Louis's story describes a dynamic process of deepening knowledge about and involvement in a specific religious culture. By his account, Louis did not simply come in and lift Vodou practices out of context. Rather, he first became familiar with African rhythms by playing with drummers in New Orleans' Congo Square and getting to know members of New Orleans Vodou and San-

Figure 15.   Louis Martinie (left) of the New Orleans Voodoo Spiritual Temple and a friend prepare drums for "Flags of the Loa" ritual, facilitated by the temple at Starwood festival in New York. Photo by Ransom Haile.

teria communities. Gradually he came to understand his attraction to Vodou in connection with other aspects of his life history. His own drumming style was then shaped by the Vodou rituals he drummed for, and he eventually became identified by members of the New Orleans Voodoo temple as a "Vodou drummer" (see fig. 15).

Louis's personal history also demonstrates what many other Neopagans attest to: they did not choose their religious identity, but rather it "chose them." In this way they avoid taking personal responsibility for borrowing; a deity or spirit contacted them, and they could not refuse its invitation. Background and experience may be important factors, but finally, a tradition's deities and teachers have to "choose you." Gus, a Gardnerian elder who worked for six years with a Brazilian shaman, according to his biographical sketch in the Pantheacon 1997 festival program, writes that he does not "think it is up to human beings to determine who has a right to a spiritual practice." Gus argues that this is up to the gods and "the gods do not respect cultural boundaries."[9]

The Vodou loa, Legba, appeared to Louis as an old black man and the "old Afro woman" chose to teach him. Neopagans describe latent affinities that are drawn out by ritual involvement, the attentions of a teacher, or "mystical" experiences. They discover connections with these traditions "that were always there" but needed to be elicited by their revised understandings of their own identities. Louis insists that the family connection is important, but not sufficient to secure cultural belonging. Louis recounts the advice of one of his teachers, a priest of Belizean *obeah*: "The power of the Vodou comes up from the ground. It's not something that someone else can initiate you in, you have to feel it, it has to come up into you."[10]

Another way of displacing responsibility and making their religious practice a fate rather than a choice is to describe it as the "unfolding of a spiritual path." Like deities who affirm a Neopagan's "fit" with a particular tradition, the path itself carries them along. And they are often surprised by the direction taken by their spiritual search. Some individuals describe a dialogical process in which their visions or intuitions are affirmed by reading books or in group experiences that then in turn affect their visions, dreams, and intuitive sense of choosing the "right path." Derek R. Iannelli described his own "path" to me:

> Currently, I am very heavily involved with the occult. Tarot cards are my form of divination, and it is through meditation, and rigourous study of the Qabalah *[sic]* that my religious views come from. . . . I am slowly teaching myself Hebrew now so that I can begin to understand some of the more ancient texts of my faith. My identity, has been shaped by such things as shamanism in which I partook in a peyote ceremony, and heavy reading of the Carlos Castenada books at that time. Later in life, cultural influences (Indian) were not as readily available as they were in earlier life, and therefore, I had to search for a new PATH. It was then that I went to Rinzai Zen. I spent an entire summer in a monastery and after my experience, still felt like I did not have what I desired out of religion. I then started studying the occult in 1990.[11]

Derek, like Louis, describes a wide range of sources that shaped his religious identity. In Derek's account, the search itself produces a new religious self, pieced together from reading, ritual practice, and learning languages and rendered coherent through narrative.

Neopagans formulate new identities by drawing correspondences between what would seem to be unrelated cultures and denying the reality of cultural or historical boundaries. Marion, who offers workshops and rituals on Tibetan subjects at Neopagan festivals, once created rituals out of the writings of early twentieth-century British occultists such as Crowley and Yeats. She regularly visits a Tibetan *stupa* (Buddhist shrine) and cultural center near her home where she circumambulates the shrine and helps care for the stupa. She practices chanting and meditation daily, and her home is decorated with Tibetan *thangkas* (Buddhist scroll paintings), statues of the Buddhist figures Amitabha and Tara, and a set of Tibetan bells. Tibetan Buddhism is incorporated into her daily life and plays an important role in Marion's personal decisions. Once she received permission from her Tibetan teacher to spend the night at the stupa in order to "do a vigil." She sought guidance in making a difficult decision: should she move back to the large city where her husband lives, but where she feels threatened by crime and violence, or should she remain in a small, safe Midwestern town? Through meditation and what she described as contact with a spirit there, she received a clear message during her night at the stupa: "If you return . . . you will grow more spiritually. If you stay here you will have access to the Tibetan cultural center and you will be secure, but you will not progress spiritually."[12] She described this incident as having further legitimated her identification with Tibetan culture. Voices and visions affirm for Neopagans that they are truly engaged in a dialogue with another culture. Their search is not solely for the self, but is significantly for them, also about relationality. What Neopagans want is to belong to a viable religious community and its gods—the gods who come into their lives to guide them along their chosen paths.

By marking their bodies with tattoos of ancient deities and calling themselves by ancient Egyptian or American Indian names, Neopagans simultaneously express their rebellion against Western monotheistic religions and constitute new identities. "I've adopted Native American culture, so I had a dreamcatcher tattoo done," Kym explains, describing her tattoo in "the gallery" of tattoos on Sacred Skin Tattoo Studio's web page.[13] In a Pagan Digest discussion of tattoos, Peta, a contributor from the British isles, commented on the Polynesian tribal design and Celtic knotwork tattoos on her back: "A tattoo changes forever the way you perceive yourself; it is a very positive reclaiming of your body, a spiritual empowerment. . . . You put it on your body with the affirmation that it is your body to do with as you want, and no one can tell you what to do. . . . It is very much a re-claiming of our bodies from societal/familial/religious repression. It is a celebration of an awakening realization that my body actually belongs to me! Not my parents or my lover or society or god."

Clothing, tattoos, and jewelry provide a bodily connection between Neopagans and their adopted cultures. They may also take on new names in order to identify more intimately with these cultures. This act of naming may be self-initiated or performed by a priest, priestess, or other leader. One Pagan Digest participant explained to me how he received the ritual name "Vegtam." "As to the name Vegtam . . . it is the name given to me by the priestess at my dedication. Names are very powerful and provide lessons for us. After my dedication (to Goddess and God) was complete, I was told that my first lesson was to learn the origin of my Craft-name . . . The name comes from the Baldur saga in Norse mythology. It was the name used by Wotan as he quested for knowledge about the impending fate of his son Baldur. As I progress to higher degrees, I will receive additional names, which are held in close secret, except to members of the particular degree and of the tradition involved."[14]

An individual is marked by the community's "parent" just as a baby is marked with a name and expectations by real parents. In a message to Pagan Digest, one Neopagan describes contemporary Neopagan tribalism as "fictive kinship."[15] Neopagans desire a family to replace the one they have rejected and a clear way to identify with chosen "families" is to separate their bodies from religious pasts. By marking their bodies, they visually display their claim to another culture and assume their place in the Neopagan tribe.

Like the symbols permanently tattooed on their bodies, extensive research into other cultures lends seriousness to Neopagan self-invention. Neopagans assure themselves and their critics that they have ways of evaluating a borrower's authenticity, and that there are other factors, besides physical appearance, that legitimate cultural belonging. They often measure authenticity solely on the basis of experience with a culture's language, history, literature, and rituals, without regard for heritage or apprenticeship to a teacher. They familiarize themselves with their adopted cultures by reading scholarly work in the fields of archaeology, religious studies, folklore, and anthropology. Most Neopagans read widely and have higher levels of education than the general public.[16] Jake, a frequent contributor to Arcana, affirms that he uses "magical operations as a way of demonstrating to [the Gods] my sincerity. The Gods apparently understand prayers in any language. Nevertheless, I think they like to be addressed in the ancient languages . . . perhaps because it is a further demonstration of sincerity." For Jake, his immersion in Latin and Greek texts provides him with the expertise as a Neopagan scholar to speak about these cultures and their ritual practices.

Neopagan ways of knowing are not what academic scholars of ancient or non-Western cultures would call "scholarship," though Neo-

pagans themselves use this term. Jake thinks of himself as a scholar because of his ability to read Homer and other Greek texts in Greek and
to compose ritual scripts that include practices taken from classical accounts of Greek festivals and other ancient celebrations. The aim of most
Neopagan scholars is to enrich ritual experiences and share information
with other Neopagans, rather than to spread historical or cultural knowledge into the academic community. Moreover, Neopagans approach their
sources less critically than academic scholars. Their writings and ritual
texts often are explicitly derivative; they place no great value on original research, though they strive to creatively synthesize myths and symbols from disparate cultures. Neopagan homes I visited generally featured several shelves of books on mythology and religion from around
the world. One Neopagan priest has an entire bookcase devoted to magic
and religion. Its titles include most of the works of Crowley; *The Egyptian Book of the Dead;* the *Tao Te Ching;* and titles by Robert Graves,
Joseph Campbell, archaeologist Marija Gimbutas, and many others.[17]
In her study of Neopagan rituals, folklorist Sabina Magliocco comments
on the depth of folklore knowledge among the Neopagans she interviewed at Pagan Spirit Gathering: "While folklore theory is not their primary concern, they are unusually knowledgeable about historical and
contemporary folk traditions, especially folk narratives and customs, and
consciously make use of this knowledge when shaping new rituals.
Among them, I have found individuals who can debate with me the relative merits of the ballad collections of Child, Bronson, and Sharp; who
can practically quote from Frazer and Mannhardt; and who recognize
in my description of an obscure Sardinian children's Easter custom the
Gardens of Adonis described by classical authors."[18]

  In order to gain knowledge about specific languages and cultures,
Neopagans may also seek academic expertise. Some Neopagans in a Midwestern college town told me they had taken courses in Ancient Near
Eastern Magic and Medieval Judaism in the Religious Studies Department of their state university. Another non-Jewish Neopagan told me
that he was studying Hebrew and Judaism with a rabbi in order to gain
a deeper understanding of Jewish Kabbalah. One Neopagan ritual group
I attended drew from biblical passages and analyses of Hebrew letters in
preparing their rituals. None of the participants were Jewish or had more
than a rudimentary knowledge of Hebrew. They were not interested in
the historical or cultural context in which the biblical passages appeared,
but rather chose them for their rich imagery. For a ritual focusing on the
sun, for example, they selected a passage from Genesis 1 ("Let there be

light," etc.). At their planning session for a ritual incorporating sacred bull motifs, the ritual facilitators brought in two articles on bull symbolism from the journal *Biblical Archaeology*.[19] Materials like these provide Neopagan rituals with historical legitimacy, while also lending themselves to being shaped to suit specific rituals. Neopagan borrowers claim that their interests in other cultures are not arbitrary, that they are committed to these cultures in profound ways. They inscribe this commitment on their bodies, reclaiming the flesh that once belonged to Christianity, and they devote years to acquiring knowledge from teachers and mythological texts. In all these ways they assure themselves that they are serious about becoming fluent in the religious cultures of the other.

"CULTURAL STRIP-MINING"

Neopagans appropriate the religious idioms of cultures all over the globe and throughout human history, but nowhere with as much resistance as they have encountered from American Indians. Dressing up like an Indian, say Native American critics of borrowing, does not make you one, but instead marks you as an impostor and neo-colonialist. In this view, imitation is not a sign of respect, but of cultural imperialism. Another way into the complexities and ambiguities of Neopagan appropriations of other cultures is to approach them from the perspectives of indigenous critics, who point emphatically to the difficulties and corruptions of the practice. American Indian critics claim that their religious practices are under siege and contend that "borrowing" perpetuates "white racism" and "genocide against Indian people."[20]

Not all Native Americans share these views. Different orientations are evident among critics of what one has called "cultural strip-mining." Some Indians are upset only by white people who are profiting from the practices they borrow, others object to all borrowing, even the most respectful. White people who have not grown up in Indian communities, listening to Indian languages, cannot hope to fully understand Native rituals, say the most severe critics. Nor can they gain an understanding of Native culture by reading books rather than establishing relationships with real Native communities. However, published material by Native writers and academics on the issue of appropriating Native traditions is overwhelmingly critical of European-American borrowers.

The "stealing" of Native practices by European-Americans is legitimated among the thieves by European colonial assumptions that they could lay claim to the lands and practices of indigenous cultures, asserts

American Indian poet and anthropologist Wendy Rose. Rose argues that
Native American cultures have come to be categorized and defined by
white people who expect Indians to dress in feathered headdresses and
talk about the meaning of their dreams or to act like the stereotypes in
1950s westerns.[21] Rose criticizes the expectations of white audiences that
she fulfill their images of an "authentic" Indian by dressing in buckskin
and turquoise. While Rose does not want to dress up as an Indian, neither
does she want to see whites pretending to be authentic Indians. She attacks "whiteshamans who aspire to 'embody the Indian,' in effect 'becoming' the 'real' Indian even when actual Native people are present."[22]
These "whiteshamans," explains Rose, are white people who in their
poems or teachings assume the persona of shaman, usually in the guise
of an American Indian medicine man. Best-selling authors like Lynn Andrews (author of *Medicine Woman, Jaguar Woman,* and other fictional
accounts of American Indian shamans and their ritual practices) and Carlos Castaneda (author of a series of books about Yaqui medicine man,
Don Juan), she argues, pretend to possess Native knowledge and to speak
for Native people. Rose believes that deciding who is an authentic Indian should be up to Natives themselves, not whites.

Critics also fear that Neopagan borrowing will jeopardize Indian rights
to their own practices. Native Americans are exempt from some endangered species laws, for example. They may be allowed to use parts of endangered hawks and eagles for ritual objects. But this exemption could
be threatened by the increasing number of Neopagans and New Agers
who also make ritual objects out of endangered animal parts. Neopagans
leaving Starwood in 1995 were stopped at a roadblock on New York's
Highway 17 by state police who confiscated many such objects. "Ownership" of ritual objects by non-Natives thus poses a concrete threat to
Native communities' access to these objects.[23] Patricia Cummings, "a public interest lawyer who represents traditional Native Americans in their
struggle to protect sacred sites and preserve their cultures," criticizes New
Age "seekers" and tourists for overusing sacred sites, trampling and killing
herbs that American Indians have gathered at specific sites for centuries,
and in other ways making it increasingly difficult for them to hold their
rituals at these sites. Two particularly egregious situations, argues Cummings, are at Panther Meadows on Mt. Shasta north of San Francisco and
at Sedona, Arizona, which one Sedona resident called "a Metaphysical
Disneyland."[24]

More threatening to Native cultures even than the loss of sacred sites
and dilution of their culture is the commercial packaging and marketing

of indigenous concepts and practices that compete with Native American capitalization of their own cultural riches. "Non-Indian charlatans and 'wannabes' are selling books that promote the systematic colonization of our Lakota spirituality" states the "Declaration of War against Exploiters of Lakota Spirituality."[25] These critics are offended by expensive weekend "vision quests" and by "bestsellers" with a "tenuous hold on facts" written by non-Natives like Lynn Andrews. For many American Indians, financial competition and the false assumption of cultural authority by outsiders make cultural appropriation intolerable. Lakota activist Martina Looking Horse, for example, finds outsiders' claims to knowledge absurd and offensive: "Our religion is being bought and sold by the *wasicu* (Whites); objects sacred to the Lakota can be found in any store. . . . Prophets for Profit . . . will take a ceremony, one they know nothing of, and sell to some poor unsuspecting soul. . . . Some will claim knowledge of the old ones and of old ancient medicine, or claim to have visions. . . . I think these people are just hallucinating."[26] As Looking Horse sees it, cultural appropriation as practiced by European-Americans is a desecration. Few Neopagans actually become wealthy by spreading their interpretations of Native American rituals, but nevertheless as Wendy Rose points out, even "whiteshamans" who are not making profits negate and subsume American Indian identities by speaking as experts *for* them.[27]

Critics charge that cultural borrowers are necessarily inauthentic and deluded because in most cases they have no direct relationship with Native communities. Looking Horse and others emphasize that they themselves speak from deep roots in ancient traditions and clearly defined communities.[28] Authenticity, they argue, must be determined by belonging to and being committed to a tradition or community by blood and heritage. Critics are particularly skeptical of Neopagan eclecticism, which removes objects and practices from their cultural and geographical contexts. As Looking Horse says, "The white man in his ignorance mocks our ceremonies and claims to be holy men, medicine men and women. They create their own pathetic ceremonies even though they can't even speak our language. . . . Our religion has become a fad."[29] Rituals and other religious practices lose much of their meaning when they are not performed in the company of other members of that particular religion in an "authentic" community. Looking Horse expresses this view succinctly: "These *wasicu* have the audacity to think they make better Indians than we do. . . . How can anybody spout off about tradition and not live it?"[30] Apache medicine woman Meredith Begay contends that Native rituals must be learned in Native communities over long stretches of time: "You cannot practice Indian medicine at all in the United States unless you have been brought up into a particular life way. You have to have a background, people in your background, people that know how to heal, that tell you the story of the medicine, the way that it was applied, how it was used. You don't learn these things in just a matter of four days or five days. You learn it over a period of time. . . . Anybody can copy a sweat . . . but if they don't have the essence, it's no use; it's no good; it's a waste of time; it's just a lot of hogwash. . . . "[31] The essence of "Indian medicine" and other religious practices, according to Begay, must be acquired through experience, history, and tribal membership. It cannot be obtained for the price of a weekend workshop or by reading anthropological accounts of early twentieth-century Native American cultures.

The most radical critics say that white outsiders cannot hope to understand their traditions. American Indian critics of "wannabes" argue that white borrowers and Indians attach very different meanings to self-identity. Critics' concerns over issues of cultural representation (or in this case, misrepresentation) stem in part from their response to the broader culture that challenges the life and significance of their identity every day through the mass media. Native Americans respond to others' claims on their cultural practices by representing Indian culture or Lakota culture as a unified body of knowledge, something that can be possessed. The need to view one's own culture as unified occurs as a response to others' claims on it. In order to challenge the practices of Neopagans, then, Native critics emphasize the collective aspects of their cultures over European-American individualism. Ines Talamantez, a scholar of Native American religions, for example, argues that "the belief that the traditions of others may be appropriated to serve the needs of the self is a peculiarly Western notion that relies on a belief that knowledge is disembodied rather than embedded in relationships, intimately tied to place, and entails responsibilities to others and a commitment and discipline in learning."[32] It is this assumption that authorizes Neopagan borrowing according to opponents. As we will see, the reasons Neopagans give for borrowing other cultural idioms emphasize the self and its needs, just as Talamantez suspects.

MAKING IT UP AS WE GO:
NEOPAGAN JUSTIFICATIONS FOR BORROWING

When they defend themselves against these criticisms, Neopagans are conflicted and ambivalent. The highly politicized and emotional nature of these debates forces them to carefully define their own position on cultural borrowing in relation to other Neopagans as well as to Native others. In a section of *Circle Network News* devoted to Pagan gatherings, a Canadian, Janice Canning, writes about her experiences at Womanhealing Conference 1992. She notes that more than half of the participants had Native blood or were working with Native American organizations. The focus of the gathering was on "healing," and workshops included body work, storytelling, yoga, journal writing, tarot, and chanting. After listening to Native women's stories, Canning decided that their message to her, a European-American, was clear: "Do not teach the sacred ways of our people. It is all we have left and it sustains us now in this time of struggle and rebirth. . . . These women wanted non-Natives not to use Native objects or ceremonies in any way whatsoever." Before attending the gathering she had "received teachings that these ways were for all in order to help build the bridges of the 'rainbow people' and to bring awareness to all people no matter what origin." But she had come to the conclusion after the weekend's meeting that as "a teacher of the ancient ways of the European tradition of magic [i.e., Wicca] . . . [she would] not teach Native ceremonies." Canning's message is "anti-borrowing," but she still purports to speak for Native women. Moreover, although Canning alludes to the range of Native views toward borrowing, the editor of *Circle Network News* felt it necessary to add his own note: "It is my impression based upon experience that considerable variability exists regarding Native attitudes about the sharing of their spiritual ways with non-Natives. For valid reasons, many Natives do share views similar to those reflected in this article. In contrast, other Native peoples seem to believe that it is appropriate for this type of sharing to occur in light of the potential that Native wisdom has in teaching respect for . . . all of Nature."[33]

As they debate issues around borrowing, Neopagans try to secure a position for themselves on the contemporary religious landscape. In response to critics of borrowing, they develop tests of authenticity, criteria for claiming an ancient or non-European religion for their own. Even among those who say they value personal choice, an important measure of authenticity seems to be "blood," meaning the specific ethnic and racial identities that they actually embody. "Blood is thicker than water" remarked one of Margot Adler's informants.[34] Snowcat, a Pagan Digest participant, writes: "I have a great mixture of blood, including one quarter Dutch and one quarter Scottish. I do think that many 'white westerners' feel a disconnection from their roots and culture. My solution to this has been to go back to my own original bloodlines—the Celts."[35]

Although their parents and grandparents, for the most part, did not practice Celtic or Norse religion, Neopagans embrace what they describe as
pre-Christian European practices such as Celtic witchcraft, Asatru
(Norse/Germanic traditions), or Druidism more than any other religious
traditions.[36] Neopagans are less uneasy about "going back" to their
"original bloodlines" than they are borrowing from other cultures.

When Neopagans explain why they have taken American Indian names
or are wearing the cowrie shells of a Santeria diviner, they describe how
they discovered ideas and practices from other cultures that resonate with
their desire for different self-identities. Individual orientation and desire
are all they have according to Maggie, a Pagan Digest participant, because Neopagans are all-American "mutts," who do not belong to any
particular culture. For this reason, they feel compelled to adopt other cultural traditions that "work" for them, seem "right," that they have dreamt
about, or belonged to in a past life. Greenleaf, a subscriber to Pagan Digest, explains this view: "As some kind of reincarnational process appears
to me to be part of being human, it doesn't make much sense to me to
limit one's intellectual and religious approach to life according to the particular origins of the current physical body."[37] The turn to reincarnation
helps explain and validate affinity to a particular culture. Sade, a frequent
contributor to Pagan Digest, sees it this way: "If one posits reincarnation
as true, then given the sheer numbers o' folks alive today, some of us must
have souls that originated in other cultures. F'rinstance, I have real ties
to India, to the ancient Near East and especially to Rom or Gypsy culture—yet I'm about as whitebread as they come."[38] Neopagans' search
for cultural roots, then, is not limited to their identity in the here and now,
but may include infinite past lives.

Neopagans who have incorporated Native American practices into
their religious identities are not surprisingly defensive when confronted
with the charges of Native critics. In response, they justify borrowing by
emphasizing what they share with the cultures they borrow from. Because they find other cultural idioms meaningful and compelling, they
reason, these idioms are appropriate for them to use. Snowcat responds
to critics of "dabbling" by explaining how he borrows another culture's
practices: "How can we contextualize? I do a little research. If I want to
use something (a song, an object, etc.) from another culture, I find out
about how it was used, viewed, and felt about by that culture. In as far
as it is appropriate for me, I adopt the way of thinking with the object.
If I cannot relate at all to the way of thinking, I do not use the object."[39]
Ran, "a shaman in training," likewise stresses the personal meanings of

"borrowed" practices, rather than their broader cultural significance: "There is nothing wrong with 'stealing' religious trappings. Each person must come to their own spiritual peace in their own time. . . . One should not have to stop what feels right just because someone else denies its validity."[40] A. Lizard, a participant on Pagan Digest, similarly emphasizes the personal "usefulness" of ritual objects in an impatient response to opponents of borrowing: "Use your dream catchers in good health. There are plenty of Native Americans using 486 based PCs made in Taiwan right now, and the fact that the i486 chip or a Taiwan assembly plant largely come from non-Native American cultural origins doesn't affect their usefulness to their Native American user base in the least. A tool is a tool is a tool. The question isn't who invented it, it is DOES IT WORK FOR YOU???"[41]

Even Neopagans who acknowledge the moral and political problems of cultural borrowing argue that others' cultural practices are appropriate for them as individuals. Moongold, a Pagan Digest participant who describes her ancestry as a mix of "Sicilian, northern Italian, blue blood New England, Swedish and French-Canadian Indian," was hesitant at first to draw on Native American practices.

> I consider myself a seeker of spiritual truth. I avoided Native American spirituality for a number of years because I felt that I had no claim to their customs. I wanted something that I felt a part of. . . . However, last weekend I participated in a sweat lodge. My rationale was that my Swedish heritage of saunas would help get me through. . . . As we search for ways that help us hear that inner voice, why would we turn away from a method just because it belongs to another culture? When I decided to make my own drum, I chose to make a Native American hoop drum with an Elk hide, because there was a teacher here willing to help me. . . . My drum, I feel, was absolutely meant for me because of the markings on the skin. I do not feel that it is any less my drum because it comes from a Native American tradition.[42]

Moongold's sense of connection with the hoop drum and the culture it comes from is justification enough, in her eyes, for borrowing. Her "inner voice" speaks resonantly with American Indian customs, so why then, she asks, should she not heed this voice? Assuming that ancestry is fluid, she establishes links between "her" culture and "theirs." In the end, Moongold's personal quest for "spiritual truths" seems more relevant to her than the arguments against making and playing a Native American drum.[43] Neopagans justify cultural appropriation in a variety of ways from inheritance to reincarnation, but all of their explanations are based on the conviction that what is at stake are the personal meanings derived from these practices and the extent to which they enrich individual lives.

Along with emphasis on personalized spirituality, Neopagans also justify their quests for knowledge by arguing that most dimensions of human
religious experience are universal. Particular cultural practices like drumming styles and sweat-lodge rituals can be shared by anyone. Neopagans
relate stories like Moongold's of following their "inner voice" or "inner
guide" to support the assumption that "the Path is one for all; the means
to reach the goal must vary with the pilgrim."[44] For some Neopagans, religious authority of this sort is derived from Jungian psychology, as Snowcat explains: "People are entitled to use other people's ideas" because
"Jung would say that every idea is a part of the collective unconscious,
therefore, it is accessible by all."[45] "We are all talking about the same creator—just a different name," Terry explains.[46] Another Neopagan puts
it more forcefully: "The KNOWLEDGE possessed by . . . a community . . .
is clearly part of the larger human heritage and I have no problem with
its being made available beyond the boundaries of that community."[47]
From this perspective, American Indian nations and Vodou communities
have no boundaries or bodies of knowledge they can call their own, which
makes their practices available to everyone. Gus, who has been initiated
as a Gardnerian Witch, explains that at first he was uneasy approaching
other cultural traditions. A Brazilian shaman who taught Umbanda
spiritism (a blend of African beliefs, European spiritism, and indigenous
Brazilian practices) told Gus that "he did not mind that the Goddess was
my major spiritual allegiance." Gus found that the spirits seemed to know
no cultural bounds, and his experiences confirmed for him the legitimacy
of borrowing. After six years of working with the shaman, Gus left and
some time later set up a "healing circle" that incorporated techniques he
had learned from the shaman with his training as a Witch. After Gus
moved away from the area, he called to see how the circle was doing: "I
was told by the woman at whose house the circle now takes place that a
very masculine black spirit with some sort of fringe over his eyes had
started showing up. After consulting with my *caboclo* [community], it became apparent that this was Xango (Chango). She said, 'Oh, that's why
Anna [another participant] kept getting the word 'chango' in her mind
whenever she saw him.' "[48]

In Neopagan accounts of their relationships with spirits and deities,
it is clear that these beings have agency beyond what Neopagans ask
them to do within a ritual context and that they even enter into ritual
space when they have not been invited. Gus was surprised to hear of
Xango's appearance: "Everything I had done [in the circle] was explicitly within a Wiccan context. Further, the people now doing the circle

had had no real experience with African practices. Now Xango, my father in the Yoruba pantheon, was showing up." So Gus concluded that "the Goddess is on good terms with Yoruba deities." For Gus, the supernatural world where spirits relate to each other has its own relationships and meanings that we can never be certain of. Moreover, humans cannot completely control their interactions with this world: "Once you've started incorporating spirits you can never really go back to where you were before." In other words, once these traditions are mixed, even unintentionally, the spirits may proceed with their own agendas. When I attended a Vodou ritual at Starwood, two Neopagans appeared at the ritual fire dressed as Gede, the Vodou spirit of the dead. They were immediately incorporated into the ritual when the priestess asked them to guard the fire. While the drumming rose to a frenzied pitch and dancers swirled around them, they remained somber and still (see fig. 16).

Neopagan understanding of culture and identity as polysemous and accumulative is consistent with certain contemporary postmodern notions of subjectivity and cultural boundaries. British cultural theorist Dick Hebdige, for instance, argues in *Cut 'N' Mix: Culture, Identity and Caribbean Music,* that rather than thinking of Caribbean music as traceable to a particular source, "The roots themselves are in a state of constant flux and change. The roots don't stay in one place. They change shape. They change colour. And they grow. There is no such thing as a pure point of origin . . . but that doesn't mean there isn't a history." Hebdige quotes a white Reggae fan:

> There's no such thing as "England" any more . . . welcome to India brothers! This is the Caribbean! . . . Nigeria! . . . There is no England, man. Balsall Heath is the centre of the melting pot, 'cos all I ever see when I go out is half-Arab, half-Pakistani, half-Jamaican, half-Scottish, half-Irish. I know 'cos I am [half Scottish/half Irish]. . . . who am I? . . . Alright, where do I belong? You know I was brought up with blacks, Pakistanis, Africans, Asians, everything, you name it. . . . Who do I belong to? . . . I'm just a broad person. The earth is mine. . . . You know we was not born in Jamaica. . . . We was not born in "England." We were born here, man. It's our right.[49]

Like Reggae fans, Neopagans argue that they are just one more element in the mix and that issues of race and class are not significant in a "melting-pot world," to borrow Moongold's phrase. While they would at first seem to be trumpeting cultural diversity and the uniqueness of the particular cultures they appropriate, in fact, Neopagans expect other cultures to open their boundaries and blend with white European-Americans.[50]

Figure 16.   Participant in "Flags of the Loa" ritual at
Starwood becomes the *Iwa* Gede, who guards the ritual
fire. Photo by Ransom Haile.

Such an assumption stands in direct contrast to the position of Native American critics that identity must be rooted in community, place,
tradition, and family. Neopagan views on borrowing emerge from a particular understanding of cultural boundaries and the relationship between individuals and their communities. This understanding "derives
from our ability continuously to reinvent ourselves out of our confused

cultural conditions."[51] The notion that cultural identities are malleable and fluid makes it difficult for oppressed populations like American Indians to create strong communities and improve their economic and social positions. This is the argument that Native American critics of borrowing make when faced with "plastic medicine men" and Neopagans who insist "on the permeability of social groups, the unboundedness of cultural unities, and the instabilities of individual selves."[52] Defenders of borrowing who suggest that syncretism is a universal human practice and characteristic of how cultural practices change over time effectively silence critical voices of those cultures they themselves claim to honor. But other Neopagans might disagree with this perspective and argue that it essentializes history and removes oppressed populations from the common human project of making and sustaining meaning.

STRATEGIES OF INTIMACY AND DISTANCE

At festivals, Neopagans imagine themselves as "a tribe" and "a chosen community." They create a collective identity out of struggles over personal meaning, sources of knowledge, and bodily experiences, and as a contrast to who and what they are not: Christians and mundania. Neopagan attitudes toward borrowing reflect their ambivalence about how to see themselves in relation to other Americans. Through a dynamic of intimacy and distance, they express guilt about their own complicity in the ongoing colonization of North America's indigenous cultures. They distance themselves from the New Age Movement and other Neopagans in order to move themselves closer to the appropriated culture. They call themselves by Indian names or participate in the life of a Vodou temple in order to assure themselves that they belong with these cultures and not, on the one hand, with "whiteshamans" or, on the other, with conservative Christians. Neopagan views on borrowing emerge from a complex process of Neopagan self-positioning. They reject Christianity and desire American Indian identities, but they also reject other white Americans who identify with Indians. At the root of this confusion is the fragility of Neopagans' own cultural position as a misunderstood religious minority. One effective way for them to construct a positive identity is by appropriating the other. But in the very process of closely identifying with Indian critics of borrowing, Neopagans reveal the distance between themselves and the other, as well as the precariousness of their invented selves. I now discuss some examples that point to the ambivalences involved in Neopagan self-positioning.

Neopagans who are uneasy about being identified as a community of borrowers respond to debates over cultural borrowing by aligning themselves with Native critics and distancing themselves from the New Age Movement. Neopagans deflect criticism of borrowing by charging that New Agers are inauthentic and by claiming more authentic borrower status for themselves. Of course Neopagans find it hard to distinguish themselves absolutely from New Agers. Clearly to them, this is a very significant boundary, because they persist in making the attempt. Terry, a Neopagan priestess, writes: "I have personal hang ups with folks that attend weekend workshops and then call themselves medicine workers."[53] One Pagan Digest correspondent describes the New Age Movement in the following derogatory way: It "is a very shallow approach to everything, taken without any real context or understanding of *anything*. It also seems to have been stripped of anything that might really challenge people or make them uncomfortable—yes, you too can achieve Total Enlightenment in about an Hour! Without ever leaving the suburbs for those nasty dark bug-filled woods, or having to confront unpleasant truths about what it is you're doing."[54] New Agers are superficial and pursue worry-free knowledge, say Neopagans. They profess to follow Native American paths, but unlike Neopagans who attend festivals to get closer to nature, New Agers hypocritically avoid any real contact with the natural world. By emphasizing some ways in which the New Age Movement is unlike the Native cultures its adherents admire, Neopagans identify with Native Americans and distance themselves from New Agers.

Neopagans acknowledge that many participants in the New Age Movement do not like *them* either. In her response to a message in Pagan Digest, Chris Carlisle, who describes herself as an "eclectic Wiccan," urges other list members to differentiate between Neopagan witchcraft and the New Age Movement: "Many of our topics of interest overlap, but many do not, and many witches wince at the mention of the New Age. One New Age organization which sponsors psychic fairs goes so far as to ban witches from participating and says in its handouts that none of the psychics involved have any truck with the Powers of Darkness. (No, they pray to the Powers of Money, instead!)"[55] According to Terry: "Wiccans generally don't accept money for teaching or helping out other people; neither will they take on just any student who can pony up a few hundred bucks for an 8-hour seminar. It's been my observation that any number of 'New Age' teachers are in precisely this position."[56] Another participant in an electronic discussion complained about "greed" in the New Age Movement: "How do you tell a New Age Witch from a neo-Pagan Witch? Put all her crystals on her and throw her in the water; if she sinks she is a New Age Witch."⁵⁷ (Since most Neopagans identify with persecuted witches of the past, it is ironic that they refer to this particular ritual of endurance.) Who is the more legitimate cultural borrower? New Agers and Neopagans want to distinguish sharply between each other and then compete for authenticity. This is not only an issue of being "better Indians than the Indians" themselves, but of being better Indians than others who are also "playing Indian." Neopagans invoke the same criticisms of the New Age Movement that Native Americans direct at all non-Native borrowers: financial exploitation and the lack of "authenticity."

Neopagans distance themselves from the negative characteristics they identify with the New Age Movement, then want to align themselves with what they see as the desirable characteristics of Native American cultures. They enter into conversations about borrowing with the assumption that American Indian cultures embody the qualities they believe Christianity and European cultures lack: Indians are close to nature and the seasonal cycles; they are respectful of women; they have feminine images of the divine such as the White Buffalo Calf Woman or the Corn Mother; and they value the body and sexuality as sacred aspects of human experience. When Neopagans reject what middle-class white society has to offer, Native cultures come "to stand for authenticity and redemption."⁵⁸ Neopagans often assume, for instance, that most non-European cultures have more positive views about the body than Christian religions and that they value "feminine" qualities such as nurturing children more highly. They also expect Native American and African cultures to be more egalitarian in the area of gender roles than the Christian traditions they have rejected. And perhaps they are, but not always in the ways that Neopagans anticipate.

Identification with Native Americans breaks down on the most intimate levels of cultural practice. Conflicts between Neopagans' "own" newly made tradition and the appropriated "other" hinge on different ideas about bodily purity and gender roles. Neopagans believe that the body is sacred, while some American Indian cultures teach that the body must be purified through the sweat lodge or menstruation. Neopagans arrive at Native American ceremonies expecting to find Native versions of their own view that the body itself is divine and that in a ritual setting the body may serve as a vessel for god or goddess. Martina Looking Horse complains about the ignorance of European-Americans: "A lot of white women come to our purification ceremonies needing help or guidance. Instead of learning about what to wear or what to do, they just come and take off all their clothes not realizing that traditional women are supposed to cover their bodies below the shoulders."[59] These white women join Native cultures of their own imaginations. Neopagans cannot participate fully in purification ceremonies because they resist the separation of men and women and look condescendingly on modest views of the human body. They may also refuse to comply with Indian practices that do not fit their expectations of what Indians should do. They may be offended by traditional strictures and protocols. Some Neopagans, for instance, are uncomfortable with rituals that segregate men and women, such as some sweat lodges, or with the idea of a moon hut to which women retreat during menstruation.

Around the evening fire at a "harvest festival" in the Midwest, a Lakota woman explained that women "on their moon" should not participate in her sweat-lodge ritual because they are already "powerful" and to ask for more power would be "greedy." Some festival goers were upset at the time and discussed their unhappiness among themselves after the sweat-lodge ritual was over. The exclusion of menstruating women was condescending and disrespectful, they felt. Why not let each individual woman decide for herself whether or not to participate in the sweat lodge? Many of the Neopagan women and some of the men complained about what they saw as evidence of "sexism." They also immediately put their discomfort about the separation of menstruating women from the ritual into a framework in which menstruation had to be clean or unclean. Festival goers thus turned this into an issue of pollution that clearly did not fit into the Native ritualist's approach to menstruation as a condition of great power. There were questions during the preritual discussion and grumbling afterward. Many Neopagans at the festival apparently wanted to enjoy the spiritual and physical benefits of a sweat lodge presented by "real" Indians but did not want to follow "real" Indian rules. They wanted to participate in an authentic sweat, but they did not want to meet the Native sweat-lodge leader's criteria for authenticity.

Neopagans approach the cultures they most want to emulate with ambivalence. They are eager to claim these traditions as their own but at the same time want to remain autonomous from them. They want to be able to experiment with Native American practices and incorporate Native ritual objects on their home altars without compromising their own ethics or politics. They also want to reject monotheistic religions but without making a formal commitment to ancient or indigenous cultures.

Although they claim to be on, for example, a "Native American path" or label themselves "Tibetan Buddhist," Neopagans generally make themselves over in the image of Native Americans, Tibetans, and others at a distance from these cultures. At Starwood, I met Tala, a young man who identified himself as a Pagan Taoist. He told me that for many months he had wanted a tattoo that would symbolize his Neopagan identity and decided on a yin-yang symbol. He then asked friends to come to the tent of tattooist Laughing Starheart, in order to drum and chant during the tattooing session. Tala went through what he called a ritual of initiation in his own eclectic Neopagan community, not in the company of a group of Taoists. At festivals, Neopagans also learn from other Neopagans who have apprenticed with Native American teachers, Santerian priests, or other religious specialists. During one Midwestern festival, I camped near Lucy, a Neopagan who had recently taken an interest in Santeria. She attended several workshops facilitated by Jerry, a white Canadian who had spent many years learning Santerian rites from a priest in New York City. By the end of the festival she was discussing the likes and dislikes of various *orisha* (Santerian spirits). When I saw her at the same festival the following year, she had constructed an elaborate altar to the *orisha* Yemaya in the front of her car. Tala and Lucy adopted Santeria and Tibetan Buddhist symbols and practices at Neopagan festivals and then brought these religious idioms into the most intimate places in their lives. Tala celebrated his identification with Taoism by marking his body with the yin-yang symbol, and Lucy roamed around the United States accompanied by her altar for the spirit Yemaya. They closely identified with other cultures, but did not live in communities with practitioners of Santeria or participate in rituals with other Taoists. And in this, they are typical of most Neopagans, but different from Louis, the Vodou temple drummer, who is immersed in the daily happenings of a New Orleans temple.

Neopagans want to adopt deities and practices of other peoples while remaining distinctly Neopagan. During Winterstar Symposium, a late-winter Neopagan gathering in northeastern Ohio, Ian Corrigan, who was lecturing on Celtic Magic and Religion, remarked that when "traditional" people use idols, they do not use them as tools for meditation, but as "avatars," by which he meant that Neopagans see their images as representations of archetypes or mythological characters, not as real beings. "They" do things differently than "we" do, in other words, and "they" are ignorant enough to believe that a god or goddess is really present in the idol he implied. In fact, Neopagans display a wide range of attitudes toward the presence of deities in symbols and rituals. Some treat these entities as psychological projections, others believe the deities they invoke are objectively real and outside the self. At Summerhawk, a small festival in southwestern New York, Roy was possessed by Dionysus during a ritual. At the end of the ritual, Dionysus did not leave Roy's body, and the next day several festival goers remarked that Roy had been acting strangely the previous night. Roy himself claimed that he was "de-stressing" from the effects of allowing his "Dionysian side" to emerge. But Peh, a Neopagan priest who was talking with him, suggested that the "real presence" of Dionysus was responsible for Roy's experience. Roy seemed to find this explanation more satisfactory, as I overheard him later that day telling the story of Dionysus's "appearance." Neopagans often show contradictory attitudes toward a deity's presence. They interact with gods and spirits as though they were part of the self as well as completely other. As often as not, proclaiming their disbelief allows Neopagans to maintain their identification with the very traditions they say they want to reject.

Their ambivalence about the presence of deity, then, is another way in which Neopagans move between intimacy and distance. Some of them are more comfortable with psychological explanations for visions of angels or the voices of spirit guides. But others, like Chris, describe the appearance of a goddess as though she is a separate being: "I was sitting under a tree reading when I heard/saw/smelled/felt the Goddess, who said, 'finally you hear me. I have been calling you always and you were deaf.'" The question of a deity's presence is one of many issues that reflect Neopagan ambivalence toward the cultures they appropriate. They look to the past and to other cultures for new identities but not necessarily for identification. While these other cultures may be distant from "us" (meaning European-Americans), they possess what we desire.[60] Anthropologist Alice B. Kehoe contends in "Primal Gaia: Primitivists and Plastic Medicine Men" that the view that Indians lead more "authentic" lives is based on assumptions of "an immense difference, a Great Gulf between 'these peoples' and the rest of us."[61]

Looking backward to a more perfect era has been a constant theme in American religious history.[62] But the result of looking to a golden age—for Neopagans, precontact Indian cultures—is to distance the self from the ideal other. Ancient Israel provided colonial New Englanders with a model for their own community of chosen people. This model also served to remind Puritans of their sinfulness and imperfections. Similarly, some contemporary Protestant fundamentalists look to New England Puritan communities as the embodiment of all that is good and perfect in American life.[63] The preoccupation with ancestors is characteristic of European-American Puritan culture that embedded this yearning deep in the American grain. The United States is a culture that simultaneously yearns for and denies its ancestors—yearns for them in order to provide some stability in a relentlessly convulsive society, rejects them as one of the preconditions for success in this economy. Neopagans thus reflect the ambivalence toward ancestors characteristic of American society when they long for cultural purity, but constantly shape and change borrowed practices to suit their needs as contemporary Americans.

Neopagans are concerned that the cultures they adopt remain "pure." They draw attention to a cultural gulf between the "pure" Indian and the "corrupt" Anglo-American. While they imbue non-European cultures with a special authenticity, they continue to act as though they themselves know best which practices are "pure," what ritual objects "authentic." In some cases Neopagans are more concerned with cultural purity than the cultures they borrow from. At an autumn harvest festival I attended, one participant was upset because the sweat-lodge ritual was not "traditional" enough. He decided not to participate in the ritual even though he had spent hours helping to build the sweat lodge. He was upset, he told me, because he felt that the Lakota teacher had not constructed the lodge using all natural materials. Instead, the teacher instructed his helpers to cover the outer layer of the structure with sheets of plastic to hold in the heat. The Neopagan "outsider" was far more concerned about cultural purity than the Native American ritualists.

Louis, the drummer, expressed similar frustration at the Vodou priestess who told him, "There's no distinction—it all goes back to the same source." He has become increasingly interested in keeping New Orleans Vodou "pure" by tracing its African and Haitian roots. He told me of hours spent in an ethnomusicology library listening to tapes of Haitian drumming recorded in the 1930s. He was practicing these styles of drumming in order to incorporate them into the New Orleans temple's rituals. Again, the Neopagan outsider is more concerned about racial or ritual purity than the African American Vodou priests and priestesses he works with: "At this point Miriam describes me as the 'high priest' of the temple and I said that I would be *a* priest, and some people think I'm racist for this because I said the priest and the priestess should be Afro. I think one of the main benefits of Vodou is to involve myself and other Anglos in it and to have images of deity that are Afro. It's hard to be a racist if your gods are Black." Louis arranged New Orleans Vodou priestess

Miriam's visit to Starwood in 1999, when she facilitated a Vodou ritual and read Neopagans' fortunes from her tent on Merchants' Row (see fig. 17). Louis went on to describe another occasion on which he resisted racial blending. His teacher who came to New Orleans from Belize as a priest of *obeah* wanted Louis to initiate a young African American man who had come to the Rampart Street Voodoo Spiritual Temple: "Oswan wanted me to do it and I thought 'no, man,' an Afro man should be initiated by an Afro man, a European man should probably also be initiated by an Afro male because it helps with the racism. But I was the one who thought it was an issue."[64] Because of the flexibility of the New Orleans Vodou community, Louis was included and allowed to become a priest. Ironically, once included, he attempted to make Vodou pure and his drumming for the temple more true to a past that only he was concerned with. By focusing on the temple's historical and cultural roots, Louis distanced himself from the present concerns of these Vodou practitioners.

When Neopagans borrow from Vodou or Native American practices, they construct an ordered space for themselves to inhabit rather than understanding other cultures on those cultures' own terms.[65] In the process of adapting the practices of other cultures to their own needs, Neopagans reveal their own deeply felt concerns about self and community identity.

CONCLUSION

At first Neopagans seem quintessentially postmodern as they deconstruct their own lives and invent new identities from American Indian cultures, religions of the African diaspora, and Eastern traditions like Taoism. At Neopagan festivals participants can shop in the "spiritual supermarket"; they can gaze at and try on a wide variety of religious styles and ritual practices without becoming committed or responsible to the communities that practice them. This kind of religious experimentation is possible from a Neopagan perspective because it is guided by an individual's spiritual needs and desires. Opponents are offended by Neopagan borrowing practices for the same reasons. They charge that borrowers are guided by the needs of the self to desecrate indigenous traditions.

Critics are correct in their observation that in the process of creating new selves, Neopagans try to personalize Native American and other borrowed cultures. Appropriated practices are shaped to suit the needs of contemporary European-Americans who say they are feminist, ecologically minded, tolerant toward other races, ethnic groups, and sexual orientations, and suspicious of rules and doctrines. On closer examination,

Figure 17.   Priestess Miriam of the New Orleans Voodoo Spiritual Temple rests outside her tent on Merchants' Row where she gives divinatory readings to festival goers. Photo by Ransom Haile.

however, Neopagan borrowing practices are rooted in the desire to belong to an *ancient* tradition in a wider cultural context that privileges
the new.[66] They may be making new identities out of the pieces of a frag-
mented world, but they search for coherence, for an ancestry that matters, for "pure" ritual practices, and a perfect past. As a result of this
tension, Neopagan involvement with other cultures is full of contradictions. Ambivalent about their own desires, they project this confusion
onto cultures they borrow from; they want them to be pliant as well as
static and pure.

Neopagans identify with American Indian cultures for the same reasons that they reclaim the role of the seventeenth-century wise women
and men who were branded "witches"; they see themselves as similarly
persecuted and oppressed. They make this parallel explicit when they de-
nounce Christians for witch burning and colonialism. When they take
up Native American and Vodou ritual objects and practices, Neopagans
emphatically claim their own place at "the fringes of the herd," to borrow the title of a discussion topic on Arcana. Neopagans dress themselves in exotic trappings while they hide the fact that their identity is a
creation of their own vision and a reaction to those churches they have
abandoned. Costumes and tattoos seem to conceal the past. The remade
self may not look the same, but it still carries a white identity within and
acts out of Anglo-American assumptions.[67]

Indigenous American peoples, European cultures, African diaspora
communities, Tibetan refugees, and new religious forms of their own
making interact in the cultural spaces where Neopagans live: books and
Neopagan publications, the Internet, festivals, and workshops. In these
sites of interaction, Neopagans draw on the power of Native American
cultures at the same time that they maintain their identity as middle-class
European-Americans. They move between intimacy and distance, between identification and difference, as they try to decide who they are
and where they stand in relation to debates about appropriation. As Neopagans articulate the reasons they appropriate the practices of other cultures, they create a uniquely Neopagan identity. Copying the other in appearance or through ritual practice is part of the improvisational process
Neopagans engage in as they create themselves and their communities.
The identities that they define for themselves challenge as well as express
the ambivalence about race and ethnic identity that they share with many
other Americans, including the Indian critics who find them pathetic and
the New Agers they ridicule.

Neopagans relate episodes of disillusionment with mainstream religion to identify more clearly with the traditions they have adopted—polytheistic and decentralized. The practice of Christian-bashing, for instance, establishes clear boundaries between their chosen Neopagan identities and a rejected religious upbringing. Their new identities become even more meaningful when contrasted to unpleasant past experiences, especially in Neopagan remembrances of growing up in strict religious households. Their new gods are more tolerant and less authoritarian. Neopagans' stories about how they came to practice Vodou or participate in Wiccan rituals often mention Christian intolerance and rigidity. By portraying the religions they were raised in negatively, Neopagans create sympathy for their appropriation of other cultures. But they also recall that as children they were drawn to tales of otherness, to mythical worlds and fantasy fiction, and they locate the origins of the self in childhood experience.

CHAPTER FIVE

Children of the Devil or Gifted in Magic?

*The Work of Memory
in Neopagan Narrative*

Festivals are an arena for self-creation as well as a space for making community, a space within which festival goers define themselves in relation to the others they encounter at festivals. But the festival self is put together and expressed outside of the festival setting as well. Neopagans' festival experiences are shaped by their pasts, and their presence at festivals is part of the larger story of their lives. When festival goers tell each other how they came to be at a festival, how they came to adopt a certain name and the ritual practices of a particular culture, or why they have tattoos of fairies covering their bodies, they situate themselves in relation to their identities both inside and outside festival bounds. Most significantly, they give meaning to the present by telling stories of their childhood that explain why they became Pagans and how they came to be at a Pagan festival. These stories indicate that the relationship between Neopagans' current identities and their remembered childhood is complex and dynamic. Neopagans' expression and performance of self at festivals may be affected by childhood experiences, but their narratives about the past are also constituted through the lens of the present.

As individuals first encounter and then become acquainted with the broader Neopagan movement, they begin to interpret their own experiences in ways that are specifically Neopagan. In their discussions of self, Neopagans draw on "frames of meaning," to borrow a phrase from anthropologists George Rosenwald and Richard Ochberg and apply "new categories for understanding social life" to describe childhood and make sense of their personal histories.[1] Storytelling among Neopagans is thus a process in which, as Rosenwald puts it, "The narrator of a life history appears as the pole in a dialogic relation. He or she responds to the particular terms of the interaction by producing successive versions of himself or herself in the given sequence, with the given unfolding of detail, the given increase of complication and simplification, the given versions of past, present, and future, the given conceptions of self and other. Subjectivity . . . displays its momentum by oscillating between telling and living."[2] In a similar fashion, Neopagans produce identity narratives as they are living them out at festivals. A woman who attends a sweat-lodge ritual for the first time and listens to the stories and songs of the sweat-lodge leader, "remembers" experiences from her past that resonate with the ritual. She describes her past during the sweat, and these memories then become part of her identity. "Living" and "telling" are constantly shaping and reshaping each other as Neopagans share their self-narratives in festival space.

When Neopagans tell each other stories about how they came to be at a festival, they tell their stories in ways they think will make sense to other festival goers. They test the intelligibility of their narratives by measuring the reactions and responses of listeners. And by hearing others' stories, they come to understand their own differently. It is not the facts of the story, but the self-construction that takes place in story-telling that is the more significant cultural act. Communicating stories to others may be an important aspect of social relationships, but "personal stories are not merely a way of telling someone (or oneself) about one's life; they are the means by which identities may be fashioned."[3] Sharing childhood stories is a Neopagan genre of storytelling that sets up childhood experiences as paradigmatic of Neopagan religious identity. The stories individuals remember from their childhood highlight Neopagan concerns such as intimacy with nature and the ability to contact a spirit world. For instance, many Neopagans describe themselves in childhood as children who were open to the spiritual world and connected with nature. "Children as seekers," to borrow psychoanalyst Robert Coles's phrase, are the central characters in Neopagan narratives.[4] The children Neopagans remembered themselves as accepted and were curious about supernatural occurrences such as the appearance of ghosts and the voices of tree spirits.

Neopagan childhood stories are narratives of loss and redemption in which childhood embodies the storytellers' most profound ideals and desires. Neopagans tell each other that innocent appreciation of nature and sensitivity to the supernatural characterized their childhood. As they were socialized into a predominantly Christian culture, they say they lost these qualities, only to regain them when, as adults, they discovered Neopaganism and began to draw on cultural traditions that resonated with their childhood world. Neopagans also tell each other that the world *should* be as they remember seeing it as children, and that childhood experiences play a central role in who they are now. And so they redeem the childhood world at festivals. As places set apart from their everyday lives, festivals allow participants to piece together fragments of the past in new ways.

The themes that emerge from their stories, then, point to issues that are important in their private worlds cast in the language of the broader Neopagan movement. In this way, Neopagans reveal in childhood stories some of the defining features of this new religion. While Neopagans place themselves in opposition to mundania and to the mainstream religious communities of Christianity and Judaism, most of them nevertheless grew up in mainstream society, attended churches and schools, and were there enculturated with the same values as their peers. Their Neopagan identities, they say, emerged out of unique episodes in their lives—exposure to certain books and family magical traditions, visions and out-of-body experiences. But these are not simply stories about conversion to Neopaganism or early affinities with magical practice. The child self and Neopagan-to-be is treated ambivalently, reflecting a much broader cultural ambivalence about childhood, and particularly children's religiosity. In these stories the child is wounded and victimized, a part of the self that needs to be healed, often through ritual practices that dredge out emotional and physical pain from the past. If the child was seen by others as evil, then this is particularly true. But childhood is also identified by adult Neopagans as a source of wonder and a time of innocence, an experience that should be recovered and celebrated.

LOOKING BACK AT THE LANDSCAPE OF CHILDHOOD

Neopagans create new religions out of the myths, deities, places, and companions of childhood. As they participate in do-it-yourself religion, Neopagans draw from the landscape of childhood—the places, people, events, and feelings that compose memories of personal pasts—in order to create stories about their lives that make sense in a Neopagan context.

When asked how they came to be involved with magic and witchcraft, Neopagans describe childhood landscapes of myth and fantasy, of nature spirits and supernatural powers, that capture the utopian vision of most Neopagan festivals.⁵ As children, many Neopagans wrote and acted out fairy tales. Their parents provided them with fantasy and science fiction books or watched Star Trek with them. They also recount episodes of isolation or ostracism from other children, special knowledge of the natural world, and supernatural occurrences such as out-of-body travel or telepathy. They imagine the past in such a way as to explain current issues in their lives, and they look to the past as a source for images and insights, for stories, costumes, personal symbols, and rituals.

Immersion in nature is one of the features of the child's world that many Neopagans most clearly remember. They recall that their childhood spirituality evolved out of a sense that nature was alive and that they were deeply connected to the natural world. They incorporate their childhood intimacy with an enchanted natural environment into nature-based religious practices. They say that they were more at home in the woods than in their families and schools. In 1992 Catherine, who had been attending Neopagan festivals for ten years, told me about childhood episodes that resulted in her becoming a Pagan: she was "an angst-filled teenager," who "used to walk along the beach dressed in black and reciting Rimbaud." She was very much an outsider at her high school and her peers called her a "witch," but she felt no connection with the label. When she was fifteen she convinced her mother to leave her alone for a few days in their cabin in the woods, rather than taking her along on a trip. Lying in the dark one night, she slipped out of her body and was able to look back on it from a great distance away. She remembers flying out of her body through a mist and into a castle. When she came back down into her body, she sat straight up in the bed and thought, "Oh, I am a Witch." Then, over the next few days she practiced leaving her body while walking through the woods: "I was looking at faces in trees while my body was several yards behind me." For the first time in a long while she felt that "everything was okay. I became aware of the vitality surrounding me. Everything was in motion, and I was a part of it all."⁶ Catherine identifies the initial awareness of "being a part of it all" as the point of origin of her Neopagan identity.

Interconnectedness—the complex relationships among humans, animals, trees, and earth—is a central belief of Neopaganism. In Catherine's out-of-body experience, the boundaries between self and other are fluid and can be made to dissolve at will. The common Neopagan chant "Earth my body, water my blood, air my breath, and fire my spirit" attests to the essential oneness between self and world and the possibility of intimacy with nature that Neopagans identify as features of childhood that are desirable for adults as well. Jerry Harding captures the importance of communion with nature in this section of his poem "Essence of Mother Earth": "I walk through the forest / Hearing the sounds of the spirits and creatures of nature / I begin to feel the essence of the forest / becoming one with the spirits of nature."[7] Neopagans describe childhood as a time of vivid imagination and of intimacy with the natural world and its powers: "The world was a magical place and we were all magicians. We played and we sang, and the Lord and Lady smiled upon us for we were Their beloved children. . . . We liked to be outside as we were one with the world."[8]

Neopagans remember themselves as visionary and unusual children powerfully affected by the places where they lived and roamed. Although many Neopagans grew up in urban areas or the suburbs, they recall special visits to the country. As children they interacted with nature spirits or left offerings for fairies in the woods. At festivals they share memories of being at home in the woods and fields where they wandered as children. As a result, Neopagans say in these stories that they feel "more themselves" in nature. For them, the remembered childhood self is like the "real self" that emerges at festivals. Cindy, who has recently quit working as a computer consultant to go back to school, explains it this way: "[Neopaganism and Wicca] seem familiar—I had long ago decided that, if there were a natural 'religion,' it would be one of the duality of nature—sun and moon, day and night, god and goddess."[9] Cindy was raised on a farm, her only sibling a much older brother, and she remembers spending most of her time alone outside. She says that much of her "inner strength and peace came from spending time by myself near a pond or in a field or by a lake and just feeling the earth."[10] Like the festival self surrounded by farmland or wilderness, the remembered child self is most comfortable in nature. Reverend Candida, an "Eclectic Wiccan High Priestess," employed as a software designer/engineer, similarly sees her experiences in nature as formative to her Neopagan identity: "I always felt the energy of living things and felt closest to deity when I was around nature. I have also ALWAYS been interested in the spiritual side of life and at the age of 12 I came up with a definition of deity that has pretty much stayed the same. I also had some psychic experiences growing up (usually feeling the energy of a plant, seeing someone out of the corner of my eye that disappeared when I looked at them, feeling energy in my hands). . . . "[11]

Neopagans, who as adults practice "earth-based" religions that incorporate natural elements and deify natural forces, give special significance to these childhood visions and contacts with nature's divinity. Their earliest experience of nature introduces them to a fundamental Neopagan belief that the earth and all life on earth are filled with "energy" that can be personified as a god or goddess. Neopagans believe that the Western world has become disenchanted due to the otherworldliness of Christianity and its focus on salvation. In their view, powerful religious experiences cannot take place in Christian churches, which they see as spiritually impoverished. Instead, sacrality can be experienced through contact with nature or by searching within oneself and one's past. Remembering childhood as a time of enchantment is a way of regaining some of what Christianity has lost. Like Reverend Candida, other Neopagans believe they developed an early definition of deity that has stayed with them or that as adults they have discovered deities that recapture childhood visions and experiences.

In these stories Neopagans do not simply remember being part of "nature" in the abstract. They also link childhood spirituality to special places from their pasts. They remember particular childhood sites as powerful places that shaped their Neopagan selves. In the same way that festival space is said to transform festival goers, Neopagans remember things happening in special childhood places, where as young boys and girls they had remarkable and formative experiences. Ranfeadhael, who tells me he is "Active Duty Air Force," claims that the presence of "ley lines"—channels of energy that criss-cross the planet—near the house he grew up in resulted in a particularly active site for supernatural occurrences.[12] Celest remembers the 170-year-old farmhouse she grew up in as "*very* active spiritually. A lot of my ancestors are there along with some unwanted or wandering spirits that scared me and my parents a lot. My mother found me at the age of three in a circle with my dolls trying to reach a lost pet."[13] Celest remembers herself as a child who responded to "spirits" in her house by doing a ritual involving a circle, a common characteristic of Neopagan ritual work. As Celest now sees it, she responded to the powers of the house with uniquely Neopagan forms because she was destined to become a Neopagan.

Neopagans often describe their child selves as unusually gifted in imagination or intelligence. They believe in a childhood way of being and knowing, which is distinct from, but can inform, the adult self. As Sara says,

> Maybe one of the reasons is adults who had an unpleasant youth, whether from illness or abuse, tend to have very well-developed imaginations. When the "here and now" is very unpleasant, a person might tend to look for realities that are "otherly," which if you're a child usually include a lot of fantasy and living in your head. Since it seems to me that a great deal of magick involves strong belief and visualizations, those of us who had a lot of practice in those things when we were children hang onto that ability as adults. I think we're also more accepting of things that are a little out of the mainstream, and more accepting of creative solutions for problems.[14]

Sara's sense of estrangement from her peers coincided with and was probably exacerbated by her interest in reading. Chris also remembers herself as a child who, like Sara, "lived in her head." She describes her "oddness" and the "transformative experiences" of her childhood: "I was (and am) an asthmatic. . . . I couldn't run well when ill, and was very, very thin, so was both bad at sports and odd looking. My breathing was funny, my looks were funny, I got out of things, so therefore was a strange creature. . . . It's hard to be odd and singled out for mockery when it's for things you can't help. At one point or another, the child in this position often says, and I certainly did, 'Well, if I can't be just like them, I'll be REALLY different.'"[15] Chris's sense of estrangement from her peers coincided with and was probably exacerbated by her interest in reading. Like many Neopagans, she was drawn to mythology: "I also read a lot of fairy tales and kiddy books on other cultures. This is where I met my first gods and goddesses and learned about places where things are done differently. Talking about such things (and trying out an occasional charm, etc.) automatically makes the strange child even stranger."[16]

Childhood ostracism is remembered ambivalently; it is connected to being special (Chris points out that she was "far ahead" of her classmates in areas such as "reading, geography, history") and yet some Neopagans also seem sad that they were identified as "a being apart." This sadness or sense of loss of what they imagine to be a "normal" childhood is assuaged by the discovery of a community to belong to that includes many others with similar memories of being ostracized from their peers during childhood or adolescence. In fact, their childhood experiences now become a source of skills and knowledge that are valued and significant in Neopagan practices. Chris's familiarity with visionary experiences facilitated her initiation into Neopaganism: "The visions taught me that the out-of-the ordinary was possible. When I started my training for initiation, I discovered that I could do things with myself simply through meditation and concentration that others could do only after taking drugs or long years of study. It mostly meant just REMEMBERING what it's like and then searching for, I guess, the paths in my brain."[17]

Childhood immersion in fictional worlds is recalled to fulfill the longings of troubled teenagers who, through their dress or behavior expressed themselves in a language their peers couldn't understand, a language derived from the books they loved, not with the interests of "normal" teenagers. For Pauline, sporting short hair, ties, and baggy men's clothes in an effort to be safe in downtown Chicago and to express her refusal to accept a "feminine" style of dress, made her a target for the misconceived stereotypes of her peers. Pauline and Chris describe themselves as alienated adolescents who were misunderstood or ignored by the people around them. They remember themselves as "social misfits," who were acutely aware of being different from their peers. They were searching for a place to belong in a world that perceived them as outsiders.

Ranfeadhael takes a slightly different perspective on being labeled "crazy" by his peers. Ostracism, he says, has its uses: "It did serve admirably as a protection both from physical harm (no one wants to beat up a crazy—you never know what they'll do), and from emotional closeness. I also got considerable attention from the adults, who I saw as my peers, while avoiding the attentions of those in my age group, who I saw as below me."[18] Catherine and Pauline explained that they eventually began to "use" their ostracism and their unique individual experiences. As they searched for an identity to claim as their own, their self-images were at first defined by their "persecutors," the other young people who taunted them. These women were regarded by others and saw themselves as strangers in a middle-class culture that valued neither individuality nor femaleness. They saw themselves as displaced outsiders, "homeless" and "rootless." They wanted to escape the limitations and misconceptions of other people's labels and categories and describe a pivotal moment when they claimed the identity of otherness as their own. At this point they realized "Oh, I am a witch," "I'm home," "This is it"— that is, the world they had been looking for. This moment of recognition is accompanied by a sense of belonging to an oppressed and persecuted tradition that has always been "part" of them, as well as a sense of liberation and empowerment at choosing their own identity.[19]

When they identify with a tradition of witchcraft and magic, they embrace the ongoing persecution involved with being other. When Katy first started calling herself a witch, her friends and acquaintances avoided her.

Similarly, when Sharon tried to bring up the subject of witchcraft, people who were interested in witchcraft were afraid to talk about it and others felt threatened by the topic or were simply not interested. These two women simultaneously experienced their own embracing of otherness and a sense of belonging. What existentialist philosopher Jean-Paul Sartre called the "project" of an individual's life seems to be, for these Neopagans, an attempt to balance their own world with the "worlds" of other people in an ongoing act of self-definition, a continuous enrichment of childhood symbols, and a reexperiencing of teenage ostracism.

Scenes of childhood places provide a context for understanding mysterious or out-of-the-ordinary experiences and for conveying these experiences to other Neopagans. Neopagans invest their stories with symbols and practices familiar and important to them now. Though they say that childhood experiences attracted them to a specifically Neopagan aesthetic, they see the past through their current interest in ley lines and circles, earth goddesses and out-of-body travel. When Neopagans create altars, shrines, and nature sanctuaries for rituals and festivals occurring in the present, they invoke childhood scenes. They try to express a childlike appreciation of nature and a sense of playfulness when they make signs, decorate campsites, and prepare ritual spaces at festivals. Festival sites are created to elicit wonder, in an attempt to bring the child self into the present. These sites help create a world that they can experience as full of spirits and unseen forces, in contrast to a spiritually deprived outside world. The "fairy woods" at Starwood are hung with Christmas tree lights; another Starwood campsite was decorated with huge cut-outs of flying saucers; and medieval pavilions reminiscent of Arthurian legends appeared at other festivals. Altars in festival woods strewn with bird skeletons, shells, crystals, and other tiny objects, recall childhood offerings to the fairies. Colorful costumes, festive campsites, the light step of a dance, or a collection of playful drummers, remind festival goers of the children they were or wish they had been (see fig. 18). For Neopagans, festival sites are an ideal world reconstructed through the work of memory, a world in which humans treat nature with reverence, and in which they can recover a lost sense of power and mystery.

VOICES AND VISIONS, GHOSTS AND SPIRITS

As they become familiar with the ways that other Neopagans remember childhood and interpret the past, newcomers tell their own stories about unusual childhood occurrences that preceded their move toward

Figure 18. "Tripsy" the fairy, outfitted with handmade bow and arrow and fairy wings, exemplifies Starwood festival goers' childlike playfulness. Photo by Ransom Haile.

Neopaganism. In Neopagans' stories about their pasts, children are not simply affected by the forces or spirits of nature; they also initiate strange events. Looking back, Neopagans see a child self who possessed powers that adult Neopagans value and desire. They say that childhood visions of the divine in nature and encounters with unusual phenomena such as ghosts, mark the very beginning of their Neopagan identities. They also say it is Neopaganism that restored to them past experiences they had repressed. In each other's company, Neopagans redefine past events, which were explained to them at the time as "silly" or "evil," as religiously significant. Now Neopagans characterize the adults who told them they were "too imaginative" as spiritually impoverished, deluded, or simply ignorant about Neopagan beliefs and practices.

Neopagans' stories of strange childhood events must be seen in the context of a larger cultural struggle over meaning. Repeatedly, Neopagans' childhood stories describe a battle between the desires of childhood selves (Pagans-to-be) and parents who sought to control them—identified with Christianity or Judaism. What Neopagans now see as early inclinations toward Neopaganism were snuffed out by concerned Christian parents or grandparents. As they explain how they came to be Neopagans, these men and women recall dramatic struggles between their own early Pagan sensibilities and broader social norms, particularly Christian values. They were frightened by their seemingly unique powers to enter a magical world, a world that their families sometimes saw as dangerous. Neopagans, who have themselves rejected Christianity, blame Christian relatives, and a society permeated with Christian values and agendas, for spoiling natural childhood gifts. Neopagan stories relate how socialization, and especially the influence of Christianity, made children lose their sense of wonder and playfulness, and caused them to ignore experiences that involved visualization or telepathy. "You see," Justyn Kinslow writes, "I was born Pagan. We all were. We were all born free of the concepts of guilt and sin that would later be indoctrinated and socialized into our hearts, bodies, minds, and souls. At birth we were free, but the churches and schools would soon move to enslave us and capture our spirits. As children we were able to visualize without even thinking about it. . . . We were imaginative and could create any reality we wished. . . . Nothing was impossible as we had not been told, yet, that it was."[20]

Neopagans also charge that family members misunderstood their activities in the same way that other Americans confuse Neopaganism with satanism. This view allows Neopagans to reinterpret traumatic child-hood experiences through the lens of contemporary struggles between Neopagans and conservative evangelical Christians. Stories reveal a bat-tle over meaning that was waged as the child's world clashed with an un-yielding adult view of the hard-and-fast line between good and evil.

In Neopagan childhood dramas, children kept quiet about what they heard and saw because they were sure their parents would be angry with them or think that they were crazy. Hedgehog, who was "raised as a con-gregationalist protestant, real old-fashioned New England puritan stock," admits that at age forty-one she has "only very recently begun to be able to touch that part of [her]self without feeling really stupid." Steeped in readings from Greek and Roman mythology and the Grimms Brothers' fairy tales, as a child she "was sensitive to other worldly things." She remembers the reactions of adults to whom she described "voices that talked to me and called my name at night." "Like most people, I had a lot of it shamed out of me by the time I was a teenager ('don't be silly' 'you're being hysterical' 'don't talk nonsense' 'you're too imaginative' 'you're too sensitive' etc., etc., ad [in]finitum, ad nau-seam)."[21] Carrie, a biology graduate student, says she was "a polter-geist" as a child and recalls "things flying through the air, crowds of faces and moving persons visible in the room, lots of out of body stuff, folks sitting on the bed, etc. I didn't have anyone to talk to about it—parents didn't notice or care. . . . It was an anxiety filled childhood!"[22] Falcon Storm explains that at age eight or nine she often "made offerings to the gods or fairy folk as a child, but never told my parents, because they'd have said I was being silly."[23]

Neopagans also recall with regret and anger what was even worse than being misunderstood: internalizing the disbelief of others. "I always saw people's 'Light,' thought that everyone could, so it was never a topic of conversation, that was until my Mother told me that not everyone could. I was 7 years old. Not wanting to be different, I tried to get rid of this curse. It never really diminished, but now I must meditate before I can see clearly. Its a scary thing to see someone walking down the street as if they were on fire, when you're a 7 year old."[24] For Falcon Storm, an engineer, the experience of being different became something to avoid, a "curse" that set her apart from other people. In this story it is her mother who disillusions her and precipitates her "fall" from the pristine world of childhood powers to a social reality that fears and denies such powers. Neopagans say that this is the consequence of a disenchanted society in which adults let children know that spiritual sensitivity and strange visions are abnormal.

While some Neopagans recall being alone much of the time, others remember the fellowship of other children who played with them in a world apart and shared with them visions of ghosts and other strange experiences.[25] Ranfeadhael reminisces about the special relationship he and his cousin shared: "My cousin, with whom I was very close, was born with one green eye and one brown eye. Traditionally, this is indicative of being able to see into both worlds. Indeed, when we were growing up, shades and other spirits were drawn to Dawn. . . . It was Dawn, her brother Chris, and I playing that first really introduced me into the occult. We all three showed some measure of talent, and with all three of us there, all Hell frequently broke loose. Once we all three witnessed what I believe to have been some spirit walking the ley lines, and other times, we talked with shades, including the ghost cats."[26] The two worlds that Ranfeadhael refers to are the spirit world and the ordinary world of everyday life. Neopagan narratives suggest that children may be particularly gifted with the ability to live in both worlds or to move more easily between these worlds than adults. This gift of moving easily between worlds is seen as an asset in Neopagan ritual work.

Because ritual can be playful and creative (the Sunday night group used finger paints for one session), it recovers moments from the past when play was a part of people's lives, and if they were "special children" as many Neopagans believe they were, this recovery nurtures their current ritual life. Men and women sometimes say that when they became Neopagans or found out about the Neopagan community, they were "coming home." As they join Neopagan ritual groups or attend festivals, they can once again participate in a shared world of meaning and action without feeling that they are "silly" or that they are doing "the devil's work." As they recreate their childhood worlds from the vantage point of the present, then, Neopagans recall children who were isolated from other people but in close contact with a spirit world; ordinary in their everyday lives but extraordinary in their secret worlds.[27]

FANTASY WORLDS AND THE "REAL" WORLD

In their stories, Neopagans were children with an inordinate love of reading and a passion for books. In a way, Neopagans are manifesting in the "real" world what they remember of the fictional worlds of their childhood:

worlds that "encourage an embracing, dream-like absorption, a dissociated daydream of dragons, powers and higher realms. . . . Magical practice attempts to elicit this uncritical, imaginative absorption in ritual, a suspension of judgmental, reality-testing criticism."[28] When Lin, a graduate student living in New England, told me that fantasy and science fiction literature such as Frank Herbert's *Dune* and Katherine Kurtz's Deryni novels were sources she drew on in her "identity-making," I asked her why she found these books especially compelling, and she explained to me that in *Dune* she was drawn to "the naturalness of the mystical feelings on the part of the characters. It is normal, a given, that prophecies are heeded, and people take them very seriously." Prophecies and other extraordinary events, then, become part of reality as well as fiction in a world constructed out of Neopagan values. By casting back through their own pasts for examples of "imaginative absorption," Neopagans recall that when they were children they often crossed the boundaries between fantasy and reality through books.

One of the central themes in Neopagan childhood stories is the child's curiosity about mythology, fantasy, and science fiction. In a message to Pagan Digest, Marilyn remembers: "I've been interested in 'all things weird and wonderful' as long as I can remember. At age 10 or so, I found the 'psychic and metaphysical' shelf in the public library and read everything from J. B. Rhine's ESP research to psychic phenomena, reincarnation, spiritualism and so on and so on."[29] Childhood interest in mythology is reenacted at festivals. During festivals, for instance, ritual participants can act out, with the approval of their peers, mythological characters such as Dionysus or Persephone, recalling the play acting they participated in as children. In this way, they bring the past to life through expressive forms. Pauline, a festival organizer, was fascinated by dragons as a child, and while in high school she researched dragon lore and assumed the character of a dragon in theatrical performances. She later created her own dragon "children" out of leather and paint to sell at Neopagan festivals.

Neopagans are drawn to books that bring alive other worlds or worlds of the past. "I was weaned on Heinlein," writes Uriel.[30] When I asked festival goers how they came to be Neopagans, many of them recalled their childhood interest in fantasy fiction. Sharon, now a self-titled witch, told me that when she accompanied her mother to the library as a child, she went straight to the books on witchcraft and astrology. Neopagans explain that magical fiction, like Ursula K. LeGuin's *Wizard of Earthsea* trilogy, described a world that reminded them of their own "odd" experiences: seeing spirits in the trees or a ghost in their house. Like their contact with ghosts and nature spirits, these books represented a reality in sharp contrast to what they were learning in school and church. Aliera explained to me that "Sci-fi and fantasy shaped me the most, mainly because I was reading that stuff so young that I didn't feel it to be as impossible as I might have."[31] As adults, Neopagans intentionally set out to create a world at festivals or in ritual work in which seeing tree spirits and talking to fairies is normal. For this reason, they remember themselves as children who were open to supernatural experiences and willing to believe in magic. Falcon Storm, a thirty-five-year old NASA engineer, writes that she has "read sci-fi and fantasy for as long as I can remember and it never has seemed neither impossible nor improbable."[32] Neopagans recall that in mythology and fantasy books they discovered a world that "made sense to them."

When remembering themselves as sickly or spiritually sensitive children, Neopagans say that their isolation in the world of books gave them significant advantages in other aspects of their lives. Involvement with books and reading contributed to their sense of being special, as in the case of Hedgehog: "I was very strongly drawn to fairy tales and mythology as a child. . . . I was an early and prodigious reader of Greek and Roman mythology, branched into Norse, read everything the brothers Grimm had ever published, including their work on linguistics, was reading science fiction (Azimov, Heinlein, etc.) by age 10, Tolkien at 13, got blown away by Hermann Hesse at 15, so you can see that I gathered an awful lot of input likely to lead a dreamy, imaginative child in the direction of paganism."[33] When they were totally immersed in fictional worlds, these children became actors, at least in their own imaginations. They remember feeling a sense of power in their early reading because, in spite of being mere children, they were in control, interpreting and imagining stories in their own ways. "I know I spent my childhood with my head in a book, any book, to escape my home life. The world I found there was so much more satisfying than the one I lived in. As an adult, I tend to read the way some people drink. Things 'supernatural' or 'magickal' aren't that hard for me to accept, because they were part of my 'reality' as a child. I guess it helped me grow an open mind," Sara writes to an Arcana discussion of children who are "open channels" for unusual events and visions.[34] For Sara, reading provided a richer and more "satisfying" emotional world than her family life, a life that she escaped through fiction.

Neopagans assume that there is a dynamic relationship between fiction and their own lives. They see their experiences reflected in

Arthurian legend, J. R. R. Tolkien's *Lord of the Rings* trilogy, and ancient Greek myths. They react as if the boundary between fictional and real worlds is fluid, and their ritual work draws heavily on the fantasy novels and myths they are familiar with. Rituals bridge fantasy and reality by making symbols and characters concrete, as when Neopagans dress up as Greek goddesses or invoke the power of Morgan le Fey during a ritual. Festival workshops also bring fairy tales to life. At ELFest 1991, Laughing Starheart approached parents and children about the Oz workshop he wanted to hold. Starheart announced the first meeting of "the Lothlorien Oz Club" in *The Elven Chronicle:* "Fans and enthusiasts of America's wonderland will gather together to share their love of OZ. Be prepared to discuss favorite characters, books, films and magic. Tea party to follow, with OZ-ade, OZ-cream + trivia contest. Bring a friend: real, stuffed or imaginary! Remember OZ is one step away from Faerie in Lothlorien."[35] In the ways Neopagans bring fiction and fantasy into their everyday lives, they overlap with reenactment organizations like the Society for Creative Anachronism (SCA), which re-creates the Middle Ages.[36] Participants in the SCA gather at "wars" where, with the help of myth and history, they dress up and perform as medieval characters. While SCA gatherings strictly adhere to rigid dress codes in order to re-create as accurately as possible an earlier era, Neopagans play with intrusions of the past into the present.

On the visual surface of festivals Neopagans present a mythological medieval past as well as a personal past. Some festival goers dress up in medieval clothing or other costumes that seem to come from fiction, and would certainly be out of place in the streets and institutions of everyday life. A pamphlet for "Gypsy Moon," a store based in Cambridge, Massachusetts, that had a booth crowded with beautiful medieval-style cloaks and gowns at Starwood, reads as follows: "Enter the romantic realm of cavalier cloaks and capes, pirate shirts and daggers; medieval garb, articles of leather and chain mail; helmets and scabbards, buckskin; silk velvets and lace; exquisite antique shawls; vintage jewels. . . . For those whose desire is for the truly unique. . . . wear your dreams, transform your reality, and find that the only boundaries are those of your imagination." Many Neopagan festivals have a medieval flavor: merchants sell steel swords and festival goers drink mead. The festival feast at Rites of Spring was served by "wenches" dressed in long, full skirts and loose blouses cinched at the waist with tight bodices. Neopagans mine memories of childhood for special sensitivities and look to past cultures as sources of wisdom.

Constructing identity by looking backward and bringing an imagined past into present ritual life has been an important aspect of Neopaganism since the first American Neopagan groups took shape during the 1960s. While some Neopagan communities looked to the future and drew on science fiction literature, others turned to the past for inspiration. And in his study of 1960s religions, Robert Ellwood observes, "The past was of help in the counterculture's quest for legitimation and authority" as it was seen as the locus of truth. Cultural historian Peter Clecak agrees that nostalgia was rampant in the sixties and seventies: "nostalgia for times past, for places either remote or undisfigured by technology, for family, and for an experience of community."[37] Typical of this quest for the past was "romantic neo-medievalism" exemplified by the popularity of Tolkien and of Lerner-Loewe's *Camelot* and fascination with ancient worlds and supernatural events, which certainly characterizes Neopagan reclaiming of the witch and the cloaked Druid.[38]

If fantasy books introduce children to Neopagan beliefs, then interest in medieval reenactment and popular role-playing games (RPG) such as Dungeons and Dragons carrries potential Neopagans deeper into the fold.[39] When Ranfeadhael first became interested in magic, he "started copying down spells from "Dragonlance" and Tolkien. "I never really got the courage to use them, but I believed in them nonetheless." Dungeons and Dragons and card games like "Magic the Gathering" offer mythic fantasy worlds analogous to those that attract readers to science fiction and fantasy novels, except that they can participate in the games. Participation in actual Neopagan ritual groups seems for some individuals the next logical step from fiction to reality. Both rituals and role-playing games are theatrical and encourage improvisation.

> I played DnD from the time I was 10 until I was 21, and would still be playing if I had the time. RPGs are simply an escape from reality. Gamers are just thespians, whose stage is in their minds. By entering the role of a character, you, in effect, become that character for the duration of play. There is nothing more occult in this than there is in being an actor. Nevertheless, you do tend to experience the same things that actors often do—you become addicted to the unreality of the character, and eventually, the character's personality begins to [a]ffect your own. . . . The only [a]ffect RPGs ever had on my spiritual development has been to give me something to believe in. From my childhood experiences, I knew there was something to the occult. I just needed to find WHAT I believed in. For a while I thought I believed in RPG-style magic. Now I know that's not how it works, but it was a starting point for my spiritual journey.[40]

Like Neopagans who claim they had childhood visions of spirits and ghosts, Ranfeadhael locates the origins of "belief" in childhood. Even though he charges that role-playing games are an escape from reality, Ranfeadhael suggests that role playing requires a kind of mental staging that is a useful skill in ritual work.

At Neopagan festivals, role playing takes place in real space and time. One first-time Rites of Spring participant describes his exhilaration while watching others perform in a large public context those things that he might have done alone at home or in a small group. He was struck by "the hair-raising experience of seeing, at last, others do things we do, of seeing others lift a weapon level and kiss it with right reverence." In the festival setting, participants can unsheathe a sword and point it in the sky to call the presence of a deity into the ritual circle or dress like a couple out of medieval times, jumping over a broomstick and being handfasted in a ring of freshly picked flowers. Not just books and stories, but the characters themselves come to life as festival goers play with the boundary between fantasy and reality.

Neopagans find reflections of their own life experiences in myths and fantasy fiction and draw on these sources to express who they have been and want to be. Bruno Bettelheim points out in *The Uses of Enchantment* that fairy tales (like fantasy and science fiction) describe children's inner lives, their greatest fears, and most profound, unconscious desires. Neopagans might say that their fairy tales and ritual performances serve the same purpose and that our culture would be improved if more people engaged in role playing. Though Bettelheim views fairy tales as an important part of children's development and enjoyable for adults to read, he assumes that growing up means leaving behind fairy tales. Neopagan childhood stories suggest that the opposite is true for Neopagans. In fact, part of the Neopagan critique of Western culture is aimed at assumptions like Bettelheim's. Neopagan rituals and festivals seek to extend and revive the childlike wonder of fictional worlds in a community of adults. Growing up does not have to mean leaving behind or denying the reality of their favorite myths and fantasy tales. If at some time in their lives Neopagans lost these worlds, they gain them back through their involvement with Neopaganism.

MY GRANDMOTHER'S MAGIC

There is a range of parental possibilities in the stories about the past that Neopagans share with each other at festivals. Considering Neopagans' ambivalence about their childhood, it is not surprising that in these stories parental figures appear as forces for good and evil. At one extreme, parents are cast as positive role models who initiate the child's interest in nature and magic; at the other they are depicted as zealous Christians who negatively affect the child.

A popular motif in Neopagan childhood stories is the significant adult who subtly directs a young child's occult interests. This kind of parent is someone who exposes the child to a sense of wonder and an appreciation of nature. Candida recalls her mother's part in her growing intimacy with the natural world: "My mother would take me outside to see the stars or point out an especially pretty flower."[41] Neopagans believe that this is one way parents play a key role in the development of a Neopagan identity that is intimate with and appreciative of nature. This kind of parent or relative can be someone who simply respects and loves nature or someone who actually works with supernatural and natural forces, such as a grandmother's "folk magic." The parent or relative gives the child mythology to read or has books available that describe magic and mysticism. These parental figures instruct their sons and daughters to appreciate nature and to be curious about diverse religious beliefs, or they play the role of wise and knowledgeable men and women, who have gifted their children and grandchildren with magical abilities. Some Neopagans also attribute their magical inclinations to family traditions of spells, healings, or special knowledge about nature. Instead of dismissing their grandmothers' "superstitions," adult Neopagans present their forbears as evidence of their own authentic magical heritage. Like the appropriation of American Indian cultures, inheritance lends self-created religious identities the power of tradition.

Neopagans may reject the formal religious affiliation of their families, but they find all sorts of ways to explain the religious significance (both positive and negative) of their parents and other important family members. Neopagans say their parents demonstrated psychic gifts or turned to spiritualism, and they describe grandmothers who practiced "folk magic."[42] Ranfeadhael writes that his grandmother's German-Irish coal-mining family from West Virginia "is rich in magic," and, while Christian, nevertheless are "rather proud of their folksy abilities. Nothing flashy, just practical empathy, telepathy, clairvoyance, wart-charming, channeling." And it was these inherited talents that Ranfeadhael experimented with as a child. While discrete practices such as these do not constitute an organized religion, Neopagans identify them as the origins of their religious identity.

Some Neopagans believe they were "destined" to become Neopagans; inherited practices and a grandparent's occult interests simply prove this. Uhlan describes himself as "a Kemetic Religionist" who "worships the Ancient Egyptian gods." He attended a Christian school as a child, but began to question "Christian dogma" when his grandmother came to visit at Christmas and brought him a book of Greek myths. "All of a sudden [the myths] made sense to me in a way Christianity never had. A few years later, when I was 8 she bought me my first book on Egypt."[43] Significant adults in Rhianna's life also created a climate in which her Neopagan identity could emerge. Rhianna had "paranormal experiences all of [her] life," including what she describes as a frightening episode of telekinesis when she was five. She grew up with a grandmother "who called herself a medium," and thus "was always exposed to the more supernatural side of life and religion," though Rhianna, like Lin, was raised Catholic. Rhianna remembers watching her grandmother "levitate a table during a seance," and she recalls "seeing spirits, feeling spirits physically, empathic and vicarious feelings, and much more," throughout her childhood.[44] She notes, however, that her grandmother "was not religious at all." It is Rhianna who identifies a loose-knit body of beliefs as a religious system—the origin of her Neopagan identity.

Family magical traditions include skills such as spell making, fortune telling, clairvoyance, and herbal knowledge, as well as a willingness to believe in the efficacy of astrology and the reality of ghosts. Lin describes herself as a "Catholic, Unitarian Pagan" and credits her father for encouraging her "religious quests and questionings." Her father, she explains, "is a big believer in the occult. . . . He believes in what he calls 'the big book' in which everyone's fate is determined. He believes in UFOs and in psychic phenomena. . . . One of his greatest wishes is to be 'abducted' by a UFO, actually, or have a 'third kind' of encounter." Lin does not attribute her own religious inclinations or her ability to see ghosts to her father, but she does, like him, have prophetic dreams. Although she claims he is a "traditional Catholic in many ways," he nevertheless encouraged her in all her "religious quests and questionings."[45] Lin does not follow her father's beliefs, but his openness to noninstitutionally sanctioned forms of knowledge and practice offered her an alternative to the institutional Catholic church. Her father was not directly responsible for her turn to Neopaganism, but he created an atmosphere in which Lin could see Neopaganism as a reasonable choice. These portraits of significant adults attest to a kind of hidden spiritual tradition in their parents' generation that Neopagans now express in a public context of festivals and newsgroups. In these stories, Neopagans' parents and grandparents participated in multiple and often contradictory practices. They shaped their children and grandchildren in ways imperceptible to themselves and often in direct contrast to what they were trying to teach the children.

Some Neopagans' memories of seances suggest that their parents and grandparents were never only churchgoers or atheists. They could be Protestant fundamentalists as well as spiritualists, Catholics as well as UFO enthusiasts. In these multiple affiliations they took advantage of the cultural and religious shifts taking place during the 1960s, as they shared in the wider religious experimentalism characteristic of American society.[46] Studies of various aspects of the 1960s, both at the time and since, note the widespread interest in occult activities among men and women of Ranfeadhael's parents' generation.[47] Robert Ellwood observes that the popular *Dark Shadows* soap opera, which ran from 1966 to 1971, depicted a family "involved with everything that made up the sixties spiritual counterculture. They did astrology and tarot cards, witchcraft, the *I Ching*."[48] American popular religion in the form of miracle lore, dowsing, almanacs, and fortune telling has long allowed multiple religious commitments. Neopagans are more likely than participants in exclusivist religions to talk openly about the range of their religious activities and to take pride in relatives who did not bow to institutional religious authority.

CHILDREN OF THE DEVIL

Some Neopagans describe their identity as "emerging" because of the encouragement of significant adults, but others maintain that important adults played darker roles in childhood dramas. They appear in childhood stories as evil stepmothers (not witches, but overly zealous Christians, in this reversal of fairy tale characters). Neopagan adults reject conservative evangelical Christian parents who, like Ranfeadhael's family, may also engage in folk-magic practices but are committed to Christianity. Ranfeadhael observes that his family's magical talents were experienced in tension with their Christian identities. On the one hand, psychic abilities are sources of pride. But, says Ranfeadhael, "Unfortunately, once the innate abilities begin to show through, their natural reaction is to turn to God." In stories about childhood experiences in their parents' churches, Neopagans identify two themes that led to their dis-illusionment with Christianity (and less often, Judaism).[49] They com-plain that their Christian families and the other Christians they knew were "hypocritical," by which they seem to mean superficial or inade-quately "religious." As these men and women describe it, their Neopagan identity emerged as a negative response to the shallowness of their fam-ily's traditional religion. They understand Neopaganism to be a religion that is inclusive, and thus enriched by other religious cultures, as well as brimming with spiritual power, in contrast to what they describe as a desiccated Christian tradition.

Neopagans argue that exposure to Christian hypocrisy pushed them out of the church. Falcon Storm writes that she "saw hypocrisy early on as a child," and then, at age thirteen, "was 'saved' (gods forbid!), but as I entered high school, began to see the hypocrisy in the church and to question my 'salvation,' I suppose that was the beginning of my search for a more realistic religion."[50] Sue says that her mother "only went to church because she thought she ought to. She wanted people to see her there. . . . Having rejected the Christian churches as shallow and occa-sionally downright wicked, I have had only myself and nature as a guide."[51] As a child attending a Scottish school, Ananga "started ques-tioning" his religious upbringing as he "learned the truth, e. g. Evolu-tion, unreliability of the Bible, evils within Christianity," and gradually "found Christianity had scant meaning for [him]. It was too cerebral, obsessed with music rather than the Word, much too materialistic in its outlook." Eventually Ananga came to see involvement with Christian-ity as a waste of time and "found a few seconds in direct contact with God was much more meaningful than hours listening to preachers, read-ing theological tomes, and singing Victorian hymns." For Ananga, Chris-tianity wasn't sufficiently engaged with what he saw as the essence of re-ligion: direct contact with the divine.

Neopagans say Christians are hypocrites because they preach love and acceptance, but the historical record reveals their prejudice and intoler-ance. Chris says she is no longer affiliated with the Catholic church be-cause it "attempted to make me inflexible and self-righteous. I try to ig-nore that, as I reject the patriarchy of Catholicism and its unhealthy emphasis on sin."[52] Airique mentioned prejudice as a central problem of contemporary Christian churches: "Being gay and Catholic never mixed well. . . . I still hold contempt for Catholics, or any other 'religious' peoples who include prejudice and hatred in their teachings."[53] Tannev remembers her growing dissatisfaction as a child with the responses she

received from her Bible teachers to questions about the origin of Christmas trees and the Easter bunny, so she went to the main research library
at Cornell University where she was living and read about the history of
Christianity.

> I did find out the answers and a whole lot more about the Christians that did
> not please me! How could these people who were supposed to be following
> the teaching of Christ treat other human beings in the way that they had. It
> made me furious! I read about the Crusades, the Witch Hunts, and the Salem
> Trials. . . . This was the turning point for me. If being a Christian meant liv-
> ing in ignorance and yet at the same time thinking that you are better than
> all other forms of life, even other people who did not believe the same as you,
> then I wanted nothing to do with it! It was then that I began my research into
> witchcraft. . . . This was at the ripe old age of 12! The more I read, the more
> I wanted to read and learn. At 13 years old, I was an agnostic, between the
> ages of 17–18 I was a Satanist, at 19 I went back to agnostic and then at 21
> I was initiated into Wicca.[54]

Neopagans describe themselves as young people who were disappointed
by inconsistencies in Christian theology and behavior and upset by their
discovery of Christian treatment of witches, gays, and other minorities.

In contrast, the other common criticism of Christians was for "shov-
ing religion down their throats," that is, being too religious. Many Neopagans describe the family religions they reject in very negative ways, recalling abuse at the hands of zealous Christian crusaders against evil.
They also charge that their Christian parents and churches prevented
them from realizing their true Neopagan identity. Episodes of abuse by
Christians is another common theme in Neopagan narratives of the self.
Instead of instilling their children with curiosity about spirits invoked at
seances or a love of nature, these Christian parents and grandparents
fought violently against any sign of interest in the occult. Uhlan describes
his seven years at "Jerry Falwell's elementary school" as "very effective
brainwashing."[55] Another Neopagan describes her early confrontations
with Christianity: "I have had an avid interest in the occult since I was
very, very young. My fundamentalist grandmother tried her damnedest
to convince me that anything to do with the occult was 'of the devil' and
that I would suffer 'eternal damnation' if I ever considered these things.
My first deck of Tarot cards was burned by this woman to prevent my
being 'demon possessed.' "[56]

Neopagans remember themselves as children who were identified as
"evil" when they expressed interest in the tarot or other "satanic" practices."[57] They became contested figures in the battle between Christian

parents and "satanic" occult activities, a battle legitimized and encouraged by conservative evangelical Christian fiction by authors like Roger Elwood and child-rearing guides by Joanna Michaelsen, discussed in chapter 3. Celest recalls her parents' attempts to fight off "satanic forces" in their home. As she remembers it, her parents had sought help from their church: "I remember some people from the church coming out to the house (two men) and going around the house thumping their bibles and screaming 'in the name of God, satan we bind you and all that you touch from this house' and the like. . . . They once took a beautiful antique picture, and a doll of mine because they were possessed, and needed to be burned. . . . I never understood this because if they could get satan out of the house, then why couldn't they get him out of my doll?"[58]

In stories about their childhood, these Neopagans lay out in detail their violent treatment at the hands of Christians. Llew claims that "If Roman Catholicism had not been shoved down my unwilling throat, I might be more inclined to accept it." Many Neopagans used the phrase "shoved down my throat" to describe aggressive proselytizing by families and churches. They remember themselves as emotionally abused children, violated by their parents' religious beliefs. Christian enemies play the same roles in childhood stories as contemporary Christian neighbors who threaten violence: both become the "other" against which the victimized self takes shape.[59]

In spite of their parents' aggressive efforts to prevent them from further investigating witchcraft and magic, Neopagans say they persisted. Derek's personal interests resulted in attempts by his parents and their church to "properly" socialize him, which had the opposite effect of causing him to reject Christianity. "The facade of 'he is always there when you need him' proved more times to be a fallacy than anything I have run into in my religious endeavors. Finally, the Mormon church cured me of my beliefs in God as a single entity, after my mother put me through a pseudo-exorcism at age 14 because I was interested in reading Revelations, and other items on the work of Beelzebub." Despite the efforts of his Mormon family, Derek became interested in a range of religious alternatives: first Native American shamanism, then Rinzai Zen, and finally Western occult traditions such as tarot, Kabbalah, and Crowley's writings. Like other Neopagans he has read widely in philosophy, religion, mythology, and anthropology, mentioning the books of Carlos Castaneda as well as influences from existentialist writers such as Kierkegaard and Nietsche.[60]

When many Neopagans tell stories about their past experiences with Christianity, they say that they pursued personal interests regardless of the obstacles in their paths. The contest with religious obstacles is what creates the tension in Neopagan autobiographical storytelling. And for some Neopagans, a good story is made by focusing on the evil ways of fundamentalist grandmothers. Episodes of conflict with Christian family members are remembered as deeply painful and correspond to the ongoing persecution many Neopagans experience in their daily lives. These stories are sagas of heroic Neopagans who overcame adversity and survived many trials and tribulations. And it is the Neopagan self, they remind each other, which was forged as they took with them the fragments of childhood that were useful to their Neopagan identity and left the rest behind.

With all this attention paid to childhood, one might expect children to be an important focus at festivals. I found a range of different strategies for addressing children's needs in what many consider to be an adult space. While adults are encouraged to be childlike and playful in rituals and workshops, opening up the boundaries between adult and child worlds, festival participants worry about exposing children to an adult world—serious issues like AIDs and sexual abuse or simply the open sexuality that characterizes most festivals. Larger festivals organize special programs for children and teenagers. PSG featured a well-organized and clearly set apart children's area, stocked with sunscreen and juice, where parents could sign up for volunteer shifts. During several ELF festivals I heard adults volunteering to watch children in a trailer set up near the front of the festival site. They even organized a children's video showing and brought in blankets and sleeping bags so that children might fall asleep while their parents attended long late-night rituals. During the six years I attended festivals, children's programming became more structured and more extensive. When I returned to Starwood in 1998, after a six-year absence, a fenced-off children's area had been built for childcare and children's workshops. The Starwood bonfire that year was topped off by a branch of wishes made by young children as well as a pentagram constructed by teenagers. Some parents told me that they left their children with relatives or friends so that they could enjoy themselves more fully and participate in long workshops and rituals.

The presence of children at festivals may trouble the boundary festival goers hope to draw between festival and mundane worlds. Neopagans want their children to learn Neopagan values—what better place to do this than at a Neopagan festival. Others fear that children cannot be expected to straddle both worlds as adults must do, worrying they will mention to classmates that they spent the weekend in the woods with a bunch of naked people. Parents told me that they did not feel free to bring their children with them because of custody issues with their ex-husbands or ex-wives. In one case after a divorce, a parent was strictly forbidden from exposing her child to Neopagan practices—festivals were entirely out of the question. If festivals are intended to recapture the landscape of childhood, then this terrain, while it shares some features with children's worlds, is more colored by adult desires and expectations.

Childhood plays a dynamic role in Neopagan self-making; the childhood self is created through stories about the past. At the same time, childhood stories are used to constitute the adult self. Narrative both constructs a coherent self and heals wounds, and narratives of the self are not static; once told, they continue to be shaped by experience.[61] Neopagans construct childhood by looking backward through their current notions about self and world. But memory is characterized by what psychologist Daniel Schacter calls a "fragile power"; it has many limitations even while its influence is pervasive in these stories. Even though "our past experiences, knowledge, and needs all have a powerful influence on what we retain," explains Schacter, remembering hinges on the "cues" that initiate recall and the environment within which memory retrieval takes place.[62] Neopagan idioms frame the past and create a child self that has Neopagan potential: an outsider in the broader Christian-dominated culture who is intimately connected with nature and the astral or spirit realm. By sharing memories of childhood with their festival friends, Neopagans try to bring back into their religious lives what they feel they lost as they became adults: a world of fantasy and role playing, connectedness with nature, and openness to supernatural events. By emphasizing lost innocence and parental betrayal, Neopagans make more powerful the religion in which they "find" their lost selves.

Since Philip Aries's groundbreaking argument in 1962 that childhood is not a timeless category, but was created in mid-eighteenth-century Europe, historians and sociologists have debated the extent to which childhood is a cultural construct.[63] Neopagans construct childhood through stories that say as much about their current desires as about their actual experiences as children. "Childhood is the difference against which adults define themselves. It is a time of innocence, a time that refers back to a fantasy world where the painful realities and social constraints of adult culture no longer exist."[64] In a *Circle Network News* article, Justyn, a Vietnam veteran and prison inmate serving a life sentence, mourns the childhood he lost and gives thanks for discovering Neopaganism while in prison: "We had no fears until the adults gave us theirs. . . . Such things as war, hatred, and intolerance did not exist in our worldview. . . . Let's open our hearts to the child within and let our love flow into the world. Let's laugh and sing again as we did when we were children."[65] For Justyn, childhood represents all that he has lost because of his war experience and the consequences it wrought in his life: depression, alcoholism, withdrawal, and crime. For him, Neopaganism offers the chance to rediscover the lost world of innocence. He imagines childhood, then, as a way of heightening the contrast between Neopaganism and mundania—a war-addicted nation that needs a strong dose of innocence.

Childhood is also powerful because of its identification with the anarchic, with potential and possibility. Children "represent a potential challenge to social order by virtue of their constant promise of liminality."[66] Again, childhood is seen as a remedy to contemporary American life, but here not so much for its innocence as for its subversiveness. Liminality is unrealized potential, neither this nor that. The liminal child holds out the promise for a different kind of world. By recovering childhood potential, then, Neopagans believe they can change the world as well as their own lives. They want to establish a utopian community at festivals that nurtures diverse selves and allows for the enchanted realm of childhood to coexist with adult concerns.

Neopagans turn to childhood for the material out of which to shape identities, bringing the child forward in time. The back and forth movement of these stories blurs the boundaries between past and present selves, and festivals are as much for expressing the child self as they are for reconstructing childhood through stories. Neopagans invoke the freshness and innocence of childhood to help them create the self anew; childhood is thus marked through narratives as the origin of a specifically Neopagan self. Sharing stories in this way is a verbal method of calling the desired self into existence. If the child's sense of wonder at nature is recalled through Neopagan genres of storytelling, then the child's sensuality and playfulness is brought back through specifically Neopagan kinds of embodiment. This is a liberated child self in an adult body, living in perfect harmony within a community. It is through the body, say Neopagans, that the past can be successfully expiated, worked on, made over, or relived. I next turn to bodily forms of self-expression: dancing, drumming, body art, and sexuality.

CHAPTER SIX

Serious Playing with the Self

Gender and Eroticism at the Festival Fire

"Late Saturday night is reserved for our now legendary Bonfire. Picture, if you will, hundreds of us, throbbing drums, moon and stars, whirling around a fire the size of a small house," reads the Starwood festival program.[1] When I attended Starwood 1992, I watched festival goers dressed in dark, ankle-length capes or gauze gowns, adorned with feathers and jewelry and holding fluorescent wands, candles, and sparklers, proceed through the festival field toward the bonfire site. Dancers perform around the fire as it is carefully lit, the flames spreading slowly at first and then blazing to the accompaniment of drumming and excited applause. A large group of men and women drumming and playing rattles and cowbells cluster along one side of the bonfire. The full and energetic sounds generated by this crowd of musicians urge on dancers as they pass. Women's and men's bodies are adorned only with jewelry or tattoos, their skin glows with sweat and the fire's light. A number of women in colorful Middle Eastern costume perform belly dances; other women and men dance in a variety of styles, some taking slow swinging steps, others leaping and skipping closer to the flames. And the festival fire goes on like this for hours, late into the night.

Even the first Starwood fire was memorable, recalls Starwood organizer Jeff Rosenbaum in his introduction to Starwood XV events. It took place during a lunar eclipse in July of 1981: "The fourth of July had been rainy, and a load of firewood and felled branches meant for a bonfire lay dry and unused in a small valley nearby." The Starwood festival crew went to their neighbors and asked to buy the wood. "We added the 18 foot planks upright to the pile Tee Pee style, not quite meeting at the top. Saturday night we lit the first Starwood Bonfire and drummed and chanted around it. When the fire peaked, a twenty foot tongue of flame shot out the top, sending us whooping and cheering in an expanding ring away from the blast of heat, under a full moon shining blue through the rising wood smoke."[2] It is at these fires that tensions between self-expression and the needs of the festival community, which have appeared at every moment of festival going, are worked on at the most intimate level of festival experience. At the boundaries of the individual body—drummer or dancer—issues of space, self, and community are particularly intense.

Like Starwood's bonfire, other festival fires serve to draw together festival communities for a free-form and festive ritual (see fig. 19). Fires begin at sundown or after the evening's formal ritual. A few drummers start a slow beat, beckoning festival goers to drum and dance around the fire. In the cooler evening air, ritual fires draw festival participants to the warmth and light. Starwood's bonfire ceremony includes a choreographed dance and procession that marks the beginning of the ritual. But once the fire is lit there is no leader, no orchestration, no focus of attention, and the ritual develops its own organic forms. Emerging structures and patterns are unplanned and unspoken, taking shape in the interplay of drums and movement. Festival goers dance around the fire for many reasons, according to festival dancer Diane Tabor. They dance for "celebration and joy, sexual enticement, inward-journeying, and for the invocation and evocation of energy."[3] Some participants seem to share one ELF elder's observation that "drumming is the heartbeat of the festival," while others would claim that dancing is as central to festival experience as drumming. But it is the ways in which these two forms of expression and performance—dancing and drumming—play off one another that creates the excitement and intensity of festival fires.

Dancing usually begins slowly and builds in response to the skill and enthusiasm of the drumming. Some dancers are particularly skilled and graceful. I met several women at festivals who had performed in ballet and modern dance troupes or were actresses accustomed to being on stage. When the drumming becomes too chaotic or uninspired, dancers fade to the edges of the circle, and everyone falls back into conversation and watches the fire. Then new dancers emerge suddenly from the dark edges beyond the firelit circle and movement begins again. All night long,

Figure 19.   This Candle Labyrinth has been added as a community tradition to celebrate Summer Solstice at Pagan Spirit Gathering sponsored by Circle Sanctuary. Participants meditatively walk the labyrinth as a ritual of inner transformation. Shown here is the Solstice Labyrinth from 1997 Pagan Spirit Gathering, which was held in Ohio. Photo courtesy of Circle Sanctuary archives. Photo by Jeff Koslow.

dancers and drummers come and go. Often a group of slowly swaying "trance dancers" forms the circle closest to the fire, while those moving with more energetic steps circle them. Many dancers who want to dance in place or do not want to be illuminated by the fire, position themselves in the shadows and among the loosely knit outer circle of people watching and talking together in small groups. On weekend nights the festival fire continues through the last few hours before dawn with the "third shift" of "crazy people who dance and drum around the bonfire until the sun comes up."[4]

The fire is a place to wear costumes or to undress, to dance extravagantly, and to play loud music in ways that are not acceptable elsewhere. Dancing around the fire can be playful or serious. At times when the beat quickens, a few dancers spontaneously leap and run around the fire, spinning with such speed that they draw out smoke and sparks. At one moment during Summerhawk's Grupple Dome fire, a few men ran around like wild animals, making animal noises and chasing each other around the fire and hanging from the Grupple "rafters" before jumping down on the people standing below them. Some participants would agree with Salome who told me that the ritual fire is an opportunity "to go really crazy."[5]

But later in the evening at Grupple, the ritual fire is quieter, a small gathering of a few women swaying slowly to soft drumming. This kind of fire is less "crazy" and more like what Diane Tabor calls "a sacred act . . . [and] a powerful means of transportation between our physical forms and other levels of existence."[6] Like the meaning of the festival as a whole, understandings and experiences of festival fires are contested by participants. Participants' impressions of the fire vary and their experiences may change from one night to the next or from one festival to another. Tabor cautions against a quick evaluation: "The next time that you're around the fire and people are dancing in their various wondrous ways, remember that more may be happening there than the casual observer might understand. A bonfire is a party, but that isn't all that it is. There is magick in the fire, the chants, the drums, and the dance."[7]

While the entire festival experience provides a space away from the patterns of everyday life, late-night fires are another step removed from participants' other life and mundane personality. "It was so nice to be able to have a thump on my djembe without worrying if I'm disturbing the neighbors," says Ian, a Pagan Digest contributor, on his return from Free Spirit Gathering, a Maryland festival.[8] Festival goers tell themselves that the fire can be anything they want to make it, and uncertainty about the fire's purpose gives it the potential to create powerful experiences, to transport participants to "higher states of consciousness." Neopagans describe the ritual fire as particularly sacred, a place where transformation is possible, where magic happens. "Dance a circle with intent and focused Will and you have created sacred ground," Tabor asserts.[9] The ritual fire "is about a different, less frequent type of experience," one festival drummer explains in an *Elven Chronicle* article about Lothlorien's dome-covered circle: "Thunder Dome is a place to set aside my personality with all of its wants, needs, desires, etc. I have many opportunities to relate through my 'personality' and enjoy satisfactions available on that level."[10] For this participant the festival fire is an opportunity to step outside of his everyday personality and to "enter into direct contact with Spirit." Ordinary desires are left at the entrance to this ritual so that extraordinary things can take place. Like the festival as a whole, then, ritual fires are spaces defined in contrast to everyday life and the mundane world.

The fire is a separate event within the festival, often announced in the festival program or schedule of events. But even though it is set apart from other festival activities, its boundaries are fluid and its organization loose. For these reasons, it is a space that encourages improvisation. "[The fire circle] is the place to go for impromptu tribal drumming and dancing," notes the nineteenth annual Rites of Spring program. The ritual fire is set apart, but not in the clearly demarcated way that a formal ritual might be. Late-night fires are not guarded and no one is excluded or needs special training to enter the fire circle, in contrast to formal collective rituals. At ELF events, for example, Thunder Dome is often used for large group rituals. On these occasions specific ritual leaders make sure that the space is marked, usually by casting a circle, calling the directions and elements, purifying the space and participants, and invoking deities. Often the late-night fire evolves from a group of people remaining in ritual space after a formal ritual has ended. At Rites of Spring 1997, on the other hand, the late-night fire space was a ten-minute walk from the main festival areas. The main path leading to it ended at a gateway that festival staff had built to mark an entrance to the circle. Standing there when I approached was a man smudging participants under the gateway, so that they would notice and think about the circle as they entered. The relatively permeable boundaries at ritual fires promote freedom of expression and a "party atmosphere," but they also result in confusion about the purpose of these spaces.

The intent for the late-night fire is usually decided silently and individually, while in more formal rituals it is vocalized publicly and collectively. While this practice creates more flexibility for individual participants, it is also a potential source of conflict because no common intent is made clear. As a participant not well versed in the kinds of visualization that might be used to create a "temple" at the fire, I nonetheless found that by moving into the ritual space and around the fire with other dancers, my perceptions of the space and people around me changed. Upon entering the circle, I was overwhelmed by heat and smoke and mesmerized by the drums, and I began to feel a sense of oneness with the dancers and drummers. We moved together but with different steps, becoming one in the drum beat, and one as a group of bodies dancing around the fire. The endless circling facilitated our disorientation in time and space. It was this disorientation that played with the boundaries between self and other, that made possible the feeling of union with others. It was at the fire more than anywhere at festivals that I separated from my identity as researcher and observer. I suspect it is in similar ways that other dancers and drummers leave their mundane habits and selves behind as they become caught up in the circle.

At Rites of Spring 1997 I eventually left the overcrowded fire circle and sat down on a log to listen and watch. I had to step outside of the circle and move beyond the outer ring of onlookers into the cold night

before I became an observer again. Only then did I become fully aware
of the sweat on my skin and the soreness of my feet. Only then could I
orient myself by the moon and the trees as a separate individual with my
feet on the ground. Evenings were often chilly, so that the outer ring of
people watching the fire was much colder than the inner ring of dancers
who felt their skin getting scorched. When I left the circle of dancers to
find a drink of water or catch my breath in the outer circle, I felt disoriented for a few moments, even though I had had nothing but water. I
came to see clearly that this was because I had lost my habitual distance
from others. At rituals I was busy trying to keep track of what was going
on, and during workshops I concentrated on what presenters had to say.
Without consciously making the decision, I approached the festival fire
at the end of the evening as a space I could enter after my "work" was
finished. I wasn't worried about keeping notes because it seemed marginal to the more structured and "important" parts of the festival. It was
at the late-night fires that I was most profoundly and most sensuously
aware of the nature of ritual space and the potential of rituals like these
to liberate participants from the "selves" they bring with them.

Festival goers place the fire at the symbolic center of their festival
memories. Ritual fires condense participants' expectations of the festival as a place apart where community and individual identity are performed and celebrated and community tensions are dissolved. Promoters highlight ritual fires in their flyers, and fires are the focus of
important memories about previous festivals. Ian sums up his first festival experience at Free Spirit Gathering in Maryland: "The nightly
drum/dance fire circle was probably the most intense experience of the
weekend."[11] Salome, a frequent participant in festivals at Lothlorien,
echoes this sentiment: "That's what festival really means—is that there's
tons of people drumming."[12] Late-night festival fires are where Neopagans' most expressive and experimental selves join for a collective
event. It is because festival fires are a public opportunity for the expression of individuality and at the same time the only large and un-
structured communal ritual gathering, that they are so important. And
for this reason they are thought to be particularly powerful and memorable. A promotional flyer for Starwood 1996 promised "the legendary
Starwood bonfire, where over a thousand joyous spirits combine their
energies by drum, dance, and song, a blazing heart of Gold to mirror
and join the stars themselves." Festival organizers hope that through
collective self-abandonment, ritual participants will be united in a common experience.

Festival goers think of the ritual fire as a point of continuity with the cultures they want to identify with. They attend workshops on Native American drumming and African dancing that they perform around the fire. At a festival site far away from the mundane world, festival participants say they feel what it means to be part of a "tribe." An announcement for EarthSpirit Community's Rites of Spring reads as follows: "In a beautiful and remote wooded area we gather once again for Rites of Spring. The sparks of the ritual fire rise into the night to the sound of ancient rhythms on the drums. Colorful ribbons flutter in the center of a vast circle, as together we weave the web of community and dance within it. . . . Be part of a Tribal Dance as we drum and chant late into the night around a ritual fire."[13] In "A Gathering Primer," J. Perry Damarru claims that festivals are "a gathering of the Tribes of the Magi," at which dancing and drumming create a sense of "tribal" identity that overcomes the isolation of individuals.[14] I attended a workshop on African dance at ELFest 1992 and another on African drumming techniques at Summerhawk 1992. I noticed later that drummers and dancers incorporated many of the methods taught at workshops into the ritual fire. Neopagans imagine that around the fire they are dancing with the steps of their ancestors and drumming in the traditions of distant cultures. In this way, involvement in late-night fires provides a concrete and embodied experience of the festival as a community created out of borrowed and revived cultural practices. At the fire, a sense of connection with the past and with other cultural traditions coexists with spontaneity and individual expression.

Neopagans gathered around the fire show their affiliation with Middle Eastern, African, Indian, and Native American cultures at the site of the body. It is also through the body that festivals are most memorable and festival memories most accessible. Trevor Marty, a participant in Pagan Spirit Gathering 1992, evokes the memories of past festivals in a letter to *Circle Network News:* "Remember as the sweat pours down naked bodies, singing to the whispering winds, dancing around flames in the sacred pit." Typically, memories of the festival fire are sensual memories. Marty continues, evoking the thick sensuality of the fire, "Where can you taste witchcraft in the night air, or feel the moonlight upon your body and dance round cauldron fires 'til dawn? Does the sound of VooDoo drums do strange things to you? Does the scent of aromatic night fires make you want to go a little crazy?"[15] Memories of ritual fires are sensual and seductive, drawing participants back to a festival year after year. In a letter to *Circle Network News,* Cain, a frequent participant in Pagan Spirit Gathering, writes, "Every year at Summer Solstice, the pagan drums beat wildly through the grapevine summoning Gypsy and professional Pagans from across the Americas and around the globe to boogie once again naked and free around the fire."

I had not attended a festival in more than a year, when I was walking down the street where I live, and the scent of sage and burning wood from a neighbor's fireplace filled the air. I was immediately transported to the night of a huge Starwood bonfire. I remembered longingly the freedom I had felt to move through the darkness; I remembered having been propelled around the fire by ecstatic drumming, heedless of the sweat soaking my clothes and the smoke burning my eyes, oblivious to the sharp stones beneath my bare feet. There is a knowledge about festivals that exists only in my body, a knowledge that I gained through movement. Performance theorist Dierdre Sklar argues that movement is "a corporeal way of knowing. It is as loaded with significance, with who people take themselves to be, as verbal media." In her essay "Can Bodylore Be Brought to Its Senses?" Sklar observes that this kind of knowledge gained through "the deep somatic experience of movement" cannot be replaced with talking, because "the medium of embodied knowledge is not words but sensations in which are stored intertwined corporeal, emotional, and conceptual memories. This is to say, that we cannot fabricate, through words and other media, sensory worlds."[16] Neopagans, it seems, construct their identities around the fire by moving back and forth between verbal and somatic ways of knowing. In order to reach a deeper understanding of their festival experiences, I have concentrated on bodily aspects of their ritual lives as well as my own embodied experience of festivals. My memories of the festival are not simply of the events I saw and the conversations I shared with other participants; they are sensual memories embedded in my body as well as written in my field notes. And so it must be, I believe, for the many Neopagans who travel to festivals every summer.

The apparent lack of structure and the deluge of images and sounds, sage burning and incense, challenges festival fire participants' personal boundaries on a physiological level. As they walk differently and dance differently, festival goers claim that the body is transformed, and so they also say, is the self. As one Lothlorien festival goer puts it, the fire "is a special place, a space to do special things," and these are "things" related to the body.[17] Costumed, tattooed, jewel covered, and glistening nude dancers, chanting, drummers and other musicians, smoke, and flame, make festival fires a feast for the senses. For many festival participants being "at home" in festival space means moving and feeling differently about their bodies, and ritual fires are places where this difference is both discovered and expressed. It is at the most intimate boundaries of the body, their stories say, that they are transformed by the festival fire. Festival participants identify their place in the festival community through their bodies and carve onto their bodies marks of their collective identity.

THE RITUAL FIRE AS A THEATER
FOR SELF-EXPRESSION

Freedom of expression and self-transformation are facilitated by the perception that ritual fires are safe and sacred places. A ritual space feels safe to Neopagans when they are able to identify their personal boundaries in a collective context. There is also an understanding among festival goers that other participants will respect their personal boundaries and that the festival community will protect them from unwelcome advances. If the fire is not formally bounded like an organized ritual in which guardians and protective spirits are called on to secure a safe space, participants have ways of making it feel safe. Dance makes the space feel safe for some participants by creating invisible boundaries. As Diane Tabor puts it: "Dancing 'O's creates a vortex of energy which acts to keep the space safe. The warding effect is amplified when the dancers are aware and focused on their purpose. I know dedicated magicians who will circle the fire for hours keeping the vortex spinning with their movement and their Wills. It is the raising and maintaining of a temple. . . ."[18] Festival participants imagine ritual fires to be invisible temples constructed by participants' intentions and maintained by their focused "wills." By "will" they mean a directed and conscious intent by which the space for a ritual is created and its goals put in place.

Salome frequently mentioned her concerns about safety during our conversations about festival fires, but she also told me that "people at ELF usually pick up on it if someone is being hurtful toward a woman."[19] She observed that "anywhere you go there are always going to be people who are going to try and hurt you. But the idea that you're in a place where there's more safety than elsewhere is a nice thing to know. . . . It's been a playground for me to be more assertive on and say, 'listen, get out of my personal space and get out of it now. I don't want you in my personal space unless I invite you in.' Most people will leave you alone then and if they don't then I'm not going to deal with them. Sometimes it's good to have a safe environment where you can just go out of control."[20] Yet how is it possible for festival fire participants to feel safe when they are going "out of control?"

Safety and loss of control seem to be in tension, but the loosely organized festival fire is a place where contradictory intentions and impulses inevitably coexist. In "Dance Work," Diane Tabor describes "dancing for joy" like "a child." She suggests that dancing around the fire, adults regain a childlike ability to "surrender to emotion," which in adults, "may stir fears of losing control." She goes on to point out that "there is, however, a powerful magick in surrendering the body to the expression of joy. It provides a balance to the stress and sorrow encountered in every life. . . . Joy and laughter are gifts from the gods."[21] At ritual fires, childhood memories become vivid, just as they do in other areas of festival experience. Here the goal is to strive for a playfulness and joy in self-expression, but in a very adult fashion—erotic dancing for example. Nudity may evoke the simplicity and innocence of childhood, but within a sexually charged setting.[22]

Loss of control and freedom have specific meanings in the context of festivals that are not always stated in festival literature but are learned through experience. Festival goers can express themselves in whatever ways they choose, as long as they do not infringe on the rights of others. Artemis, a public librarian, explained to me that freedom to dance around the fire is one of the main reasons she goes to festivals. I asked her if there were other places that she also enjoyed dancing: "Not with the freedom that I feel at Lothlorien or at any other festival, Rainbow or whatever, just because I know that nothing I do down there is going to be looked down upon. It doesn't matter how I dance, nobody's going to go 'oh my God,' and like look at me like that because when I dance I don't think. . . . I have problems dancing in other public arenas like bars. I'm not the kind of person who dances with other people. I dance by myself and that can be a problem when going to bars by yourself as a woman, and I get hassled all the time."[23]

Many women and men describe feeling "freer" at festivals. At the fire they become less inhibited and more comfortable with their bodies. In this way the fire becomes a theater for self-invention, an improvisational space to be "outrageous" and "attention-grabbing." Men and women immerse themselves in the performance of dancing and drumming, releasing their bodies in ways unique to the festival setting. In so doing they make this space their own and redefine their bodies and movements to fit the space.

Drumming plays an important role in defining festival space and inspiring festival dance and movement. I was welcomed by drums in the distance as I walked through the woods of Lothlorien. On each of my many returns to this festival site, the drums signaled to my body a different way of moving. Unconsciously I relax, my movements become more fluid, my posture more erect. The drums have communicated to my body that I am entering a different kind of space. Flutes and cowbells ask me to leave my worries in mundania and beckon me to enter a world of movement that is not like normal life. Longtime festival goer Peh told me that drumming was not originally part of festivals, but for many Neopagans it has come to symbolize festival experience, and if they are drummers, to locate their place in and importance to the festival community. Drumming has become one of the most important activities at festivals. Louis, the Vodou temple drummer, believes that the festival fire is a "major happening . . . shared by all who attend these Festivals." He claims that the "shared experience of the fire and the language of the fire is drumming."[24]

Various drum techniques are taught in festival workshops—Starwood XV offered "Drum-making," "Music of the Bodhran," "Middle Eastern Rhythms," "Creative Drumming," "Traditional Rhythms of Guinea," "Rhythms of the Rampart St. Voodoo Temple" and "Kung Fu for Drummers"—and drummers are essential to festival fires and other rituals. At most of the large festivals I attended, drumming could be heard throughout the day and night. Anyone can drum at festivals, and more experienced drummers are available to guide beginners. Many sizes and styles of drums can be bought from festival merchants by anyone who wants to participate in festival drumming. At some festivals, drumming workshops during the day provide a core group of drummers who have practiced together and discussed guidelines. But drumming at the fires is open, and anyone is welcome to join. This inclusivity is both a strength and a potential problem for participants in ritual fires. The authors of the booklet "Festival Drumming" recognize that because of the "eclectic nature of festivals, the deities and spirits worshipped by the various esoteric groupings . . . differ widely," and symbol systems used to communicate experiences often are particular to specific groups or solitary individuals. Because of these conditions drumming becomes "an arena of both contention and cooperation." The authors point out that drumming should encourage festival participants to find "unity in diversity": "There is a need for a form of expression which transcends the intellectual barriers that weigh so heavily upon verbal communication. A nonverbal communion open to all who would partake of its magickal involvement." It is drumming and listening to the drums, they believe, that best reflect "the diversity of religious elements brought together in unison around the Festivals' great fire. . . . The beats and styles of playing are open to all who find, or wish to find, the language of the Festival within themselves."[25] Drumming and dancing around the fire aim for a balance between individual expression and collective comfort.

Specific forms of festival dancing have developed alongside festival drumming. Dancing around the fire, like drumming, generates energy for the ritual and helps the ritual work as a collective experience. Festival goers can dance around the fire in any style, or, if they want, learn specific skills in festival workshops set aside for this purpose. The program for Starwood XV lists the following dance workshops: "Celtic Dance Music," "African Dance," "Ritual Dance Technique," "Dances of Universal Peace," and "Tslagi Dance of Life." The fire is conducive to many kinds of dance, including the expression of sexuality through what Diane Tabor describes as "erotic dancing." Festival goers talk about the fire as a space in which they can express their sexuality and the pleasure they take in their bodies without necessarily having their movements interpreted as sexually inviting: "In most cases, dancers who are dancing for the purpose of generating energy for the fire are not interested in getting picked up, but rather in amplifying the collective energy flow. This is a valuable gift and deserves to be appreciated as such. By calling up the kundalini energy, the dancer becomes a channel for his or her own sexual energies. The feeling aroused in the observers may also be used to contribute to the personal and general energy flow."[26]

Neopagans believe that sexuality is sacred—"the Goddess is immanent in flesh," writes Starhawk in *Dreaming the Dark*—and they experiment with different forms of sexual expression in the safe space of the fire.[27] Because they are in the process of redefining the relationship between sexuality and spirituality in a reaction to what they see as the negative influence of Christianity and other religions—Starhawk counsels her readers to "reject spiritual systems that further the flesh/spirit split"—this community-in-the-making does not have a common tradition that dictates rules of sexual behavior.[28] In their books on contemporary witchcraft, Janet Farrar and Stewart Farrar discuss the sexual elements of ritual practice: "Witches regard sex as something both holy and natural . . . any activity as intense as sex on the physical level will echo on the other levels—astral, mental, and spiritual." Ritual sex, then, can be used to direct power toward specific ends, such as conception. Ritual sex within some Wiccan covens, called "the Great Rite," may be symbolic, "in which the union of the male and female principles is symbolised by the insertion of the athame [ritual knife] in the chalice to bless the wine. In the 'actual' Great Rite, the rest of the coven leave the room before the couple embrace."[29] Perhaps this attitude that sex is powerful and sacred is best summed up in witchcraft's "Charge of the Goddess": "All acts of love and pleasure are my rituals."

But who decides which acts of pleasure are acceptable at an eclectic Neopagan festival? Festival fire participants are required to make up the rules as they go. While some participants find this challenge intimidating, others experience it as liberating. The fire provides a space in which they can be sexually playful without committing themselves. They can flirt with other dancers and drummers within the circle without expecting anything to happen after they leave the fire. I have seen men and women who told me they were heterosexual engaging in homoerotic play around the fire—looking and moving seductively with same-sex partners. Generating "sexual energy" does not necessarily lead to sexual involvement with other participants, caution veteran festival goers. In "A Festival Primer," Damarru tells readers that the festival fire may be one of the few opportunities that participants have to express themselves sexually without being misinterpreted: "More often than not, it's one of the only chances the person gets to leave all that behind."[30]

Within the ritual space of the late-night festival fire, men and women must work on their own boundaries and find ways to communicate those boundaries to other people. If they dance and move in ways that seem sexually suggestive, they are encouraged by others to clarify their intentions. Sexually expressive dancers who gyrate suggestively "amplify the collective energy flow," according to Tabor. For her, erotic dancing creates a powerful ritual experience and generates energy for the ritual's work. Starhawk emphasizes that in ritual dance "the circles we spin can become erotic structures."[31] Tabor describes it this way: "As one watches a woman who is skilled in Middle eastern dance, one might feel sexually aroused. If all one does with that energy is get horny, that's okay, but it is also an opportunity to let the energy rise up through the body, activating the higher chakric centers."[32] Sexual self-expression draws on powerful human emotions and sexual feelings that challenge participants' habitual sense of body boundaries and create memorable experiences.

Dance and movement around the fire are not only forms of self-expression and sexual experimentation, but also methods of healing. The body takes center stage at ritual fires and becomes a tool for healing the self. "You come into the Pagan community—most of us weren't born and raised in the Pagan community—with a whole lot of wounds. We live in a society that's constantly inflicting wounds, so we need healing, and I think as we heal, it will help our images of community."[33] Some participants attribute the healing of deep emotional wounds to dancing around the festival fire. Salome told me about going to Chants to Dance immediately after her release from a psychiatric hospital where she had been treated for depression: "It really helped—drumming around the fire, being able to dance, to cut loose, because I'd been under a doctor and my parents' care for six months at that point." She bemoaned the fact that therapists tend to overlook the physical aspects of healing because, for her, dancing at festival fires was effective therapy: "I use the festivals a lot for that, trying to free up my body. I concentrate on that a lot, but mostly at festivals because it's a very safe environment."[34] Salome credited the healing power of festival going in part to the effects of psychedelic mushrooms she took on her way to the festival. By the time she entered the ritual fire, "It was really wild. I ended up with two people, one who did not exist and had on this rainbow mask. . . . I forgot where I was." She confessed that she "started becoming really violent. . . . I guess I was trying to feed the fire. I was beating on rocks and throwing them in the fire. I took all these drums and started beating on them." She remembers that at that point another ritual fire participant made her sit down at the outskirts of the fire where she would not get hurt or damage anyone's drum. She stayed by the fire throughout the night, and in the morning, she recalls, "I was standing by the fire and I was really lost. Someone came over to me and said, 'Salome, are you back yet?' And he said 'Let me do some energy work on you so that you can get back.' And he did something over me, adjusting auras or something." When he was finished working with her, she began to realize what had come out of the night's experience. "I remember feeling much better after that. It was very spiritual but it was a lot of stuff—abuse issues coming out. It was very intense, but it resolved a lot of things for me."[35]

Although many festival goers approach the fire as a space for play, it also provides a place for work on health problems and emotional issues.

Salome's experience is not unique. Some men and women come to festivals intentionally to work on healing emotional wounds, while others find that festival going and involvement in Neopaganism opens up wounds and forces them to seek healing. "When we first come into Paganism, we meet the underworld," said Miriam, a Neopagan psychologist who was giving a workshop on healing at Pantheacon. The focus on sexual and bodily expression in ritual requires self-examination and can trigger painful issues. Embodying deities can also be exhausting

and disturbing to some people, explained Miriam. Some ritual participants report becoming sick or being exhausted afterward, because
"deities have a different vibration." Participants in the Pantheacon workshop emphasized the importance of Neopagans taking care of each other
and dealing with safety issues.

Many workshops I attended at festivals created safe spaces in which
to focus on healing emotional wounds through the body—usually
troubled relationships or sexual abuse. At Rites of Spring 1997 the
Women's Healing Circle (a woman-only workshop) was similar to the
many other women's circles I attended at festivals in that it provided a
safe space for women to talk about painful aspects of their lives. All participants were smudged with burning sage at the beginning of the ritual
and led through a "tree of life" guided meditation in which we were
asked to stand in a circle and feel our roots going down through our feet
into the molten fire of the earth's core. We stretched our arms up to reach
the sky. Some women volunteered to be healers, and others to be healed.
The workshop leader asked healers to "channel the healing energy"
through each woman's body and down into the earth or up into the sky.
The first group of five women to be healed lay on the floor like the spokes
of a wheel. The group of healers sat at their heads and put their hands
on places that they thought needed "healing energy." The workshop
leader moved around the room to help where she thought she was
needed, especially with the less experienced "healers," all the while
singing Neopagan chants. When the first group was finished we all sat
in a circle for a few minutes and then switched places, the healers lying
on the floor, and the group that had been on the floor taking their turn
as healers. One woman on the floor began crying and later told the circle that she had "a lot of abuse in my past." At the end of the circle,
everyone participated in a group hug and a chant; we then dispersed into
the festival night. Healing is the central festival discourse; festival workshops and rituals return repeatedly to the theme of healing, and it is often
the topic of informal conversations throughout the festival site.

As a space that is both "safe" and "free," the fire allows for a kind of
healing that might not occur elsewhere. It is much less structured than
the Women's Circle at Rites of Spring, and no one facilitates the healing
process. Salome's physical presence at the fire, and the effects of the fire,
other ritual participants, and the psychedelics on her physical experience
facilitated a healing process. Anthropologist Frederick Lamp describes
the importance of the body as a tool in ritual work among the Temne of
Sierra Leone: "In ritual dance the body is the medium of spiritual uni-

verse and a tool of artistic conception. Just as the body is used as a microcosm of the universe, and a tool of the arts that reflect it, so it is also a cultural artifact, a functional effect of cosmological thought."[36] Neopagans want to remake the body given to them by socialization and the religious institutions that shaped their upbringing into a symbol of a future society more in keeping with Neopagan values such as the sacred sexuality. At ritual fires, the body both expresses and constructs meaning. Diane Tabor explains that "ritual dance may also be used to work on personal issues which are too threatening or deeply buried to address in our everyday consciousness. Emotions which have been repressed in the interest of preserving our lives and relationships can be allowed expression and worked through in the safe space created by dance."[37] It is the movement of dance, suggests Tabor, that draws out participants' most deeply buried and painful emotions and experiences. In Salome's case, drugs facilitated the release of pent-up emotions.

Drugs and alcohol are treated ambivalently by festival goers and festival organizers. Just as there is more tolerance for appearance and behavior that is not acceptable in the broader society, so is there tolerance for drug and alcohol use as long as it does not impinge on the experiences of other festival goers. While some drug use at festivals is purely recreational, psychedelics in particular are looked upon as spiritual tools. Neopagans take drugs like LSD and psychedelic mushrooms as another way of traveling "into faerie," of opening their emotional and physical boundaries to the festival experience. Ideally, at least, the festival also provides a safe space for this kind of experimentation. Drugs can enhance the sense of festival as a place apart from ordinary life, while they may also help bring about personal transformation. Like dance, drugs shift the body out of habitual ways of moving and sensing. Although some festival goers turn to psychedelics to facilitate their entry into festival or ritual space, costumes, body paint, nudity, drumming, and dance are more typical techniques.

Dance, psychedelics, and ritual can heal past traumas, especially those involving sexuality and body image. In a letter to *Circle Network News*, a festival participant named Godric discusses his first encounter with festival drumming and dancing. At first he felt intimidated by the dancers' grace and remembered a childhood incident in which someone had made him feel ashamed of dancing at a wedding: "For many years, this vague and chilling memory has recurred whenever I've tried or been asked to dance. It turns my feet to stone and my coordination to chaos." Godric describes joining the dancers at Pagan Spirit Gathering as a step toward healing old fears: "I had absorbed enough PSG atmosphere to realize that fear of ridicule had been banished from this place, along with indoor plumbing and telephones. This time I left my drum at my camp. I noticed people with bodies no less clumsy or attractive than mine dancing in the fire circle, and they didn't look ridiculous. They looked beautiful, happy, entranced, and ecstatic. I closed my eyes and slipped into the pattern of the music, trying it on. It welcomed me. I retreated briefly and left clothing and inhibitions under a nearby tree, then joined the dance." Godric's story echoes other men's accounts of working with body image around the festival fire. Michael, an architect from the East Coast, self-consciously makes use of the festival fire to explore body movement and sexuality: "While I was going to these festivals, I was working magically to bring sex into my life, not to specifically get sexual experience, but to find it within myself and to learn to express it." I asked him what changes came about in his life as a result of festival going: "I dance differently. I look at women differently. I look at their faces; I listen to their voices; I'm not afraid of them anymore. I'm not afraid of myself when I'm around them."[38] For Michael, festivals in general, and the ritual fire in particular, made possible the changes he sought in his sense of self and body image. Michael tells me that now at home he dances each morning before work because, "my body knows what it needs. It's such a pleasure to be in my body." Festival goers report that surrendering to the experience of the ritual fire allows them to trust their bodies in ways that are new for them. Their enhanced sensitivity to the needs of the body, they say, is something they carry home with them.

Healing at festival fires is helped along by the creative use of costume and body marking. Festival goers' bodies become the canvas on which self-images can be painted with the boldest strokes. Ritual fire participants present their innermost fantasies and hidden selves in a public space. They convey with their appearance who they want to be, what character or persona they want to take on at the festival. In "A Pilgrim's Guide to Pagan Festivals," Richard Keenan describes Free Spirit Gathering participants' "sense of costuming and theatre": "One woman got into character as a pict warrior dressed in nothing but full body blue paint; another dressed only in paint as a flame."[39] Costumes, nudity, jewelry, tattoos, body paint, body piercing, and styles of dancing and drumming are all methods of communicating about the self through the body.

Festival goers arrive at festivals adorned with tattoos and piercings, and they take costumes from home, but they also create costumes and mark their bodies during the festival. The elements participants put to-

Figure 20.   An Elf Lore Family masking workshop takes place at Samhain
Fest. Courtesy Marty Laubach. Photo by Bethany Curtiss.

gether to express their festival selves are usually available from merchants
and other festival goers. On Merchant's Row cloaks, masks, and body
jewelry are readily available; hair wrapping specialists and body painters
also set up in the merchants' area; and professional tattoo artists and
piercing specialists are present at large festivals like ELFest, Starwood,
and PSG. Like hidden selves, tattoos and piercings covered in everyday
life are revealed at festivals. In a *Mezlim* article called "Why We Mark
Our Bodies," Tath Zal asserts, "It is the view of many that an unmarked
body is an inarticulate form, separated from its social/cultural identity;
and that only when the body acquires the 'marks of civilization' does it
begin to communicate and become an active part of the greater social
experience."[40] Festivals encourage participants to experiment with body
paint, create colorful masks and costumes, have their hair wrapped with
colorful threads, or get tattoos (see figs. 20 and 21). The culture of display at festivals provides a perfect opportunity for the communication
of personal identity through the body.

Neopagan bodies articulate specific cultural and religious identities
with symbols that are recognizable to most Neopagans. Tattoos of
yin/yang symbols or pentagrams and Celtic brooches pinning back long,
hooded cloaks signify particular cultural and religious affiliations within

Figure 21.   Masked participants gather after a nocturnal masked ritual at the 1998 Front Range Pagan Festival in Colorado. Courtesy Chas Clifton. Photo Chas Clifton.

the larger Neopagan world. For Zal, "self-identity" is one of the most common reasons why Neopagans get tattoos and piercings: these kinds of markings, he explains, "represent an aspect of the recipient's personal identity and/or emblem of accomplishment. A tattoo may represent a picture of this aspect (astrological signs, nicknames, personal strengths/ weaknesses of an influential nature), while a piercing can convey a sense of ownership over one's body and the related pains and pleasures derived therefrom."[41] Sindi explains it this way in a message to Pagan Digest: "I got my first mark (pentagram, left breast) to celebrate going back to college and my affiliation with Wicca simultaneously. . . . I'm finishing grad school this December & I want to get another to celebrate that. Celtic knotwork, possibly. . . . Contrary to popular belief, the terms 'librarian' and 'dead-from-the-neck-down' are not interchangeable! A concealable/displayable piece of body art allows me to take people's preconceptions and do a mental cream-pie on them."[42] For Sindi, tattoos mark a rite of passage and symbolize a hidden self.

   Some festival goers make the tattooing process into a rite of passage. When I was sitting outside Laughing Starheart's tattoo parlor at Starwood, many people came by to look through Starheart's tattoo books and magazines, to talk about their tattoos, and to imagine getting new ones. That day, Wendy got a "triskalion" depicting three phases of the moon. Though this was her first year at Starwood, she told us that she had been waiting to get her tattoo at the festival. She asked people who were talking outside the tattoo parlor to chant, and her husband drummed constantly until Starheart had finished. Common tattoos include the Chinese yin/yang symbol—Michael has a yin/yang tattoo because he considers himself Taoist as well as Pagan—Celtic knotwork, animals, dragons, unicorns, and astrological signs. Laughing Starheart has tattoos of angels and a phoenix. Cary explains the significance of his tattoos: "I'm planning on getting a couple of tattoos as a way of ritualizing certain aspects of my life. . . . I have an idea for a very large one that came to me in a vision. . . . I'm planning on getting a much smaller one on my arm, a Sanskrit 'OM' which has religious significance for me."[43] Dave also told Pagan Digest readers that by inscribing his religious identity on his body, he would be transformed "forever": "Originally I wanted a tiger design, because this is my Chinese birth sign, but I settled eventually for a dragon, because the flowing, curving design seemed to encapsulate the taoist philosophy which influences me."[44] Chris elaborates further on the connection between tattooing and Neopaganism: "This [tattoo] is very much a pagan/shamanistic (and indeed Magickal) activity. . . . Talk about being changed fundamentally! talk about pain and altered states of consciousness!"[45] For most Neopagans, magic is a process of self-transformation, which in this case is visibly marked with a tattoo or piercing. In "Healing Tattoo," tattooist Crow, whom I saw at ELFest and Starwood, observes that "the vast majority of persons seeking a tattoo do so with the very conscious intention of changing themselves. They enter into the process, a truly symbiotic joining of the energies of artist and wearer, consciously seeking to manifest a chosen vision of themselves."[46] Tattoos, then, distinguish the self of the past from the self envisioned for the future, the self one wants to become.

Festival fires are an opportunity to make the hidden self visible, to show off and talk about tattoos and piercings. During our interview, Michael showed me his recent nipple piercings, which were decorated with shiny blue metallic rings. He told me he had never displayed them in public and had not yet decided whether or not to bare his chest at the festival fire. That Saturday night though, I noticed him dancing in the fire light, with his nipple rings exposed. Many women and men have one or both nipples pierced; I have also seen lip, nose, navel, and genital piercings at festivals. Festivals are one of the few environments where people can proudly display their piercings in public. Experimentation with dress and appearance, with movement and gender roles, is less possible in their mundane lives. In this way Neopagans are like other subcultures that mark their divergence from social norms with visible signs like unusual dress and body jewelry.[47] More than anything else, Neopagans use appearance to raise questions about their nature—who they are in terms of gender and religious identity.

GENDER PLAY

At festival fires Neopagan men and women play with gender distinctions, reveal tattoos, cross-dress, exaggerate femininity and masculinity, or try to look androgynous. Men as well as women use dancing and partial nudity to display the self, play with sexual orientation and work on body image. Sometimes the dancers are predominantly women, at other times men and women are equally represented. At a distance the half-nude bodies with their skirts flowing are almost indistinguishable, men moving as gracefully and sensually as women. During my first Lothlorien festival, I was struck by the dancers' bare feet, the variety of costumes, and the complete lack of clothes worn by many participants. When she was not playing her flute to accompany the drums, Leona leapt gracefully around the fire. A tall and slender dancer with long red hair, she went topless, wearing only lace-trimmed white tights, pink leg warmers, and over-the-knee black suede boots. Kenn wrapped a cloth around his waist and swung his hips like a belly-dancer, prancing sensuously around the fire. Marie was dressed in white gauze skirt and veil, her large breasts uncovered and swaying to the beat.[48]

Many men wear loose, flowing skirts, caftans, or brightly colored cloths wrapped around their waists. Putting on clothing marked as female is an ambiguous statement in the festival setting. Like nudity it is a rejection of mundane style and an assertion of difference, but it doesn't necessarily signal a change in gender or sexual identity. In her study of cross-dressing in literature and popular culture, Marjorie Garber argues that "transvestism is a space of possibility structuring and confounding culture: the disruptive element that intervenes. . . . "[49] Cross-dressing at festivals is practiced by gays, lesbians, bisexuals, and transgendered people, as well as straight men and women who are playing with assumptions about gender that participants bring with them. Salome says she likes to see "all the guys running around in skirts. It's nice because they don't have to worry about being called fag. Heterosexual and homosexual men dress in the same type of outfits and it's really nice for people to be able to get in touch with that feminine side of themselves."[50]

Gender play, dress and undress, erotic dancing, and body art all express the body's challenge to social norms of beauty and decorum. "Piercing enthusiasts are coming out of the closet and showing off their gold," Cain Berlinger writes in "The Other Alternative: Piercing as Body Art." Physical beauty, Berlinger points out, is redefined by piercings: "These people had long since discovered the beauty of their own bodies . . . Older bodies, overweight bodies. . . . [They] had long believed in their own brand of beauty, sexuality, worth. Tattoos and piercings, for them, are creative art; their bodies are their canvases."[51] In the limited time and space of festivals, participants replace mundania's ideals of beauty with a reality characterized by dress-up, personal creativity, body art, and erotic dancing.

By bringing out their hidden identities and marking their bodies with the signs of festival culture, Neopagans express identities that contrast sharply to the outside world. They do this by revealing hidden features of their bodies and by covering themselves with unusual body paint or costumes. Reflecting on Brazilian *Carnaval*, Victor Turner describes costuming as "serious play." Neopagan festivals, like *Carnaval* or Mardi Gras, are intended to be visually exciting and playful, but they may also bring about changed understandings of self or other. At festivals, "people 'play' with the elements of the familiar and defamiliarize them. Novelty emerges from unprecedented combinations of familiar elements."[52] Anthropologist Tanya Luhrman takes up a related notion of serious play when she explains that Neopagan ritual is like children's "make-believe," except that it involves serious personal and societal concerns.[53] At first glance Neopagan costuming and body painting might appear arbitrary, but festival goers speak through their bodies about their most serious and profound desires. During his research on *Carnaval*, Turner learned that "It is a Brazilian point of honor that if one is going to wear a costume or *fantasia*, it must communicate one's most private or intimate fantasy in the most artistic way possible. Repression must be lifted. One might even talk about the aestheticization of the repressed, making the very private public in the mode of beauty."[54] I suspect that many festival participants would agree with this observation, although Neopagans also approach costuming as an opportunity to express aspects they lack. They take on a persona with characteristics they "need." For instance, a man may cross-dress to explore his femininity, or a woman may clothe herself as a virgin bride, belly dancer, earth mother, or seductress as a way of playfully exploring an aspect of herself that she normally does not show.

One year at Rites of Spring, Michael told me he attended a "sexy underwear dance. . . . The most popular costume was trashy underwear, people dressing up as Elizabethan sex fantasies." I asked Peh, a "magician" and teacher who has designed and facilitated many festival rituals and workshops, why he did not dress up for festivals: "I don't costume very well. It's not something that I've been able to develop. It's interesting because they push it so much in ELF, you know, to get your fantasy, to get your persona. . . . I was walking around last night looking at all these people in wonderful costumes wondering well, what would I wear, what would I look like? What persona would I take? Would I take a strong leather kind of bondage thing or would I take a more feminine one. Maybe I'm so split between them—I know [laughs], maybe I'm so balanced that I don't need either one."[55] When they put on costumes and dance in unusual ways, festival goers take risks by exposing inner fantasies and desires.

This is perhaps most obvious in the case of festival nudity. Nudity is a familiar part of everyday life and common in private spaces like homes and bathrooms. But nudity is a public statement of personal freedom at festivals. In this way, it is one of the most striking and unfamiliar features of the festival landscape. It seems to be a stripping away of culture, a freeing of the self, and yet it is at the same time a "costume" that communicates something about the person who wears it. What seems to be the utter simplicity of nakedness is in fact the hardest to read of all festival self-representation. Neopagans' comments on festival nudity suggest that it is normal and comfortable to festival goers who are accustomed to it: "How can you tell you're at a Pagan festival?" jokes Pine after returning from Free Spirit Gathering; "A naked man has to be walking an inflated dinosaur to get anyone to pay attention to him."[56] For Michael, nudity at festivals signals a healthy acceptance of the body: "It's a pleasure to see naked people walking around as if it was the most normal thing to do in the world. One of my images of it is a woman sitting on a folding chair in the rain with a red umbrella, stark naked—an acceptance of the weather, an acceptance of the body."[57]

As a form of self-expression and a statement of personal freedom, nudity also seems to have a healing effect on those who practice it. The Starwood XV program advises, "You'll be surprised how quickly you get used to it! Relax, enjoy the freedom, and wear good sun-block, especially on parts that rarely see the light of day . . . and remember—if you don't wanna, you don't gotta!" Michael recounts another example of what he believes are the healing effects of nudity.

> There's no real pressure to take off your clothes, some people do, some people don't. One year there was a ritual in which we smeared mud on each other. We got naked and smeared mud on each other and it was wonderful. We smeared mud all over our bodies. We were squatting in this mud and cheeping like monkeys and showing each other stones and just playing with this. And we were naked. A friend of mine was there, a lesbian woman who has got real concerns about her body and said to me afterwards that that was the first mixed group that she had ever felt safe being naked in and that really is the sense you get at these festivals."[58]

Festival goers suggest that, like provocative dancing around the fire, nudity is more an experience of and for the self, than it is for the enjoyment of others. For this reason it challenges the assumptions that people bring with them from the outside world. But to what extent do the assumptions of mundania intrude on festival goers' ideal views of the festival fire?

COMMUNITY CONFLICTS
AND CONTESTED BEHAVIOR

As Neopagan festivals have developed over the past fifteen years, the varied interests and commitments with which people arrive come into conflict with each other, and in this way, festivals have become spaces in which highly personalized religious identities take shape within and against a temporary community. Festival fires provide an inviting space for self-performance within the broader context of the festival community. At the fire, individuals play with and express different aspects of their identity: magical practice, sexuality and gender, body image, humor—all express participants' sense of how they fit into the larger Neopagan movement. But because of their diversity, ritual-fire participants inevitably disagree in many ways. In contrast to expectations of unconstrained self-expression, these festivals are actually highly structured settings, and this contrast is particularly clear in the area of gender roles and techniques of the body.

In the stories that men and women tell about self-transformation, issues of conflict and points of contention blur the boundaries between festival and mundane worlds. While participants expect that gender will be more fluid at Neopagan festivals, they often encounter the same assumptions about masculinity and femininity that characterize mundania. Ritual fires, while supposedly the most free-form of all festival activities, in certain instances replicate gender roles in the outside society. Men tend to be the more aggressive dancers and drummers, dominating ritual space and taking more risks, such as jumping over the fire, while women dance more slowly and sensuously. Festival goers also expect festivals to be egalitarian; in this too they fall short of the ideal. Ritual work at the festival fire involves gender play and gender reversal. Although some men and women say they are healed and transformed by their experiences at the ritual fire, there are other stories about the fire, stories that suggest its transformative effects are sometimes more limited than participants anticipate. Personal boundaries are not always recognized or respected by others and wounds are not always healed. The festival fire can be a painful or frightening experience as well as a pleasurable one. Again, the body is the site at which effects of the ritual fire are most visible and its failures most acute.

At the fire, there is an expectation that participants perform and display themselves for an audience and that they contribute to the collective experience. Apparent freedom of individual choice may in actuality mean conforming to the most acceptable Neopagan styles, such as "going sky-clad." Contributing to the fire's "energy" may be assumed by some to mean that women should go bare breasted or dance in a seductive manner. Normlessness prevails on the surface, but at second glance, specifically Neopagan norms become more visible. Native American jewelry and buckskins, pentagrams and crystals, anything in black or purple, flowery gauze skirts and "ethnic" clothes, leather bodices, boots, or other medieval wear borrowed from the Society for Creative Anachronism aesthetic—all of these are part of a distinctively Neopagan style. Experimenting with degrees of nudity may express a newly discovered acceptance of one's body; it may also constitute a kind of conformity. Several festival goers conveyed to me the discomfort they felt about keeping on their clothes. In my role as participant-observer, I too sometimes felt that by remaining clothed I was not completely participating in the festival experience. I also feared that my clothed body sharpened the boundary between my status as an outsider and other festival participants.[59] But I gradually realized that many other festival goers did not take off their clothes. They also sometimes felt that nudity, or at least partial nudity, was the expectation, and that they were being looked down upon for not conforming to the "un-dress code."

Ritual fires seem free of expectations; however, self-expression can itself become a kind of norm. Many festival goers are reluctant participants at late-night fires, preferring to observe from the sidelines, while not feeling entirely comfortable about their nonparticipation. In *Mezlim*'s "Gatherings Issue," Aravah admits that she initially felt "uptight and afraid" at the fire. Her daughter, she reports, "was dancing joyously around the fire," while she herself "sat miserably on a log thinking how much I wanted to dance, too." She credits her discomfort to "fear of being myself. The rituals and workshops quite often pulled this out of me in one way or another."[60] Festival rituals and workshops offered Aravah an opportunity to "be herself," but "being herself" was not as simple as festival literature suggests. The "real self" cannot always appear on demand, nor is it always clear what this "real self" is. Men and women who attend festival fires often feel compelled to be someone different from their everyday self. In Aravah's experience, the requirements of making oneself anew, of setting one's own boundaries, was demanding. In a letter to Kevin, a longtime festival goer and ritual facilitator, I expressed my sense that the "ethic of self-fulfillment" at festivals can be a problem for some participants. Kevin responded: "I think that I was seduced by this ethic for many years. It's a strange and dangerous game—at least emotionally and psychologically. There is a sense of 'it's okay for me to go after what my most primal urges tell me that I want'. . . . Many—or most—of the social boundaries that these people work with in their ordinary lives are torn apart, melted away and otherwise disrupted by 'festival space.' I think that this is one of the most virulent aspects of liminal space—that it disrupts the ordinary boundaries and definitions, causing new ones to arise."[61] As Kevin sees it, when, as at the fire, festival space destroys boundaries, it does a kind of violence to festival goers' sense of self.

The area in which boundary negotiation is most difficult is sexuality. Nudity, sexy dressing, provocative dancing, and the sensual excitement of the fire send conflicting messages to participants. "Some people become confused when they see others dancing in a sexually provocative (evocative) way. There is a tendency in our culture to equate highly sensual dance with a sexual invitation," warns Diane Tabor in her article on "Dance Work" for the *Mezlim* Gatherings Issue. Like other areas of the festival, erotic dance is fraught with tension because of its seeming lack of rules and boundaries. On several occasions, festival goers told me that they did not have the requisite "energy" for the festival fire; a kind of sexual performance was expected that they did not feel prepared to deliver. The morning after a big Friday night festival fire at ELFest 1992, Juliet told me she did not have any "kundalini energy" (erotic performance) for the fire that night and had felt compelled to leave the

Figure 22.   Starwood's ritual fire circle, once called Grupple, is reconstructed as the Roundhouse. The fire pit is in the center of the circle; covered drums ring the outside.

ritual circle and "pout in her tent." I talked with ELF elder Peh about the problem of sexual boundaries, and he told me of a similar incident when a woman he knew was overwhelmed by the sexual energy around the fire and returned to her campsite.[62] At Summerhawk 1992 I was invited to join "a nest" at the outskirts of the fire. Kenn and his friends explained to me that they set up the nest to be an explicitly nonsexual space in which people could be physically intimate without pressure to be sexual. The nest gathered in a corner of Grupple Dome and watched the fire together, massaging each other and talking quietly (see fig. 22).

As they become more familiar with the unique kind of theater that takes place around the late-night fire, participants master a language of body and gesture that identifies sexual boundaries. But many festival goers are surprised to discover that guidelines for dancing and sexual behavior are still in the process of being created at festivals. And in this process, dancing around the fire can be a frustrating experience. Tabor goes on to point out that erotic dance is often "for the power of the fire," not as an invitation to sex: "I have a friend who is both a beautiful woman and an exciting dancer, who has become reluctant to share her gift around the fire. She explains that the men think she's out to get laid and the women hate her for getting all the attention. A man I know, who is a powerfully erotic dancer, often finds himself surrounded by women who interpret his dancing as a sexual comeon."[63] Participants are on their own to negotiate these boundaries every time they approach the fire. Damarru cautions festival goers about miscommunication: "Respecting each other's boundaries also means listening to what is being said. 'No' means 'NO.' It doesn't mean, 'follow me back to my tent and let's talk about it.' "

Creating "safe space" necessitates boundaries, limits, and rules, all of which are approached ambivalently in the permissive festival atmosphere. Many festivals have established policies to deal with sexual harassment, and the covens and ritual groups whose members attend festivals also find ways to address treatment and prevention of sexual harassment.[64] A Wiccan priestess whose daughter had "experienced unwanted overtures during a festival, designed a ritual to raise the coven's awareness of sexual harassment and to help the young woman overcome the unpleasant experience."[65] Because many festivals have dealt with an occasional incident of sexual harassment, festival organizers have attempted to create guidelines for behavior. According to Loretta Orion, EarthSpirit publishes a "guide to appropriate behavior" for Rites of Spring.[66] In the Spring 1992 *Elven Chronicle*, Ms. Manners' column entitled "Do Me, Do Me, Do Me, Good Touching" confronts the issue of bodily boundaries.

> Let me begin by saying everyone is capable of both experiencing and pressing sexual harassment and rape. While most people would agree that women don't want to be raped, the question of how a woman could possibly rape or sexually harass a man is still up for grabs, so to speak. . . . Sexual come-ons, rude flirting and pressing sex can be suffered by both men and women. Just how do you know when someone doesn't like what you're doing? How do you know when your flirting is 'Bad touch'? One easy way to tell is if the person says, 'Stop,' 'No thank you, I'm not interested,' or 'Get your hands off me.' It is less easy to tell if the person tries to be 'polite' and just avoids you. You might misunderstand and think they are playing hard to get. When in doubt ask, 'Excuse me, but I've been flirting with you. Have you enjoyed it?' They only have to say 'Yes' or 'No.' It might be embarrassing if they say no, but it is better than getting kicked out of the festival for sexual harassment.

Ms. Manners' column was written in response to an incident of sexual harassment at an ELF festival. Kristina, who had previously attended several festivals at Lothlorien, lodged a complaint with the community elders about a male festival goer who would not leave her alone. One of the elders attempted to resolve the problem by bringing the two people together for a discussion. The man claimed that the woman, Kristina, had attacked *him*, and she refused to further discuss the matter. She later complained to other members of the festival community that the organizers had not adequately responded to her charges. Some of Kristina's female friends boycotted the next festival, protesting that the festival atmosphere did not ensure their safety. But another festival participant criticized Kristina for not taking a more "egalitarian" and more "appropriately Neopagan approach" to the incident of harassment. He asked why she had not gathered together a group of women to confront the man in question, rather than complaining to an authority figure—one of the festival organizers.[67]

In this case and in other festival incidents, the habitual turn to authority is not easily broken.[68] Assumptions about power and authority that festival goers carry with them into festival space are sometimes inconsistent with the egalitarian image the festival community presents.[69] Rose, whose friend complained she was sexually harassed, decided to stay away from ELFest for a year at least. She told me that she had come to realize the limits of her community and drifted back to Christianity for the first time since childhood. She pointed out that in Neopaganism, people experience change "on the astral," but are unable to realize these changes in material ways, in everyday life. In Rose's view, this failing was due to the overemphasis on self-realization and the neglect of the needs of the community. When individuals are given complete freedom, she implied, substance abuse, sexual harassment, and other problems are often not dealt with, undermining Neopagan efforts to build community.[70] The constant refrain of "Do as thou will as long as thou harm none," or Aleister Crowley's often-repeated, "Do what thou wilt" downplay community responsibility and disregard the subtle ways in which communities are harmed.

In a community that takes a proactive stance toward healing sexual abuse and in which participants are encouraged to share stories of abuse and victimization, it is surprising to find sexual and spousal abuse. While reading through festival organizers' websites, I came across a moving example of this paradox—the openness and desire to help each other heal and the denial that serious spousal abuse could exist within their community. On EarthSpirit's public website—available to anyone surfing the Internet, I read a letter an EarthSpirit member had sent "to my community" in which she detailed a history of abuse by her male partner and coven mate, as well as her discovery that her partner, who had refused to participate in an open relationship with her, had sexual relationships with many of her friends and other participants at festivals.

These examples suggest how difficult it is to unlearn behavior, to be new selves and to form ideal communities at festivals and in the Neo-pagan movement generally. Neopagan festivals try to institute new rules and guidelines. They expect festival goers to act differently on cue, through acts of self-will. But the lack of boundaries at ritual fires may force people to fall back on habitual behaviors. In "an unruly mass of strangers," as Damarru characterizes the festival fire, participants may forget that the erotic dancer in front of them may be dancing "for the fire" and not for their personal entertainment. Others doubt festival or-ganizers' assurances that sexual harassment will be severely dealt with. The ritual fire is characterized by ambiguity; it is for "letting loose," but also for "direct contact with Spirit." Clearly not everyone attends the fire to work on personal transformation and "the attainment of higher states of consciousness." Some come to "trance dance" or engage in what they call "shamanic journeying"; others approach the fire to express themselves with a physical freedom impossible in other social contexts. Late-night fire participants may be looking for a party atmosphere, pro-vided by the spectacle of dancing bodies and fire jumping.

One of the ongoing conflicts at ritual fires is between festival goers who want to use the space for late-night parties and those who want to keep it a sacred space for ritual work. Salome characterizes the ambigu-ous nature of the fire's "party atmosphere": "I think it's so great after a big ritual and people are throwing whatever they throw into the fire. They have sparklers and they throw stuff that sparkles into the fire and every-body's all painted up and people have wands and all their ceremonial clothes on. It's really like a big party."[71] At Pagan Spirit Gathering, sev-eral announcements about "abuse" of the ritual space were made at daily village meetings. At ELFest 1992, Chris, who was attending her second Lothlorien festival, complained to me that the previous year "biker-looking" men were staggering drunk around the fire and getting in the way of dancers. Concerns about inappropriate behavior at festival fires were voiced at several festivals I attended during my field work in 1992. An article in *The Elven Chronicle* suggested that drinking parties should be banned from the ritual circle. While the fire is certain to mean differ-ent things to different people, there are some activities, participants argue, which violate its sacredness and cannot be tolerated. The "ELF91 Grand Council report" includes several comments about the problematic nature of the fire: "Dana said she feels the drums are too loud at night. . . . Deb-orah said she doesn't like hooping and hollering. . . . Midnight stated that Thunder was built as a shrine. She doesn't like the 'party' or 'theatre' atmosphere. She asked that people be respectful—keep the tourist energy down."[72] Festival goers are asked by festival sponsors not to bring bottles into the ritual space or throw cigarette butts in the fire. The *Elven Chronicle*'s Ms. Manners and other critics of party behavior identify issues of purity that are central to the ritual fire as a sacred place. "Tourist energy," as they put it, identifies some ritual fire participants as outsiders who do not really belong at the festival in the first place.

These criticisms are meant to guide and define the festival community by drawing lines between appropriate and inappropriate behavior. The *Chronicle* reported that at the Grand Council meeting, Midnight asked "that there be no cigarette butts, and to start fires organically (no kerosene)." Ms. Manners similarly wants the ritual circle to be a place set apart from the profane activities taking place on the rest of the festival grounds. Ms. Manners sums up questionable behavior at the late night festival fire:

> Third shift, as we understand it, is ritual space where the drum's voices are mingled with the ritualists' heartbeats in a trance inducing a mixture of beats, silence, sweat, smiles and rhythmic community chants designed to intertwine with the quiet magic of the angels' drumming. . . . Ms. Manners must ask the question: do these lovely angels really want to come to an atmosphere of: loud, show-off blasts on congas; drying wet sox (etc.); cooking hot dogs over the ritual fire (unless it is Friday) . . . overt sexual grabbing; drinking songs; exaltations of how late it is and isn't it great to be part of third shift; getting falling down drunk; suggesting women have no right to drum and should let the MEN do it; and lover's quarrels. Are these really conducive to keeping the community trance energy?

For many festival participants, music and nude dancing signify an atmosphere where "anything goes," while for other late-night drummers and dancers, the festival fire is a sacred space in which self-transformation occurs in other ways. As festival communities attempt to resolve these differences and create guidelines for behavior, they engage in an ongoing process of self-definition.

The booklet "Festival Drumming" warns that because of the diversity of interests that converge at the festival fire, "differences, if not problems, in communication are likely."[73] Longtime festival drummer Ranger Rick sees the problem of the fire this way, "Everybody marches to the beat of a different drummer, but what happens when they all show up at the same time?"[74] Attempts to unify diverse styles and levels of skill through "the language of drumming" do not always transcend the various systems of belief and practice that men and women bring with them

to the festival fire. While cooperation does occur, dissatisfaction and tension are as likely. Some participants find community in the drumming
experience, while others experience frustration and a sense of isolation.

During Summerhawk 1992 I camped with Peh, who was often consulted about controversial issues. Early one afternoon Maddog stopped
by our campsite to give Peh his side of the story about a drumming controversy that took place the previous summer at a festival that Peh helped
organize. This controversy in particular and Maddog's drumming in general became the subject of an exchange of letters in *Mezlim*. He told Peh
that he wrote to *Mezlim* in order to draw attention to the unfair treatment he received at the hands of festival authorities. Maddog, a self-
described "chaos magician," claimed that his aggressive drumming style
is how he "prays" to his "gods and goddesses," and is "one of the oldest ways to reach oneness with the universe." He resents the efforts by
some festival organizers to limit his rights to self-expression and worship: "This festival-goer is sorry to experience and witness Drummers
being kicked around, badgered, bad mouthed and falsely accused of malicious mischief." The problem, argues Maddog, is not with the drumming, but with the festival goers who are disturbed by it. "I'm tired of
hearing the same line, 'We can't sleep!' Now, I know for a fact, you could
sleep if you'd stop fighting the beat and merge with it." Even "small children" he claims, "have slept under my drum on several occasions."
Raven Greywalker comes to Maddog's defense in another letter to *Mezlim*, in which she affirms his right to be "hard core," because "the oldest school or tradition of drumming is the inspired do-it-till-you-drop-
then-get-up-and-do-it-again school." She also points out that other
festival goers could benefit from "the all night drumming," instead of
complaining about it: "The shamanic technique that feeds gatherings
some of that good energy we take home when it's over. Those who don't
enjoy it and would rather sleep(?!) might wish to camp far away. I suggest ear plugs." Most festival drummers would probably agree that many
types of drumming are methods of worship, but according to Peh, other
festival goers see Maddog's reasoning as an excuse for self-indulgence.
According to Ms. Manners, "Thunder shrine is a community area where
events occur of a magical nature." This is all well and good, she says,
except for the fact that "some people's 'magickal nature' is other people's
'pain in the neck.' "

But tensions around drumming do not arise only between people who
want to stay up and drum and those who want to sleep; they are about
the meaning of drumming itself. Much of the negotiation concerning

drumming etiquette at the festival fire centers around defining what is
"proper" festival drumming. "As a practicing Shaman," Crow writes in
the *Elven Chronicle,* "drumming is a constant part of my relatedness to
the sacred. It feels to me both powerful and appropriate for the good of
all that there be a special and separate place during festivals for those of
us who wish to drum in a sacred way." At an ELF festival in 1993, I witnessed another episode in the ongoing struggle to clarify the meaning of
drumming at the late-night fire. ELF had spent thousands of dollars to
construct a dome over Thunder Shrine that they hoped would somewhat
contain the sound of drums. Festival organizers came up with some
guidelines, which they handed out to other festival participants. "Quiet
time begins at 11 P.M. and extends to 9 A.M." stated the guidelines, "We
have neighbors and some elves who need to sleep. This is not a totally
remote wilderness. We are not trying to be drunken primitives." But this
is exactly what some festival goers are "trying to be." For Maddog,
chaotic behavior of this sort is sacred. But the rules insist that "it is fine
to stay up late, drum & dance lightly in Thunderdome, play guitars, sing
or converse around the campfire circles." ELF organizers emphasize that
they want to control late-night activity and that those who do not comply "will be warned," and if they persist, "rejected without a refund."
According to ELF's rules the proper late-night behavior is to "keep it low
and easy, smooth as silk, gentle and peaceful (no war drums and animal
yells) so we have no troubles."

The "selves" who come together at the fire are not uncorrupted by the
world outside the festival; inevitably they bring it with them. They share
traumas from the past and play out childhood fantasies, they dance in
American Indian clothes and experiment with African drum beats. In the
struggle over the festival-fire experience at Lothlorien, all aspects of the
ritual came under scrutiny. Critics called into question styles of drumming
and dancing, and authority figures drew up rules of comportment. For
some festival goers the free-form circle at ELFest became a painful reminder
of divisiveness and contention within the community. It also came to represent the authority of some voices over others. A few Neopagans who
had participated in ELF events for years decided not to return to ELFest.
Instead of attending ELFest, a small group of dissatisfied festival goers held
their own "counter-fest," an all-night drumming and dancing ritual fire,
in another dome that one of them had built on his private property.

I was able to watch ELF's troubles with drumming come to a head
over a period of four years, during which time the dome over Thunder
was slowly constructed and rules were clarified. Several drummers told

me they would never again attend another ELF-sponsored festival, while other drummers formed an organization within ELF to consult with festival organizers on drumming issues. At Lothlorien, drumming controversies are likely to continue. While some former Lothlorien festival goers may start their own festivals elsewhere, others insist they will remain in the community to fight over these issues. At the nineteenth annual Rites of Spring, I learned that Rites staff had also experienced and dealt with problems around the late-night ritual fire. In response, they came up with several methods of making their late-night fire circle into a distinctly sacred space. "Please don't use this fire for casual socializing," warns the festival program. They also established late-night spaces specifically for socializing: "Late Nites at Rites Cafe" is described in the festival program as "a great space to hear good music, storytelling, poetry, and hang out with new friends." The Rites of Spring fire circle is located a ten-minute walk away from the main festival area and cannot be heard from most camp sites, so noise is not a problem. Rites of Spring staff found a solution to the conflicts over late-night fires by clarifying their intent for the fire and thus more tightly defining participants' experiences. They solved the noise problem and keep away "tourist energy" by removing the fire from the center of the festival site and placing it in an isolated circle in the woods, which they marked with a gateway and gatekeeper. But other festivals—Starwood, for example—seem committed to the notion of the free-form fire that never feels completely in control. This risks conflict and discomfort among some participants, but at the same time leaves open a range of late-night fire experiences.

Regardless of tensions around the fires, individual festival goers continued to tell me how much they benefited from drumming and dancing. It is possible for them to leave worries outside the walls of Thunder and other ritual spaces, to enter the ritual circle and forget about last year's arguments, to surrender to the drums and dance the night away. In the aftermath of conflicts and power struggles, Neopagans assure each other that festivals are for community renewal and individual growth. More than simply allowing their "real selves" to come out in wild dancing and frenzied drumming, festival goers work on transforming the pain, illness, awkwardness, and wounds they bring with them. Certainly festival goers experience transformative moments, and these moments may even occur as a result of community tensions and ongoing power struggles.

Individual stories like Salome's and Michael's convey this sense of personal change most vividly. They remembered ELFest as a turning point in their personal journeys. Each of them performed around the fire in his or her own way. Salome "went crazy" and then lay down by the fire in a trance for hours. Michael took off his clothes, exposing his recent nipple piercings for the first time, and joined the dancers circling the fire. At the end of the four-day ELFest, Salome returned to her college dorm from the festival, certain that her experiences at the fire had helped along her recovery from a long bout of mental illness and hospitalization. Michael returned to the office where he works as an architect feeling that his sense of his own body had undergone a transformation. As he wears his blue steel nipple rings under his normal office clothes, he is reminded of what it was like to dance around the fire. Michael assures me, "I have come through a mountain pass into a new country that was different from where I had been before." In *Between Theater and Anthropology*, performance theorist Richard Schechner distinguishes between two kinds of performances, both of which occur at Neopagan festivals. "Transportive" performance, writes Schechner, temporarily transports the performer, but at the end of the performance, he or she returns to the starting point. On the other hand, "transformative" performance irrevocably changes the performer.[75] In Neopagan terms a "new self" emerges at festivals: new ways of moving and tattoos transform the body; new friendships and relationships are forged and old relationships ended—there is no going back to the "old" self; and lives are irrevocably changed. As they expected when they set out on the journey to a festival, "Anything that happened there could not help but transform me."[76]

As we have seen, this transformation takes place on many levels, as Neopagans locate themselves in relationship to their neighbors and to other religions, as they decide whom to include and exclude from their communities, and as they set limits on appropriate behavior. Neopagan festivals take shape in a dynamic network of meaning that is discursive, experiential, and contestational. Neopagans are highly self-reflective; they engage in an ongoing conversation about their own actions. As with other festival issues, they make meaning out of the festival fire by gossiping, complaining, protesting, and sharing stories about others' behavior as well as their own and divulging details of their sensual, bodily experience. Discussions about behavior, sexuality, identity, and spirituality occur before, during, and after rituals, in small group meetings, in newsletters, on websites, and in nationally distributed Neopagan periodicals. At the Church of All Worlds "May Queen and King" meeting at Ancient Ways 1997, one participant remarked, "We are all fringe people and we want others to be tolerant, but sometimes we tolerate too much." In most cases, as I have argued, the meanings of their stories are contested and ambiguous. As women dance around the fire, they look relaxed and beautiful, but the following day one of them may confess that she experienced harassment or felt forced to leave the intensity of the fire and retreat to the safety of her tent. Different strategies for resolving issues around the festival fire reflect broader trends in the Neopagan movement. If the fire is to feel safe for everyone, then the behavior of some participants must be controlled. But any effort to restrict self-expression is seen by some festival goers as a failure to realize the Neopagan value of individualism. Conflicts and debates such as those around the festival fire are largely responsible for bringing forth new understandings of self and community at Neopagan festivals.

Conclusions

The Circle Is Open but Never Broken

Throughout this study I have raised issues concerning the creation of new selves within Neopagan festival communities, and I have argued that the most important problems of self-invention emerge at boundaries.[1] Questions about self-identity are most troubling and conflicted during boundary work because drawing boundaries necessitates defining one space against another, one community against neighboring communities, and the self in relation to ancient or marginalized cultures. At the boundaries, endless possibilities seem to exist, but so do their limits. Dancing oneself into a trance state at the festival fire or borrowing deities from an array of different cultures can open up the boundaries of the self and make all things seem possible. However, while taking off one's clothes seems the ultimate freedom, it may also result in sexual harassment, just as free-form drumming may elicit angry reactions from other festival goers who are trying to sleep, and referring to one's past life as an American Indian may incite critics of cultural "genocide." At many different festival boundaries, festival goers encounter and explore possibilities for self-transformation, only to discover limits where they least expected them.

In this final discussion, I bring Neopagan self-making strategies into relation with contemporary theories of subjectivity and use the Neopagan case to reflect on the fate of the self in late twentieth-century American religion and society. In order to do this I first turn to some of the ways in which Neopaganism diverges from its roots in the 1960s. I suggest some directions for future research on new religious movements that developed during the decade or so following the 1960s. What we have seen of Neopagan self-creation in festival rituals like the late-night fire and in discussions of cultural borrowing and accounts of childhood, indicates a tension between two understandings of self. The first kind of self might be called the fluid, "post-modern self" described by French philosopher Jean-François Lyotard in *The Postmodern Condition.* The second view of the self is the deep, inward, "modern self" identified by philosopher Charles Taylor in *Sources of the Self: The Making of the Modern Identity.* [2]

John, one of my first Neopagan informants, told me that Neopaganism is the ideal postmodern religion; that is, the eclecticism of borrowing and other Neopagan practices follow from the belief that identity and tradition are not fixed but malleable.[3] As Lyotard puts it, "Eclecticism is the degree zero of contemporary general culture"; it is the attitude that "anything goes."[4] Cultural geographer Rob Shields characterizes postmodernism with the same kind of self-making that takes place at festivals: "New modes of subjectivity . . . are thus being experimented with, browsed through, and tried on, in much the same way that one might shop for clothes."[5] Festival goers "try on" selves by shopping for costumes, masks, jewelry, and ritual tools along Merchants' Row. This kind of postmodern self is also consciously pursued by Neopagans who "browse through" local sites of knowledge, such as childhood memories and small-town occult shops or ritual groups, as well as global sites— websites that make available Victorian occult texts and museum displays on ancient Egypt.[6] Back at home from the festival, Neopagans invent Internet personas and participate in discussions about mythology, magical techniques, cultural borrowing, and ritual practices with other Neopagans from around the world.[7]

Many Neopagans would probably agree that lifestyle choices are the tools of self-experimentation and that an individual's "multiple identifications form a private *dramatis personae*—a self which can no longer be simplistically theorized as unified, or based solely on an individual's job or productive function."[8] Neopagan literature and stories discussed over the Internet and at festivals share with other contemporary American biographies the assumption that they can start over, be "reborn," change their gender, and leave behind their past. This free-flowing, decentered view of subjectivity is based in part on the notion of a self with no depth or essence. That Neopagans have been affected by this view is evident from their many comments about remaking the self in festival space, about the changeable nature of religious identity, and especially about shaping the body through tattoos and costumes. In debates about cultural borrowing, Ranfeadhael, the "shaman-in-training," argues that nothing—neither self, nor culture—is pure. Neopagans try on personas at festivals with the assurance that they can become different selves at will, that they can surround themselves with newly invented families and throw off their Christian pasts without looking back.

Although at festivals Neopagans play with endless possibilities for remaking the self, this apparent fluidity of self is in tension with another characteristically Neopagan view that places a "deep" self in the center of the Neopagan world. In ritual work Neopagans act as though the self has depths and as if essential truths about the "real" self are there to be discovered. Neopagan technologies of the self focus on what Taylor describes as two important characteristics of modern self-identity: multiple layers and inwardness.[9] Neopagans are interested in digging into the depths of the self, unearthing childhood mysteries, and experimenting with "archetypes" that they "need." In Kenn Deigh's ELFest 1991 ritual, participants were asked to descend into the underworld of the self to meet the goddess who dwells there. This is not a new approach to self-understanding. It was St. Augustine (354–430 C.E.), argues Taylor, "who introduced the inwardness of radical reflexivity and bequeathed it to the Western tradition of thought." Like Augustine's approach to knowledge of self and God, Neopagan rituals are characterized by the assumption that "the route to the higher passes within," and it is this assumption that places Neopagans in the very tradition they work so hard to reject.[10] They pursue the "higher" or "real" self in ritual work and at festivals. However, Neopagans might go beyond the Augustinian version of self by arguing that the goddess *is* within and one need continue no farther along "the route."

Neopagans tell stories of past lives and childhood experiences that suggest that the self has many layers, and their festival rituals encourage journeys inward to seek divinity. It is this sense of inwardness and depth, argues Taylor, that builds up through the whole modern period in writers like Thomas Mann and James Joyce, whose work shows "an awareness of living on a duality or plurality of levels, not totally compatible, but which can't be reduced to unity."[11] Neopagans speak directly to the experience of living with multiple selves when they describe "real," "mundane," "higher," and "child" selves. They tend to be acutely aware of shifts between selves and contexts and even make these shifts explicit.

For instance, they say they are "in the closet" when they haven't revealed their beliefs to their families and hide pentacles beneath their clothes when at work. But at festivals their clothing, jewelry, and behavior identify Neopagan selves: Druids, Witches, Greek goddesses, and Native American shamans.

Taylor is critical of the displacement of the solidarities of birth and family by personal goals of self-realization, but on this Neopagans would disagree with him. They might argue that Taylor's understanding of these solidarities neglects to take into account how abusive and distressing families can be, especially to homosexuals who seek new families and "tribes" in the Neopagan community. Remembering their ostracism from family members and their discomfort in a world defined by what they see as rigid Christian doctrines and morality, many Neopagans feel they have no choice but to seek alternative families and communities. Invented families and new religious forms or pantheons of deities are more hospitable places for these men and women. "Family" and "tribe" have not disappeared as the locus of moral authority, but they have been redefined, no longer determined by birth, blood, name, and institutional affiliation.

By setting my observations of Neopagan techniques of the self in relation to what others have said about subjectivity in the contemporary West, I argue that Neopagans exemplify the modern self as it is conceived by these thinkers and that Neopagan efforts at self-creation show that a location in space and within a defined religious community is necessary for, even when it conflicts with, the inward turn to self-excavation.

Neopagans would seem to be extreme religious postmodernists. Their religious forms would also seem to embody shifts that American religions went through during and after the 1960s and 1970s. But Neopagans' emphasis—especially at festivals—on creating home and tribe is often in conflict with the demands of personal autonomy, and what seems to be a free-floating, constantly reinvented self is quickly constrained by the desire for authenticity and tradition. The needs of the self are always being circumscribed by the needs of others and by conditions set in the larger community. Festival programs and the content of festival workshops suggest that Neopagans have a strong sense of collective as well as individual identity, often forged in conflicts against the other: suspicious Christian neighbors and an ignorant public that assumes that Neopaganism is satanic. It may also be the case that the focus within the Neopagan movement has shifted away from unlimited individual freedom toward the needs of community, as many of the older festivals have been running for more than fifteen years. A participant in Rites of Spring

1997 said to me that the festival is "growing up." Back in its early years, he explained, it was about debauchery and wife-swapping, but now it offers children's programs and twelve-step groups.

While Neopagans at first seem to have picked up the trend toward personal autonomy identified by analyses of the sixties, they embed this trend in a framework of interconnectedness. Because of their desire to connect with ancient others and today's marginalized cultures, Neopagans locate the self in a network of relationships. They may even contextualize the self in relation to authentic sweat lodges, as some festival goers have done, and "pure" African drumming techniques, as Louis does in his involvement with the New Orleans Vodou community. They connect their religious lives to the holidays of Ancient Celts and Romans, the persecution of American Indians or Salem witches, early childhood experience, and the parents and grandparents who modeled the religious quest for them. Their personal journeys are intimately related to the divine in self, other, and in nature—located by definition outside the self. Neopagan festivals make it clear that the self is rooted in special places and connected to important others.

Neopaganism poses some questions about the relationship between personal autonomy and commitment to community in late twentieth-century American religion. I propose that the individualism that emerged in the 1960s was coupled with the desire to belong to a self-chosen religious community, not to the church of one's parents. For Neopagans, personal autonomy is both a turning inward to one's own moral authority *and* the outward expressions of self that take place in relation to others and within a larger community. Neopagans constantly negotiate between the authority of the self and requirements for community life. The assumption that governs writing about contemporary moral life, namely that personalized religion necessarily means that each self is in its "own moral universe," neglects to consider the importance of relational factors to contemporary moral agents.

I bring my observations about the two kinds of Neopagan selves—the nonessential, free-floating self and the deep self—into conversation with sociologist Anthony Giddens's understanding of self-identity in "late modernity." Giddens argues that the search for an autonomous self-identity in late modernity is giving way to the attempt to situate the self in new social movements, religions, and contexts.[12] New narratives of self are thus required to replace traditional contexts of locating the self in the world. The issues Neopagans work on as they construct identities are specific to the late twentieth century or to the situation of "high modernity," as Giddens calls it: "In the post-traditional order of modernity, and against the backdrop of new forms of mediated experience, self-identity becomes a reflexively ordered endeavour. The reflexive project of the self, which consists in the sustaining of coherent, yet continuously revised, biographical narratives, takes place in the context of multiple choices as filtered through abstract systems."[13] Neopagans are experts on "the reflexive project of the self" as it is described by Giddens. They make the project of self-construction seem less arbitrary by sharing coherent stories about themselves that progress in a linear fashion. They gather pieces of identity from different cultures, from fiction and from fantasy, and put these pieces together into a coherent whole by referring to childhood. The stories Neopagans tell about their lives focus on the meaning of self and attest to the significance of individuality within the Neopagan community. But these personal stories are told in order to highlight common themes and experiences that have value for most Neopagans. Personal narrative works to shape a common cultural and moral universe.

Like Neopagans, Giddens views the body as an essential factor in the project of self-making: "An important feature of a society of high-reflexivity," explains Giddens, is "the open character of self-identity and the reflexive nature of the body." Giddens's comments on the role of the body in self-reflexivity can be grounded in Neopagan practice, especially in drummers' and dancers' self-descriptions. "Experiencing the body is a way of cohering the self as an integrated whole, whereby the individual says 'This is where I live.' " Erotic dance and body art tell Neopagans "where they live," and tattoos and piercings mark the body as a dwelling for the self. Neopagan bodies "carry identity," to borrow a phrase from Giddens, in erotic dance, drumming, costuming, and body art. But the body is much more than a carrier; the body is also "a site of interaction, appropriation and re-appropriation."[14] Neopagans appropriate cultural idioms with body art and costume, and they interact with other festival goers through ritual movement and dance.

By putting the festival fire last, I pointed to the fact that the most apparently liberating form of bodily self-expression must be contextualized by the requirements of community life. Michael's story of baring his nipple rings in public suggests again that the self must be recognized by and performed for the community in order to be "real." While body transformations like tattoos are personal statements, they are statements that take on significant meaning in a community that admires and appreciates these tattoos. Dancing erotically and exposing tattoos and piercings are signs of belonging at the same time that they are intimate expressions of personal identity.

At a midsummer Neopagan festival, I was standing in the dark outer circle of the festival fire when I was approached by someone I had interviewed that morning. This black-hooded man from an army base in Maine pointed out to me a friend of his who had worked as an exotic dancer. Her female lover, he said, had been encouraging her to dance more loosely. She had been feeling inhibited about taking off her clothes at the festival and in particular while dancing around the fire. She had told him that she wanted to learn how to dance for herself instead of an audience. Her desire to replace the sense of herself as a performer for an audience's enjoyment with less self-conscious movement was realized by the end of the festival. He later asked that I watch her dance, that I notice how she seemed to be lost in her own movement without awareness of herself as a body observed. By then she had removed all her clothes and joined the other nude and half nude dancers closest to the fire. She was both a female body displayed before an audience and a woman dancing for her own pleasure. She made use of the fire to reshape her past and experiment with a new kind of self. And her black-shrouded friend used this opportunity to create a story about her movement between different identities, a story that highlighted for me both the possibilities and limitations of festivals.

The tension between the pursuit of self-realization and the desire for a place in community is most sharply defined where the self encounters limits in the community. Neopagans seem to have taken the postmodern creed and run with it, only to find that there were limits to where they could go: limits set by their neighbors and limits set by other cultures on the margins of American society. The apparent freedom to reimagine the self at festivals, for instance, in erotic dancing, is an ambiguous freedom, casting Neopagans back onto traditional assumptions about gender and sexuality at the same time that gender flexibility and sexual self-definition seem most attainable. Although self-exploration and sexual expression are promoted at festivals, they must be limited by the needs of others, by sexual-harassment policies and advice on safe sex. Rather than an untrammeled realm of sexual and social freedom, sexual and self-experimentation at Neopagan festivals necessitates hard work and results in new regulations of behavior. I do not want to eclipse the sense

of wonder and enchantment, the visual beauty, the powerful ritual experiences, the pleasure of festivals, and the utopian possibilities imagined at festivals. Neopagans testify that festivals are transformative, that
they further relationships with spirits and goddesses, that healing takes
place, that they experience liberation and renewed self-confidence, and
that they, however temporary it may be, provide an ideal community in
an imperfect world.

Notes

PREFACE

1. The term "Neopagan" signifies that these men and women are reinventing ancient pagan traditions or creating entirely new ones. Their religious beliefs and practices are usually self-consciously shaped to meet the needs of contemporary Americans and Europeans rather than to remain true to specific ancient religions.

2. Throughout this chapter about Neopagan stories, I use "Christian" as they do—to signify an all-encompassing category to which they contrast themselves.

3. Michael Kelly, "The Witches in the Whirlwind: Disfavor, Fame Find Arkansas Group Pursuing Beliefs," *The Commercial Appeal* (20 Oct. 1994). I found this story at http://www.raccoon.com/~aiko/news/commercial.html, though I read several other accounts of the Rileys' troubles during 1993 and 1994.

4. Kelly, "The Witches," n.p.

5. I chose these festivals for two reasons. I attended festivals that were the largest and longest running: Starwood, Rites of Spring, Pagan Spirit Gathering, Ancient Ways. I also attended those that were convenient to my location: ELFest, Wild Magick Gathering, Chants to Dance, and Sun Fest. These festivals were held at Lothlorien, a nature sanctuary in southern Indiana owned by the Elf Lore Family (ELF). Pagan Spirit Gathering was held at a privately owned campground near Madison, Wisconsin; Circle Harvest Fest was at Neopagan–owned Circle Sanctuary, also near Madison; Starwood and Summerhawk were held at Brushwood, a privately owned campground in southwestern New York; WinterStar, an indoor festival, took place at Atwood ski resort in northern Ohio; Ancient Ways was at Harbin Hot Springs, a New Age resort in northern California; Pantheacon, another indoor festival, was at the Oakland downtown Marriott hotel.

Regarding the spelling of "magick" (e.g., Wild Magick Gathering), some Neo-pagans spell it with a "k" to distinguish their ritual practices from stage magic. This spelling is used most often by ceremonial magicians who draw from the works of Victorian British occultist Aleister Crowley, who adapted this spelling in his important work *Magick in Theory and Practice* (New York: Dover Publications, 1929, reprint 1976).

6. Because this is a decentralized movement with little institutional structure and many people practicing as "solitaries" apart from covens or study groups, it is difficult to obtain an accurate membership number. In *A Community of Witches: Contemporary Neo-Paganism and Witchcraft in the United States*, sociologist Helen Berger estimates that there are 150,000–200,000 Neopagans in the United States (Columbia: University of South Carolina Press, 1999), 9.

7. Margaret A. Murray, *The Witch-Cult in Western Europe* (Oxford: Oxford University Press, 1921); Gerald B. Gardner, *Witchcraft Today* (New York: The Citadel Press, 1954. Reprint 1955). The best general introduction to Neopaganism is Margot Adler's *Drawing Down the Moon: Witches, Druids, Goddess-Worshippers, and Other Pagans in America Today* (Boston: Beacon Press, 1986). Others have described in detail the origins of contemporary Neopaganism, and I have no wish to duplicate their work. For instance, see Ronald Hutton, "The Roots of Modern Paganism," in *Paganism Today,* ed. Graham Harvey and Charlotte Hardman (London: Thorsons, 1996); Howard Eilberg-Schwartz, "Witches of the West: Neo-Paganism and Goddess Worship as Enlightenment Religions," *Neo-Paganism: A Search for Religious Alternatives* (Women's Studies Program, Indiana University, Occasional Series No. 3 [1988]): 93–120. Michael York provides helpful distinctions between Neopagan and New Age origins in *The Emerging Network: A Sociology of the Neo-Pagan and New Age Networks* (Lanham, Md.: Rowman and Littlefield, 1995). Aidan Kelley has written a detailed but controversial treatment of Pagan origins in *Crafting the Art of Magic: A History of Modern Witchcraft, 1939–1964* (St. Paul, Minn.: Llewellyn Press, 1991). See Donald H. Frew, "Methodological Flaws in Recent Studies of Historical and Modern Witchcraft," *Ethnologies* 20, no. 1 (1998): 33–65. Historian Keith Thomas describes popular occult practices in *Religion and the Decline of Magic* (New York: Charles Scribner's Sons, 1971).

8. Sources on Renaissance magic include: Ingrid Merkel and Allen G. Debus, eds., *Hermeticism and the Renaissance: Intellectual History and the Occult in Early Modern Europe* (Washington, D.C.: Folger Press, 1988); Wayne Shumaker, *The Occult Sciences in the Renaissance: A Study in Intellectual Patterns* (Berkeley and Los Angeles: University of California Press, 1972); Brian Vickers, ed., *Occult and Scientific Mentalities in the Renaissance* (Cambridge, Eng.: Cambridge University Press, 1984); D. P. Walker, *Spiritual and Demonic Magic from Ficino to Campanella* (London: The Warburg Institute, University of London, 1958); and Frances A. Yates, *Giordano Bruno and the Hermetic Tradition* (New York: Vintage, 1964). Prudence Jones and Nigel Pennick claim that Wicca derives much of its ritual framework from the Cambridge "myth and ritual school," and especially from the work of Jane Ellen Harrison (*A History of Pagan Europe* [London: Routledge, 1995]). Other helpful histories of ritual magic are E. M. Butler, *Ritual Magic* (Cambridge, Eng.: Cambridge University Press, 1979),

and Ellic Howe, *The Magicians of the Golden Dawn: A Documentary History of a Magical Order* (London: Routledge, 1972).

9. David Hall, *Worlds of Wonder, Days of Judgment: Popular Religious Belief in Early New England* (Cambridge, Mass.: Harvard University Press, 1989); Jon Butler, *Awash in a Sea of Faith: Christianizing the American People* (Cambridge, Mass.: Harvard University Press, 1990).

10. Robert Ellwood Jr., "The American Theosophical Synthesis," in *The Occult in America: New Historical Perspectives,* ed. Howard Kerr and Charles Crow (Urbana: University of Illinois Press, 1983), 111–34.

11. Catherine L. Albanese, *Nature Religion in America: From the Algonkian Indians to the New Age* (Chicago: University of Chicago Press, 1990).

12. Robert Ellwood Jr., *Alternative Altars: Unconventional and Eastern Spirituality in America* (Chicago: University of Chicago Press, 1979).

13. femrel-l@mizzou1.bitnet; Pagan Digest's e-mail address is brown. edu.uther+pagan@drycas.club.cc.cmu.edu; Arcana's e-mail address is arcana@brownvm. By the end of this project almost all the large festivals—Starwood, Ancient Ways, and Rites of Spring—had set up websites from which I also downloaded information. These sites are mentioned in footnotes.

14. I asked all Neopagans whom I quoted from interviews or the Internet if they would like me to use their magical name (a special name given them by their priest or priestess or assumed in ritual contexts) or a pseudonym. In several instances, Neopagans who practice openly, especially those who function as media experts, told me to use their real names. I have followed their wishes. I also changed some identifying factors that might threaten the safety and anonymity of my informants.

15. Janet H. Murray, *Hamlet on the Holodeck: The Future of Narrative in Cyberspace* (New York: The Free Press, 1997), 252. For another important study of Internet communities, see Sherry Turkle, *Life on the Screen: Identity in the Age of the Internet* (New York: Simon & Schuster, 1995). Although both Murray and Turkle examine the ways in which narrative is used in MUDs and other computer-created realities, neither of these authors looks at the ways in which real communities are extended into the virtual space of the Internet.

16. Robert Ellwood Jr., *The Sixties Spiritual Awakening: American Religion Moving from Modern to Postmodern* (New Brunswick, N.J.: Rutgers University Press, 1994), 9.

17. Peter Clecak, *America's Quest for the Ideal Self: Dissent and Fulfillment in the 60s and 70s* (New York: Oxford University Press, 1983), 22. In *The Sixties: Years of Hope, Days of Rage* (New York: Bantam Books, 1987), Todd Gitlin sees the cultural context from which the sixties counterculture assumed responsibility for its contradictions (hope followed by rage being just one of these): "This generation was formed in the jaws of an extreme and wrenching tension between the assumption of affluence and its opposite, a terror of loss, destruction, and failure" (12). At rock concerts and other large gatherings as well as in communes and individual lives, the 1960s counterculture expressed a similar innocence and hope equated with childhood. Writing in 1977, Morris Dickstein agreed that "the sixties were a period that believed in magic and innocence, that had a touching faith in the omni-potence of individual desire" (*Gates of Eden:*

American Culture in the Sixties [New York: Penguin Books, 1977], 210). In his analysis of 1960s writers, Dickstein identifies a pervading belief that individuals could shape reality at will and that the most effective sources for social change are individuals, not institutions. Many commentators on the legacies of the 1960s agree that these goals failed and that disillusionment characterized the late 1960s (see Gitlin, Clecak).

18. Phillip E. Hammond, *Religion and Personal Autonomy: The Third Disestablishment in America* (Columbia: University of South Carolina Press, 1992), 10. Although Hammond concludes that the "third disestablishment" is "another step in the direction of secularization" (175), the New Age and Neopagan movements that are characterized by a high level of personal autonomy are hardly "secular," any more than widespread beliefs in astrology and ghosts.

19. Sociologist Steven Tipton criticizes the stripping away of moral authority from major institutions and withdrawal into the refuge of private life in *Getting Saved from the Sixties: Moral Meaning in Conversion and Cultural Change* (Berkeley and Los Angeles: University of California Press, 1982).

20. While anthropologists such as Clifford Geertz and Marilyn Strathern have argued that Westerners have a unified and coherent sense of self in contrast to the "others" of ethnographic inquiry, my research supports recent arguments by Michele Stephen and Katherine P. Ewing that in most cultures, "People can be observed to project multiple, inconsistent self-representations that are context-dependent and shift rapidly," while they experience the self as whole and consistent (Katherine P. Ewing discusses the shortcomings of Geertz's and Strathern's understandings of self-identity in "The Illusion of Wholeness: Culture, Self, and the Experience of Inconsistency," *Ethos* 18, no. 3 [Sept. 1990]: 251–78). Neopagans make the self seem consistent by telling stories that bring adult self and childhood experience together into a coherent identity. Stephen's study of Mekeo people's (of Papua New Guinea) views of the self as put forth in *A'Aisa's Gifts: A Study of Magic and the Self* (Berkeley and Los Angeles: University of California Press, 1995), xii, demonstrates the role of magic in self-construction.

21. Some of these self types are described in Diane Rothbard Margolis, *The Fabric of Self: A Theory of Ethics and Emotions* (New Haven: Yale University Press, 1998). Rothbard draws on George Herbert Mead's views of the self as something that "occurs in human interaction"—the first kind of self in my list. The astral plane is described by many Neopagans as a realm where humans meet and interact with spirits or deities. My understanding of the relationship between self and culture is informed by the essays in *Culture Theory: Essays on Mind, Self, and Emotion,* ed. Richard Shweder and Robert Levine (Cambridge, Eng.: Cambridge University, 1984).

22. For analysis and case studies of this trend, see Robert N. Bellah, Richard Madsen, William M. Sullivan, Ann Swidler, and Steven M. Tipton, *Habits of the Heart: Individualism and Commitment in American Life* (San Francisco: Harper and Row, 1985); and Wade Clark Roof, *A Generation of Seekers* (San Francisco: Harper, 1993).

23. See, for example, Harvey Cox, *Fire from Heaven: The Rise of Pentecostal Spirituality and the Reshaping of Religion in the Twenty-First Century* (Reading, Mass.: Addison-Wesley, 1995); and Elaine Lawless's work on Pentecostals,

God's Peculiar People: Women's Voices and Folk Tradition in a Pentecostal Church (Lexington: University Press of Kentucky, 1988).

24. I met Neopagan festival goers who also attended Lilith Fair, Lollapalooza, raves, the Burning Man festival, Grateful Dead shows, Rainbow gatherings, and the original Woodstock. See the Lilith Fair website: http://lilithfair.com. This is a more recent, female version of the earlier touring music festival, Lollapalooza, created by musician Perry Farrell and friends in 1991. For an analysis of the Burning Man festival as sacred space, see Sarah Pike, "Desert Gods, Apocalyptic Art and the Making of Sacred Space at the Burning Man Festival," in *God in the Details: Popular Religion and Everyday Life,* ed. Kate McCarthy and Eric Mazur (New York: Routledge, 2000). Information about raves is easily available on the Internet; for example, a rave network with many links is at http://www.hyperreal.org/raves/. Michael I. Niman, *People of the Rainbow: A Nomadic Utopia* (Knoxville: The University of Tennessee Press, 1997) is an academic study of Rainbow Festivals. Like festivals, outdoor concerts like Woodstock and Woodstock II were countercultural in terms of both appearance and behavior; nudity, unusual clothing, and experiences brought on by psychedelic drugs occurred at both kinds of events. In England, summer solstice gatherings at Stonehenge similarly celebrate pre-Christian religions, as well as being celebrations of a more general alternative culture. Christopher Chippendale's description of contemporary events at and conflicts over Stonehenge is outlined in the final chapter of *Stonehenge Complete* (Ithaca: Cornell University Press, 1983), 253–63.

INTRODUCTION

1. Neopagans create images of festivals as magical worlds out of the mythological stories, fantasy, and science fiction that many of them have loved since childhood. In her ethnography of Neopagans in contemporary England, T. M. Luhrman argues that Neopagan rituals recreate the experience of reading childhood fantasies like C. S. Lewis's Narnia stories, J. R. R. Tolkien's *Lord of the Rings,* Ursula LeGuin's *Earthsea Trilogy,* Marion Zimmer Bradley's *Mists of Avalon,* Dion Fortune's *Sea Priestess* and *Moon Magic,* and Dennis Wheatley's *The Devil Rides Out.* "These are probably the novels most magicians would choose as the most important fictional works about magic. . . . Most of them say that they loved these books or that these novels were what excited them about the idea of practicing magic" (T. M. Luhrman, *Persuasions of the Witch's Craft: Ritual Magic in Contemporary England* [Cambridge, Mass: Harvard University Press, 1989], 87). Most of Luhrman's findings can be applied to American Neopagans. Festivals, however, seem to be much more central to the Neopagan movement in the United States; one exception is the huge yearly festival that takes place near Stonehenge.

2. Circle Sanctuary, which sponsors PSG, revolves around Selena Fox, Dennis Carpenter, and other paid staff members who live or work at Circle Sanctuary in Mt. Horeb, Wisconsin (http://www.circlesanctuary.org/page2.html). Rites of Spring and Twilight Covening are sponsored by the EarthSpirit Community: Deirdre Pulgram Arthen, Andras Corban Arthen, and a close group of Arthen friends and family, originally based in the Boston area, but now living in western

Massachusetts (http://www.earthspirit.com/). Starwood is organized by the Association for Consciousness Exploration (ACE) and is primarily held together by Jeff Rosenbaum (home base in Cleveland, Ohio) and other members of the Chameleon Club (http://www.rosencomet.com/LINKS/index.html). Ancient Ways and Pantheacon are organized by the Ancient Ways store in Berkeley, California, whose owner Glenn Turner is the main organizer (http://www.conjure.com/AW/). These important people are usually acknowledged in festival programs, as are other staff. The Rites of Spring XIX program lists the following staff positions: coordinators, program coordinators, operations, registration, Healers Hall coordinator, Late Nite at Rites, volunteer coordinators, family programming, performances, feast coordinators, EarthSpirit store, merchants coordinator, fire circle guardian, broadsheet, sound and light technicians, chefs, fair coordinator, ground central, newcomer coordinator, Guiser's Ball, rides coordinator, website, mask making and ritual installations, and program book production.

3. For an excellent discussion of Neopagan rituals as an art form, see Sabina Magliocco, "Ritual Is My Chosen Art Form: The Creation of Ritual as Folk Art among Contemporary Pagans," in *Magical Religion and Modern Witchcraft*, ed. James R. Lewis (Albany: State University of New York Press, 1996): 93–119.

4. Starwood XV festival program.

CHAPTER 1. DRIVING INTO FAIRIE

1. Kenn Deigh, letter to author, 2 June 1992.

2. For general, cross-cultural studies of "magic" as a category, see Daniel O'Keefe, *Stolen Lightning: A Social Theory of Magic* (New York: Continuum, 1982), and Marcel Mauss, *A General Theory of Magic* (London: Routledge, 1972).

3. John Symonds and Kenneth Grant, eds., *Magic* (London: Routledge and Kegan Paul, 1973), 131. Also see Starhawk, *Dreaming the Dark: Magic, Sex and Politics* (Boston: Beacon Press, 1982); Doreen Valiente, *Natural Magic* (New York: St. Martin's Press, 1975); and Isaac Bonewits, *Real Magic* (New York: Berkly Publishing, 1972).

4. Mary K. Greer, *Women of the Golden Dawn: Rebels and Priestesses* (Rochester, Vt.: Park Street Press, 1995), 64. Greer's book provides an insider's perspective of the ways in which women involved in the Golden Dawn used ritual and magic to transform their lives.

5. Quotation from Loretta Orion, *Never Again the Burning Times* (Prospect Heights, Ill.: Waveland Press, 1995), 262.

6. Yi-Fu Tuan, *Space and Place: The Perspective of Experience* (Minneapolis: University of Minnesota Press, 1977), 6. Other important works on the construction of place and space are Gaston Bachelard, *The Poetics of Space*, trans. Maria Jolas (New York: The Orion Press, 1958, reprint 1964); Henri Lefebvre, *The Production of Space*, trans. Donald Nicholson-Smith (Oxford: Blackwell, 1974, reprint 1992); and Edward W. Soja, *Postmodern Cartographies: The Reassertion of Space in Critical Social Theory* (New York: Verso, 1989).

7. R. Laurence Moore discusses Chautauqua Sunday School Institutes in *Selling God: American Religion on the Cultural Marketplace* (New York: Oxford

University Press, 1994). Moore writes that the institutes "lasted for two weeks and were organized around lessons, sermons, devotional meetings, *plus* concerts, fireworks, bonfires, humorous lectures, and music" (151). In 1998, a Starwood participant pointed out to me that Chatauqua was ten miles down the road from Brushwood, Starwood's current site.

8. An anonymous message on the electronic "Arcana Discussion List for the Study of the Occult" (6 March 1994).

9. In *Alternative Altars*, Robert Ellwood Jr. identifies a stream of alternative religious expression, including Spiritualism, to which contemporary Neopaganism clearly belongs (*Alternative Altars: Unconventional and Eastern Spirituality in America* [Chicago: University of Chicago Press, 1979]).

10. See R. Laurence Moore, *In Search of White Crows: Spiritualism, Parapsychology, and American Culture* (New York: Oxford University Press, 1977).

11. Neopagans typically go by pseudonyms or first names only at festivals, both to protect anonymity and to reflect the informality and intimacy of festivals' atmospheres.

12. Rhianna, e-mail to author, 25 April 1995.

13. When talking about where their own dead have gone, some Neopagans use the term "Summerland," borrowing Spiritualists' name for the land of the deceased.

14. Neopagans are active in a wide variety of causes; environmentalism is probably the most common. Dennis Carpenter proposes in *Spiritual Experiences, Life Changes, and Ecological Viewpoints of Contemporary Pagans* (Ph.D. diss , Saybrook Institute, 1994) that environmental concerns arise among Neopagans as a direct response to their spiritual experiences.

15. Ann Braude, *Radical Spirits: Spiritualism and Women's Rights in Nineteenth-Century America* (Boston: Beacon Press, 1989), 19.

16. Outside criticism did not succeed in disrupting Spiritualist gatherings. Moore suggests that attacks against Spiritualists resulted in bonding and solidarity. See his "The Occult Connection? Mormonism, Christian Science, and Spiritualism," in *The Occult in America,* ed. Howard Kerr and Charles Crow (Urbana: University of Illinois Press, 1983), 135–61.

17. Braude, *Radical Spirits,* 43; Moore, *In Search of White Crows,* 40–69.

18. Neopagans make a point of disavowing other available religious options and affirming their individualized religious practices, whereas participants at Spiritualist gatherings might identify themselves as Christians or Quakers as well as Spiritualists. Neopagans are also generally much less concerned with social acceptance. Spiritualists worked hard to gain acceptance, to prove that their practices were scientifically verifiable, but Neopagans seem to celebrate and thrive on their own difference.

19. Moore, *Selling God,* 45–46. See also Leigh Eric Schmidt, *Consumer Rites: The Buying and Selling of American Holidays* (Princeton, N.J.: Princeton University Press, 1995).

20. Philosopher of "place" Eugene Walter argues in *Placeways* that "A place is a unity of experience, organizing the intercommunication and mutual influence of all beings within it" (Walter, *Placeways: A Theory of the Human Environment* [Chapel Hill: University of North Carolina Press, 1988], 23). See also John

F. Sears, *Sacred Places: American Tourist Attractions in the Nineteenth Century* [Oxford: Oxford University Press, 1979]).

21. Nathan Hatch, *The Democratization of American Christianity* (New Haven: Yale University Press, 1989), 50–52.

22. Flyer advertising "Harvest of Light: A Pagan Retreat," held near Columbia, Missouri, on Labor Day Weekend, 1993.

23. Sears, *Sacred Places*, 8–9. See also D. W. Meinig, ed., *The Interpretation of Ordinary Landscapes: Geographical Essays* (New York: Oxford University Press, 1979).

24. Historian Richard Slotkin argues in *Gunfighter Nation: The Myth of the Frontier in Twentieth-Century America* that the frontier myth is the United States' most characteristic one (New York: Atheneum, 1992). The frontier myth was originally detailed in Frederick Jackson Turner, *The Frontier in American History* (New York: Holt, Rinehart and Winston, 1920, reprint 1962).

25. Winthrop set out his vision in "A Model of Christian Charity," in *Puritan Political Ideas, 1558–1794,* ed. Edmund S. Morgan (Indianapolis: Bobbs-Merrill, 1965).

26. Alexis de Tocqueville, *Democracy in America*, trans. George Lawrence, ed. J. P. Mayer (New York: Doubleday, Anchor Books, 1969).

27. Roderick Nash, *Wilderness and the American Mind* (New Haven: Yale University Press, 1967, reprint 1973), 89. Nash traces this theme through the writings of John Muir and Aldo Leopold and discusses its manifestation in the 1960s counterculture.

28. My understanding of festivals as "places apart" has been helped by Beverly Stoeltje, "Festival," in *Folklore, Cultural Performances, and Popular Entertainments: A Communications-Centered Handbook,* ed. Richard Bauman (Oxford: Oxford University Press, 1992); Jean Duvignaud, "Festivals: A Sociological Approach," *Cultures* 3, no. 1 (Unesco Press, 1976): 13–25; Alessandro Falassi, *Time out of Time: Essays on the Festival* (Albuquerque: University of New Mexico Press, 1987); and Frank Manning, ed., *The Celebration of Society: Perspectives on Contemporary Cultural Performance* (Bowling Green, Ky.: Bowling Green University Press, 1983).

29. Neopagan festivals are marginal sites, or "heterotopias," to borrow Michel Foucault's term. There are places in every culture, says Foucault, "which are something like counter-sites, a kind of effectively enacted utopia in which . . . all the other real sites . . . are simultaneously represented, contested, and inverted." "Of Other Spaces," *Diacritics* 16 (1986): 24. Other kinds of heterotopias that Foucault discusses in this essay include fairgrounds on the outskirts of cities and Polynesian "vacation villages." Much of Foucault's work is taken up with issues of power and space. My understanding of festivals and power has also been helped by Derek Gregory, *Geographical Imaginations* (Oxford: Blackwell, 1994).

30. Rob Shields, *Places on the Margin: Alternative Geographies of Modernity* (London: Routledge, 1991), 112. G. Rinschede and S. M. Bhardwaj describe "place mythologies" as narratives of the virtues and sanctities of specific sites (Introduction to *Pilgrimage in the United States* [Berlin: Reimer Verlag, 1990], 11). But the sites they identify, like Neopagan festivals and the seaside retreats

described by Shields, probably have negative associations as well. Other studies of place mythologies that have helped me understand festivals include John A. Agnew and James S. Duncan, eds., *The Power of Place: Bringing Together Geographical and Sociological Imaginations* (Boston: Unwin Hyman, 1989); Anne Buttimer, *Geography and the Human Spirit* (Baltimore: Johns Hopkins University Press, 1993); James Duncan and David Ley, eds., *Place/Culture/Representation* (London: Routledge, 1993); and Tony Hiss, *The Experience of Place* (New York: Knopf, 1990). For some good examples of place myths see James Griffith, *Beliefs and Holy Places: A Spiritual Geography of the Pimeria Alta* (Tucson: University of Arizona Press, 1992); David Chidester and Edward T. Linenthal, eds., *American Sacred Space* (Bloomington: Indiana University Press, 1995); and Jamie Scott and Paul Simpson-Housley, eds., *Sacred Places and Profane Spaces: Essays in the Geographies of Judaism, Christianity and Islam* (New York: Greenwood Press, 1991).

31. Arnold van Gennep, *The Rites of Passage* (Chicago: University of Chicago Press, 1960), 21.

32. Ibid., 115. The importance of the liminal phase in ritual is most thoroughly explored in the work of Victor Turner, and especially in *The Ritual Process: Structure and Anti-Structure* (Ithaca: Cornell University Press, 1969).

33. Barbara Myerhoff, "Rites of Passage: Process and Paradox," in *Celebration: Studies in Festivity and Ritual,* ed. Victor Turner (Washington, D.C.: Smithsonian Institution Press, 1982), 116–17.

34. In *Dramas, Fields, and Metaphors: Symbolic Action in Human Society* (Ithaca: Cornell University Press, 1974), Victor Turner contrasts flexible, egalitarian liminal events to the stratified, normal world (200–201). Neopagans explore a similar contrast in their literature about festivals.

35. Stoeltje, "Festival," in Bauman, *Folklore,* 268. In his study of Brazilian *Carnaval*, anthropologist Roberto DaMatta describes the process by which a "special space" is "produced" for *Carnaval* by opposing "street" to "home" in the same way that Neopagans oppose festival to mundania (*Carnivals, Rogues, and Heroes: An Interpretation of the Brazilian Dilemma* [Notre Dame: University of Notre Dame Press, 1991], 81–84).

36. Margot Adler, *Drawing Down the Moon: Witches, Druids, Goddess-Worshippers, and Other Pagans in America Today* (Boston: Beacon Press, 1986), 424.

37. Salome, interview by author, 9 July 1993.

38. Margaret Thompson Drewel, *Yoruba Ritual: Performers, Play, Agency* (Bloomington: Indiana University Press, 1992), 174.

39. Quoted in Orion, *Never Again the Burning Times,* 146.

40. Vyvien, a Neopagan from Canberra, Australia, describes her first trip to a Church of All Worlds gathering (Pagan Summer Gathering 1992) in Australia (*Green Egg* 26, no. 101 [summer 1993], 30).

41. I heard this chant at many festivals, but most recently at Ancient Ways, 1997.

42. This places Neopagans in an American tradition of nature religion described by historian Catherine L. Albanese in *Nature Religion in America: From the Algonkian Indians to the New Age* (Chicago: University of Chicago Press, 1990). The concept of a "tribe" also turns up in an important phenomenon

closely related to Neopagan festivals: the Rainbow Gatherings. Rainbow gatherings are held on both regional and national levels and sponsored by a loose network of people called the "Rainbow Tribe." I have met many Neopagans at festivals who had attended at least one Rainbow Gathering; some festival participants even became exposed to Neopaganism through their involvement with the Rainbow Tribe. The national meetings are much larger than Neopagan festivals, with more than 10,000 participants.

43. *The American Heritage College Dictionary*, 3d ed. (Boston: Houghton Mifflin Company, 1993).

44. Moonstar, Introduction to "Reader's Forum," *Circle Network News* 7, no. 3 (fall 1985): 9.

45. Caitlin, *Circle Network News* 7, no. 3 (fall 1985): 10.

46. Starhawk discusses the links between changing consciousness and social change throughout *Dreaming the Dark,* but especially 114–34.

47. Lothlorien is the home of ELF festivals as well as festivals sponsored by other Neopagan groups such as The Trolls, who put on a spring festival called "Chants to Dance" or the Illuminati of Indiana, who have held several solstice festivals at Lothlorien. Wotanwald is based on an old Norse design and is the site for yearly gatherings "with a strong Norse/Teutonic flavoring" (*Circle Network News* 7, no. 3 [fall 1985]: 4).

48. Roberto DaMatta, "Carnaval, Informality, and Magic: A Point of View from Brazil," in *Text, Play and Story: The Construction and Reconstruction of Self and Society,* ed. E. M. Bruner (Washington, D.C.: American Ethnological Society, 1984), 230–46.

49. Announcement for Spiral Gathering, Atlanta, Georgia.

50. Orion, *Never Again the Burning Times,* 133.

51. Michael, cassette tape to author, 9 June 1992.

52. See for instance Victor Turner and Edith Turner, *Image and Pilgrimage in Christian Culture: Anthropological Perspectives* (New York: Columbia University Press, 1978); Robert A. Orsi, "The Center out There, in Here, and Everywhere Else: The Nature of Pilgrimage to the Shrine of Saint Jude, 1929–1965," *Journal of Social History* 25, no. 2 (winter 1991): 213–32; Alan Morinis, ed., *Sacred Journeys: The Anthropology of Pilgrimage* (Westport, Conn.: Greenwood Press, 1992); David L. Haberman, *Journey through the Twelve Forests: An Encounter with Krishna* (New York: Oxford University Press, 1994); and Barbara G. Myerhoff, *Peyote Hunt: The Sacred Journey of the Huichol Indians* (Ithaca: Cornell University Press, 1974).

53. Morinis, *Sacred Journeys,* 2.

54. Carpenter, *Spiritual Experiences,* 8–9.

55. Orion, *Never Again the Burning Times,* 154.

56. *Circle Network News* (published by Circle Sanctuary), "Pagan Gatherings Issue" (summer 1992).

57. Kenn Deigh, *Mezlim* 3, no. 2 (1992).

58. Anne Buttimer, "Home, Reach, and the Sense of Place." Many of the essays collected in *The Human Experience of Space and Place,* ed. Anne Buttimer and David Seamon (New York: St. Martin's Press, 1980) deal with the relationship between place and self-understanding (167). See also Winifred Gallagher,

The Power of Place: How Our Surroundings Shape Our Thoughts, Emotions, and Actions (New York: Poseidon Press, 1993).

59. Robert N. Bellah et al, *Habits of the Heart: Individualism and Commitment in American Life* (San Francisco: Harper and Row, 1985). Other commentators on late twentieth-century American religion and culture have made similar observations. See for instance Wade Clark Roof, *A Generation of Seekers* (San Francisco: Harper, 1993); and Walter Truett Anderson, *Reality Isn't What It Used to Be: Theatrical Politics, Ready-to-Wear Religion, Global Myths, Primitive Chic, and Other Wonders of the Postmodern World* (San Francisco: Harper and Row, 1990).

60. Spiral Gathering announcement, 1999.

61. PSG 1993 "Village Guide."

62. J. Milton Yinger observes in his study of "countercultural" religions that New Religious Movements tend to move in two directions, often both strands of movement within one group: "One branch adapting in some measure to the world around it while another pushes strongly against the dominant norms." J. Milton Yinger, *Countercultures: The Promise and the Peril of a World Turned Upside Down* (New York: The Free Press, 1982), 247. Movement in both directions is evident at Neopagan festivals.

63. Kenn Deigh, interview by author, November 1992.

64. Peh, conversation with author, 1 July 1993.

65. "Pagan Gatherings—Discovering Spiritual Homeland," flyer for 1993 Pagan Spirit Gathering.

66. From a mailing announcing Pagan Spirit Gathering 1995.

67. Orion's discussion of kinship and rites of passage is in *Never Again the Burning Times*, 244–54.

68. Flyer for Lumensgate 1994: "Opening the Way." Lumensgate is a small festival held at Brushwood Folklore Center in southwestern New York and sponsored by N'Chi, publishers of the Neopagan magazine *Mezlim*.

69. Adler, *Drawing Down the Moon*, 424.

70. Flyer for Harvest of Light, 1993.

71. Several of the festivals I attended held workshops that dealt with issues concerning religious freedom and alternative families, such as homosexual partnerships and polyamorous arrangements, where multiple sexual partners were described as an extended family. I also attended gay handfastings.

72. Rose, conversation with author, 29 May 1992.

73. Roger D. Abrahams, "Shouting Match at the Border: The Folklore of Display Events," in *"And Other Neighborly Names": Social Process and Cultural Image in Texas Folklore,* ed. Richard Bauman and Roger D. Abrahams (Austin: The University of Texas Press, 1982), 303–21.

74. Orion, *Never Again the Burning Times,* 262–64. My understanding of boundary making has been informed by Anthony P. Cohen, ed., *Symbolising Boundaries: Identity and Diversity in British Cultures* (Manchester, Eng.: Manchester University Press, 1986), and by David S. Hess's study of boundaries and the construction of self against other in *Science in the New Age: The Paranormal, Its Defenders and Debunkers and American Culture* (Madison: University of Wisconsin Press, 1993).

75. *Circle Network News,* "Pagan Gatherings Issue" (summer 1992), 17.

76. *Green Egg* 26, no. 101 (summer 1993): 30.

77. Orian, *Never Again the Burning Times,* 140.

78. Anthropologist Alan Morinis describes the continuity between pilgrimage and home: "While the sacred place is the source of power and salvation, it is at home once again that the effects of power are incorporated into life and what salvation is gained is confirmed" (*Sacred Journeys,* 27).

CHAPTER 2. SHRINES OF FLAME AND SILENCE

1. Conversation with author, Bloomington, Ind., November 1993.

2. Folklorists and anthropologists have studied issues of power in ritual and festival, paying particular attention to the ways in which social conflicts are expressed and resolved through ritual action. Folklorist Beverly J. Stoeltje describes three levels of "the circulation of power" in ritual genres: form, production, and discourse ("Power and the Ritual Genres: American Rodeo," *Western Folklore* 52, nos. 3–5 [April, July, Oct. 1993], 135–56). Analyses of power relations at festivals in the work of David Kertzer, Jean Duvignaud, Alessandro Falassi, and others have tended to look for public statements of authority and overt uses of power. My study builds on this work, but pays more attention to the ways in which conflicts are worked out within a small community as it makes meaning of sacred woods and shrines, rather than analyzing ritualized conflict between political institutions and their opposition. Duvignaud, "Festivals: A Sociological Approach," *Cultures* 3, no. 1 (Unesco Press, 1976): 13–25. Falassi, *Time out of Time: Essays on the Festival* (Albuquerque: University of New Mexico Press, 1987); and Manning, ed., *The Celebration of Society: Perspectives on Contemporary Cultural Performance.* Bowling Green, Ky.: Bowling Green University Press, 1983.

3. "In any society," Foucault observes, "there are manifold relations of power which permeate, characterise and constitute the social body, and these relations of power cannot themselves be established, consolidated, nor implemented without the production, accumulation, circulation and functioning of a discourse" (*Power/Knowledge: Selected Interviews and Other Writings, 1972–1977,* ed. Colin Gordon [New York: Pantheon Books, 1980], 93).

4. In *Dreaming the Dark,* Starhawk provides many examples of ways to replace relations characterized by "power-over" with "power-from-within."

5. Foucault, *Power/Knowledge,* 69.

6. Jeffrey, conversation with author, Needmore, Ind., 14 May 1992.

7. Salome, interview by author, Bloomington, Ind., 9 July 1993.

8. natrcl-l@uscolo.edu, 5 January 1999.

9. Ibid., 12 January 1999.

10. Colin, ibid., 5 January 1999.

11. Macha, e-mails to author on 30 November 1999 and 8 December 1999.

12. Pauline Campanelli and Don Campanelli, *Circles, Groves and Sanctuaries* (St. Paul, Minn.: Llewellyn Publications, 1994), 120.

13. Ibid., 125.

14. De-Anna Alba, "Gaia," *Circle Network News* 7, no. 3 (fall 1985): 14.

15. Michael, cassette tape to author, 9 June 1992.

16. Pagan Spirit Gathering 1993 Village Guide, 2.

17. While most Neopagans talk about energy in similar ways, they have a range of opinions about it. Some see it as a mental construct; others say it is the influential power of nature or deities.

18. Flyer for 1993 Pagan Spirit Gathering.

19. The quotation is from Starhawk, *Dreaming the Dark*, 10.

20. Peh, conversation with author, Bloomington, Ind., 31 May 1992.

21. In response to questions by readers of the listserve Arcana, folklorist Lee Irwin identifies sweetgrass as "heirochloe odorata." Translation something like Hier-sacred, chloe-grass, odorata-smell . . . or "sacred, great-smelling, grass" (e-mail to author, 14 September 1993).

22. Caitlin Johnson, *Circle Network News* 7, no. 3 (fall 1985): 9.

23. Gary, e-mail to author, 5 January 1997.

24. Adler, *Drawing Down the Moon*, 25.

25. At coven or other small group meetings devoted to the deities of a specific tradition, participants are less likely to call on another culture's spirits, though the more eclectic pagan groups do just that.

26. Internationally distributed *Circle Network News* fulfills a similar function by networking Neopagans scattered around the world. Every issue includes a large section devoted to "passages": announcements of births, handfastings, deaths of people and animals, and initiations.

27. *The Elven Chronicle* (summer 1991): 5.

28. James Fernandez, *Bwiti: An Ethnography of the Religious Imagination in Africa* (Princeton, N.J.: Princeton University Press, 1982).

29. The Pagan Federation website, http://www.paganfed.demon.co.uk/.

30. Contemporary Druid revival groups in the United States have their origins in the imaginative rituals organized by a group of students at Carleton College in Northfield, Minn., in 1963, according to Margot Adler (*Drawing Down the Moon*, 323–24).

31. A "grove," like a witchcraft coven, is a small group that meets for rituals and networking. While covens are independent communities, groves compose a larger organization, such as Ar nDraiocht Fein, which is under the direction of the "Mother Grove." Similarly, the Church of All Worlds is made up of "nests," which are largely independent, but share news and information as well as common values and guidelines.

32. On the Druids, see Peter B. Ellis, *The Druids* (London: Constable, 1994); and Ronald Hutton, *The Pagan Religions of the Ancient British Isles* (London: Blackwell, 1991).

33. Bryan Perrin, "Dialog with the Earth Mother," *News from the Mother Grove* 4, no. 6 (June-July 1992), n.p.

34. Scott Pollack, "1,000 Pagans Running around Naked in the Forest: Let's Build It!" in *Fireheart* 7 (1993): 13–22.

35. Perrin, Dialog with the Earth Mother," n.p.

36. Traditional Wiccan altars generally contain some variation on the following lesson from Raymond Buckland: "The 'Altar Furniture' consists of a candle, or candles; incense burner (known variously as a 'censer' or 'thurible');

two dishes, one for salt and one for water; libation dish; goblet(s); and figures
to represent the deities. Of course this is not a hard-and-fast list. Feel free to add
or subtract according to your needs"(*Buckland's Complete Book of Witchcraft*
[St. Paul, Minn.: Llewellyn Publications, 1986], 22).

37. Ibid., 32 .

38. Leslie Petrovski, "Altars: Personal Areas Reflect '90s Spiritual Signature"
(*The Denver Post*, 7 February 1999).

39. Ramon A. Gutierrez, "Conjuring the Holy: Mexican Domestic Altars,"
in *Home Altars of Mexico,* ed. Dana Salvo (Albuquerque: University of New
Mexico Press, 1997), 39. Salvo's beautiful book features photographs and es-
says about home altars throughout Mexico. Vodou altars also share some of the
characteristics of Neopagan altars. For excellent photographs and discussion of
Vodou altars, see Mama Lola and Karen McCarthy Brown, "The Altar Room:
A Dialogue," in *Sacred Arts of Haitian Vodou,* ed. Donald A. Cosentino (Los
Angeles: UCLA Fowler Museum of Cultural History, 1995), 227–39.

40. Kay Turner and Suzanne Seriff, " 'Giving an Altar': The Ideology of Reproduction in a St. Joseph's Day Feast," *Journal of American Folklore* 100, no.
398 (Oct.-Dec. 1987): 446–60. See also Anne Lafferty, "How We Braid Our
Lives Together with Our Ancestors," *Ethnologies* 20, no. 1 (1998): 129–49.

41. Cynthia Eller, *Living in the Lap of the Goddess: The Feminist Spirituality Movement in America* (New York: Crossroad, 1993), 107–8. Eller's study
gives an excellent overview of feminist spirituality, which includes many Neopagan women.

42. In a study of Santeria festival altars, art historian David Brown argues
that altar making can be seen as "aesthetically marked, practical strategies of empowerment, advancement, and securing life's social and spiritual goods, within a
community of emergent relationships" ("Toward an Ethnoaesthetics of Santeria
Ritual Arts," in *Santeria Aesthetics in Contemporary Latin American Art*, ed. Arturo Lindsay [Washington, D.C.: Smithsonian Institution Press, 1996], 119).

43. Kevin, personal correspondence to author, 4 August 1992.

44. Ibid., 10 October 1991.

45. Pagan-Digest, 6, no. 23, 14 February 1999.

46. Pagan-Digest 6, no. 24, 20 February 1999.

47. Lunae Mica Alicia, ibid.

48. J. Perry Damarru, *Mezlim* 3, no. 2 (1992): 5.

49. For a discussion of Neopagan foodways, see Kerry Noonan, "May You
Never Hunger: Religious Foodways in Dianic Witchcraft," *Ethnologies* 20, no.
1 (1998): 151–73.

50. Eller, *Living in the Lap of the Goddess,* 1.

51. "A History of Circle Sanctuary and its Contributions to Wiccan Spirituality and Pagan Culture," Circle Sanctuary website, http://www.circlesanctu-
ary.org/page2.html, 1996.

52. Radical Faeries were a presence at most of the gatherings I attended. The
Radical Faerie movement began around 1978, according to Margot Adler, as an
attempt to infuse gay men's spirituality with elements of "the old Pagan nature
religions" (*Drawing Down the Moon,* 341–48).

53. "Fairy" and "Faerie" have confusing meanings, not corresponding to their spellings in any way. Lothlorien's "Faerie," the enchanted woods, have no associations with gay and lesbian identities, but refer to fairy tales and myths of magical lands and spirits. In recent years, however, Lothlorien also has a "fairy camp" for gay men and their friends.

54. Published in the Pagan Spirit Gathering 1993 Village Guide by Circle Sanctuary.

55. "A Gathering Primer" in *Mezlim* 3, no. 2 (1992): 5.

56. *The Elven Chronicle* (summer 1991): 2.

CHAPTER 3. THE GREAT EVIL
THAT IS IN YOUR BACKYARD

1. Peter Edwards, e-mail to author, 12 February 1991. Iain Walker, John Quinn, and Peter Day's long article details the destructive effects of rumors perpetuated by social workers, "The Attack on Innocence," *The Mail on Sunday* (England), 21 October 1990.

2. The quotation is from a "Religious Freedom Update" sent to various Internet listserves in order to gain support for The Church of Iron Oak's hearing with Palm Bay City's Planning and Zoning board (info@delphi.com, 1 July 1994).

3. Quotation from Jan Corrigan, *Green Egg* 26, no. 102 (autumn 1993): 58. The "fundies" quote is from Maethyn, femrel-l@mizzou1.bitnet, 9 February 1993.

4. Leo Louis Martello, *Witchcraft: The Old Religion* (Secaucus, N.J.: Citadel Press, 1973), 88.

5. Numerous examples of Neopagan press releases responding to accusations that they are "satanists" are mentioned in each issue of *Circle Network News*.

6. Llyselya, *Green Egg* Forum 25, no. 96 (1992): 41.

7. I consistently capitalize "Satanist" and "Witch" when referring to a chosen religious identity that has some institutional affiliation, just as I would capitalize "Baptist" or "Unitarian." I use a lower-case "s" when describing the popular view of satanists that is based on images from horror movies. I also use lower-case "w" in "witch" when discussing the image of the witch constructed in the minds of seventeenth-century witch hunters.

8. A similar example of police harassment was reported in Pagan Digest: "Last Beltane, the Yellow Springs Police Department paid a visit to our [outdoor] circle, asked us if we were performing human sacrifice, threatened to confiscate our sword, athames, etc." (Dan, *Pagan Digest*, 6 October 1991).

9. *The Herald Telephone* 19, no. 6 (September 1985).

10. Adler, *Drawing down the Moon*, 453.

11. Chris Carlisle, e-mail to author, 2 December 1991.

12. J. Gordon Melton, "Satanism," *The Encyclopedia of American Religions* (Wilmington, N.C.: McGrath, 1978), 301.

13. Jeffrey S. Victor, *Satanic Panic: The Creation of a Contemporary Legend* (Chicago: Open Court, 1993); James T. Richardson, Joel Best, and David G. Bromley, eds., *The Satanism Scare* (New York: A. de Gruyter, 1991); and

Robert D. Hicks, *In Pursuit of Satan: The Police and the Occult* (Buffalo: Prometheus Books, 1991).

14. An excellent short summary of the forces behind and facts about "the satanism scare" is John Johnson and Steve Padilla's, "Satanism: Skeptics Abound," *Los Angeles Times*, 23 April 1991.

15. Ibid.

16. Late twentieth-century rumors about satanic cults had their beginning in 1980 with the release of *Michelle Remembers* by Michelle Smith and Lawrence Pazder (New York: Congdon and Latté, 1980), one woman's account of being trapped in a satanic cult. More recent accounts, such as Lauren Stratford's 1988 book, *Satan's Underground,* which sold 140,000 copies, have continued to spread stories of satanic ritual abuse and entrapment (Johnson and Padilla, "Satanism"). For a critical analysis of sexual abuse and ritual abuse cases based on recovered memories see Elizabeth Loftus and Katherine Ketcham, ed., *The Myth of Repressed Memory: False Memories and Allegations of Sexual Abuse* (New York: St. Martin's Griffin, 1994).

17. See, for example, *Green Egg* 26, no. 101 (summer 1993): 46.

18. *Circle Network News* 17, no. 2 (1995): 7.

19. Chris Carlisle, Arcana, 5 March 1993.

20. Quoted in Catharine Cookson, "Reports from the Trenches: A Case Study of Religious Freedom Issues Faced by Wiccans Practicing in the United States," *Journal of Church and State* 39, no. 4 (autumn 1997): 723 48. Cookson describes many more cases of persecution—both court cases and stories shared with her by Neopagan informants.

21. Iron Oak website: http://ddi.digital.net/~ironoak/ (January 1997).

22. *The Martinsville* [Ind.] *Reporter* (29 September 1989).

23. The quotation comes from Melton's excellent entry on "Satanism" (*Encyclopedia of American Religion*) in which he carefully distinguishes between witchcraft, Neopaganism, and different kinds of practitioners of Satanism, 301.

24. Lowell D. Streiker, "The Opening of the American Mind: A Fresh Look at Cults of Persecution," *Journal of Ecumenical Studies* 27, no. 4 (fall 1990): 732.

25. Thomas A. Tweed and Stephen Prothero, eds., *Asian Religions in America: A Documentary History* (Oxford: Oxford University Press, 1999), 62.

26. See, for example, James B. Tabor and Eugene V. Gallagher, *Why Waco? Cults and the Battle for Religious Freedom in America* (Berkeley and Los Angeles: University of California Press, 1995). Other scholars of new religions have made similar observations about the social function of persecution. See for example, J. Gordon Melton and Robert L. Moore, eds., *The Cult Experience: Responding to the New Religious Pluralism* (New York: Pilgrim Press, 1982); and Robert Bellah and Frederick Greenspahn, eds., *Uncivil Religion: Interreligious Hostility in America* (New York: Crossroad, 1987).

27. Don Hudson Frew, "A Brief History of Satanism," *Witchcraft, Satanism and Occult Crime: Who's Who and What's What,* Starwood Festival program, 4th ed., n.p., n.d., 4.

28. According to Wuthnow, "conservatives" and "liberals" face off on most important social and religious problems (*The Restructuring of American Religion* [Princeton, N.J.: Princeton University Press, 1988], 10). Sociologist James

Davison Hunter characterizes these two competing visions as "orthodox" and "progressive" (*Evangelicalism: The Coming Generation* [Chicago: The University of Chicago Press, 1987], 44).

29. The cooperation of Protestant evangelicals with conservative Catholics on moral issues such as abortion and the dangers of Neopaganism are part of what Mark J. Rozell and Clyde Wilcox call "the second coming of the Christian Right" (*Second Coming: The New Christian Right in Virginia Politics* [Baltimore: Johns Hopkins University Press, 1996], 215).

30. Fiction and nonfiction authored by conservative Catholics that demonize Neopaganism and "occult" practices and consider religions like Neopaganism dangerous includes the following: Bud Macfarlane, *Pierced by a Sword* (Cleveland: Saint Jude Media, 1995); Michael O'Brien, *Father Elijah: An Apocalypse* (San Francisco: Ignatius Press, 1996); and Michael H. Brown, *The Final Hour* (Milford, Oh.: Faith Publishing, 1992). Books by conservative evangelical Protestants that identify Neopaganism and occult practices as evidence of a satanic conspiracy include Jerry Johnston, *The Edge of Evil: The Rise of Satanism in North America* (Dallas: Word Publishing, 1989); Randall N. Baer, *Inside the New Age Nightmare* (Lafayette, La.: Huntington House, 1984); and Constance Cumbey, *The Hidden Dangers of the Rainbow: The New Age Movement and Our Coming Age of Barbarism* (Shreveport, La.: Huntington House, 1983).

31. See Ted Peters, *The Cosmic Self: A Penetrating Look at Today's New Age Movements* (San Francisco: HarperSanFrancisco, 1991).

32. Rogers is also the founder of Media House International, a clearing house for conservative Christian news. His web page is at http://forerunner.com/jaysbio.html. A Pagan Digest member alerted other readers of the Digest to an article linking abortion (described as "child sacrifice") and Wicca. The article linking Neopaganism to abortion was found at URL http://forerunner.com/champion/X0038.html.

33. From *Green Egg* 25, no. 97 (summer 1992): 55.

34. Cookson, "Reports from the Trenches," 730.

35. Ibid., 736.

36. Elendil, Pagan Digest, 31 March 1994.

37. Nancy Tatom Ammerman, *Bible Believers: Fundamentalists in the Modern World* (New Brunswick, N.J.: Rutgers University Press, 1987), 97.

38. Battles against Neopaganism and rumors about satanic neighbors take place in an apocalyptic framework described by Nancy Ammerman in *Bible Believers,* 5. Hal Lindsey, author of the best-selling *The Late Great Planet Earth* links "the rise of Satanism to the Last Days prophesied in the Book of Revelation" (*The Late Great Planet Earth* [New York: Bantam Books, 1970, reprint 1973]). See also Roger Elwood's Christian horror novel, *The Christening* (Eugene, Or.: Harvest House Press, 1989) that links occult interests with the apocalypse.

39. Nineteenth-century captivity narratives such as Maria Monk's *Awful Disclosures of the Hotel Dieu Nunnery* (Hamden, Conn.: Archon Books, 1836, reprint 1962) share many common themes with contemporary satanic fears. Jenny Franchot explores the cultural anxieties behind anti-Catholic captivity stories: for instance, "The Catholic body marked the boundaries of a normative Protestant self intent on a purity that would signal the attainment of perfection"

(*Roads to Rome: The Antebellum Protestant Encounter with Catholicism* (Berkeley and Los Angeles: University of California Press, 1994), xxv.

40. James Dobson and Gary Bauer, *Children at Risk: The Battle for the Hearts and Minds of Our Kids* (Dallas: Word Publishing, 1990) and Johanna Michaelsen's *Like Lambs to the Slaughter: Your Child and the Occult* (Eugene, Or.: Harvest House, 1989) are two examples.

41. This strategy was also adopted by Eric Pryor, who claimed he converted from Paganism to Christianity and is now located at the "Christian Gladiator Ministries." In his response to Pryor's letter to *Green Egg*, Otter Zell, founder of the Church of All Worlds, which publishes *Green Egg*, accused Pryor of spreading stories that he even "ate cat innards" when he was a Pagan and "ripped off the heads of chickens and drank their blood."

42. The letter was not dated, but it was given to me during the summer of 1992.

43. *Lady Liberty League Special Bulletin* (Mt. Horeb, Wis.: Circle Sanctuary), 9 December 1992. The Lady Liberty League is one of a few religious freedom groups organized to support Neopagans who experience job discrimination, religious discrimination in custody battles, and other forms of harassment. The Association of Magical and Earth Religions (AMER) is another such organization.

44. Starfeild, Pagan Digest, 18 November 1995.

45. Although I focus here on Neopagans' views of what their neighbors think about them and some of the evidence in print and electronic media, I have talked to only a handful of the neighbors. I have read their letters of warning and their press releases, as well as the broader range of Christian literature mentioned in this chapter. My intent in this chapter is to make some suggestions of directions for further investigation of these issues. My interests lie in Neopagan stories of persecution at the hands of Christians and the strategies Neopagans use to draw boundaries between themselves and their neighbors. Questions about the extent to which Christian neighbors act consistently in the negative ways Neopagans suggest they do are best left for another study.

46. Bryan Wilson, *The Social Dimensions of Sectarianism* (Oxford: Clarendon Press, 1990), 49.

47. "Elf Lore Family Inc. Press Release" (October 1985).

48. The Gnostic Mass is one of the central rituals performed by the Ordo Templi Orientis (OTO), founded by Aleister Crowley. The mass I attended at Summerhawk was solemn and theatrical, actors performed their parts and recited memorized lines. Others attending were as much audience as participants. The Gnostic Mass is described in Crowley's *Magick in Theory and Practice*, 345–61. In *Ritual Magic in England: 1887 to the Present Day* (London: Neville Spearman Limited, 1970), historian Francis King gives a clear discussion of the origins of Crowley's OTO as well as other important ritual magic groups, such as Dion Fortune's "Fraternity of the Inner Light," that have had significant influences on many contemporary Neopagan communities.

49. OTO Grand Lodge website: http://otohq.org/oto/.

50. Summerhawk 1993 promotional material makes explicit its debt to Crowley. The "Illuminati of Indiana," another Crowley-influenced organization,

has held its Sunfest at Lothlorien for several years. My information about the festival is for 1993 and 1994.

51. Chris Carlisle, Arcana, 15 November 1993.

52. Peh was on many mailing lists and pulled this letter out of his files when I expressed interest in harassment of Neopagans.

53. *Green Egg* 26, no. 103 (winter 1993–94): 51.

54. Sabina Magliocco, letter to author, 6 August 1993.

55. Elsie, a college student who grew up in a rural community near Lothlorien, told me that as a teenager she was warned about satanic activities taking place at the site (conversation with author, May 1992).

56. A look through ELF's newsletters and festival flyers reveals that, in response to ongoing border conflicts, ELF has been constantly involved with discussing and implementing ways of appeasing neighbors.

57. *The Elven Chronicle* (winter 1991): 14.

58. Rowan, conversation with author at Chants to Dance 1992.

59. Other new religious movements have also banded together under persecution in order to establish an identity separate from the rest of society. Older movements like the Church of Jesus Christ of Latter-day Saints (Mormons), as well as more recent new religious movements like the Branch Davidians in Texas and Elizabeth Clare Prophet's Church Universal and Triumphant in Montana, have tried to escape the unfriendly eyes of neighbors by removing their communities to relatively less-populated regions of the country.

60. Women and nature quotation from Jan Corrigan, *Green Egg* 26, no. 102 (autumn 1993): 58; letter from Noadia, *Green Egg* 26, no. 101 (summer 1993): 54.

61. Other Neopagan organizations have responded similarly to misrepresentation by the media. AppleMoon Coven of New Hampshire reported in Pagan Digest that a local radio station newscast referred to them as "a bunch of Satanists," after which they called the station manager and told him "to get his facts straight." They also listed the address and phone number for the station so that other Pagans could call or write (4 February 1996).

62. Alyssa, Pagan Digest, 6 December 1991.

63. Carpenter, *Spiritual Experiences,* 42.

64. Adler, *Drawing Down the Moon,* 45.

65. Adler, *Drawing Down the Moon,* addresses disagreement over the accuracy of pagan revivals on pages 41–93 and 233–82.

66. The most infamous construction of witchcraft as evil is Dominicans Heinrich Institoris and Jacobus Sprenger's *Malleus Maleficarum* ("hammer of witches"), which included tales of witches' perverse pacts with the devil (trans. Montague Summers [London: Hogarth Press, 1969 [1487]). For historical accounts of the witch persecutions see Keith Thomas, *Religion and the Decline of Magic* (New York: Charles Scribner's Sons, 1971); and Brian P. Levack, *The Witch-Hunt in Early Modern Europe* (London: Longman, 1995). For two excellent studies of the witch trials in colonial New England, see Carol Karlsen, *The Devil in the Shape of a Woman* (New York: W. W. Norton, 1987); John Demos, *Entertaining Satan: Witchcraft and the Culture of Early New England* (New York: Oxford University Press, 1982).

67. Quotations "this long holy war" and "our Pagan Holocaust" are from Otter Zell, *Green Egg* 25, no. 96 (Ostara 1992): 2.

68. Historian Philip Greven argues in *Spare the Child: The Religious Roots of Punishment and the Psychological Impact of Physical Abuse* (New York: Alfred A. Knopf, 1991) that physical discipline as practiced by contemporary conservative Protestants can be shown to be abusive and has led to the deaths of children in extreme cases.

69. E-mail to author, 2 December 1991.

70. The Sourceress (a Neopagan who wrote me on this topic) e-mail to author, 1 December 1991.

71. Martello, *Witchcraft*, 16–17.

72. Loretta Orion describes a similar dynamic in *Never Again the Burning Times:* "Christian Fundamentalists and Earth-Healers (such as Neopagans, New Age enthusiasts, and the like) are one another's devils"(65).

73. Melissa, Arcana, n.d.

74. R. G., Arcana, n.d.

75. *Green Egg* 25, no. 96 (Ostara 1992): 36.

76. Wol, Pagan Digest, 28 April 1996.

77. Quotation is from Steve Posch-Coward, *Green Egg* 25, no. 96 (Ostara 1992): 38.

78. Burkel, alt.pagan, 19 March 1993.

79. Ibid.

80. Another example of boundary crossing is a fascinating panel discussion in *Green Egg*: "The Christo-Pagan Panel," an "interfaith dialogue" in which fifteen Neopagan and Christian panelists consider the possibility (or impossibility) of "building bridges" (*Green Egg* 26, no. 103 [winter 1993–94]).

81. *Green Egg* 26, no. 101 (summer 1993): 54.

82. Ellenie, Pagan Digest, 18 November 1985.

83. Neopagans' treatment of Crowley is highly complex. Many of the Neopagans I have met are familiar with and consult his books in creating rituals. Wiccans and other witches are less likely to draw from Crowley's teachings directly and distance themselves from him. However, many of their own rituals and other religious practices are influenced by Crowley and his work. Adler quotes one source who suggested that "fifty percent of modern Wicca is an invention bought and paid for by Gerald B. Gardner from Aleister Crowley" (*Drawing Down the Moon*, 64). Doreen Valiente, Gardner's most important successor, wrote Adler in 1985 that she believed Gardner's rituals "were heavily influenced by Crowley and the O.T.O." (*Drawing Down the Moon*, 85).

84. Mary Ann, Pagan Digest, 9 December 1991.

85. http://otohq.org/oto/thclcma.html.

86. For a fuller account of Satanic beliefs, see Anton LaVey, *The Satanic Bible* (New York: Avon Books, 1969).

87. Llyselya, *Green Egg* 25, no. 96 (Ostara 1992): 41.

88. Martello, *Witchcraft*, 37. Goode quoted in Helen Knode, "Out of the Broom Closet: Portrait of an L. A. Coven," *L. A. Weekly* (19–25 Jan. 1990): 20.

89. Martello, *Witchcraft*, 16.

90. Ibid., 27.

91. The Covenant of the Goddess ("an international organization of cooperating, autonomous Wiccan congregations and solitary practitioners") website, www.cog.org/, 17 May 1999.

92. Knode, "Out of the Broom Closet," 20.

93. On this point, Thelemic groups (named after the Abbey of Thelema, where Crowley experimented with some of the rituals he describes in his books), who draw heavily from Crowley's teachings, diverge from other Neopagans, the Gnostic Mass being the most obvious example.

94. Martello, *Witchcraft*, 88.

95. Eric, Pagan Digest, 15 November 1993.

96. *Green Egg* 25, no. 96 (Ostara 1992): 41.

97. Martello's label for fundamentalists (*Witchcraft*, 88).

98. *Sunday Herald-Telephone*, 29 September 1985, 1.

99. Kenn Deigh, interview by author, 23 October 1992.

100. Peh, conversation with author, 25 March 1992.

101. I heard this complaint several times during ElFest and Wild Magick in 1992.

102. The *Bedford Times-Mail* (Bedford, Ind.), 21 April 1992.

103. Roman and Jasper, conversation with author, June 1994.

104. *Green Egg* 26, no. 103 (winter 1993–94): 53.

105. Peh, conversation with author, 1 July 1993. The "old hippies" analogy works because the 1960s counterculture has become an established piece of cultural history. The documentary "Woodstock" is shown on public television, and in 1994, a highly publicized and commercialized second Woodstock took place. The hippies of the 1960s, as a social phenomenon, have a familiar and well-defined place in American culture.

CHAPTER 4. BLOOD THAT MATTERS

1. Many other religious traditions were also represented at PSG 1993: "Ritual & Dance to the Goddess Yemaya," "Beginning Martial Arts," "Bayou Folklore and Gris Gris." Starwood XII included workshops on "Celtic Sacred Enclosures," "Chinese Six Healing Sounds," and "Reiki." Native American groups and individuals are sometimes present at festivals.

2. "From a Declaration of War against Exploiters of Lakota Spirituality" (ratified by the Dakota, Lakota, and Nakota Nations, June 1993), quoted in Cherie Parker, "Playing Indian," in *Twin Cities Reader* (Minneapolis, Minn., 29 Nov.–5 Dec., 1995). Essays in M. Annette Jaimes, ed., *The State of Native America: Genocide, Colonization, and Resistance* (Boston: South End Press, 1992) and James A. Clifton, ed., *The Invented Indian: Cultural Fictions and Government Policies* (New Brunswick, N.J.: Transaction Books, 1990) discuss the negative effects of cultural borrowing on Native Americans. Other critical views of representations of American Indians include Mark Wallace's essay, "Black Hawk's 'An Autobiography': the Production and Use of an 'Indian' Voice," *The American Indian Quarterly* 18, no. 4 (fall 1994). Important articulations of a critical Native American perspective are Ward Churchill, "Another Dry White Season," *Z Magazine* 6, no. 10 (Oct. 1993), 43–48 and "Spiritual Hucksterism,"

Z Magazine 3, no. 12 (Dec. 1990), 94–98; and Ines Maria Talamantez, "Seeing Red: American Indian Women Speaking about Their Religious and Political Perspectives," *In Our Own Voices: Four Centuries of American Women's Religious Writing,* ed. Rosemary Radford Ruether and Rosemary Skinner Keller (San Francisco: Harper, 1995), 383–423.

3. Moongold, Pagan Digest, 26 May 1995.

4. I spoke with Sherry at several festivals in 1992: Elfest and Wild Magick Gathering in Indiana and Starwood in New York. Anthropologist Alice Kehoe writes disparagingly of Sun Bear in an essay on "plastic medicine men" ("Primal Gaia: Primitivists and Plastic Medicine Men," in *The Invented Indian*).

5. Interview by author, Bloomington, Ind., 27 June 1995.

6. According to anthropologist Karen McCarthy Brown, Legba is "the guardian of crossroads and doorways" (*Mama Lola: A Vodou Priestess in Brooklyn* [Berkeley and Los Angeles: University of California Press, 1991], 54).

7. Louis Martinie, interview by author, Bloomington, Ind., 27 June 1995.

8. Ibid.

9. Gus, e-mail to author, 6 January 1997.

10. Louis Martinie, interview by author, Bloomington, Ind., 27 June 1995. In *Working the Spirit: Ceremonies of the African Diaspora* (Boston: Beacon Press, 1994), Joseph Murphy defines *obeah* as "sorcery," a tradition taken from Africa to Jamaica and characterized by "the preparation of symbolic, therapeutic, and toxic medicines," sometimes involving dance and interaction with spirits (115–22).

11. Derek R. Ianelli, e-mail to author, 13 April 1995.

12. Marion, conversation with author, Bloomington, Ind., July 1995.

13. http://www.sacredskin.com/html/gallery.html.

14. Ash, e-mail to author, 22 May 1995. Neopagans may have more than one name or some of their names may be secret, known only to themselves or members of a certain level of initiation.

15. Pagan Digest, 20 October 1994. Neopagan groups often describe themselves as "tribes."

16. "As readers, they are an elite," writes Adler (*Drawing Down the Moon,* 36).

17. Some popular titles among Neopagans are: Robert Graves, *The Greek Myths* (New York: G. Braziller, 1957); Joseph Campbell, *Creative Mythology* (New York: Penguin, 1976); and Marija Gimbutas, *The Language of the Goddess: Unearthing the Hidden Symbols of Western Civilization* (San Francisco: Harper and Row, 1989).

18. Sabina Magliocco, "Ritual Is My Chosen Art Form: The Creation of Ritual as Folk Art among Contemporary Pagans," in *Magical Religion and Modern Witchcraft,* ed. James R. Lewis (New York: State University of New York Press, 1996), 93–119.

19. Published in Washington, D. C., by The Biblical Archaeology Society.

20. Patricia Cummings, "Native Religion, New-Agers, and the Forest Service," *Inner Voice* (Sep./Oct. 1992), 8.

21. Rose notes, for example, that Leslie Silko's novel *Ceremony* is classified with "Native American literature" rather than with other works of fiction. These

quotes and observations are taken from Rose's essay "The Great Pretenders: Further Reflections on Whiteshamanism," in *The State of Native America,* ed. Annette M. Jaimes (Boston: South End Press, 1992), 403–21.

22. Ibid., 45.

23. Peh, interview with author, Bloomington, Ind., 21 August 1995.

24. Cummings, "Native Religion," 8.

25. Parker, "Playing Indian," 11.

26. Looking Horse, "Lakota Spirituality, Lakota Sovereignty," *Colors* (Minneapolis, January 1995), 14.

27. And further, Rose adds that "not all whiteshamans are Americans, poets, or even white." "The Great Pretenders," 403–4.

28. In many of these attacks, it is interesting to note that Native critics collapse distinctions among Indian nations. Some Neopagan borrowers also fail to recognize that all Native Americans are not the same. In this way, Neopagans replicate the Christians who classify them with all other non-Christian religions (particularly satanism).

29. Looking Horse, "Lakota," 14.

30. Ibid., 15–16.

31. Meredith Begay (an Apache medicine woman) interview by Ines Maria Talamantez, "Seeing Red," 382.

32. Talamantez, "Seeing Red," 384.

33. All quotations *Circle Network News* (1993), 17.

34. In her 1986 edition of *Drawing Down the Moon,* Adler argues that most Neopagan groups are not concerned with their own religious heritage, although Nordic Pagans are an exception.

35. Snowcat, Pagan Digest, May 1995. Bron Taylor describes a similar approach at a gathering of environmental activists and American Indians where the Indians advised, "Go back to your traditions. . . . Know yourself first" ("Earthen Spirituality or Cultural Genocide?: Radical Environmentalism's Appropriation of Native American Spirituality," *Religion* 27 (1997): 190.

36. Adler makes this point repeatedly in *Drawing Down the Moon.* Here I want to acknowledge that some Neopagans develop their identities from family magical traditions, which are not usually recognized as such and certainly are not seen as religious systems by older family members. What a Neopagan would call "magic" is usually described by other family members as "lore": herbal healings, beliefs about ghosts and spirits, and ritual interactions with nature are a few examples. On Asatru see Jeffrey Kaplan, "The Reconstruction of the Asatru and Odinist Traditions," in *Magical Religion and Modern Witchcraft,* ed. James R. Lewis (Albany: State University of New York Press, 1996), 193–236.

37. Greenleaf, Pagan Digest, 23 February 1992.

38. Sade, Pagan Digest, 7 April 1992.

39. Snowcat, Pagan Digest, May 1995.

40. Ranfeadhael, e-mail to author, 21 April 1995.

41. A. Lizard, Pagan Digest, 7 April 1992.

42. Moongold, Pagan Digest, 26 May 1995.

43. Neopagans determine a source's validity on the basis of its usefulness to individual or group rituals, not by historical accuracy. They collect information

from popular sources such as Barbara G. Walker, *The Woman's Encyclopedia of Myths and Secrets* (San Francisco: Harper and Row, 1983), or widely discredited classics like Sir James Frazer's *The Golden Bough: A Study in Comparative Religion* (New York: Macmillan, 1894).

44. Jeffrey Smith, quoted by Robert, 21 May 1995.

45. Snowcat, Pagan Digest, 26 May 1995.

46. Terry, e-mail to author, 21 April 1995.

47. Pagan Digest, 23 February 1992.

48. Gus, e-mail to author, 5 January 1997.

49. Dick Hebdige, *Cut 'N' Mix: Culture, Identity and Caribbean Music* (London: Methuen, 1987), 10, 158–59.

50. This view is related to American "melting-pot" ideology as it appeared in assimilationist discourse at least as far back as the eighteenth century. According to anthropologist Anya Peterson Royce, this ideology hinged on the view of America "as a melting pot that would, out of the diverse raw materials of its citizens, create a totally new blend, culturally and biologically" (*Ethnic Identity: Strategies of Diversity* [Bloomington: Indiana University Press, 1982], 132).

51. Talal Asad, *Genealogies of Religion: Discipline and Reasons of Power in Christianity and Islam* (Baltimore: Johns Hopkins University Press, 1993), 263. In the context of North America, Joel Martin takes a similar approach in *Sacred Revolt: The Muskogee's Struggle for a New World,* (Boston: Beacon Press, 1991).

52. Like Neopagans, some cultural theorists describe elements of culture as though they are "up for grabs." See, for example, Leonard Grossberg, "The Formation of Cultural Studies: An American in Birmingham," *Strategies: A Journal of Theory, Culture and Politics* 2 (1989): 114–48.

53. Terry, e-mail to author, 21 April 1995.

54. Sade, Pagan Digest, 23 February 1992.

55. Chris Carlisle, Pagan Digest, 23 February 1992.

56. Terry, e-mail to author, 21 April 1995, and Pagan Digest, 23 February 1992.

57. Alt.pagan, 3 January 1992.

58. Deborah Root, " 'White Indians': Appropriation and the Politics of Display," in *Borrowed Power: Essays on Cultural Appropriation,* ed. Bruce Ziff and Pratima V. Rao (New Brunswick, N.J.: Rutgers University Press, 1997), 226.

59. Looking Horse, "Lakota," 15.

60. It should be noted here that there are African American and American Indian Neopagans, but they are very much in a minority. African Americans who practice Vodou or Santeria have occasionally led workshops or performed at festivals.

61. Kehoe, "Primal Gaia," 195.

62. See, for example, Richard T. Hughes and C. Leonard Allen, *Illusions of Innocence: Protestant Primitivism in America, 1630–1875* (Chicago: University of Chicago Press, 1988).

63. Nancy Ammerman mentions this tendency on pages 17 and 199 of *Bible Believers.*

64. Louis Martinie, interview by author, Bloomington, Ind., 27 June 1995.

65. For a discussion of a similar kind of distancing in the field of anthropology, see Johannes Fabian, *Time and the Other: How Anthropology Makes Its Object* (New York: Columbia University Press, 1983).

66. Charles Taylor, *Multiculturalism and the Politics of Recognition* (Princeton, N.J.: Princeton University Press, 1992). Neopagans desire "recognition" as a persecuted minority that seeks to define itself rather than to be defined by others.

67. For an example of the inverse of Neopagan borrowing, the copying of white men by indigenous cultures, see Michael Taussig, *Mimesis and Alterity: A Particular History of the Senses* (New York: Routledge, 1993), xiii, 129–33.

CHAPTER 5. CHILDREN OF THE DEVIL OR GIFTED IN MAGIC?

1. George C. Rosenwald and Richard L. Ochberg, introduction to *Storied Lives: The Cultural Politics of Self-Understanding*, eds. George C. Rosenwald and Richard L. Ochberg (New Haven: Yale University Press, 1992), 2.

2. Rosenwald, conclusion to *Storied Lives*, 286.

3. Rosenwald and Ochberg, "Introduction," 1.

4. Coles's book *The Spiritual Life of Children* (Boston: Houghton Mifflin Company, 1990) is one of the few studies of children's religiosity. Although Coles's work is mostly about Christians and Jews, he also spoke with American Indian, atheist, and agnostic children.

5. I use the concept of a landscape to indicate emotional terrain as well as geographical.

6. Catherine, interview by author, 5 March 1992.

7. Jerry B. Harding III, *Circle Network News* 16, no. 3 (fall 1994), 10.

8. Rev. Justyn Wayne Kinslow, "Paganism in Daily Life," *Circle Network News* 16, no. 4 (winter 1994–95), 20.

9. Cindy, e-mail to author, 16 April 1995. A large proportion of the Neopagans I have corresponded with over e-mail are in computer-related or scientific fields. Adler found through her 1985 survey of Neopagans that "their job profiles are pretty unusual, with an amazingly high percentage in computer, scientific, and technical fields" (Adler, *Drawing Down the Moon*, 446).

10. Cindy, e-mail to author, 16 April 1995.

11. Rev. Candida, e-mail to author, 17 April 1995.

12. At Winterstar 1993 I attended a workshop on "Pagan Taboos" in which "pagans in the military" was one of the topics discussed. Although many Neopagans call themselves pacifists, I have met quite a few who are in the military.

13. Celest, e-mail to author, 15 April 1995.

14. Sara, Arcana, 5 October 1993.

15. Chris, e-mail to author, 20 April 1995.

16. Ibid.

17. Ibid.

18. Ranfeadhael, e-mail to author, 21 April 1995.

19. In *Saint Genet: Actor and Martyr*, Jean-Paul Sartre describes the moment when Jean Genet claimed "I am a thief" as an act of self-definition. Sartre argues that Genet can only regain his subjectivity by objectifying himself. Like Genet, who claims, "I decided to be what crime made of me," the "witches" who were identified by their peers as outsiders, "themselves assume the ostracism of

which they are victims, so as not to leave the initiative to their oppressor" (*Saint Genet: Actor and Martyr* [New York: G. Braziller, 1963], 54). Even Neopagan chants express an oppositional attitude. See, for instance, Sabina Magliocco and Holly Tannen, "The Real Old-Time Religion: Towards an Aesthetics of Neo-Pagan Song," *Ethnologies* 20, no. 1 (1998): 175–201.

20. Kinslow, "Paganism in Daily Life," 20.

21. Hedgehog, e-mail to author, 19 April 1995.

22. Carrie, e-mail to author, 21 April 1995.

23. Falcon Storm, e-mail to author, 11 April 1995.

24. Lilith on Pagan Digest.

25. Certainly children's literature is full of such tales. For example, Frances Hodgson Burnett's *The Secret Garden* (New York: Random House, 1987) portrays this world apart, as do C. S. Lewis's Narnia books, such as *The Lion, the Witch and the Wardrobe* (New York: Macmillan, 1950).

26. Ranfeadhael, e-mail to author, 10 April 1995.

27. In her study of "spiritual feminists," Cynthia Eller describes similar childhood stories circulating among her informants (*Living in the Lap of the Goddess,* 25–31).

28. Luhrman, *Persuasions of the Witch's Craft,* 87.

29. Marilyn, Pagan Digest, n.d.

30. Uriel, e-mail to author, May 1995.

31. Aliera, e-mail to author, 23 April 1995.

32. Falcon Storm, e-mail to author, 11 April 1995. Another Pagan Digest introduction mentions the influence of George Lucas's *Star Wars* (12 April 1992).

33. Hedgehog, e-mail to author, 19 April 1995.

34. Sara, Arcana, 5 October 1993.

35. Laughing Starheart, *The Elven Chronicle* (summer 1991), 15.

36. The SCA official website states that the organization was started in Berkeley in 1966 and is "dedicated to the study and recreation of the European Middle Ages" (http://www.sca.org).

37. Peter Clecak, *America's Quest for the Ideal Self: Dissent and Fulfillment in the 60s and 70s* (New York: Oxford University Press, 1983), 93. On pages 145 and 203, Clecak also discusses nostalgia and romanticism. The sixties counterculture is described in detail by sixties cultural analyst Theodore Roszak in *The Making of a Counter Culture* (Garden City, N.Y.: Doubleday, 1969). My analysis of innocence and nostalgia in the 1960s and early 1970s is also informed by Robert S. Ellwood, *The Sixties Spiritual Awakening: American Religion Moving from Modern to Postmodern* (New Brunswick, N.J.: Rutgers University Press, 1994); Morris Dickstein, *Gates of Eden: American Culture in the Sixties* (New York: Penguin Books, 1977); and Todd Gitlin, *The Sixties: Years of Hope, Days of Rage* (New York: Bantam Books, 1987).

38. Ellwood, *Sixties Spiritual Awakening,* 134.

39. "Dungeons and Dragons is a fantasy role-playing game developed primarily by Gary Gygax (registered trademark TSR Hobbies, Inc.) in which a person takes on the characteristics of a certain character, like a warrior, wizard, thief and so forth. . . . Players choose many parameters of the game—there is no board,

players can choose their own abilities—and the imagery and scenery is taken from Tolkienesque science fiction" (Luhrman, *Persuasions of the Witch's Craft*, 106).

40. Ranfeadhael, e-mail to author, 10 April 1995.

41. Candida, e-mail to author, 17 April 1995.

42. Almost no Neopagans mentioned learning magical skills or herbal remedies from their father's side of the family.

43. Uhlan, e-mail to author, 15 April 1995.

44. Rhianna, e-mail to author, 25 April 1995.

45. Lin, e-mail to author, 10 April 1995. Dreams and visions are generally ignored by scholars of American religions, and yet they play an important role in the belief systems of many Americans. For examples, see James McClenon, *Wondrous Events: Foundations of Religious Belief* (Philadelphia: University of Pennsylvania Press, 1994).

46. Sydney Ahlstrom contends that the sixties experienced "a fundamental shift in American religious and moral attitudes." See pages 1080–82 in Sydney E. Ahlstrom, *A Religious History of the American People* (New Haven: Yale University Press, 1972).

47. For example, see William Braden, *The Age of Aquarius: Technology and the Cultural Revolution* (Chicago: Quadrangle Books, 1970); Gini Scott, *Cult and Countercult: A Study of a Spiritual Growth Group and a Witchcraft Order* (Westport, Conn.: Greenwood Press, 1980); Edward A. Tiryakian, *On the Margin of the Visible: Sociology, the Esoteric, and the Occult* (New York: John Wiley and Sons, 1974); and Marcello Truzzi, "The Occult Revival as Popular Culture: Some Random Observations on the Old and Nouveau Witch," *Sociological Quarterly* 13 (1972): 16–36.

48. Ellwood, *Sixties Spiritual Awakening*, 202.

49. My own research bears out the evidence in surveys of Neopaganism by J. Gordon Melton (1980) and Margot Adler (1985). Both Adler and Melton discovered that "the religious background of the Pagan community mirrored the national religious profile of America very closely, the only departure was that Jews were doubly represented." Jews made up 6.2 percent of Melton's survey respondents and 5.4 percent of Adler's. Neopagans from Christian backgrounds were 68.5 percent of Melton's and 74.7 percent of Adler's (Adler, *Drawing Down the Moon*, 446).

50. Falcon Storm, e-mail to author, 11 April 1995.

51. Cindy, e-mail to author, 16 April 1995.

52. Chris, e-mail to author, 10 April 1995.

53. Airique, e-mail to author, 17 April 1995.

54. Tannev Abt-Mu, letter to author, 21 April 1995.

55. Uhlan, e-mail to author, 15 April 1995.

56. Wendy, Arcana, 1995.

57. Children and their perverse interests appear as dangerous and satanic forces in many novels popular among fundamentalist Christians, such as the works of Frank Peretti and Roger Elwood. Elwood's and Peretti's fictional tales are of children who are corrupted by occult activities such as astrology.

58. Celest, e-mail to author, 15 April 1995.

59. Cynthia Eller's informants (many of them were Witches) told her similar stories of abuse. One woman was "kidnapped" and taken to exorcists (*Living in the Lap of the Goddess*, 13–14).

60. Derek R. Iannelli, e-mail to author, 13 April 1995.

61. Cheryl Mattingly, *Healing Dramas and Clinical Plots: The Narrative Structure of Experience* (Cambridge, Eng.: Cambridge University Press, 1998), 84.

62. Daniel L. Schacter, *Searching for Memory: The Brain, the Mind, and the Past* (New York: Basic Books, 1996), 7, 52.

63. Philip Aries, *Centuries of Childhood* (London: Cape, 1962).

64. Lynn Spigel, "Seducing the Innocent," in *The Children's Culture Reader*, ed. Henry Jenkins (New York: New York University Press, 1998), 110.

65. Kinslow, "Paganism in Daily Life," 20.

66. Allison James, Chris Jenks, and Alan Prout, *Theorizing Childhood* (New York: Teacher's College Press, 1998), 198.

CHAPTER 6. SERIOUS PLAYING WITH THE SELF

1. Starwood XV program.

2. Starwood XV program.

3. Diane Tabor, "Dance Work," *Mezlim* 3, no. 2 (Beltane 1992), 13.

4. J. Perry Damarru, "A Gathering Primer," *Mezlim* 3, no. 2 (Beltane 1992), 3–6.

5. Salome, interview by author, 9 July 1993.

6. Tabor, "Dance Work," *Mezlim* 3, no. 2 (Beltane 1992), 13–14.

7. Ibid., 15.

8. Ian, Pagan Digest, 25 June 1995.

9. Tabor, "Dance Work," 13.

10. *The Elven Chronicle* (summer 1991).

11. Ian, Pagan Digest, 25 June 1995.

12. Salome, interview by author, Bloomington, Ind., 9 July 1993.

13. From EarthSpirit Community web page: http://www.earthspirit.com/ (3 December 1996).

14. Damarru, "A Gathering Primer," 3.

15. elemental, alt.magick, 4 April 1993.

16. Dierdre Sklar, "Can Bodylore Be Brought to Its Senses?" *Journal of American Folklore* 107, no. 423 (winter 1994): 9–22.

17. *The Elven Chronicle* (summer 1991).

18. Tabor, "Dance Work," 13–14

19. Salome, interview by author, Bloomington, Ind., 9 July 1993.

20. Salome, interview by author, Bloomington, Ind., 9 July 1993.

21. Tabor, "Dance Work," 14–15.

22. Occasionally older children and infants attend the ritual fire early in the evening, but I never saw children around the fire in the more intense later hours. I can only remember once seeing a girl of eight or nine dancing around the fire with her mother; children usually sit at the outskirts. I never saw a child involved with the sexually provocative dancing. In general, festival communities are particularly protective toward children and designate separate spaces for children's activities.

23. Artemis, interview by author, Needmore, Ind., 2 May 1992.

24. Drumspeak, *Festival Drumming* (Cincinnati, Oh.: Black Moon Publishing, 1991), 4. Black Moon is an enterprise founded by Louis Martinie and Mishlen Linden that publishes elegantly produced "chapbooks" on topics of interest to Neopagans and keeps an archive of Neopagan material.

25. Ibid.

26. Tabor, "Dance Work," 15.

27. Starhawk, *Dreaming the Dark,* 140.

28. Ibid.

29. Janet Farrar and Stewart Farrar, *The Life and Times of a Modern Witch* (Custer, Wash.: Phoenix Publishing, 1987), 74, 76.

30. *Mezlim,* 3, no. 2 (Beltane 1992): 4.

31. Starhawk, *Dreaming the Dark,* 143.

32. Tabor, "Dance Work," 15.

33. Starhawk, "Healing Our Wounds, Healing the Earth," interview by Deirdre Pulgram Arthen, *Fireheart* 7 (1993), 36.

34. Salome, interview by author, Bloomington, Ind., July 1993.

35. Ibid.

36. Frederick Lamp, "Heavenly Bodies: Menses, Moon, and Rituals of License among the Temne of Sierra Leone," in *Blood Magic,* ed. Thomas Buckley and Alma Gottlieb (Berkeley and Los Angeles: University of California Press, 1988), 231.

37. Tabor, *Mezlim* 3, no. 2 (Beltane 1992), 14.

38. Personal correspondence, June 1992.

39. Richard Keenan, "A Pilgrim's Guide to Pagan Festivals," *Mezlim* 3, no. 2 (Beltane 1992), 18.

40. Tath Zal, "Why We Mark Our Bodies," *Mezlim* 3, no. 1 (1992), 12.

41. Ibid., 10–13.

42. Sindi, Pagan Digest, 8 November 1992.

43. Cary, Pagan Digest, 14 November 1996.

44. Dave, Pagan Digest, 3 November 1992.

45. Chris, Pagan Digest, 8 November 1992.

46. Crow, "Healing Tattoo," *Mezlim* 3, no. 1 (1992), 7.

47. British cultural studies scholar Paul Willis describes similar ways in which groups of "hippies" and "biker boys" protest "normality" through clothing and appearance: "The most direct expression of their nature was in their appearance and their bodily movement" (*Profane Culture* [London: Routledge, 1978], 95). Also see Dick Hebdige, *Subculture: The Meaning of Style* (New York: Methuen, 1979).

48. Marie grew up at festivals, attending them with her mother who makes a living as a merchant. I learned several years later that Marie was working as a dancer in a topless bar. Some of her female friends who had seen her dance there told me, that unlike most of the other dancers, when Marie danced for money, she still "invoked the goddess" and "ran goddess energy."

49. Marjorie Garber, *Vested Interests: Cross-Dressing and Cultural Anxiety* (San Francisco: Harper, 1993), 17. See also Gaylyn Studlar's study of how actress Marlene Dietrich cross-dressed "to create herself" ("The Metamorphoses

of Marlene Dietrich," in *Fabrications: Costume and the Female Body,* ed. Jane Gaines and Charlotte Herzog [New York: Routledge, 1990], 229–49).

50. Salome, interview by author, Bloomington, Ind., 9 July 1993.

51. Cain Berlinger, "The Other Alternative: Piercing as Body Art," *Mezlim* 3, no. 1 (1992), 14–17.

52. Victor Turner, "*Carnaval* in Rio: Dionysian Drama in an Industrializing Society," in *The Celebration of Society: Perspectives on Contemporary Cultural Performance,* ed. Frank Manning (Bowling Green, Ky.: Bowling Green University Press, 1983), 27.

53. Luhrman, *Persuasions of the Witch's Craft,* 324–36.

54. Turner, "*Carnaval* in Rio," 123. Turner's essay furthermore suggests that license and the expression of "the repressed" are made possible by the highly structured planning that precedes the *Carnaval.* While much planning precedes pagan festivals as well, the relationship between structure and antistructure is more parallel than linear; boundary enforcement and boundarylessness may take place simultaneously.

55. Peh, interview by author, en route to Starwood, July 1992.

56. Pine, Pagan Digest, 25 June 1995.

57. Interview by author, 6 September 1992.

58. Michael, interview by author, Needmore, Ind., 20 June 1992.

59. In fact, I was more likely to have the opposite problem—blending in too well. After a public talk on my research at festivals, a woman in the audience asked me, "Well, what did you wear?" I realized later that this was not a frivolous question. Appearance is an important factor in identifying self and other at festivals. I rummaged through my closets before festivals to find the many vintage silk and velvet dresses I collected scavenging thrift stores during my college years, that were not in good enough shape to wear in mundania but would work well for a weekend at a carnival in the woods. I too separated festival wardrobe from mundane clothes.

60. Aravah, "The First Festival" *Mezlim* 4, no. 2 (Beltane 1993), 41–45.

61. Kevin, personal correspondence, 4 August 1992.

62. Peh, interview by author, Bloomington, Ind., July 1992

63. Tabor, "Dance Work," 15.

64. At the beginning of several ELF festivals one of the ELF elders gave a talk about inappropriate sexual behavior at the festival fire.

65. Sabina Magliocco, "Ritual Is My Chosen Art Form: The Creation of Ritual as Folk Art among Contemporary Pagans," in *Magical Religion and Modern Witchcraft,* ed. James R. Lewis (New York: State University of New York Press, 1996), 107.

66. Loretta Orion, *Never Again the Burning Times* (Prospect Heights, Ill.: Waveland Press, 1995), 134.

67. According to Michael, at Starwood 1991 this kind of approach was used when a man was harassing women in the women's shower.

68. Three years later, another festival member was accused of sexual harassment and ordered not to set foot in any Lothlorien festivals.

69. My account of the story is based on conversations with this festival organizer, Peh, and Kristina's friends, Rachel and Jason (summer 1992).

70. Rose, conversation with author, 31 May 1992.

71. Salome, interview by author, Bloomington, Ind., 9 July 1993.

72. *The Elven Chronicle* (summer 1991).

73. Drumspeak, "Festival Drumming," 4.

74. Ranger Rick, "Festival Drumming," in *Mezlim* 3, no. 2 (Beltane 1992), 4.

75. Richard Schechner, *Between Theater and Anthropology* (Philadelphia: University of Pennsylvania Press, 1985), 41–42, 117–50.

76. Kenn Deigh, letter to author, 2 June 1992. Neopagans describe ritualized experiences at festivals as journeys. Anthropologist Margaret Drewel explains how ritual works as a dynamic process that resembles a "journey-like experience" in *Yoruba Ritual: Performers, Play, Agency* (Bloomington: Indiana University Press, 1992), 28.

CONCLUSIONS

1. The title of this chapter, "The Circle Is Open but Never Broken," is a standard Neopagan ritual ending; "Merry Meet and Merry Part and Merry Meet Again" is also usually added.

2. Charles Taylor, *Sources of the Self: The Making of the Modern Identity* (Cambridge, Mass.: Harvard University Press, 1989). Jean-François Lyotard, *The Postmodern Condition: A Report on Knowledge* (Minneapolis: University of Minnesota Press, 1979, reprint 1984).

3. In *Reality Isn't What It Used to Be,* Walter Truett Anderson identifies three characteristics of the postmodern worldview that Neopagans seem to be working with: 1) changes in identity and boundaries; 2) changes in morals, ethics, and values; and 3) changes in relationship to traditions, customs, and institutions (San Francisco: Harper and Row, 1990).

4. Lyotard, *The Postmodern Condition*, 76. See also pages 15, 30–31, 81.

5. Rob Shields, *Lifestyle Shopping: The Subject of Consumption* (London: Routledge, 1992), 15.

6. A quick glance at World Wide Web materials related to Neopaganism demonstrates the immense range of possible sources. Texts of rituals can be downloaded from individual home pages; entire books by Neopagan authors are available at sites for file transfer protocol (ftp).

7. Subscribers to the list Arcana, for instance, are located all over North America and in countries such as Brazil, Japan, Poland, New Zealand, and Australia.

8. Shields, *Lifestyle Shopping*, 16.

9. Taylor, *Sources of the Self*, 177, 480.

10. Ibid., 131.

11. Taylor, *Sources of the Self*, 480.

12. Anthony Giddens, *Modernity and Self-Identity: Self and Society in the Late Modern Age* (Stanford: Stanford University Press, 1991).

13. Ibid., 5.

14. Ibid., 78, 217–18.

Bibliography

BOOKS AND ARTICLES

Abrahams, Roger D. "The Language of Festivals: Celebrating the Economy." In *Celebration: Studies in Festivity and Ritual*, edited by Victor Turner. Washington, D.C.: Smithsonian Institution Press, 1982.

———. "Shouting Match at the Border: The Folklore of Display Events." In *"And Other Neighborly Names": Social Process and Cultural Image in Texas Folklore*, edited by Richard Bauman and Roger D. Abrahams. Austin: The University of Texas Press, 1982.

Adler, Margot. *Drawing Down the Moon: Witches, Druids, Goddess-Worshippers, and Other Pagans in America Today*. Boston: Beacon Press, 1986.

Agnew, John A., and James S. Duncan, eds. *The Power of Place: Bringing Together Geographical and Sociological Imaginations*. Boston: Unwin Hyman, 1989.

Ahlstrom, Sydney E. *A Religious History of the American People*. New Haven: Yale University Press, 1972.

Albanese, Catherine L. *Nature Religion in America: From the Algonkian Indians to the New Age*. Chicago: University of Chicago Press, 1990.

Ammerman, Nancy Tatom. *Bible Believers: Fundamentalists in the Modern World*. New Brunswick, N.J.: Rutgers University Press, 1987.

Anderson, Walter Truett. *Reality Isn't What It Used to Be: Theatrical Politics, Ready-to-Wear Religion, Global Myths, Primitive Chic, and Other Wonders of the Postmodern World*. San Francisco: Harper and Row, 1990.

Aries, Philip. *Centuries of Childhood*. London: Cape, 1962.

Asad, Talal. *Genealogies of Religion: Discipline and Reasons of Power in Christianity and Islam*. Baltimore: Johns Hopkins University Press, 1993.

Bachelard, Gaston. *The Poetics of Space*. Translated by Maria Jolas. New York: The Orion Press, 1958. Reprint 1964.

Baer, Randall N. *Inside the New Age Nightmare.* Lafayette, La.: Huntington House, 1984.

Bauman, Richard, ed. *Folklore, Cultural Performances, and Popular Entertainments: A Communications-Centered Handbook.* Oxford: Oxford University Press, 1992.

Bauman, Richard, and Roger D. Abrahams, eds. *"And Other Neighborly Names": Social Process and Cultural Image in Texas Folklore.* Austin: The University of Texas Press, 1982.

Bellah, Robert N., Richard Madsen, William M. Sullivan, Ann Swidler, and Steven M. Tipton. *Habits of the Heart: Individualism and Commitment in American Life.* San Francisco: Harper and Row, 1985.

Bellah, Robert N., and Frederick Greenspahn, eds. *Uncivil Religion: Interreligious Hostility in America.* New York: Crossroads, 1987.

Berger, Helen. *A Community of Witches: Contemporary Neo-Paganism and Witchcraft in the United States.* Columbia: University of South Carolina Press, 1999.

Bharati, Agehananda. "The Hindu Renaissance and Its Apologetic Patterns." *Journal of Asian Studies* 39, no. 2 (Feb. 1970).

Bonewits, Isaac. *Real Magic.* New York: Berkly, 1972.

Boyer, Paul, and Stephen Nissenbaum. *Salem Possessed: The Social Origins of Witchcraft.* Cambridge, Mass.: Harvard University Press, 1974.

Braden, William. *The Age of Aquarius: Technology and the Cultural Revolution.* Chicago: Quadrangle Books, 1970.

Bradley, Marion Zimmer. *The Mists of Avalon.* London: Sphere, 1982.

Braude, Ann. *Radical Spirits: Spiritualism and Women's Rights in Nineteenth-Century America.* Boston: Beacon Press, 1989.

Brown, David. "Toward an Ethnoaesthetics of Santeria Ritual Arts." In *Santeria Aesthetics in Contemporary Latin American Art,* edited by Arturo Lindsay. Washington: Smithsonian Institution Press, 1996.

Brown, Karen McCarthy. *Mama Lola: A Vodou Priestess in Brooklyn.* Berkeley and Los Angeles: University of California Press, 1991.

Brown, Karen McCarthy, and Mama Lola. "The Altar Room: A Dialogue." In *Sacred Arts of Haitian Vodou,* edited by Donald A. Cosentino. Los Angeles: UCLA Fowler Museum of Cultural History, 1995.

Brown, Michael H. *The Final Hour.* Milford, Oh.: Faith, 1992.

Buckland, Raymond. *Buckland's Complete Book of Witchcraft.* St. Paul, Mn.: Llewellyn Publications, 1986.

Burnett, Frances Hodgson. *The Secret Garden.* New York: Random House, 1987.

Burtner, Rev. Wm. Kent, O.P. *Cults, Sects, and the New Age.* Edited by James J. LeBar. Huntington, Ind.: Our Sunday Visitor, 1989.

Butler, E. M. *Ritual Magic.* Cambridge, Eng.: Cambridge University Press, 1979.

Butler, Jon. *Awash in a Sea of Faith: Christianizing the American People.* Cambridge, Mass.: Harvard University Press, 1990.

Buttimer, Anne. *Geography and the Human Spirit.* Baltimore: Johns Hopkins University Press, 1993.

———. "Home, Reach, and the Sense of Place." In *The Human Experience of Space and Place,* edited by Anne Buttimer and David Seamon. New York: St. Martin's Press, 1980.

Campanelli, Pauline, and Don Campanelli. *Circles, Groves and Sanctuaries.* St. Paul, Mn.: Llewellyn Publications, 1994.

Campbell, Joseph. *Creative Mythology.* New York: Penguin, 1976.

Carpenter, Dennis. *Spiritual Experiences, Life Changes, and Ecological Viewpoints of Contemporary Pagans.* Ph.D. diss., Saybrook Institute, 1994.

Chidester, David, and Edward T. Linenthal. *American Sacred Space.* Bloomington: Indiana University Press, 1995.

Chippendale, Christopher. *Stonehenge Complete.* Ithaca: Cornell University Press, 1983.

Churchill, Ward. "Another Dry White Season." *Z Magazine* 6, no. 10 (Oct. 1993): 43–48.

———. "Spiritual Hucksterism." *Z Magazine* 3, no. 12 (Dec. 1990): 94–98.

Clecak, Peter. *America's Quest for the Ideal Self: Dissent and Fulfillment in the 60s and 70s.* New York: Oxford University Press, 1983.

Cohen, Anthony P., ed. *Symbolising Boundaries: Identity and Diversity in British Cultures.* Manchester, Eng.: Manchester University Press, 1986.

Coles, Robert. *The Spiritual Life of Children.* Boston: Houghton Mifflin, 1990.

Conway, Flo, and Jim Siegelman. *Holy Terror: The Fundamentalist War on America's Freedoms in Religion, Politics and Our Private Lives.* Garden City, N.Y.: Doubleday, 1982.

Cookson, Catharine. "Reports from the Trenches: A Case Study of Religious Freedom Issues Faced by Wiccans Practicing in the United States." *Journal of Church and State* 39, no. 4 (autumn 1997): 723–48.

Cox, Harvey. *Fire from Heaven: The Rise of Pentecostal Spirituality and the Reshaping of Religion in the Twenty-First Century.* Reading, Mass.: Addison-Wesley, 1995.

Crowley, Aleister. *The Book of Lies.* York Beach, Me.: Samuel Weiser, 1913. Reprint 1984.

———. *Magick in Theory and Practice.* New York: Dover Publications, 1929. Reprint 1976.

Crumrine, N. Ross, and Alan Morinis, eds. *Pilgrimage in Latin America.* New York: Greenwood Press, 1991.

Cumbey, Constance. *The Hidden Dangers of the Rainbow: The New Age Movement and Our Coming Age of Barbarism.* Shreveport, La.: Huntington House, 1983.

Cummings, Patricia. "Native Religion, New-Agers, and the Forest Service." *Inner Voice* (Sep./Oct. 1992).

Cuneo, Michael W. *The Smoke of Satan: Conservative and Traditionalist Dissent in Contemporary American Catholicism.* New York: Oxford University Press, 1997.

DaMatta, Roberto. "Carnaval, Informality, and Magic: A Point of View from Brazil." In *Text, Play and Story: The Construction and Reconstruction of Self and Society,* edited by Edward M. Bruner. Washington, D.C.: American Ethnological Society, 1984.

———. *Carnivals, Rogues, and Heroes: An Interpretation of the Brazilian Dilemma.* Notre Dame: University of Notre Dame Press, 1991.

Demos, John. *Entertaining Satan: Witchcraft and the Culture of Early New England.* New York: Oxford University Press, 1982.

De Parrie, Paul, and Mary Prind. *Unholy Sacrifices of the New Age.* Westchester, Ill.: Crossway Books, 1988.

Diamond, Sara. *Spiritual Warfare: The Politics of the Christian Right.* Montreal: Black Rose Books, 1990.

Dickstein, Morris. *Gates of Eden: American Culture in the Sixties.* New York: Penguin Books, 1977.

Dobson, James, and Gary Bauer. *Children At Risk: The Battle for the Hearts and Minds of Our Kids.* Dallas: Word Publishing, 1990.

Douglas, Mary. *Purity and Danger: An Analysis of the Concepts of Pollution and Taboo.* London: Routledge, 1966

Drewel, Margaret. *Yoruba Ritual: Performers, Play, Agency.* Bloomington: Indiana University Press, 1992.

Drumspeak. *Festival Drumming.* Cincinnati, Oh.: Black Moon Publishing, 1991.

Duncan, James, and David Ley, eds. *Place/Culture/Representation.* London: Routledge, 1993.

Duvignaud, Jean. "Festivals: A Sociological Approach." *Cultures* 3, no. 1 (Unesco Press, 1976): 13–25.

Ebersole, Gary L. *Captured by Texts: Puritan to Postmodern Images of Indian Captivity.* Charlottesville: University Press of Virginia, 1995.

Eilberg-Schwartz, Howard. "Witches of the West: Neopaganism and Goddess Worship as Enlightenment Religions." *Neo-Paganism: A Feminist Search for Religious Alternatives.* Women's Studies Program, Indiana University, Occasional Series No. 3, 1988.

Eller, Cynthia. *Living in the Lap of the Goddess: The Feminist Spirituality Movement in America.* New York: Crossroads, 1993.

Ellis, Peter B. *The Druids.* London: Constable, 1994.

Ellwood, Robert S., Jr. *Alternative Altars: Unconventional and Eastern Spirituality in America.* Chicago: University of Chicago Press, 1979.

———. "The American Theosophical Synthesis." In *The Occult in America: New Historical Perspectives,* edited by Howard Kerr and Charles Crow. Urbana: University of Illinois Press, 1983.

———. *The Sixties Spiritual Awakening: American Religion Moving from Modern to Postmodern.* New Brunswick, N.J.: Rutgers University Press, 1994.

Elwood, Roger. *Angelwalk.* Westchester, Ill.: Crossway Books, 1988.

———. *The Christening.* Eugene, Or.: Harvest House Press, 1989.

Enroth, Ronald. *The Lure of the Cults.* Chappaqua, N.Y.: Christian Herald Books, 1979.

Ewing, Katherine P. "The Illusion of Wholeness: Culture, Self, and the Experience of Inconsistency." *Ethos* 18, no. 3 (Sep. 1990): 251–78.

Fabian, Johannes. *Time and the Other: How Anthropology Makes Its Object.* New York: Columbia University Press, 1983.

Falassi, Alessandro. *Time out of Time: Essays on the Festival.* Albuquerque: University of New Mexico Press, 1987.

Farrar, Janet, and Stewart Farrar. *The Life and Times of a Modern Witch.* Custer, Wash.: Phoenix Publishing, 1987.

Fernandez, James. *Bwiti: An Ethnography of the Religious Imagination in Africa.* Princeton, N.J.: Princeton University Press, 1982.

Flynn, Ted, and Maureen Flynn. *The Thunder of Justice: The Warning, the Miracle, the Chastisement, the Era of Peace: God's Ultimate Acts of Mercy.* N.p.: MaxKol Communications, 1993.

Fortune, Dion. *Moon Magic.* York Beach, Me.: Samuel Weiser, 1956. Reprint 1985.

———. *The Sea Priestess.* York Beach, Me.: Samuel Weiser, 1959. Reprint 1985.

Foucault, Michel. *The Foucault Reader.* Edited by Paul Rabinow. New York: Pantheon, 1984.

———. "Of Other Spaces." *Diacritics* 16 (1986): 22–27.

———. *Power/Knowledge: Selected Interviews and Other Writings, 1972–1977.* Edited by Colin Gordon. New York: Pantheon Books, 1980.

Franchot, Jenny. *Roads to Rome: The Antebellum Protestant Encounter with Catholicism.* Berkeley and Los Angeles: University of California Press, 1994.

Frazer, Sir James. *The Golden Bough: A Study in Comparative Religion.* New York: Macmillan, 1894.

Frew, Don Hudson. "A Brief History of Satanism." *Witchcraft, Satanism and Occult Crime: Who's Who and What's What,* 4th ed. N.p., n.d.

———. "Methodological Flaws in Recent Studies of Historical and Modern Witchcraft." *Ethnologies* 20, no. 1 (1998): 33–65.

Gallagher, Winifred. *The Power of Place: How Our Surroundings Shape Our Thoughts, Emotions, and Actions.* New York: Poseidon Press, 1993.

Garber, Marjorie. *Vested Interests: Cross-Dressing and Cultural Anxiety.* San Francisco: Harper, 1993.

Gardner, Gerald B. *Witchcraft Today.* New York: The Citadel Press, 1954. Reprint 1955.

Giddens, Anthony. *Modernity and Self-Identity: Self and Society in the Late Modern Age.* Stanford: Stanford University Press, 1991.

Gilmore, Mikal. *Shot in the Heart.* New York: Doubleday, 1994.

Gimbutas, Marija. *The Language of the Goddess: Unearthing the Hidden Symbols of Western Civilization.* San Francisco: Harper and Row, 1989.

Ginzburg, Carlo. *The Cheese and the Worms: The Cosmos of a Sixteenth-Century Miller.* Translated by John Tedeschi and Anne Tedeschi. Baltimore: Johns Hopkins University Press, 1980.

———. *The Night Battles: Witchcraft and Agrarian Cults in the Sixteenth and Seventeenth Centuries.* London: Routledge and Kegan Paul, 1966. Reprint 1983.

Gitlin, Todd. *The Sixties: Years of Hope, Days of Rage.* New York: Bantam Books, 1987.

Grant, Kenneth, and John Symonds, eds. *Magic.* London: Routledge and Kegan Paul, 1973.

Graves, Robert. *The Greek Myths.* New York: G. Braziller, 1957.

Greer, Mary K. *Women of the Golden Dawn: Rebels and Priestesses.* Rochester, Vt.: Park Street Press, 1995.

Gregory, Derek. *Geographical Imaginations.* Oxford: Blackwell, 1994.

Greven, Philip. *Spare the Child: The Religious Roots of Punishment and the Psychological Impact of Physical Abuse.* New York: Alfred A. Knopf, 1991.

Griffith, James. *Beliefs and Holy Places: A Spiritual Geography of the Pimeria Alta.* Tucson: University of Arizona Press, 1992.

Grossberg, Leonard. "The Formation of Cultural Studies: An American in Birmingham." *Strategies: A Journal of Theory, Culture and Politics* 2 (1989): 114–48.

Gutierrez, Ramon A. "Conjuring the Holy: Mexican Domestic Altars." In *Home Altars of Mexico,* edited by Dana Salvo. Albuquerque: University of New Mexico Press, 1997.

Haberman, David L. *Journey through the Twelve Forests: An Encounter with Krishna.* New York: Oxford University Press, 1994.

Hall, David. *Worlds of Wonder, Days of Judgment: Popular Religious Belief in Early New England.* Cambridge, Mass.: Harvard University Press, 1989.

Hammond, Phillip E. *Religion and Personal Autonomy: The Third Disestablishment in America.* Columbia: University of South Carolina Press, 1992.

Harrison, Jane Ellen. *A History of Pagan Europe.* London: Routledge, 1995.

Harvey, Graham, and Charlotte Hardman, eds. *Paganism Today.* London: Thorsons, 1996.

Hatch, Nathan. *The Democratization of American Christianity.* New Haven: Yale University Press, 1989.

Hebdige, Dick. *Cut 'N' Mix: Culture, Identity and Caribbean Music.* London: Methuen, 1987.

———. *Subculture: The Meaning of Style.* New York: Methuen, 1979.

Hess, David S. *Science in the New Age: The Paranormal, Its Defenders and Debunkers and American Culture.* Madison: University of Wisconsin Press, 1993.

Hexham, Irving. "The Evangelical Response to the New Age." In *Perspectives on the New Age,* edited by James R. Lewis and J. Gordon Melton. New York: State University of New York Press, 1992.

Hicks, Robert D. *In Pursuit of Satan: The Police and the Occult.* Buffalo: Prometheus Books, 1991.

Hiss, Tony. *The Experience of Place.* New York: Knopf, 1990.

Howe, Ellic. *The Magicians of the Golden Dawn: A Documentary History of a Magical Order.* London: Routledge, 1972.

Hughes, Richard T., and C. Leonard Allen. *Illusions of Innocence: Protestant Primitivism in America, 1630–1875.* Chicago: University of Chicago Press, 1988.

Hunter, James Davison. *Evangelicalism: The Coming Generation.* Chicago: The University of Chicago Press, 1987.

Hutton, Ronald. *The Pagan Religions of the Ancient British Isles.* London: Blackwell, 1991.

———. "The Roots of Modern Paganism." In *Paganism Today,* edited by Graham Harvey and Charlotte Hardman. London: Thorsons, 1996.

Institoris, Heinrich, and Jacobus Sprenger. *Malleus Maleficarum.* Translated by Montague Summers. 1487. Reprint London: Hogarth Press, 1969.

Jaimes, M. Annette, ed. *The State of Native America: Genocide, Colonization, and Resistance.* Boston: South End Press, 1992.

James, Allison, Chris Jenks, and Alan Prout. *Theorizing Childhood.* New York: Teacher's College Press, 1998.

Johnston, Jerry. *The Edge of Evil: The Rise of Satanism in North America.* Dallas: Word Publishing, 1989.

Jones, Prudence, and Nigel Pennick. *A History of Pagan Europe*. London: Routledge, 1995.

Kaplan, Jeffrey. "The Reconstruction of the Asatru and Odinist Traditions." In *Magical Religion and Modern Witchcraft*, edited by James R. Lewis. Albany: State University of New York Press, 1996.

Karlsen, Carol. *The Devil in the Shape of a Woman*. New York: W. W. Norton, 1987.

Kehoe, Alice B. "Primal Gaia: Primitivists and Plastic Medicine Men." In *The Invented Indian: Cultural Fictions and Government Policies*, edited by James A. Clifton. New Brunswick, N.J.: Transaction Books, 1990.

Kelley, Aidan. *Crafting the Art of Magic: A History of Modern Witchcraft, 1939–1964*. St. Paul, Minn.: Llewellyn Press, 1991.

Kessler, Lauren. *After All These Years: Sixties Ideals in a Different World*. New York: Thunder's Mouth Press, 1990.

King, Francis. *Ritual Magic in England: 1887 to the Present Day*. London: Neville Spearman, 1970.

Klaits, Joseph. *Servants of Satan: The Age of the Witch Hunts*. Bloomington: Indiana University Press, 1985.

Lafferty, Anne. "How We Braid Our Lives Together with Our Ancestors." *Ethnologies* 20, no. 1 (1998): 129–49.

Lamp, Frederick. "Heavenly Bodies: Menses, Moon, and Rituals of License among the Temne of Sierra Leone." In *Blood Magic*, edited by Thomas Buckley and Alma Gottlieb. Berkeley and Los Angeles: University of California Press, 1988.

Lasch, Christopher. *The Culture of Narcissism: American Life in an Age of Diminishing Expectations*. New York: W. W. Norton, 1978.

LaVey, Anton. *The Satanic Bible*. New York: Avon Books, 1969.

Lawless, Elaine. *God's Peculiar People: Women's Voices and Folk Tradition in a Pentecostal Church*. Lexington: University Press of Kentucky, 1988.

———. *Joy Unspeakable*. Produced by Elaine Lawless and Elizabeth Peterson. Indiana University Television, 1981. Videocassette, 50 min.

Lefebvre, Henri. *The Production of Space*. Translated by Donald Nicholson-Smith. Oxford: Blackwell, 1974. Reprint 1992.

LeGuin, Ursula. *A Wizard of Earthsea*. Emeryville, Cal.: Parnassus Press, 1968.

Levack, Brian P. *The Witch-Hunt in Early Modern Europe*. London: Longman, 1995.

Lewis, C. S. *The Lion, the Witch and the Wardrobe*. New York: Macmillan, 1950.

Lindsey, Hal. *The Late Great Planet Earth*. New York: Bantam Books, 1970. Reprint 1973.

Loftus, Elizabeth, and Katherine Ketcham, eds. *The Myth of Repressed Memory: False Memories and Allegations of Sexual Abuse*. New York: St. Martin's Griffin, 1994.

Looking Horse, Martina. "Lakota Spirituality, Lakota Sovereignty." *Colors*. Minneapolis: January 1995.

Luhrman, T. M. *Persuasions of the Witch's Craft: Ritual Magic in Contemporary England*. Cambridge, Mass: Harvard University Press, 1989.

Lyotard, Jean-François. *The Postmodern Condition: A Report on Knowledge*. Minneapolis: University of Minnesota Press, 1979. Reprint 1984.

MacAloon, John J., ed. *Rite, Drama, Festival, Spectacle: Rehearsals toward a Theory of Cultural Performance.* Philadelphia: Institute for the Study of Human Issues, 1984.

Macfarlane, Bud. *Pierced by a Sword.* Cleveland: Saint Jude Media, 1995.

Magliocco, Sabina. "Ritual Is My Chosen Art Form: The Creation of Ritual as Folk Art among Contemporary Pagans." In *Magical Religion and Modern Witchcraft,* edited by James R. Lewis. New York: State University of New York Press, 1996.

Magliocco, Sabina, and Holly Tannen. "The Real Old-Time Religion: Towards an Aesthetics of Neo-Pagan Song." *Ethnologies* 20, no. 1 (1998): 175–201.

Manning, Frank, ed. *The Celebration of Society: Perspectives on Contemporary Cultural Performance.* Bowling Green, Ky.: Bowling Green University Press, 1983.

Margolis, Diane Rothbard. *The Fabric of Self: A Theory of Ethics and Emotions.* New Haven: Yale University Press, 1998.

Marrs, Texe. *Dark Secrets of the New Age: Satan's Plan for a One World Religion.* Westchester, Ill.: Crossway Books, 1987.

Martello, Leo Louis. *Witchcraft: The Old Religion.* Secaucus, N.J: Citadel Press, 1973.

Martin, Joel. *Sacred Revolt: The Muskogee's Struggle for a New World.* Boston: Beacon Press, 1991.

Mattingly, Cheryl. *Healing Dramas and Clinical Plots: The Narrative Structure of Experience.* Cambridge, Eng.: Cambridge University Press, 1998.

Mauss, Marcel. *A General Theory of Magic.* London: Routledge, 1972.

McClenon, James. *Wondrous Events: Foundations of Religious Belief.* Philadelphia: University of Pennsylvania Press, 1994.

Meinig, D. W., ed. *The Interpretation of Ordinary Landscapes: Geographical Essays.* New York: Oxford University Press, 1979.

Melton, J. Gordon. "Satanism." In *The Encyclopedia of American Religions,* edited by J. Gordon Melton. Wilmington, N.C.: McGrath, 1978.

Melton, J. Gordon, and Robert L. Moore, eds. *The Cult Experience: Responding to the New Religious Pluralism.* New York: Pilgrim Press, 1982.

Merkel, Ingrid, and Allen G. Debus, eds. *Hermeticism and the Renaissance: Intellectual History and the Occult in Early Modern Europe.* Washington, D.C.: Folger Press, 1988.

Michaelsen, Johanna. *Like Lambs to the Slaughter: Your Child and the Occult.* Eugene, Or.: Harvest House, 1989.

Miller, Timothy. *The Hippies and American Values.* Knoxville: University of Tennessee Press, 1991.

Monk, Maria. *Awful Disclosures of the Hotel Dieu Nunnery.* 1836. Reprint Hamden, Conn.: Archon Books, 1962.

Moore, R. Laurence. *In Search of White Crows: Spiritualism, Parapsychology, and American Culture.* New York: Oxford University Press, 1977.

———. "The Occult Connection? Mormonism, Christian Science, and Spiritualism." In *The Occult in America,* edited by Howard Kerr and Charles Crow. Urbana: University of Illinois Press, 1983.

————. *Selling God: American Religion on the Cultural Marketplace.* New York: Oxford University Press, 1994.

Morinis, Alan, ed. *Sacred Journeys: The Anthropology of Pilgrimage.* Westport, Conn.: Greenwood Press, 1992.

Murphy, Joseph. "Black Religion and 'Black Magic': Prejudice and Projection in Images of African-Derived Religions." *Religion* 20 (1990): 323–37.

————. *Working the Spirit: Ceremonies of the African Diaspora.* Boston: Beacon Press, 1994.

Murray, Janet H. *Hamlet on the Holodeck: The Future of Narrative in Cyberspace.* New York: The Free Press, 1997.

Murray, Margaret A. *The Witch-Cult in Western Europe.* Oxford: Oxford University Press, 1921.

Myerhoff, Barbara G. *Peyote Hunt: The Sacred Journey of the Huichol Indians.* Ithaca: Cornell University Press, 1974.

————. "Rites of Passage: Process and Paradox." In *Celebration: Studies in Festivity and Ritual,* edited by Victor Turner. Washington, D. C.: Smithsonian Institution Press, 1982.

Namias, June. *White Captives: Gender and Ethnicity on the American Frontier.* Chapel Hill: The University of North Carolina Press, 1995.

Nash, Roderick. *Wilderness and the American Mind.* New Haven: Yale University Press, 1967. Reprint 1973.

Niman, Michael I. *People of the Rainbow: A Nomadic Utopia.* Knoxville: University of Tennessee Press, 1997.

Noonan, Kerry. "May You Never Hunger: Religious Foodways in Dianic Witchcraft." *Ethnologies* 20, no. 1 (1998): 151–73.

O'Brien, Michael. *Father Elijah: An Apocalypse.* San Francisco: Ignatius Press, 1996.

O'Keefe, Daniel. *Stolen Lightning: A Social Theory of Magic.* New York: Continuum, 1982.

Orion, Loretta. *Never Again the Burning Times.* Prospect Heights, Ill.: Waveland Press, 1995.

————. "The Center Out There, In Here, and Everywhere Else: The Nature of Pilgrimage to the Shrine of Saint Jude, 1929–1965." *Journal of Social History* 25, no. 2 (winter 1991): 213–32.

Orsi, Robert A. *The Madonna of 115th Street: Faith and Community in Italian Harlem, 1880–1950.* New Haven: Yale University Press, 1985.

Parker, John. *At the Heart of Darkness: Witchcraft, Black Magic and Satanism Today.* London: Sidgwick & Jackson, 1993.

Peretti, Frank. *Piercing the Darkness.* Westchester, N.Y.: Crossway, 1986.

————. *This Present Darkness.* Westchester, N.Y.: Crossway, 1989.

Peters, Edward. *The Magician, the Witch and the Law.* Philadelphia: University of Pennsylvania Press, 1981.

Peters, Ted. *The Cosmic Self: A Penetrating Look at Today's New Age Movements.* San Francisco: HarperSanFrancisco, 1991.

Pike, Sarah. "Desert Gods, Apocalyptic Art and the Making of Sacred Space at the Burning Man Festival." In *God in the Details: Popular Religion and*

Everyday Life, edited by Kate McCarthy and Eric Mazur. New York: Routledge, 2000.

———. "Magical Selves, Earthly Bodies: Self-Identity and Religious Community
at Contemporary Pagan Festivals. Ph.D. thesis. Indiana University, 1998.

Quaife, Geoffrey. *Godly Zeal and Furious Rage: The Witch Hunts in Early Modern Europe.* New York: St. Martin's Press, 1987.

Regardie, Israel, ed. *777 and Other Qabalistic Writings of Aleister Crowley.* York
Beach, Me.: Samuel Weiser, 1973.

Richardson, James T., Joel Best, and David G. Bromley, eds. *The Satanism Scare.*
New York: A. de Gruyter, 1991.

Rinschede, G., and S. M. Bhardwaj, eds. *Pilgrimage in the United States.* Berlin:
Reimer Verlag, 1990.

Roof, Wade Clark. *A Generation of Seekers.* San Francisco: Harper, 1993.

Root, Deborah. " 'White Indians': Appropriation and the Politics of Display."
In *Borrowed Power: Essays on Cultural Appropriation,* edited by Bruce Ziff
and Pratima V. Rao. New Brunswick, N.J.: Rutgers University Press, 1997.

Rose, Wendy. "The Great Pretenders: Further Reflections on Whiteshamanism."
In *The State of Native America,* edited by Annette M. Jaimes. Boston: South
End Press, 1992.

Rosenwald, George C. "Introduction." In *Storied Lives: The Cultural Politics of
Self-Understanding,* edited by George C. Rosenwald and Richard L. Ochberg.
New Haven: Yale University Press, 1992.

Roszak, Theodore. *The Making of a Counter Culture.* Garden City, N.Y.: Doubleday, 1969.

Rowlandson, Mary. *The Captive.* Tucson, Ariz.: Eagle Publications, 1990.

Royce, Anya Peterson. *Ethnic Identity: Strategies of Diversity.* Bloomington: Indiana University Press, 1982.

Rozell, Mark J., and Clyde Wilcox. *Second Coming: The New Christian Right
in Virginia Politics.* Baltimore: Johns Hopkins University Press, 1996.

Salvo, Dana. *Home Altars of Mexico.* Albuquerque: University of New Mexico
Press, 1997.

Sartre, Jean-Paul. *Saint Genet: Actor and Martyr.* Translated by Bernard Frecht-
man. New York: G. Braziller, 1963.

Schacter, Daniel L. *Searching for Memory: The Brain, the Mind, and the Past.*
New York: Basic Books, 1996.

Schechner, Richard. *Between Theater and Anthropology.* Philadelphia: University of Pennsylvania Press, 1985.

Schmidt, Leigh Eric. *Consumer Rites: The Buying and Selling of American Holidays.* Princeton, N.J.: Princeton University Press, 1995.

Scott, Gini. *Cult and Countercult: A Study of a Spiritual Growth Group and a
Witchcraft Order.* Westport, Conn.: Greenwood Press, 1980

Scott, Jamie, and Paul Simpson-Housley, eds. *Sacred Places and Profane Spaces:
Essays in the Geographies of Judaism, Christianity and Islam.* New York:
Greenwood Press, 1991.

Sears, John. *Sacred Places: American Tourist Attractions in the Nineteenth Century.* Oxford: Oxford University Press, 1979.

Shields, Rob. *Lifestyle Shopping: The Subject of Consumption.* London: Routledge, 1992.

———. *Places on the Margin: Alternative Geographies of Modernity.* London: Routledge, 1991.

Shumaker, Wayne. *The Occult Sciences in the Renaissance: A Study in Intellectual Patterns.* Berkeley and Los Angeles: University of California Press, 1972.

Shweder, Richard, and Robert Levine, eds. *Culture Theory: Essays on Mind, Self, and Emotion.* Cambridge, Eng.: Cambridge University Press, 1984.

Sklar, Dierdre. "Can Bodylore Be Brought to Its Senses?" *Journal of American Folklore* 107, no. 423 (winter 1994): 9–22.

Slotkin, Richard. *Gunfighter Nation: The Myth of the Frontier in Twentieth-Century America.* New York: Atheneum, 1992.

Soja, Edward. *Postmodern Cartographies: The Reassertion of Space in Critical Social Theory.* New York: Verso, 1989.

Spigel, Lynn. "Seducing the Innocent." In *The Children's Culture Reader,* edited by Henry Jenkins. New York: New York University Press, 1998.

Starhawk. *Dreaming the Dark: Magic, Sex and Politics.* Boston: Beacon Press, 1982.

Stephen, Michele. *A'Aisa's Gifts: A Study of Magic and the Self.* Berkeley and Los Angeles: University of California Press, 1995.

Stoeltje, Beverly J. "Festival." In *Folklore, Cultural Performances, and Popular Entertainments: A Communications-Centered Handbook,* edited by Richard Bauman. Oxford: Oxford University Press, 1992.

———. "Power and the Ritual Genres: American Rodeo." *Western Folklore* 52, nos. 3–5 (April, July, Oct. 1993).

Streiker, Lowell D. "The Opening of the American Mind: A Fresh Look at Cults of Persecution." *The Journal of Ecumenical Studies* 27, no. 4 (fall 1990): 731.

Studlar, Gaylyn. "The Metamorphoses of Marlene Dietrich." In *Fabrications: Costume and the Female Body,* edited by Jane Gaines and Charlotte Herzog. New York: Routledge, 1990.

Symonds, John, and Kenneth Grant, eds. *Magic.* London: Routledge and Kegan Paul, 1973.

Tabor, James B., and Eugene V. Gallagher. *Why Waco? Cults and the Battle for Religious Freedom in America.* Berkeley and Los Angeles: University of California Press, 1995.

Talamantez, Ines Maria. "Seeing Red: American Indian Women Speaking about Their Religious and Political Perspectives." *In Our Own Voices: Four Centuries of American Women's Religious Writing,* edited by Rosemary Radford Ruether and Rosemary Skinner Keller. San Francisco: Harper, 1995.

Taussig, Michael. *Mimesis and Alterity: A Particular History of the Senses.* New York: Routledge, 1993.

Taylor, Bron. "Earthen Spirituality or Cultural Genocide?: Radical Environmentalism's Appropriation of Native American Spirituality." *Religion* 27 (1997): 183–215.

Taylor, Charles. *Multiculturalism and the Politics of Recognition.* Princeton, N.J.: Princeton University Press, 1992.

———. *Sources of the Self: The Making of the Modern Identity.* Cambridge, Mass.: Harvard University Press, 1989.

Thomas, Keith. *Religion and the Decline of Magic.* New York: Charles Scribner's Sons, 1971.

Tipton, Steven. *Getting Saved from the Sixties: Moral Meaning in Conversion and Cultural Change.* Berkeley and Los Angeles: University of California Press, 1982.

Tiryakian, Edward A. *On the Margin of the Visible: Sociology, the Esoteric, and the Occult.* New York: John Wiley and Sons, 1974.

Tocqueville, Alexis de. *Democracy in America.* Translated by George Lawrence. Edited by J. P. Mayer. New York: Doubleday, Anchor Books, 1969.

Tolkien, J. R. R. *The Lord of the Rings.* 3 vols. New York: Houghton Mifflin, 1965.

Truzzi, Marcello. "The Occult Revival as Popular Culture: Some Random Observations on the Old and Nouveau Witch." *Sociological Quarterly* 13 (1972): 17–24.

Tuan, Yi-Fu. *Space and Place: The Perspective of Experience.* Minneapolis: University of Minnesota Press, 1977.

Turkle, Sherry. *Life on the Screen: Identity in the Age of the Internet.* New York: Simon & Schuster, 1995.

Turner, Frederick Jackson. *The Frontier in American History.* 1920. Reprint New York: Holt, Rinehart and Winston, 1962.

Turner, Kay, and Suzanne Seriff. " 'Giving an Altar': The Ideology of Reproduction in a St. Joseph's Day Feast." *Journal of American Folklore* 100, no. 398 (Oct.-Dec. 1987): 446–60.

Turner, Victor. "*Carnaval* in Rio: Dionysian Drama in an Industrializing Society." In *The Celebration of Society: Perspectives on Contemporary Cultural Performance,* edited by Frank Manning. Bowling Green, Ky.: Bowling Green University Press, 1983.

———. *Dramas, Fields, and Metaphors: Symbolic Action in Human Society.* Ithaca: Cornell University Press, 1974.

———. *The Ritual Process, Structure and Anti-Structure.* Ithaca: Cornell University Press, 1969.

Turner, Victor, and Edith Turner. *Image and Pilgrimage in Christian Culture: Anthropological Perspectives.* New York: Columbia University Press, 1978.

Tweed, Thomas A., and Stephen Prothero, eds. *Asian Religions in America: A Documentary History.* Oxford: Oxford University Press, 1983.

Valiente, Doreen. *Natural Magic.* New York: St. Martin's Press, 1975.

Van Gennep, Arnold. *The Rites of Passage.* Chicago: University of Chicago Press, 1960.

Vickers, Brian, ed. *Occult and Scientific Mentalities in the Renaissance.* Cambridge, Eng.: Cambridge University Press, 1984.

Victor, Jeffrey S. *Satanic Panic: The Creation of a Contemporary Legend.* Chicago: Open Court, 1993.

Walker, Barbara G. *The Woman's Encyclopedia of Myths and Secrets.* San Francisco: Harper and Row, 1983.

Walker, D. P. *Spiritual and Demonic Magic from Ficino to Campanella*. London: The Warburg Institute, University of London, 1958.

Wallace, Mark. "Black Hawk's 'An Autobiography': The Production and Use of an 'Indian' Voice." *The American Indian Quarterly* 18, no. 4 (fall 1994): 481–95.

Walter, Eugene. *Placeways: A Theory of the Human Environment*. Chapel Hill: University of North Carolina Press, 1988.

Weimann, Gabriel. "Mass-Mediated Occultism: The Role of the Media in the Occult Revival." *Journal of Popular Culture* 18, no. 4 (spring 1985): 81–88.

Wheatley, Dennis. *The Devil Rides Out*. New York: Arrow Books, 1954.

Willis, Paul. *Profane Culture*. London: Routledge, 1978.

Wilson, Bryan. *The Social Dimensions of Sectarianism*. Oxford: Clarendon Press, 1990.

Winthrop, John. "A Model of Christian Charity." In *Puritan Political Ideas, 1558–1794*, edited by Edmund S. Morgan. Indianapolis: Bobbs-Merrill, 1965.

Wuthnow, Robert. *The Restructuring of American Religion*. Princeton, N.J.: Princeton University Press, 1988.

Yates, Frances A. *Giordano Bruno and the Hermetic Tradition*. New York: Vintage, 1964.

Yinger, J. Milton. *Countercultures: The Promise and the Peril of a World Turned Upside Down*. New York: The Free Press, 1982.

York, Michael. *The Emerging Network: A Sociology of the Neo-Pagan and New Age Networks*. Lanham, Md.: Rowman and Littlefield, 1995.

PERIODICALS

Circle Network News (1991–94)
The Elven Chronicle (1991–92)
Enchanté (1989–95)
Fireheart (1988–93)
Green Egg (1990–96)
Mezlim (1992–94)

Index

abortion, 95, 96, 243n29
accumulation, places of, 56, 59. *See also* altars; shrines
ADF (Ar nDraiocht Fein), 62–64, 239nn30–31
Adler, Margot, 20–21, 33–34, 57, 89, 108, 138, 139, 239n30, 240n52, 246n83, 249nn34,36
African Americans: cultural borrowing from, xxi; as Neopagans, 250n60; presence at festivals, 151, 152, 250n60. *See also* racism; Santeria; Vodou
Airique, 176
Alba, DeAnna, 50
Albanese, Catherine L., xiv, 235n42
alcohol, use of, 54, 118, 197, 211, 212, 214
Alicia, Lunae Mica, 69
Aliera, 169
altars, 61, 65–70, 68, 71, 72, 79; as architectonic space, 59–60; at home, 66–69, 68, 147, 240n39; in cars, 69–70, 148; child self and, 163; collective and individual identities and, 64–65, 70; as communication, 66; community, 64–65; cultural borrowing and, 148; Elvis, 78, 79; "energy charging" at, 64, 67; etiquette surrounding, 70; function of, 66–70, 240n42; identity and, 66, 70; locations of, 65–66; private vs. public, 66, 70; of Santeria, 240n42; shrines distinguished from,

56, 65; vandalizing of, 102–3; of Vodou, 240n39; of Wicca, 239n36. *See also* rituals; shrines
Amelia, 82, 83
AMER (Association of Magical and Earth Religions), 244n43
American Indians. *See* Native Americans
American Psychological Association (APA), 90
Ammerman, Nancy, 94
Ananga, 176
Anath, 69
ancestors, 15, 56, 150
Ancestors' Shrine, 49, 59, 60, 61
Ancient Ways, 23, 216, 227n5, 232n2
Anderson, Walter Truett, 257n3
Andrew, 41–43
Andrews, Lynn, 135, 136
animal sacrifice, 101, 113
Anna, 48
APA (American Psychological Association), 90
appearance, use of, 202, 255n47. *See also* body; clothing and costume; piercing; tattoos
AppleMoon Coven, 245n61
Aquino, Michael, 113
Aravah, 207
Arcana (e-mail list), xvii, 229n13, 257n7; discussion on, 91, 105, 110, 132, 169
archetypes, xxii, 69, 141
architectonic spaces, 59–60
architecture of belief, xviii–xix

Aries, Philip, 180
Ar nDraiocht Fein (ADF), 62–64,
  239nn30–31
Artemis, 191
Arthen, Andras Corban, 5, 30,
  231–32n2
Arthen, Deirdre Pulgram, 7, 231–32n2
Asatru, 139
Asian religions: cultural borrowing and,
  xii, 130–31, 148; persecution and, 93;
  as source, xiv
assimilationism, 250n50
Association for Consciousness Exploration (ACE), 232n2
Association of Magical and Earth Religions (AMER), 102, 109, 244n4
astral plane, xxii, 230n21. See also spirit
  world
astral projection, 67
astrology, xxii, 72–73
Augustine, Saint, 221
authenticity, cultural: ambivalence toward criteria, 125, 127, 147, 150–51;
  bloodlines as providing, 138–39, 173,
  253n42; individuality limited by desire
  for, 222, 223; knowledge as providing,
  132–34; Native American criticisms of
  pretensions to, 135, 136–37; Neopagan superiority and, 148, 149; and
  New Age, distancing from, 146; teachers as providing, 126–27
authority: drumming conflicts and,
  214–15; in Neopaganism and Christianity, compared, 121; resentment of,
  105–6, 107, 118; security at festivals
  and, 105–6; of self, xx–xxi, 223;
  sexual harassment and, 210,
  256nn67–68. See also power; rules
  and policies
Awful Disclosures of the Hotel Dieu
  Nunnery (Monk), 243–44n39

baby blessing ceremonies, 56–57, 58–
  59
Baldur, 132
bartering, 3, 74–75
beauty norms, challenging of, 197–98,
  203
Bedford Times-Mail, 118
Begay, Meredith, 136–37
behavior: freedom from mundane requirements of, 25–26, 31, 101, 184;
  unlearning, difficulty of, 210–11
Behavior (music group), 5
belief, xviii–xix. See also deities; God,
  Christian; Goddess; Judaism; spirits;
  spirit world

Bellah, Robert, 29
Berger, Helen, 228n6
Berlinger, Cain, 203
Beth, 78
Bettelheim, Bruno, 172
Between Theater and Anthropology
  (Schechner), 216
Bible, consultation of, 133–34
bisexuality. See gay male, lesbian, bisexual, and transgendered community
  (GLBT)
Black Moon, 255n24
body: attitudes toward, and cultural borrowing, 146–47; beauty norms, challenging of, 197–98, 203; child self of
  adults and, 181; identity construction
  and, 189–90; knowledge gained
  through, 189; marking of, 131, 132,
  190, 198–202 (see also piercing; tattoos); memories stored in, 188–89; as
  sacred, xiii; self as communicated
  through, 198–202, 224; self as healed
  through, 194; as tool in ritual work,
  196–97. See also nature; nudity
Bonewits, Isaac, 119
books, 132–34, 139, 178, 249n43; childhood reading, 158, 161, 162, 167–72,
  173, 174, 252n25; fantasy and fiction
  as influences, 1, 140, 168–72, 231n1;
  text of, on Internet, 257n6
boundaries, xi, 12, 71; and children,
  presence of, 179–80; between Christianity and Neopaganism, 112,
  246n80; contradictions and drawing
  of, 13–14; as crucial, 84–85; dance as
  creating, 190; definitions made via, 37;
  denial of, and cultural borrowing, 130,
  141; drug use and, 197; expression of
  the repressed and, 256n54; within festival, 40, 84–86; fire ritual and, 190,
  207, 211; limitations vs. possibilities
  at, 219; marginality and, 122; between
  mundania and festival, 31, 37–39, 42;
  persecution and (see persecution and
  harassment); and satanism, accusations
  of, 87–88; of self, 28–29, 207; between self and others, 158–59,
  186–87, 207; sexuality and, 190–91,
  194, 207; toilets and, 71; transformation facilitated through, 13–14, 18,
  19; transgression of, 85, 207, 209–11.
  See also collective vs. individual identities; rules and policies
Bradley, Marion Zimmer, 231n1
Branch Davidians, 100
Braude, Ann, 15
Braun, Bennett, 90

British Neopagans, 231n1
Brown County Democrat, 88, 89, 101
Brown, Karen McCarthy, 248n6
Brushwood: Druid nemeton, 49, 59,
    62–64; harassment of, 99, 101–2; loca-
    tion and background of, 24, 227n5;
    marking of space within, 50; security
    measures taken by, 105–6; toilets, 71, 72
Buckland, Raymond, 65, 239n36
Buddhism, xxii, 130–31, 148
building, spirituality and, 64
bumper stickers, 69–70
Burning Man festival, xxiii, 231n24
burnout, festival, 74
Butler, Jon, xiv, 14

Cain, 188–89
Caitlin, 23–24
calendar, 62
Cally, 83
Camelot, 171
Campanelli, Dan, 49
Campanelli, Pauline, 49
campsites, 3–4, 70, 80, 81–85, 163
Campus Crusade for Christ, 97
"Can Bodylore Be Brought to Its
    Senses?" (Sklar), 189
Candida, Reverend, 159–60
Canning, Janice, 138
Carlisle, Chris, 109, 110, 145
Carnaval, 25, 203, 235n35
Carpenter, Dennis, 27, 108, 231n2,
    233n14
Carrie, 166
cars, altars in, 69–70, 148
Cary, 201
Castaneda, Carlos, 135
Catherine, 158–59, 162
Catholics: persecution of, 243–44n39;
    persecution of Neopagans and, 94–98,
    243nn29,30. *See also* Christianity; per-
    secution and harassment
Ceil, 16
Celest, 160, 178
Celtic witchcraft, 139
Cernunnos, 114
Cerridwen, xviii
Chameleon Club, 232n2
chants: "Air I Am, Fire I Am . . . ,"
    5; "Earth my body, water my
    blood . . . ," 23, 159; oppositional atti-
    tudes of, 252n19; sources of, 5; "We
    are the old people . . . ," 123;
    "Weavers . . . ," 7–8
Chants to Dance, 195, 227n5, 236n47
Chautauqua Institutes, 14, 232–33n7
Cheri, 66

child abuse: Christian inculcation and,
    177, 178, 254n59; Christians and,
    109, 246n68; satanic ritual abuse, con-
    troversy of, 90–91, 94, 99, 109,
    242n16, 246n68
childhood, as construction, 180–81
childhood stories: ambivalence toward,
    157; books, importance of, 158, 161,
    162, 167–72, 173, 174, 252n25; con-
    sistency of self and, 230n20; construc-
    tion of, 155–57, 164–65, 180–81,
    224; family of origin and, 165–67,
    175–79; fire ritual and, 191; gifted
    abilities and, 160–62; landscape of,
    157–63, 251n5; loss and recovery of,
    180–81; nature, appreciation of, 157,
    158–60; obstacles, overcoming of,
    178–79; ostracism and, 158, 161,
    162–63, 222; spirit world, contact
    with, 167, 252n27; supernatural, sen-
    sitivity to, 157, 160, 165–66. *See also*
    family of origin
childlike wonder, 163, 164, 167, 168,
    172
children and adolescents: abuse of (*see*
    child abuse); control of, and persecu-
    tion, 98–99, 102; custody of, and per-
    secution, 91, 180; fairy tales and, 172,
    fire ritual and, 254n22; interests of,
    demonization of, 177–78; programs for,
    at festivals, 179–80, 254n22; spiritual-
    ity of, 156, 251n4; vandalism by, 102–3
Children of the Laughing Greenwood
    coven, 6
chosen family. *See* family of choice
Chris, 91, 161–62, 176, 201, 211
Christianity: aggressive proselytizing of,
    177–78; backgrounds in, coming to
    terms with, 111–13; childhood strug-
    gles with, 165–66, 175–79; "Christian-
    bashing," 104, 107–13, 121; fear of
    difference and, 93–94, 96–98; as hypo-
    critical, 176–77; as impoverished, 160,
    176; marginal movements in, xiv,
    14–19; population of Neopagans with
    backgrounds in, 253n49; rejection of
    (*see* Christianity, distancing from); Sa-
    tanism as related to, 114; unification of,
    by persecution of others, 95, 243n29
Christianity, distancing from, xiii, 16, 18,
    111–12, 175–79, 193, 233n18; and
    cultural borrowing, 123–24, 126, 144,
    149, 153, 154
Christians: abuse by, 109, 246n68; perse-
    cution of Neopagans by (*see* persecu-
    tion and harassment); as term, 227n2
church buildings, 49, 58

Church of All Worlds, xviii, xx, 216, 244n41

Church of Satan, 90, 113, 115

Church Universal and Triumphant, 100

cigarettes, 212

circle: casting of/calling the quarters, 7, 57–58; childhood awareness and, 160; closing of, 257n1; importance of, 29; as protection, 52; as symbol of community, 29–31, 37–38. *See also* rituals

Circle Harvest Fest, 24, 227n5

Circle Network News, xviii, 23, 239n26; as source, 23–24, 45, 50, 56, 91, 138, 181, 188–89, 197, 241n5

Circle Sanctuary, 16, 45, 99–100, 227n5, 231n2. *See also* Pagan Spirit Gathering

clan, of ELF, 2

cleansing rituals, 54, 55, 186, 196

Clecak, Peter, xx, 171

closet, being in the, 83, 222

clothing and costume: childlike wonder evoked through, 163, 164; as concealing the past, 153; cultural borrowing and, 126, 147, 153; fiction as influencing, 170; fire ritual and, 182; healing and, 198–99; medieval flavor of, 170, 172; merchants selling, 76, 78, 198–99; methodology and, 206, 256n59; norms of, 206–7; ostracism and, 162; role playing and, 172; security of festival and, 105, 106, 107; self-transformation and, 202–5, 255nn47,49

Coles, Robert, 156, 251n4

collective vs. individual identities: altars and, 64–65, 70; ambivalence toward individuality, 113; autonomy and, xx–xxii, 222–23; boundaries and, 225–26; campsites and, 81; as central contradiction, 13–14; conflicts and, 210, 211; and cultural borrowing, criticism of, 137, 143–44; differences between people and, 37–38; "Do as thou will as long as thou harm none," 210; eclecticism and, 53–54, 57; fire and, 183, 187, 224–25; public relations and, 105–6, 107, 117–20; safety and, 217; Satanism distinguished from Neopaganism and, 113; self-transformation and, 13, 29–38; shrines and, 56, 59, 60; value of community and, xxi–xxii, xxiii, 222–26. *See also* authority; community; self

Commercial Appeal, xi–xii

commercialization: cultural borrowing and, 134, 135–36; of festivals, 74–75, 85; and New Age movement, distancing from, 145–46

communication: drumming as, 193–94, 212–13; electronic (*see* Internet)

community: altar for, 64–65; healing amplified through, xxi–xxii, xxiii; home vs. festival, encounters of, 31–32; identity of, vs. individual (*see* collective vs. individual identities); rule-breaking and, 42; self as requiring, xxi–xxii, 224–25; shrines and, 59

A Community of Witches (Berger), 228n6

"Conjuring the Holy: Mexican Domestic Altars" (Gutierrez), 66

contests, 4

contradictions, central, 13–14. *See also* collective vs. individual identities

Corrigan, Ian, 148

counterculture, 1960s, 229–30n17; appeal to, and public relations, 120, 247n105; authority of self and, xx, 223; and desire for self-chosen religion, 223; and 1990s countercultural festivals, 231n24; nostalgia and, 171; religion following, xxii–xxiii; as source, xiv; wilderness and, 234n27

covens, groves compared to, 239n31

crime, 90, 94

cross-dressing, 202–4, 255n49

Crow, 201, 214

Crowley, Aleister, xiv; and magick, spelling of, 228n5; teachings of, 13, 102, 113, 210, 244nn48,50, 246n83, 247n93

Crystal, 73

cultural borrowing, xii–xiii, 123–26; authenticity and (*see* authenticity, cultural borrowing and); bloodlines and, 128, 130, 138–39, 249nn34–36; body and, 224; criticism of, 138, 151; criticism of, by Native Americans, 124–25, 134–37, 138, 249n35; criticism of, by Neopagans, 144–51, 153–54; as fate, 129–30; fire and, 188; fluid boundaries and, 142–44, 250n52; justification of, 128, 129–30, 137–44; knowledge and, 132–34, 139, 249n43; lack of culture and, 125–26, 139; openness to, by Native Americans, 125, 126–27, 134, 138; and self, needs of, xxi, 137, 139 40, 151; universals, appeal to, 141, 142–44; workshops and, 123, 125, 247n1

cultural imperialism, 134–37. *See also* cultural borrowing

cultural theory, 142, 144, 250n52, 255n47. *See also* postmodernism

Cummings, Patricia, 135

Cut 'N' Mix (Hebdige), 142

Damarru, J. Perry, 70, 84, 188, 194
DaMatta, Roberto, 25
"Dance Work" (Tabor), 207
dancing: children and, 254n22; costuming and, 182, 202, 255n48; erotic, 193, 194, 206, 207–9, 211, 217, 225; as essential, 5, 183; gender and, 184, 202, 206; healing and, 194–98, 225; safety and, 190–91, 193, 194, 195, 207–9; styles of, 182, 183–85, 193; workshops on, 188, 193
darkness, 23
Dark Shadows (television program), 175
Darling, Diane, 16
Dave, 201
David, 84–85
Davis, Pete Pathfinder, 111
death: memorials, 49, 56, 59, 60, 61; views of, 60, 62
"Declaration of War against Exploiters of Lakota Spirituality," 124, 136
Deigh, Kenneth, xvii, 11–12, 14, 27, 28, 31–32, 202, 208, 221
deities: as accessible, 15; archetypes and, xxii, 69, 141; attitudes toward nature of, 148–49, 160; childhood conceptions of, 159, 160; cultural borrowing and, 131, 148–49; cultural boundaries as disregarded by, 129, 141–42; cultural study and, 132; disbelief in, and Christian identification, 149; eclecticism and relationship to, xiii, 40, 57, 123, 239n25; embodiment of, xxi, 149, 195–96; energy personified by, 160; as immanent, 23, 193; meeting of new, 39; nature as value and, 49–50; oneness with, xxii; persecution based on, 97–98, 114, 121; polytheism and, 57, 97; transformation of, by Christianity, 114. *See also* God, Christian; Goddess
Denise, 115
Derek, 178
The Devil Rides Out (Wheatley), 231n1
Diana, 85
Dickstein, Morris, 229–30n17
difference. *See* other
Dionysus, 149
Discipline and Punish (Foucault), 43
discrimination in employment, 83, 244n43. *See also* persecution and harassment
Djoliba, 5
dog altar, 60, 61
Drawing Down the Moon. See Adler, Margot
Dreaming the Dark (Starhawk), 238n4
dreams, 174, 253n45

Drewel, Margaret, 257n76
drugs, use of, 195, 196, 197; alcohol, 54, 118, 197, 211, 212, 214; persecution and, 101; policy on illegal, 118, 119; as public relations issue, 117, 118–19
Druids, 49, 59, 62–64, 139, 239nn30–31
drumming: conflicts involving, 117–18, 192–93, 212–15; cultural borrowing and, 128–29, 151; as essential, 5, 183, 187, 191–92; identity and, 5; neighbor complaints and, 106, 117–18; ritual structure and, 7; styles of, 182, 183–85; workshops on, 188, 192
Dune (Herbert), 168
Dungeons and Dragons (game), 90, 171, 252–53n39
Duvignaud, Jean, 238n2

Earth First!, 48
earth religions (nature religions), xiv; as term, use of, 23, 235n42. *See also* Neopaganism
EarthSpirit Community, xviii, 64, 209, 210
eclecticism, xii–xiii; collective and individual identities and, 53–54, 57; and cultural borrowing, criticism of, 136, deities and, xiii, 40, 57, 123, 239n25; drumming and, 192–93; flexibility as necessitated by, 57; merchants and, 75–76, 78; nineteenth-century antecedents and, 14; persecution based on, 95–96; as postmodern, 220–21; public relations and, 116–17; purity issues and, 53–54; sexuality and, 194. *See also* cultural borrowing
egalitarianism, and the real vs. ideal, 43, 106, 206
elders, 2, 34, 43, 116–17
electronic communication. *See* Internet
ELFest: intimacy of strangers, 7; location and background of, 1, 227n5; meal arrangements, 5, 22, 73; merchants of, 85; rituals of, 6, 23, 221
Elf Lore Family (ELF): and children's activities, 179; elders, 2, 34, 43, 116–17; fire, 211–12, 214–15; persecution and, 88–89, 106, 245n56; public relations of, 116–20; security measures taken by, 106–7; structure and background of, 2
Ellenie, 112–13
Eller, Cynthia, 66, 74, 252n27, 254n59
Ellwood, Robert, xx, 15, 171, 175
Elven Chronicle, xviii; as source, 58, 106, 170, 185, 209, 211–12, 214

Elvis altar, 78, 79
Elwood, Roger, 178, 253n57
Emerson, Ralph Waldo, xiv, 18
employment, xv, 251n9; discrimination
    in, 83, 244n43
Enchanté, xviii
The Encyclopedia of American Religions
    (Melton), 93
endangered species, cultural borrowing
    and, 135
energy: nature of, 160, 239n17; of tem-
    ple, as continuous, 67
environmentalism: cultural borrowing and,
    125; political involvement with, 48;
    public relations and, 116; spiritual basis
    of, 233n14; as wide-ranging, 45, 48
ethics: and ambivalence toward cultural
    borrowing, 147; postmodernism and,
    257n3; sacred space and, 49–50; tree-
    cutting incident and, 42
etiquette: of altars, 70; dancing, 193,
    194; fire and drumming, 212, 213–15;
    privacy, 84–85; of touch, 209–10. See
    also safety
European-Americans, fear of difference
    and, 92–94
evangelical camp meetings, 14, 16–17
Ewing, Katherine P., 230n20

Faerie Woods, 41–45, 53, 241n53
fairy/faerie, as term, 241n53
fairy tales, function of, 172
fairy woods, 83–84, 163
Falassi, Alessandro, 238n2
Falcon Storm, 166, 169, 176
family of choice, 132; necessity of, xiii,
    222; workshops supporting, 35,
    237n71
family, festival, 32–37; defined, 83; im-
    portance of, 83; merchants as facilitat-
    ing, 80–81; private campsites and, 82
family of origin, 172–79; Christianity in-
    culcated by, 165–66; control exerted
    by, 165–67, 175–79; distancing from,
    83, 222; inheritance from, authenticity
    and, 138–39, 173, 253n42; support
    given by, 158, 173–75, 223, 253n42
fantasy fiction, as influence, 1, 168–72
Farr, Florence, 13
Farrar, Janet, 193
Farrar, Stewart, 193
Farrell, Perry, 231n24
fate, 129–30, 174
feasts, 3, 5, 72–73
feminist gatherings, 74, 252n27
feminists, spiritual, 66, 254n59. See also
    women

femrel-l (e-mail list), xvii, 229n13
Fenholdt, Jeff, 100
Fernandez, James, 59
Festival Drumming (Black Moon), xv,
    212, 255n24
festivals, 1–9; church buildings compared
    to, 49, 58; hierarchy of, 2–3 (see also
    authority; power); inclusiveness of, xv,
    15, 116–17; maturing of, 222–23;
    meal arrangements, 5, 22, 54, 72–73;
    music and dance (see dancing; drum-
    ming; fire, ritual); nineteenth-century
    antecedents to, xiv, 14–19; parking, 2;
    participants of (see participants); as pil-
    grimage, xxi, 27–29, 39, 238n78; plan-
    ning of, xvii–xviii, 2–3, 6, 231–32n2;
    preregistration for, 6; purity and (see
    purity); rituals (see altars; rituals;
    shrines); safety in (see safety); security
    at, 101–3, 105–6; self-transformation
    and (see self-transformation); sites (see
    sites; and specific festival sites); spaces
    within (see spaces within festival site);
    women's, 39, 74, 84, 252n27
Ficino, Marsilio, xiv
fiction, as influence, 167–72
field notes, xvi–xvii
fire, ritual, 8, 182–90; ashes of, 38, 51,
    58; body and, 183, 188–90; conflicts
    at, 117–18, 207–15; continuity and,
    51; dancers and (see dancing); diversity
    and, 192–93, 205, 212–15; drumming
    and (see drumming); gender roles and,
    205–6; improvisation/structurelessness
    and, 183, 185–86, 190, 191, 196, 211;
    methodology and, 186–87; norm ex-
    pectations and, 206–8; purity issues
    and, 54, 211–15; purpose of, 185,
    186, 190, 211–13; safety and,
    190–91, 196, 217; self-transformation
    and, 189–90, 206, 215–17, 224–25;
    sexuality and, 190–91, 193–94, 206,
    207–11, 217, 225; as space apart,
    185–87; space designated for, 53; third
    shift, 184, 212; tribe and union with
    others, 186–88
Fireheart, xviii, 64
flirting, 194, 209
folklore, 116, 133
folk magic, xiv, 173–75, 249n36,
    253n42
food, 5, 22, 54, 72–73
Fortune, Dion, 231n1, 244n48
Foucault, Michel, 43, 234n29, 238n3
four directions, 7, 52, 57–58, 62–63, 67
Fox, Selena, 16, 105, 231n2
Franchot, Jenny, 243–44n39

Fred (owner of Brushwood), 99, 102, 105, 120–21
freedom: limitations on (*see* collective vs. individual identities; rules and policies); meaning of, 191; nudity as statement of, 204–5; of self-expression, 33–37
Free Spirit Gathering, 187, 198
Freud, Sigmund, 28
Frew, Don, 94
frontier, 18–19, 234n24

Gaia, xxi, 50
Garber, Marjorie, 202
Gardner, Gerald B., xiv, 246n83
Gardnerian Wicca, xiv, 246n83
"Gathering Primer" (Damarru), 70, 188, 194
gay male, lesbian, bisexual, and transgendered community (GLBT): campsites for, 83–84; Christianity and, 176, 177; cross-dressing and, 202–3; family and, 33, 222; homophobia and, xiii, 222; merchants and, 78; population of, 84; Radical Faeries, 78, 84, 240n52; safety and, 84, 205; workshops and, 98
Gede, 142, 143
Geertz, Clifford, 230n20
gender: attitudes toward, and cultural borrowing, 146–47; playing with distinctions in, 202–3, 206, 255n49; roles of, conventional assumptions about, 205–6, 225. *See also* women
Genet, Jean, 251n19
Gennep, Arnold van, 20
Giddens, Anthony, 223–24
Gitlin, Todd, 229n17
Gnostic Mass, 101–2, 244nn48,50, 247n93
God, Christian: persecution and, 97–98, 121
Goddess: "All acts of love and pleasure . . . ," 194; Earth as (Gaia), xxi, 50; eclecticism and, xiii, 141, 142; triple aspect of, 62; within self, 221. *See also* deities
Godric, 197–98
Golden Dawn, xiv, 13
good and evil, struggle between, 97
Goode, Starr, 114
Graham, Billy, 114
Great Rite, 193–94
Green Egg, xviii, 16, 22; as source, 96, 105, 111, 112, 115, 119, 244n41, 246n80
Greenleaf, 139
Green Man, 42

Greven, Phillip, 246n68
Greywalker, Raven, 213
grief rituals, 41
groves, 239n31
Gus, 141
Gutierrez, Ramon A., 66
Gygax, Gary, 252–53n39

Habits of the Heart (Bellah), 29
Hall, David, xiv
Halloween, 108. *See also* Samhain
Hamlet on the Holodeck (Murray), xvii–xviii
Hammond, Phillip E., xx–xxi, 230n18
handfasting/marriage, 33, 35, 98, 172
Harding, Jerry, 159
Harvest of Light, 34
healing: alternatives, 74; of child self, 157; community and, xxi–xxii; fire ritual and, 194–98, 215–16; as focus of festival, xiii, xxi, 28, 74, 138, 196; merchants and, 74–75; Native American, 136–37; nudity as, 204–5; psychological, 74, 194–97, 215–16; space for, 22, 28, 73–75
"Healing Tattoo" (Crow), 201
Hebdige, Dick, 142
Hedgehog, 166, 169
Herald Telephone, 89, 116
Herbert, Frank, 168
heterosexuality, as less emphasized, 84
heterosexuals: cross-dressing by, 202–3; homoerotic play by, 194
hierarchy, 2–3, 14–15. *See also* authority; power
higher self, 35–37, 221
Hinduism, xiv, xxii
hippies, 119–20, 247n105, 255n47
history: campsites and, 82; "golden age" phenomenon of, 149; identity construction and imagined, 170–71; life-passage rituals and, 58–59; memory and, 38, 50; of pre-Christian traditions, xiv, 48–49, 62, 63, 114, 138–39
holiday, pagan origins of, 108, 176–77
home: body and, 188–89; campsites, 3–4, 70, 80, 81–85, 163; coming home, 162, 167; contradiction of leaving one to find one, 13; dynamic relationship of, 39–40; effects of pilgrimage and, 238n78; family formation and, 82–84; festival as, 13, 32–37; of merchants, 80–81; public sites as, 51; as retreat, 82; special designations for, 82–83; welcome home, 32. *See also* family, festival
homophobia, xiii, 222

homosexuality. *See* gay male, lesbian, bisexual, and transgendered community (GLBT)
horned god, 114
humor, 72, 101, 110, 117
hybridization, 15

Ian, 185, 187
Iannelli, Derek R., 130
ideal vs. real, xix–xx, 43, 111–12
identity, xix; altars and, 66, 70; cars and, 69–70; creation of (*see* childhood stories; cultural borrowing; self-transformation); cultural borrowing and, 137, 153–54; as fate, 174; frontier and, 18–19; modernist, 223–24; music and dance and, 5; the other and, 121–22, 123–24, 126, 144, 149, 153, 162–63; participant-observer status and, xvi; persecution and, 87–88, 108, 121–22, 162–63, 178, 245n59, 252n19; realization of, 158, 162–63; white middle-class, as ever-present, 153. *See also* self *and related entries*
Illuminati of Indiana, 236n47, 244–45n50
imagination, childhood and, 160–61
immanence, 23
individualism, 113. *See also* collective vs. individual identities
interconnectedness, as central belief, 24, 158–59, 223. *See also* collective vs. individual identities; relationships
International Society for Krishna Consciousness, 100
Internet: communication via, 2–3, 104–5, 111; postmodern self and, 220; sources on, xvii, 220, 229nn13–14, 257nn6–7
intimacy: campsites and, 82; distance and, 144–51, 153; facilitation of, 32; of strangers, 73, 80, 83
intolerance, 111–12, 154, 176
The Invented Indian (Clifton), 124
Iron Oak Coven, 92
Islam, 114

Jade, 73
Jake, 132–33
Jeffrey, 44
Jerry, 127
Johnny, 41, 83
Johnson, Caitlin, 56
Jonesboro, Arkansas, xi–xii
journeys, 211, 216, 257n76. *See also* pilgrimage
joy, 191

Joyce, James, 221
Judaism, xiii, 176, 253n49
Jung, Carl, xxii, 28, 69, 141
Justyn, 181

Katy, 162–63
Keenan, Richard, 198
Kehoe, Alice B., 149
Kertzer, David, 238n2
Ketcham, Katherine, 242n16
Kevin, 67, 69, 207
King, Francis, 244n48
kinship: fictive, 132; home altars and, 66, 240n39. *See also* family *entries*
Kinslow, Justyn, 165
Knode, Helen, 114
knowledge: of body, 189; cultural borrowing and, 132–34, 139, 249n43. *See also* books
Koslow, Jeff, xviii–xix
Kouyate, Lansana, 5
Kristina, 209–10
Kurtz, Katherine, 168
Kym, 131

Lady Liberty League, 244n43
Lamp, Frederick, 196–97
LaRouche, Lyndon, 115
Larry, 78
Larry, 106–7
late-night activities, 8, 215; fire (*see* fire, ritual)
La Vey, Anton, 90, 113, 115
L.A. Weekly, 114
Leaf, 27
Legba, 128, 130, 248n6
LeGuin, Ursula K., 168, 231n1
Leona, 202
Leopold, Aldo, 234n27
lesbians. *See* gay male, lesbian, bisexual, and transgendered community (GLBT)
Lewis, C. S., 231n1
ley lines, 160
life passages, xx; death (*see* death); handfasting/marriage, 33, 35, 98, 172; loci of, 58–59, 239n6; naming ceremonies, 56–57, 58–59; spaces for, 56; tattoos commemorating, 199–202
Lilith Fair, xxiii, 231n24
liminality, 20, 181, 207, 235n34
Lin, 168, 174
Linden, Mishlen, 255n24
lingerie, 25, 204
Lizard, A., 140
Llew, 178
Loftus, Elizabeth, 242n16
Looking Horse, Martina, 136, 146–47

The Lord of the Rings (Tolkien), 1
Lothlorien: Ancestors' Shrine, 49, 59, 60, 61; campsites at, 82–83; drumming, dome for, 118, 185, 186, 214; Faerie Woods of, 41–45, 53, 241n53; fairy camp of, 241n53; Heart Tree Circle, 56–57; location and background of, xv, 2, 24, 236n47; nudity policy, 107; persecution and, 106; space designations in, 44, 46–47, 50–51; toilets, 71, 72
LSD, 197
Lucy, 149
Luhrman, Tanya M., 203, 231n1
Lumensgate, xvii, 11, 27, 237n68
Lyotard, Jean-François, 220

Maddog, 213, 214
Maggie, 139
magic: ceremonial, xiv; definitions of, 12–13, 249n36; folk, xiv, 173–75, 249n36, 253n42; intention as determining nature of, 64; spelled magick, meaning of, 228n5; stage magic, 5, 228n5
Magick in Theory and Practice (Crowley), 228n5
Magic—The Gathering (game), 171
Magliocco, Sabina, 133
Malleus Maleficarum (Institoris and Sprenger), 114, 245n66
Mann, Thomas, 221
maps, 44, 46–47
marginality: embracing of, 16, 122; ostracism, 158, 161, 162–63, 222; as unifying, 31, 32. *See also* the other: identification with; persecution and harassment: identity and
Margolis, Diane Rothbard, 230n21
Marie, 202, 255n48
Marilyn, 168
Marion, 130–31
marketplace, 74–81, 76, 77, 85, 198–99, 200–201
marriage/handfasting, 33, 35, 98, 172
Martello, Leo, 109, 114, 115
Martinie, Louis, 127–30, 129, 148, 150–51, 192, 223, 255n24
Martinsville Reporter, 92
Marty, Trevor, 188
Mary-Ann, 113–14
massage practitioners, 22
McBride, Jeff "Magnus," 5
meal arrangements, 5, 22, 54, 72–73
media: misrepresentation by, xi–xii, 93, 99, 108, 245n61; of Neopagans, as source, xvii–xviii; occult interest and,

175; and persecution, xii, 88–89, 91–93, 94, 100, 101, 103–4, 106, 175; rumors and, 101. *See also* books
medieval representations, 170, 171, 172, 206
meditation, 979
mediums, 15
Melissa, 110
melting-pot ideology, 126, 142, 250n50
Melton, J. Gordon, 93
memorials, 49, 56, 59, 60, 61
memory: body and, 188–89; fire as central to, 187; forgetting, importance of, 25; as fragile, 180; history and, 38, 50; recovered, 242n16; self-transformation and, 39; and temporary sites, 50
men. *See* gender
menstruation, cultural borrowing and, 146, 147
merchants, 74–81, 76, 77, 85, 198–99, 200–201
methodology, xii, xv–xviii, xix–xx, 186–87, 206, 229n14, 244n45, 256n59
Mezlim, xvii, xviii, 11, 199, 207, 213
Michael, 26, 50, 51, 201, 204, 205, 215–16
Michaelsen, Joanna, 178
Michelle Remembers (Smith and Pazder), 98, 242n16
Michigan Women's Music Festival, 84
Midnight, 212
military, Pagans and, 160, 181, 225, 251n12
Miriam (psychologist), 195–96
Miriam (Vodou Priestess), 150–51, 152
The Mists of Avalon (Bradley), 231n1
Monk, Maria, 243–44n39
Moongold, 126, 140, 141, 142
Moon Magic (Fortune), 231n1
Moonstar, 23
Moore, R. Laurence, 232–33n7
moral issues, persecution and, 94–95, 96, 98, 121. *See also* ethics
Morinis, 238n78
Mormons, 178
Mt. Horeb, Wisconsin, 99–100
movies, portrayals in, 93, 99
Ms. Manners, 209, 212, 213
mud, 205
Muir, John, 234n27
"mundania": connection to, 38–39; defined, 13; merchants and boundary with, 75–78; separation from, 13–14, 20–21, 37–40, 235n34. *See also* boundaries
Murray, Margaret, xiv, xvii–xviii

music, 5–6, 142. *See also* dancing; drumming
The Myth of Repressed Memory (Loftus and Ketcham), 242n16

names, 131–32, 248n14; cultural borrowing and, 131–32; at festivals, 233n11; methodology and, xvii, 229n14
national parks, 17
Native Americans: cultural borrowing from (*see* cultural borrowing); nations of, distinctions between, 249n28; pipe ceremony, 84; presence at festivals, 32, 125, 247n1, 250n60; ritual objects and sacred sites of, 135, 147; smudging, 55; sweat lodge, 127, 146–47, 150, 223; whites speaking for, 136, 138, 249n27
natrel-l (e-mail list), xvii, 48
Natural Health (magazine), 95
nature: childhood valuing of, 157, 158–60; hyperreality of festival and, 22–23; immanence in, 23; importance of valuing, 45, 159; pilgrimages to, 27; as sacred, 23–24; Satanism distinguished from Neopaganism and, 113–14; as spiritual frontier, 17–19, 234n27. *See also* body; environmentalism
nature religions. *See* earth religions (nature religions)
neighbors: methodology and, 244n45; persecution by (*see* persecution and harassment); support or neutrality from, 119–21, 247n105
Neopaganism: dismissal of, 25; interconnectedness and, 24, 158–59, 223; and life passages (*see* life passages); New Age compared to, 95–96, 145–46; norms of, conformity to, 206–9; origins of, xiii–xiv; persecution of (*see* persecution and harassment); Satanism compared to, 113–15; SCA compared to, 170
Neopagans: avoidance of term, 116–17; books and (*see* books); culture of origin, uniformity of, xv, 123, 153, 157; identity of (*see* identity; self *entries*); literacy of, 132, 133; names of (*see* names); the other and (*see* other); as population, xii–xiii, xv, 228n6; publications of, as source, xvii–xviii; public relations by, 116–20, 247n105; recognition as persecuted minority desired by, 153, 251n66; scholarship of, 132–33, 249–50n43; as term, 116–17, 227n1. *See also* participants

New Age (magazine), 95
New Age movement, 95–96; cultural borrowing and, 125, 135; distancing from, by Neopagans, 144–46; Neopaganism compared to, 95–96, 145–46; religious right and, 95, 96, 97
New Religious Movements (NRMs), 31, 237n62
News from the Mother Grove, 62–63
newspapers, 88–89, 92–93, 101, 106
Nicole, 45, 48
nineteenth-century antecedents, of Neopagan festivals, xiv, 14–19
Noadia, 108
noise, conflicts over, 101, 106, 117–18, 214–15
non-Christian religions: identification with (*see* cultural borrowing); persecution of, as uniting Christians, 95, 243n29. *See also* pre-Christian religions; *specific religions*
non-European cultures: attitudes toward body and gender in, 146–47; identification with (*see* cultural borrowing)
Norse religion, 132, 249n34
nostalgia, 171
nudity: attitudes toward, and cultural borrowing, 147; childlike wonder and, 191; control of, 107; as expectation, 206–7; fire rituals and, 191, 192, 198; function of, 204–5; persecution and, 97, 107; public relations and, 120, 247n105. *See also* body; clothing and costume

obeah, 130, 151, 248n10
Ochberg, Richard, 155
The Omen, 93
Ordo Templi Orientis (OTO), 113, 244nn48,49
Orion, Loretta, 24–25, 27, 33, 38, 209
orisha, 39
Oshun, 39
ostracism, 158, 161, 162–63, 222. *See also* marginality
the other: exclusion of, 113–15, 147n93, 178; fear of, and persecution of Neopagans, 89–90, 93–94, 98, 121; identification with, 121–22, 123–24, 126, 144, 149, 153, 162–63. *See also* cultural borrowing
"The Other Alternative: Piercing as Body Art" (Berlinger), 203
OTO (Ordo Templi Orientis), 113, 244nn48,49
outcasts. *See* marginality
out-of-body experiences, 44, 158

pacifism, 251n12
Pagan, xii, 116–17. *See also* Neopaganism; Neopagans
Pagan Digest (e-mail list), 229n13; discussion on, 15, 69, 105, 111, 112–13, 126, 138, 139, 140, 145, 169, 185, 200, 201, 245n61
"Pagan Gatherings—Discovering Spiritual Homeland" (Threlfall), 27–28
Pagan Spirit Gathering (PSG): activities offered by, 5; campsites at, 81, 82; Candle Labyrinth, *184*; children's activities at, 179; community altar, 64–65; dancing at, 197–98; drug policy of, 119; family of choice, 35; fire of, 54, 211, 288; folklore knowledge, 133; healing space at, 22; identification of participants, 3; location and background of, 227n5; marking of space at, 51–52; meal arrangements, 5, 72–73; merchants of, 75–76; nudity policy, 107; persecution and, 105; rituals at, 6, 8, 29–30, 38; sexual orientation survey results, 84; tornado experience at, 51–52
"Pagan Standard Time," 26
Palm Bay, Florida, 92
Pan, 114
Pantheacon, 4, 195, 227n5, 231–32n2
pantheism, 57
participant-observer status, xv–xvi, xix, 186–87
participants, xv; arrival of, 1, 3–4; camping and, 3–4, 70, 80, 81–85, 163; differences between, 37–38; festival virgins, 13; identification of, 3, 105–6; names of (*see* names); volunteer activities of, 2–3; work shifts required of, 3; world brought with them, 31–32. *See also* Neopagans
path, spiritual, 130–31
Pauline, 162, 168
Pazder, Lawrence, 242n6
Peale, Norman Vincent, 95
peers, ostracism by, 158, 161, 162–63, 222
Peh, xvii, 22, 32, 34, 36–37, 53–54, 67, 68, 92–93, 117, 119–20, 149, 204, 208
Pentecostalism, xxiii, 83
Peretti, Frank, 253n57
performance, 216
Perrin, Bryan, 63
persecution and harassment: accusations of satanism, 87–94; child-custody and, 91, 180; Christian-bashing and, 104, 107–13, 121; coming out and,

162–63; conflict with Neopagan communities and, 116–20; identity and, 87–88, 108, 121–22, 162–63, 178, 245n59, 252n19; methods of, 89–90; organizations to combat, 102, 109, 244n43; ostracism, 158, 161, 162–63, 222; power dynamics of, 121; reasons for, 89–90, 93–98, 99–100; responses to, 87–88, 89, 93, 99–101, 104–15, 121–22, 241n5, 244n43, 245n56; rumor and spectacle and, 87, 98–104; self-representation and, 116–20; and unification of persecuting religion, 95, 243n29; and unification of religions persecuted, 108, 122, 245n59. *See also* festivals: security at; sexual harassment
Persephone, 23
Peta, 131
Phil's Grill, 73
piercing, 198, 199, 201–2, 203, 224
pilgrimage, xxi, 27–29, 39, 238n78
place: definition of, 233n20; myths of, 19–20, 85, 234–35n30; a place apart, 19–26, 27–29, 31, 234n29. *See also* behavior; sacred space; sites
play, 184, 195, 203
police: festivals and, 106, 118–19; harassment and, 88–89, 90, 92, 106, 241n8
politics, withdrawal from, 48
Pollack, Scott, 64
polyamory, 35, 98, 237n71
polytheism, 57, 97
popular culture, 78, 79
The Postmodern Condition (Lyotard), 220
postmodernism, 220–21, 222, 257n3; cultural boundaries and, 142, 144, 250n52; eclecticism and, 220; self and, 151, 220, 257n3
power: defined, 43, 238nn2,3; egalitarianism vs. assumptions about, 210; hidden forms of, 43, 238n4; of place apart, 19–20, 234n29; politics of persecution and, 121; spatial relations and, 42–43. *See also* authority; rules and policies
pre-Christian religions: connection with, xiv, 48–49, 62, 63, 114, 138–39; persecution and loss of, 108–9, 114. *See also* non-Christian religions
"Primal Gaia: Primitivists and Plastic Medicine Men" (Kehoe), 149
promotional material, 24, 29, 34, 35, 116–20, 185–86, 187, 188, 247n105
prostitution, sacred, 98

Protestants: child abuse and, 109,
246n68; "golden age" remembered by,
149–50; persecution of Neopagans
and, 94–98, 243nn29,30, 243–44n39.
See also Christianity; persecution and
harassment
Prothero, Stephen, 93
Pryor, Eric, 96, 244n41
psychedelic mushrooms, 195, 196, 197
psychological healing, 74, 194–97,
215–16
Puritans, 149–50
purity: cultural borrowing and, 146–47,
150–51; as nonexistent, 221; of ritual
space, 53–55, 211–15; self-definition
and, 53
Pwa, 39

Rachel, 91
racism, cultural borrowing and, 134,
150, 151
Radical Faeries, 78, 84, 240n52
Rainbow Gatherings, xxiii, 231n24,
235–36n42
Ran, 139–40
Ranfeadhael, 160, 162, 167, 171–72,
173, 175, 221
Ranger Rick, 212
raves, 231n24
real vs. ideal, xix–xx, 43, 111–12
reality, heightened, 21–23, 25
Reality Isn't What It Used to Be (Anderson), 257n3
Reck, Larry, 92–93
Reclaiming Coven, 48
Reggae, 142
reincarnation, xxii, 139
relationships: complexity of, 40; importance of, xxi–xxii, 29; interconnectedness of, 24, 158–59, 223. *See also* collective vs. individual indentities;
community; deities; intimacy; nature
religion: authority of self and, xx–xxi,
223; counterculture of 1960s and,
xx–xxi, 223; disestablishment of,
xxi–xxi, xxi–xxiii, 223onn18–19;
dreams/visions and, 253n45; experimentation in, 151; frontier and,
18–19; as hidden, effects of, 100–101;
history and (*see* history); multiple commitments to, 15, 175; Neopaganism as,
88, 121; nineteenth-century movements in, xiv, 14–19; persecution and
(*see* persecution and harassment); popular, American, 175; space designations and control of meaning of,
85–86. *See also* non-Christian reli-

gions; pre-Christian religions; *specific
religions and organizations*
Religious Freedom Restoration Act
(RFRA), 92
representation, xi–xii, xix–xx; persecution and, 89, 116–20, 247n105. *See
also* persecution and harassment; promotional material
responsibility, 210
Rhianna, 15, 174
Riley, Terry and Amanda, xi–xii, 105
Rinsa, 58
rites of passage. *See* life passages
Rites of Spring: behavior guidance, 209;
car altars at, 69; fire and late nights of,
185–86, 188, 215; location and background of, 227n5, 231–32n2; meal
arrangements, 5; music and dance at,
5–6; rituals at, 4, 6–8, 9, 55; workshops of, 196
ritual objects, Native American, 135, 147
rituals, 6–9; attendance as optional, 8;
authenticity and meaning of, 136;
baby-blessing/naming, 56–57, 58–59;
casting the circle, 7, 57–58; childlike
wonder evoked in, 163, 167, 168,
172; child self, healing of, 157; Christian tradition of self in, 221; cleansing, 54, 55, 186, 196; closing ceremonies, 9, 39; continuing effects of,
58; cultural borrowing and, 133–34,
135, 148; dance and (*see* dancing);
drumming and (*see* drumming); end-
ings of, traditional, 257n1; fiction and
fantasy and, 170; fire (*see* fire, ritual);
Flags of the Loa, 129, 142, 143; formal vs. improvisatory, 186; Gnostic
Mass, 101–2, 244nn48,50, 247n93;
grief, 41; healing as focus of,
xxi–xxii, 28, 74, 196; as journey, 216,
257n76; methodology and, xvii;
opening ceremonies, 4, 29–30, 30;
phases of, and liminality, 20; planning
of, 6; play as preparation for, 172;
self-transformation, 28; as serious
play, 203; sexuality and, 193–94;
texts of, on Internet, 257n6; visualization and, 52; Web Ritual, 6–9. *See
also* altars; circle; shrines
ritual space: gateways and gatekeepers,
54–55, 186; outdoor, 49; purity and
proper use of, 53–55, 211–15; safety
of (*see* safety). *See also* sacred space;
spaces within festival site
Rivera, Geraldo, 94
Robertson, Pat, 100
Rogers, Jay, 96, 243n32

Roland, 127
role playing, at festival, 172
role-playing games (RPG), 171–72
roles, lack of, 36–37. *See also* gender
Romantics, 18
Ron, 54
Rose, 35–36, 210
Rosemary's Baby, 93, 99
Rosenbaum, Jeff, 21–22, 182, 232n2
Rosenwald, George, 155
Rose, Wendy, 125, 134–35, 136, 248n21, 249n27
Rowan, 112
Roy, 149
Royce, Anya Peterson, 250
Rozell, Mark J., 243n29
rules and policies: breaking of, 41–43; and fire ritual, 212, 213–15; habitual behavior vs., 211; on nudity, 107; and persecution, response to, 88, 107, 117–20; resentment of/ambivalence toward, 105–6, 107, 117, 209, 213–15, 217. *See also* authority; boundaries; collective vs. individual identities; power

Sacred Skin Tattoo Studio, 131
sacred space: alternative, xxiii, 231n24; architectonic, 59–60; Christian loss of, 160; as container for divine energy, 50; defined, 44–53; ethics and values of, 49–50; festival as, 21, 23–24; fire as, conflicts over, 211–15; function of, 24; nineteenth-century religiosity and, 19; purity of (*see* purity); unexpected, 70–71. *See also* rituals; spaces within festival site
Sade, 139
safe sex, 98, 225
safety: defined, 190; fire ritual and, 190–91, 196, 217; of gay men and lesbians, 84, 205; healing work and, 196; nudity and, 205; sexuality and, 190–91, 193, 194, 196, 209–11, 256nn64,67,–68
sage, 55, 189, 196
Salem witch hunts, 31
Salome, 21, 44, 184, 187, 190–91, 195, 196, 202–3, 211, 215–16
Salvo, Dana, 240n39
Samhain, 62, 99–100
Sandy, 15
Santeria, 39, 101, 113, 240n42; cultural borrowing and, 139, 141–42, 148. *See also* Vodou
Sara, 161, 169
Sartre, Jean-Paul, 163, 251–52n19

Satan: as Christian concept, 114; persecution of Neopagans and, 97
satanic ritual abuse, 90–91, 94, 99, 109, 242n16, 246n68
satanism: accusations of (*see* persecution and harassment); children's interests labeled as, 177, 178, 253n57; vs. Satanism, as term, 241n7; Neopaganism compared to, 113–15; as religion, 90, 114; as term, 241n7
Satan's Underground (Stratford), 242n16
SCA (Society for Creative Anachronism), 75, 78, 170, 206, 252n36
Schacter, Daniel, 180
scholarship, Neopagan, 132–33, 249–50n43
science fiction, 168–72
seances, 15, 174, 175
Sea Priestess (Fortune), 231n1
secularism, 97, 98
Sedona, Arizona, 135
self: assumptions about, shared, xxii, 230n21; Augustinian version of, 221; authority of, xx–xxi, 223; body and (*see* body); boundary loss and, 207; community as necessary to, xxi–xxii, 224–25; consistency of, 230n20; higher, 35–37, 221; layers of, 24, 221–22, 230n21; modernist, 220, 221–22, 223–24; postmodernist, 220–21, 222–23; real, xxi, 207, 221; in relationship (*see* collective vs. individual identities; community; deities; nature; relationships); temples as extension of, 67, 69. *See also* identity
self-examination, 195, 216, 221, 222, 224
self-expression, as norm, 206–8
self-narratives: childhood and (*see* childhood stories); persecution and, 108–9
self-transformation, 216–17; as assumed goal, 13, 20; authenticity and, 126; authority of self and, xx; body marking and, 200–202; clothing and costumes and, 202–5, 255nn47,49; and community (*see* collective vs. individual identities); conflict and, 215; contradictions and, 13–14; cultural borrowing and, xxi, 126–34, 143–44, 148, 151; departures and, 38–39; fire and, 189–90, 206, 215–17, 224–25; fluidity of self and, 220–21; home temples and, 67, 69; magic and, 12–13; pilgrimage and, 27–28; safety and, 190
sexual abuse, 196, 210. *See also* child abuse

sexual harassment, 2, 190–91, 209–11, 217, 225, 256nn64,67,–68
sexuality: boundaries and, 190–91, 194, 207; fire ritual and, 190–91, 193–94, 206, 207–11, 217, 225; Great Rite, 193–94; persecution and, 98, 101; population statistics and, 84; presence of children and, 179; as sacred, 98, 193–94; safety and, 190–91, 193, 194, 196, 209–11, 256nn64,67,–68
sexual orientation, 35, 84, 237n71
Shadowfox, 69
shamanic journeying, 211
Sharon, 168
Sherry, 112
Shields, Rob, 85, 220
shrines, 55–70; altars and temples distinguished from, 56, 65; child self and, 163; definition of, 56; individual vs. collective identity and, 56, 59, 60; life passages and, 56–57, 58–59; location of, 56, 65; nature as basic to, 45; participant involvement in creation of, 50–51, 55–56, 59–60, 63–65. See also altars; rituals
Silver Moon, 78
Sindi, 200
sites, 227n5; isolation of, 24–25; private (permanent), 50–51, 71–72; public (temporary), 50, 51–53, 71–72, 107; spaces in (see spaces within festival site). See also specific sites
Sklar, Dierdre, 189
Smith, Michelle, 98, 242n16
smudging, 55, 186, 196
Snowcat, 138, 139, 141
social problems: Christian-bashing and, 109, 112; scapegoating of Neopagans for, 89–90, 94–95, 96–98
Society for Creative Anachronism (SCA), 75, 78, 170, 206, 252n36
solitaries, 228n6
soul, xxii
Sources of the Self (Taylor), 220
souvenirs, 3, 39
spaces within festival site: belief structures and, xviii–xix; childlike wonder evoked through, 163; conflicts over use of, 54, 101, 105–6, 116–20, 192–93, 207–15; fire (see fire, ritual); healing (see healing); marketplace, 74–81, 76, 77, 85, 198–99, 200–201; marking of, 50–53; meals, 5, 22, 54, 72–73; ritual (see altars; ritual space; shrines); toilets, 71–72; women's, 196. See also sacred space

Spiral Dance, 9
Spiral Gathering, 12, 16, 24, 52
spirit bags, 3
spirits: agency of, 141–42; leave-taking and, 39; unfamiliar, 40. See also deities; spirit world
Spiritualist movement, xiv, 14–17, 18, 19, 233nn16,18
spirit world: as accessible, 15, 23; childhood contact with, 167, 252n27; self and, xxii
spousal abuse, 210
Spurr, Jessica, 91
Starfeild, 100
Starhawk, 16, 43, 48, 193, 194, 238n4
Starheart, Laughing, 53, 56–57, 58, 60, 70, 71, 75, 78, 80, 84–85, 170, 200–201
Starwood: campsites at, 81–83, 163; children's activities at, 179; cultural borrowing and, 135; fire of, 182–83, 187, 208, 215; locals, policy toward, 107; location and background of, xx, 227n5, 232n2; meal arrangements, 5; merchants of, 77; music and dance at, 5; nudity and, 204–5; purity issues and, 54; rituals of, 62; workshops at, 35, 119, 247n1
The State of Native America (Jaimes), 124
Stephen, Michele, 230n20
Stoeltje, Beverly J., 238n2
Stonehenge, 59, 231nn24,1
storytelling, 156. See also childhood stories
Strathern, Marilyn, 230n20
subjectivity, 142, 144, 220. See also identity; postmodernism
Sue, 176
Summerhawk: deities, varying attitudes toward, 149; drumming conflict, 213; fire of, 184–85, 208; Gnostic Mass and, 102, 244n50; harassment of, 101–2; location and background of, 227n5; workshops of, 127
Sun Bear, 126–27
Sun Fest, 227n5, 244–45n50
supernatural beings. See deities; spirits. See also ancestors
sweat lodge, 127, 146–47, 150, 223
sweetgrass, 55
Syrylyn, 69

Tabor, Diane, 183, 185, 190, 193, 194, 197, 207, 208
Tala, 148
Talamantez, Ines, 137
Tammy, 83

Tannev, 176–77
Taoism, 148
tarot cards, 97, 177
tattoos: community belonging and, 224–25; as concealing the past, 153; cultural borrowing and, 131, 132, 148; merchants offering, 75, 78, 80, 200–201; self as communicated through, 198, 203, 224; significance of, 131, 132, 134, 199–202. *See also* body
Taylor, Bron, 249n35
Taylor, Charles, 220, 221
teachers, authenticity and, 126–27
television, xii, 91–92, 94, 100, 103–4, 175
Temne, 196–97
temples, 56, 67
Temple of Set, 113
Terese, 83
Terry, 141, 145
Thelemic groups, 247n93
Theosophy, xiv
Thoreau, Henry David, 18
Threlfall, John, 27–28, 32
Tibetan Buddhism, xii, 130–31, 148
time, 26
Tindome, 117
Tipton, Steven, 230n19
Tocqueville, Alexis de, 18
toilets, 71–72
tolerance, 216–17. *See also* intolerance
Tolkien, J. R. R., 1, 171
"To Save a Child," 92
tourist attractions, 14, 17–18, 19
tree-cutting incident, 42–43
tribe: chosen, 222; fire ritual and, 188; Rainbow Gatherings and, 235–36n42; term, use of, 248n15. *See also* family *entries*
The Trolls, 236n47
Tuan, Yi-Fu, 13
Turner, Glen, 231–32n2
Turner, Victor, 203, 235n34
Tweed, Thomas A., 93
twelve-step programs, 3, 119
Twilight Covening, 231–32n2

Uhlan, 174, 177
Umbanda spiritism, 141
unity, 20, 37–38
Uriel, 168
The Uses of Enchantment (Bettelheim), 172
utopia, 78; childhood ideals and, 181; forgetting and, 25; heterotopias, 234n29

Valiente, Doreen, 246n83
values. *See* freedom; nature; relationships; spaces within festival site
Vegtam, 132
victimization. *See* persecution and harassment
Victor, Jeffrey, 90
Vietnam veterans, 181
visions: childhood skills in, 161–62, 165; cultural borrowing and, 131; as important in belief systems, 253n45
visualization, 52
Vodou, 39, 101, 113, 240n39; adoption of culture, 127–30, 150–51, 223; cultural borrowing and, 142. *See also* Santeria
voices, 131, 140, 141, 149
volunteers, 2–3
voodoo. *See* Vodou
Voodoo Spiritual Temple, 129, 129, 151
Vyvien, 22, 39

Walter, Eugene, 233n20
Waterhawk, Don, 32–33
Watersnake, 39
Wendy, 201
Wheatley, Dennis, 231n1
wheel of life, 60, 62
Whitefeather, Terry, 2, 116–17
"whiteshamans," 125, 135, 136, 144, 249n27
Wicca: altar construction in, 239n36; cultural boundaries and, 141–42; Gardnerian, xiv, 246n83; Great Rite, 193–94; persecution, understanding of, 108
Wilcox, Clyde, 243n29
wilderness, 17–19, 234n27. *See also* nature
Wild Magick Gathering, 2, 56, 227n5
"Wild Magick Guidebook," 42, 49, 56
will, 190
Willow, 82, 84
Wilson, Bryan, 101
WinterStar, 119, 148, 227n5
Winthrop, John, 18
witchcraft, avoidance of term, 116–17
Witchcraft Today (Gardner), xiv
The Witch-Cult in Western Europe (Murray), xiv
witch hunts, 31, 108–9, 146, 153, 241n7, 245n66. *See also* persecution and harassment
Witch vs. witch, as terms, 241n7
A Wizard of Earthsea (LeGuin), 168, 231n1
Wol, 111, 112

Womanhealing Conference, 138
women: devaluation of, and childhood ostracism, 162; devaluation of, and rejection of Christianity, xiii, 126; festivals for, 39, 74, 84, 252n27; leadership by, 16; respect for, and cultural borrowing, 146; rights of, 15, 16; sexual harassment of, 2, 190–91, 209–11, 217, 225, 256nn64,67,68; space for, 196. *See also* gender
Womon-gathering, 39
Woodstock (I and II), 231n24, 247n105
workshops, 4; alternative families/sexualities, 35, 237n71; cultural borrowing and, 123, 125, 247n1; dancing, 188, 193; drug and alcohol use and recovery, 119; drumming, 188, 192; fantasy and fiction and, 170; healing and, xiii, xxi–xxii, 74, 138, 196; methodology and, 187; planning of, 2; sexuality, 98; on taboos, 251n12

World Trade Organization protests, 48
World Wide Web. *See* Internet
Wotan, 132
Wotanwald, 24, 236n47
Wuthnow, Robert, 94
Wyrd Sisters, 16

Xango, 141–42
The X-Files, 103–4

Yeats, William Butler, xiv
Yellowwood incident, 88–89, 106, 108, 120
Yemaya, 148
Yinger, J. Milton, 237n62
Yohalem, John, xviii

Zaleski, Jacque Omi, 92
Zal, Tath, 199
Zell, Otter, 244n41
Zoroastrianism, 114

Text: 10/13 Sabon
Display: Sabon
Composition: Impressions Book and Journal Services, Inc.
Printing and binding: Edwards Brothers
Index: Victoria Baker